A NOBLE CAUSE?
AMERICA AND THE VIETNAM WAR

MODERN WARS IN PERSPECTIVE

General Editors: *H.M. Scott and B.W. Collins*

This ambitious new series offers wide-ranging studies of specific wars, and distinct phases of warfare, from the close of the Middle Ages to the present day. It aims to advance the current integration of military history into the academic mainstream. To that end, the books are not merely traditional campaign narratives, but examine the causes, course and consequences of major conflicts, in their full international political, social and ideological contexts.

ALREADY PUBLISHED

Mexico and the Spanish Conquest
Ross Hassig

The Anglo–Dutch Wars of the Seventeenth Century
J.R. Jones

The Wars of Louis XIV
John A. Lynn

The Wars of Frederick the Great
Dennis Showalter

The Wars of Napoleon
Charles J. Esdaile

The Spanish–American War: Conflict in the Caribbean and the Pacific 1895–1902
Joseph Smith

China at War, 1901–1949
Edward L. Dreyer

The Wars of French Decolonization
Anthony Clayton

A Noble Cause? America and the Vietnam War
Gerard J. DeGroot

A NOBLE CAUSE?
AMERICA AND THE VIETNAM WAR

Gerard J. DeGroot

LONGMAN

Pearson Education Limited
Edinburgh Gate
Harlow
Essex CM20 2JE, England
and Associated Companies throughout the world.

*Published in the United States of America
by Pearson Education Inc., New York.*

First published 2000

ISBN 0-582-28718-9 CSD
ISBN 0-582-28717-0 PPR

Visit our world wide website at http://www.awl-he.com

British Library Cataloguing in Publication Data

A catalogue entry for this title is available from the British Library

Library of Congress Cataloging-in-Publication Data

A Catalog entry for this title is available from the Library of Congress

Set by 35 in 10/12pt Sabon
Produced by Addison Wesley Longman Singapore Pte Ltd.
Printed in Singapore

To my big brother,
Hans DeGroot,
who, by accident of birth, had cause to worry
about the Vietnam War

CONTENTS

LIST OF MAPS

PREFACE

Vietnam is my war as much as any war is ever likely to be. I was born in 1955 in San Diego, California, a city which back then had little identity beyond the military and defence industries. San Diegans knew that they lived in a major fortress of the Cold War. My father made missiles for General Dynamics, and enjoyed steady work and unaccustomed prosperity because of the war. As I am blessed (or cursed?) with a lively memory, I can vividly recall the night Kennedy defeated Nixon in 1960. A short time later I was bewildered by television reports of what I now realize was the self-immolation of a Buddhist bonze on a Saigon street in 1963. After Kennedy's assassination came the first conversation about Vietnam that I can recall. A family friend, who happened to be a member of the right-wing John Birch Society, spoke of the need to stop the communist guerillas in Vietnam. Few eight-year-olds know the difference between guerrillas and gorillas. I certainly didn't. From the beginning, the war seemed confusing.

The summary execution of a communist guerrilla on a Saigon street by General Nguyen Ngoc Loan during the Tet Offensive (which produced perhaps the most famous photograph from the war) is a milestone of my past. So is Lyndon Johnson's astonishing announcement that he would not seek re-election in 1968. For me, the war was always present; it was around when I first became aware of events in the outside world and still there when I was a 20-year-old university student. Mine was the last year of the Vietnam draft lottery. Numbers were drawn (mine was frighteningly low) but no one was actually drafted. In that sense, 1955 was a good year to be born.

Vietnam is part of me. It has, in ways I cannot entirely understand, shaped me. But it is also, for me at least, the past. I left the United States in 1980 to do postgraduate work in British history at the University of Edinburgh. I have resided in Scotland ever since. Thus, I missed the celebrations and controversy surrounding the building of the Vietnam War Memorial in Washington DC in November 1982 – the black granite wall which has inspired both reverence and condemnation. I also missed Ronald Reagan's reference to the war as 'a noble cause' during the 1980 presidential election. I was aware of both events, but separated from the emotions they engendered among the American people. The Vietnam syndrome, which has deeply affected so many citizens of the United States, is for me a phenomenon which exists in another country, far away.

For a large part of my academic career I have studied the effect of the Great War upon the British people. That war is a useful foundation upon which to base one's understanding of war's destructive power. The number of Americans who died during the worst year of the Vietnam War is roughly similar to the number of British who died on the first day of the battle of the Somme. The Great War provides a valuable guide with which to measure futility, carnage, suffering and loss. Perspective is important.

I would like to think that my absence from the United States over the last two decades was an advantage in writing this book. Historians should try to rise above the fray, but, sadly, cannot always do so. There is too much insularity and self-indulgence in the Vietnam scholarship produced in America today. There is also far too much manipulation of the subject (and the evidence) for wider political purposes. The war has become a battleground on which rival factions argue their contradictory visions of America. Though I would not be so presumptuous as to claim that my book is free of bias, I can assure the reader that I have no political agenda.

I would like to thank a number of people who helped bring this book into being. The archivists and librarians at the Bancroft Library (University of California, Berkeley), the Hoover Institute (Stanford University) and the Lyndon Johnson Library (University of Texas, Austin) were very gracious with their assistance and advice. James Reckner of the Texas Tech University Vietnam Center directed me to some useful sources on a few occasions. My good friend Clare White provided some gems from the Kennedy papers and Corinna Peniston-Bird advised me on how best to present a vast mountain of information in a manner accessible to lay students. Colonel Frederic Borch, US Army, provided some illuminating material from the legal files of the war and allowed me to borrow insights from his forthcoming book on the JAG Corps.

My colleague Hamish Scott was there at the beginning, encouraging me to write about Vietnam for the *Modern Wars in Perspective* series which he edits with Bruce Collins. Bruce provided encouragement at every stage along the way, but especially kept me in line at the very end, when impatience sometimes encourages haste. But I must thank especially Eric Bergerud, who has few equals in the depth of his knowledge of this subject. Eric's praise for the manuscript did much to lift a tired soul. At the same time, the care with which he read the draft and the acuity of his suggestions for improvement undoubtedly made this a better book than it would have been. I must emphasize, however, that any errors or omissions which remain in the text are my own, and in no way the fault of the various readers.

My dear wife Sharon Roe kept me sane during a punishing production schedule and provided welcome encouragement whenever spirits flagged. My son Joshua, born during the writing of the first draft, helped by keeping me awake and working at hours when most sane historians are safely tucked in bed. He and his sister Natalie were an effective curb on the obsession which afflicts any writer. It is, fortunately, nearly impossible to tell a child under four that Daddy needs to write.

Dr Gerard J. DeGroot
St Andrews, Scotland
December 1998

ACKNOWLEDGEMENTS

We are grateful to the following for permission to reproduce copyright material:

John Balaban for his poem 'After Our War' from *Locusts at the Edge of Summer: New and Selected Poems* (Port Townsend: Copper Canyon Press); Eastaboga Entertainment Corporation and IMP Ltd for the lyrics to 'The Ballad of the Green Berets' by Barry Sadler and Robin Moore (words and music by Barry Sadler and Robin Moore © 1963 Music-Music-Music Inc., USA, Peter Maurice Music Co Ltd, London WC2H 0EA, reproduced by permission of IMP Ltd); Bernard Edelman for the poem 'Ambush' by James McLeroy, which appeared in *Dear America: Letters Home from Vietnam* edited by Bernard Edelman for the New York Vietnam Veterans Memorial Commission, published by W. W. Norton & Company in 1985; 'Guerilla War' by W. D. Ehrhart is reprinted from *Beautiful Wreckage: New & Selected Poems* (Easthampton, MA: Adastra Press, 1999) and appears by permission of the author; McAvoy Layne for his poem 'Guns'; Harmony Music Ltd (UK) for the lyrics to 'Draft Dodger Rag' by Phil Ochs (©1964 "Draft Dodger Rag" by Phil Ochs, Appleseed Music Inc., assigned to Harmony Music Ltd for the UK and Eire, 11 Uxbridge St, London W8 7TQ); Gerald McCarthy for his poem 'The Sound of Guns'; words by Merle Haggard taken from the song 'Okie from Muskogee', by kind permission of Song/ATV Music Publishing.

Whilst every effort has been made to trace owners of copyright material, in a few cases this has proved impossible and we would like to take this opportunity to apologise to any copyright holders whose rights we may have unwittingly infringed.

ABBREVIATIONS

AA	anti-aircraft
AID	Agency for International Development
APC	armoured personnel carrier
ARVN	Army of the Republic of Vietnam
ASV	Associated State of Vietnam
AWOL	absent without leave
CIA	Central Intelligence Agency
CINCPAC	Commander-in-Chief, Pacific
CIP	Commercial Import Program
COSVN	Central Office of South Vietnam
DIA	Defense Intelligence Agency
DMZ	demilitarized zone
DOD	Department of Defense
DRV	Democratic Republic of Vietnam
EDC	European Defence Community
FCC	Federal Communications Commission
FSM	Free Speech Movement
FUNK	National United Front for Kampuchea
GI	Government Issue (i.e. serviceman)
GVN	Government of Vietnam (South Vietnam)
HES	Hamlet Evaluation Survey
HUAC	House Un-American Activities Committee
ICP	Indochinese Communist Party
IDA	Institute of Defence Analysis
INR	Bureau of Intelligence and Research
IPC	Interprovincial Party Committee
JAG	Judge Advocate General
JCS	Joint Chiefs of Staff
JFK	John F. Kennedy
KCP	Kampuchean Communist Party
LBJ	Lyndon Baines Johnson
LZ	landing zone
MAAG	Military Assistance Advisory Group

MACV	Military Assistance Command, Vietnam
MIA	missing in action
NCO	non-commissioned officer
NEZ	New Economic Zones
NLF	National Liberation Front
NSAM	National Security Action Memorandum
NSC	National Security Council
NVA	North Vietnamese Army
NVN	North Vietnam
OOB	order of battle
OSS	Office of Strategic Service
PAVN	People's Army of Vietnam
PLAF	People's Liberation Armed Forces
POL	petroleum, oil and lubricants
POW	prisoner of war
PRU	People's Reconnaissance Unit
PTSD	post-traumatic stress disorder
PX	post exchange
REMF	'rear echelon mother fucker'
RFK	Robert F. Kennedy
RF/PF	Regional Forces/Popular Forces
ROTC	Reserve Officer Training Corps
RPG	rocket-propelled grenade
RVN	Republic of Vietnam
RVNAF	Republic of Vietnam Armed Forces, Republic of Vietnam Air Force
SAM	surface-to-air missile
SCUM	Society for Cutting Up Men
SDS	Students for a Democratic Society
SVN	South Vietnam
TVA	Tennessee Valley Authority
UN	United Nations
USA	United States of America
USSR	Union of Soviet Socialist Republics
VA	Veterans Administration
VC	Viet Cong
VCP	Vietnamese Communist Party
VDC	Vietnam Day Committee
VFW	Veterans of Foreign Wars
VN	Vietnam
VNA	Vietnamese National Army
VNQDD	Viet Nam Quoc Dan Dang

A NOTE ON NOMENCLATURE

The multitude of acronyms and abbreviations can further cloud an already confusing war. The forces of the Vietnamese revolution consisted of the People's Army of Vietnam (PAVN), also known as the North Vietnamese Army (NVA); and the People's Liberation Armed Forces (PLAF), commonly known as the Viet Cong (VC). PAVN was a force raised and trained in the North and sent into South Vietnam to fight, while the PLAF was the military wing of the National Liberation Front, a revolutionary movement indigenous to South Vietnam. For the purpose of clarity, PAVN and PLAF will be used exclusively, except where NVA and VC are used in quotation.

There are times when a collective term is necessary to describe the political and military forces of the revolution – North and South. No adequate term exists. I have occasionally used 'the revolution' even though it can be confusing and unspecific. Generally speaking, however, I have used 'the communists' as a collective term for those groups who opposed the United States and her ally, the government of South Vietnam. I use this term in full knowledge of its flaws (not all southern revolutionaries were communists), in the absence of a suitable alternative.

It's time we recognized that ours was, in truth, a noble cause.

Ronald Reagan, speech to the Veterans of Foreign Wars, 1980

Vietnam was regarded primarily as a geopolitical abstraction, a factor in the play of American global interests. That was true about the way the United States intervened in the war with its land army. It was true about the way the United States conducted the war. And it was especially true about the way the United States left the war.

Bui Diem, former South Vietnamese ambassador to the United States, 1987

INTRODUCTION: HISTORIANS AT WAR

Those coming to the Vietnam War for the first time might start with a little experiment. Get on the World Wide Web, choose a search engine and key in 'Vietnam War'. Press return, then wait while thousands of 'matches' are brought forward. The results defy categorization; the websites of academics, journalists and earnest researchers mingle with those of cranks, delusionists and paranoiacs. Exact reproductions of important documents can be found amidst counterfeit data purporting to prove the latest crackpot conspiracy theory. One finds invitations to join discussion groups devoted to every miniscule aspect of the war. When this line of enquiry grows dull, log on to the website of a major online bookseller and again key in 'Vietnam War'. Wait. No microprocessor, no matter how fast, can answer such a search request quickly. If the bookseller is a big one, the results will eventually number in the thousands. The evidence suggests an obsession.

How else can one describe such a vast outpouring of literature which shows no sign of abatement? This obsession takes many forms. Some seek explanation – of America's involvement in the war, or of the reasons for her defeat. For others, writing about the war is a necessary act of closure in response to the pain it has caused. Others still are keen to use the war as a morality tale through which to peddle a particular vision of America. And then there are those for whom the war offers an opportunity to make money in a book market which has yet to reach saturation. So great is the desire to stamp one's authority on this market by writing the 'definitive' analysis, that some have been tempted to claim an authority which they do not possess. During the writing of this book, for instance, it was discovered that a respected scholar of the war had not been entirely truthful about his combat experience. He has yet to provide proof that he actually served in Vietnam, as he so often claimed. Subterfuge of this type is not uncommon in this field. The danger of discovery is great, but the benefits of 'authority' are manifold.

1

The field is full of cynics and frauds, but is also distinguished by some of the most talented and dedicated historians who practice the craft. Their motivation seems primarily to be to resolve the confusion which surrounds involvement in such a strange and ultimately futile conflict. Their abundant energy and prodigious output is a measure of the bewilderment felt by Americans about this war. Authors repeatedly boast that their books are based on a 'meticulous combing of previously classified documents', as if, somewhere, deep in the bowels of the National Archives or the Johnson Library, there lies a document which points to the moment of madness which took America into this war. But, as any historian worth his/her salt knows, archives never provide a final verdict. Perhaps no other war has been so well documented as Vietnam. For instance, never have historians had such early access to the sequence of decisions as was provided by the controversial release of the Pentagon Papers in 1971. But while the Papers (published in many different forms) provide incredible detail of the period 1945–67, they are still open to wide interpretation by analysts keen to prove a preconceived theory. The Papers generate more heat than light. The struggle for their release added to the legendary nature of the war, casting a conspiratorial air over the events and stimulating the adversarial inclinations of subsequent analysts. What has resulted from this frenetic search is a great deal of evidence and a deep collective knowledge, but an incomplete understanding of the war.

WRONG WAR?

Retrospective judgements on a war which was lost lead naturally to an assumption that it should perhaps never have been fought. The issue which troubles historians the most is how to explain America's involvement. Those who deal with the origins question best start at the beginning and present the war as a gradually evolving problem exacerbated by American mistakes, misconceptions and hubris. Thus, Lloyd Gardner's *Approaching Vietnam*, George McT. Kahin's *Intervention*, Arthur Schlesinger's *The Bitter Heritage: Vietnam and American Democracy, 1941–1966* and Anthony Short's *The Origins of the Vietnam War* concentrate on the tide of events and resist the temptation to identify a point of no return, nor indeed a guilty party. Blame, where appropriate, is collective. Kahin's account is particularly useful because his description of machinations in Washington is complemented by a deep understanding of what was happening on the ground in Vietnam.

Other historians prefer to personalize the origins issue. The terms of the various presidents provide neat boundaries for blame. Harry

Truman gets off very lightly perhaps because, up until 1952, the war was quite clearly an affair involving the French and the British, with the American role rather marginal. But, as Gardner, Schlesinger and Short, among others, show, it was Truman's policy of containment which gave Vietnam an importance within American foreign policy which it perhaps never deserved. As for Dwight Eisenhower, he generally receives praise from historians (see Melanie Billings-Yun, *Decision Against War: Eisenhower and Dien Bien Phu, 1954*), but David Anderson, in *Trapped by Success: The Eisenhower Administration and Vietnam, 1953–1961*, does demonstrate that the President's tendency to evade problems meant that he bequeathed a much more intractable dilemma to John Kennedy than he inherited from Truman.

It is in the examination of John Kennedy's role that the argument turns nasty. Many Americans want to believe that, if not for Kennedy's assassination in Dallas, the United States would be a better place today. Camelot would have been realized, so the fantasy goes, in part because Kennedy would have been clever and wise enough to avoid a futile war in Vietnam. This argument has been presented most forcefully in John Newman's *JFK and Vietnam*, a well-researched but disappointingly one-sided treatment. Newman demonstrates that there is enough evidence in the archives to present a credible case for Kennedy the dove. But there is even more evidence for Kennedy the hawk; to ignore it requires a suspension of logic. The latter position was first articulated by David Halberstam in *The Making of a Quagmire*, originally published in 1964. As the title implies, the author argues that policy-makers during the Kennedy era 'responded with clichés to desperately complicated and serious challenges'.[1] While his somewhat casual approach to evidence (and his venom) aroused the suspicions of subsequent historians, recent research by, among others, Larry Berman, suggests that the general thrust of the Halberstam thesis is sound.[2]

Halberstam bequeathed the quagmire thesis to those historians who have attempted to measure Lyndon Johnson's culpability. Because Johnson was the first President to send combat troops to Vietnam, his involvement seems the most controversial and has therefore attracted the most attention. When the argument is distilled, the operative question becomes: did Johnson have the opportunity to extricate the United States from the quagmire? Berman, in *Planning a Tragedy* and *Lyndon*

---

1 David Halberstam, *The Making of a Quagmire* (New York, NY, 1964), p. 338.
2 See Larry Berman, 'NSAM 263 and NSAM 273: manipulating history', in Lloyd C. Gardner and Ted Gittinger, eds, *Vietnam: The Early Decisions* (Austin, TX, 1997).

Johnson's War, argues that he did, but lacked the wisdom to see a way out or the courage to pursue it. Berman feels that Johnson, often for noble reasons, sought compromise rather than resolution. George Herring, in *LBJ and Vietnam*, is rather more unforgiving than Berman, as is H.R. McMaster in the vitriolic *Dereliction of Duty*. Those more charitable to Johnson argue that there was no obvious exit from the quagmire. Brian VanDeMark (*Into the Quagmire*) and David M. Barrett (*Uncertain Warriors*) take this line, as does Schlesinger to an extent. Lawrence Gelb and Richard K. Betts, on the other hand, present an interesting twist on the argument in *The Irony of Vietnam: The System Worked*. They argue that the Johnson administration was kept fully informed of the nature of the conflict through pessimistic State Department and Central Intelligence Agency (CIA) reports. In other words, Johnson understood the war to be a quagmire, but felt that the United States still needed to show the world that it was prepared to defend South Vietnam. Within this context, he sought a middle way between advocates of escalation and of disengagement. The most exhaustive study of the Johnson years is Gardner's *Pay Any Price*, which is also sufficiently non-judgemental to allow readers to decide for themselves the issue of culpability.

The Nixon years have not received even close to the same amount of attention. This seems strange given the bitter controversies of those years – the invasions of Cambodia and Laos, the Phoenix programme of covert assassination and coercion, and the Linebacker bombings, to name but a few. Those separate controversies have their analysts, but the period as a whole has, until recently, lacked comprehensive examination. As a result, the account provided by Nixon in his various postwar books (including *RN: The Memoirs of Richard Nixon*), which is backed up by Henry Kissinger's *White House Years*, has gone largely unchallenged. Nixon and Kissinger argue that by 1973, after exhaustive effort, they had achieved a settlement which preserved American honour, left the South Vietnamese regime intact, and kept North Vietnam's aggression in check. According to their scenario, this precarious peace was, however, squandered when, in a fit of post-Watergate pique, Congress decided to withhold the financial and military support to the South which was essential to make it work. Nixon's determined effort at rehabilitating his image meant that by the time of his death he was regarded in many quarters as a foreign policy genius. This further enhanced the popularity of his 'stab in the back' thesis. Fortunately, this dangerous fantasy has finally received a worthy and suitably damaging rebuttal with the recent publication of Jeffrey Kimball's *Nixon's Vietnam War*.

Missing from almost all of these efforts to blame or absolve America's leaders is an understanding of the war from the Vietnamese point of view. Yet if intervention was indeed a mistake, it was so because the revolution was so formidable. Leaders from Truman to Nixon erred in part because they failed to understand the Vietnamese variant of Maoist revolution and did not appreciate the strength of nationalism within Vietnam. Subsequent historians have made the same mistake. Analysis of the war is too often excessively American-centred, implying that it was within the power of the United States to shape the fate of Vietnam, as long as she chose the proper way to do so. One of the first to correct this misconception was Jeffrey Race, whose *War Comes to Long An* offers a detailed analysis of the war as it affected a single province. The book remains as indispensable and unassailable today as when it was published in 1972. Douglas Pike's studies (*PAVN: People's Army of Vietnam* and *Viet Cong: The Organization and Techniques of the National Liberation Front of South Vietnam*) demonstrate just how formidable was the military power of the revolution. *PAVN*, in particular, explains the symbiotic relationship between politics and violence, which produces a revolutionary synthesis for which 'no comprehensive counter-strategy was ever developed'.[3]

The great problem which any historian encounters in studying the war from the Vietnamese point of view is how much credence to give to communist accounts. The line between history and propaganda in books emerging from Hanoi is not distinctly drawn. For instance, James Harrison's otherwise excellent *The Endless War: Vietnam's Struggle for Independence* suffers because the author often takes at face value communist accounts of revolutionary successes. Yet Hanoi freely admitted that, since propaganda is central to the success of any revolution, hyperbole is a legitimate weapon of war. William Duiker takes a more sceptical view of the revolution, but his *Sacred War* lacks the passion of Harrison's book. The dilemma which plagues any historian of the revolution is to convey its ardour without being duped by its counterfeit romance.

ANOTHER WAY?

An understanding of the Vietnamese communist revolution often leads one to the conclusion that America's defeat was inevitable. This is essentially the line espoused by Eric Bergerud in *Dynamics of Defeat*,

---

3 Douglas Pike, *PAVN: People's Army of Vietnam* (Novato, CA, 1986), p. 251.

without doubt one of the best books on the military aspects of the war. Bergerud is one of the few historians who understand the American military *and* the Vietnamese. While he has no sentimental attachment to the revolution, he is respectful of its strength. He also questions received wisdom about the weakness of the Republic of Vietnam (RVN) and its military force. The RVN, a country without a history, has proved a handy scapegoat for those keen to explain America's defeat.

Dynamics of Defeat, along with Bergerud's *Red Thunder, Tropic Lightning*, also demolishes the myth that American defeat resulted because a mediocre force, riddled with indiscipline, was sent to Vietnam. That myth has arisen largely because so many Americans get their history of the war from sensationalist Hollywood productions. It is popular because it allows Americans to sidestep a painful realization, namely that they were defeated by a movement more formidable than their own brand of liberal democracy. Disaster, so the story goes, resulted because of the cruel coincidence of a hard war and a dysfunctional generation, weakened by Sixties excesses.

The power of this myth perhaps explains the popularity of alternative scenarios. Historians are not supposed to speculate on what might have been, yet few who have studied this war can resist the temptation. One senses, within the American mind, a desperate desire to believe that a different army or a different strategy could have won the war. Rather like Scooby Doo, fantasists wave their arms and imagine a different end which allows American omnipotence to remain intact, undented by the embarrassment of defeat by a third-rate power. Immediately after the war, the futility of the conflict and the nefarious nature of the American effort made speculation about an alternative ending seem automatically suspect. But revisionists came out of the closet after the Vietnamese invasion of Cambodia provided a shot of adrenalin to old assumptions about communist devilry. The 'true nature' of the Hanoi regime rendered it acceptable again to support American involvement and to speculate on how the United States might have won the war.

The most popular example of this genre is Harry Summers's *On Strategy*, which proposes that the Americans could have won, quickly and at relatively low cost, if only they had stuck to a conventional strategy directed against main force units of the North, instead of fighting a low-level insurgency conflict against southern guerrillas. In other words, victory would have come easily if American forces had simply done what they do best. The argument is echoed in General Bruce Palmer's *The 25 Year War*, though with somewhat more subtlety and reserve.

As is discussed in Chapter 10, the Summers thesis is pure bunk, all the more dangerous because it is so popular. It has been skilfully demolished in a number of studies which argue the centrality of the guerrilla war and the unsuitability of conventional strategy to this conflict. In *The Army in Vietnam*, Andrew Krepinevich contends that Army doctrine was heavily orientated toward a conventional war in Europe and was not sufficiently modified to the Vietnam context. In other words, the US lost because it failed to adopt counter-insurgency tactics, rather than because, as Summers argues, it did so too wholeheartedly. The Krepinevich thesis has been buttressed by a number of scholars, among them Larry Cable (*Unholy Grail*) and Richard Hunt (*Pacification*), who have condemned America's neglect of the 'other war'. The most stimulating example of this argument is Neil Sheehan's *Bright Shining Lie*, a brilliant book which exposes the inadequacies of the US war effort by recounting the career of the maverick Colonel John Paul Vann, who suffered at first hand the blinkered attitude of his superiors.

Krepinevich's impact is, however, miniscule in comparison to that of Summers, perhaps because acceptance of the former's thesis requires an understanding of the mechanics and culture of the Vietnamese revolution which American insularity does not always permit. Stated simply, the Summers explanation for defeat is easier to swallow and does not leave a bitter after-taste. But the Krepinevich thesis is not without its own flaws. Bergerud has convincingly demonstrated that the US did in fact devote a great deal of effort and money to the 'other war', but to no avail. He also feels that, while counter-insurgency tactics were necessary, it was at the same time essential to neutralize enemy main force units, which could only be achieved through conventional tactics. In other words, both Krepinevich and Summers display a one-sided understanding of the war. Both also assume that it was within the power of the United States to win, if only different decisions had been made, an assumption which does not accord with the evidence presented by Race, Bergerud and Pike. In *Backfire*, Loren Baritz also argues that American defeat was inevitable, but for very different reasons. Rather than arguing that the revolution was invincible, he contends that cultural conditioning (the tyranny of technology) rendered Americans incapable of fighting the war in a way which would cause significant injury to the enemy. The argument is stimulating and sometimes insightful, and certainly useful for sparking debate. But the book ultimately reveals that there are few scholars who are adept at both military and cultural history. Baritz is not one of them.

SCAPEGOATS

The arena of Vietnam history is heavily populated with those who, unable to accept defeat by a ragtag collection of 'barefoot guerrillas', seek scapegoats at home. Such arguments are popular because, as with the Summers thesis, they provide a detour around the painful contradictions of American power. In fact, Summers and Palmer are among the loudest voices condemning those homefront traitors who inhibited the American military from achieving success in Vietnam. Among the favourite culprits are the press, for presenting a false picture of the war; the peace protesters, for spreading dissension and undermining confidence among the soldiers; and Presidents Johnson and Nixon for failing to bring both under control. Johnson is also roundly condemned for pursuing a limited war strategy which forced the military to fight with one hand tied behind its back.

The culpability of the press is a favourite theme of the journalist Peter Braestrup. His *Big Story* argues that false reporting of the Tet Offensive turned ordinary people against the war at the very moment when the tide had turned in favour of the US. Don Oberdorfer takes an opposite view in *Tet!*, but does not manage to destroy the notion of a traitorous press. Daniel C. Hallin (*The Uncensored War*) and Kathleen Turner (*Lyndon Johnson's Dual War*) take a more sober, balanced view of the media's actual effect. By focusing on the entire war, Hallin shows that the media willingly took on a propagandist role in support of the war until the watershed years of 1968 and 1969. For those on the ground, defeat was apparent long before the media started reporting it. Negative reporting, where it existed, reflected public opposition instead of shaping it.

Those who condemn the peace protesters (and most revisionists do) argue a similar line to those who castigate the press. In other words, the war could have been won if only a united front had been established at home. Peaceniks are roundly condemned, as are Johnson and Nixon for failing to establish, through law or propaganda, a single-minded commitment to the war. Apparently, basic American freedoms (of expression and dissent) should have been sacrificed in order to defeat 'tyranny' in Vietnam. But, again, there lies behind these condemnations the assumption that the American military was actually capable of victory, if not for a disloyal media, oppositional students or pusillanimous presidents. In truth, the war was lost on the ground in Vietnam, not on the college campuses or on the front page of the *New York Times* and *Washington Post*. It is in the nature of scapegoats that they distract attention from painful realities.

Former peace protesters are pleased to be assigned such a major role in the tale of defeat, and historians of the 'movement' have happily granted it to them. The field is popular. Charles DeBenedetti (*An American Ordeal*), Tom Wells (*The War Within*), Kenneth Heinemann (*Campus Wars*), Terry Anderson (*The Movement and the Sixties*) and Melvin Small (*Johnson, Nixon and the Doves*) all deserve praise for careful research and illuminating insights. But the subject attracts all too much sentimentality from chroniclers who lived through the period or wished they had. All histories of the movement, in varying degrees, tend to admire its commitment and praise its success. Because peace is good, peace protesters are deemed virtuous. But just because the biggest anti-war movement in American history coexisted with the first defeat of the US in a foreign war does not mean the two phenomena were intrinsically connected.

It is no coincidence that praise of the movement has come from historians, who have been influenced by its romance, and criticism mainly from social scientists, who cannot ignore the raw data showing the limited influence it had upon public opinion. Polls show that in the later stages of the war the public's growing opposition to the war coexisted with an abhorrence of protesters. William Lunch, William Sperlich, Justin Gustainis, Howard Schuman and E.M. Schreiber, among others, have convincingly demonstrated that the tactics and character of the protesters severely impeded their effectiveness. The cause may have been noble, but those who espoused it were not. This is the theme driven home by Adam Garfinkle in *Telltale Hearts*, a brave demolition of the glorious myths that Sixties worshippers chant like mantras. Garfinkle argues that just because McNamara was wrong does not mean that Tom Hayden, Devid Dellinger and the other anti-war activists were right. Many people will find the book disturbing, for good reason. Others will dismiss it as the rantings of a unrepentant hawk. Though the book is an effective antidote to the romantic fantasies dominant in this area of Vietnam scholarship, there is still room in the field for a dispassionate history which chronicles the movement while analysing its strengths *and* its limitations. Such a history would have to pay attention to the huge group of Americans who loyally supported the war but who have since been largely ignored because their cause eventually became so unpopular. The historian who takes on such a project would also have to look beyond the campuses and rallies to the real war in Vietnam. It is impossible to assess accurately the achievements of the protesters without understanding why the United States was losing the war and why her leaders decided to withdraw. Few historians of the anti-war movement seem to realize that, given the mood in the United States, the protesters would have remained a tiny insignificant minority if American soldiers had been winning in Vietnam.

PURGATION

Running parallel to the search for understanding evident in the flood of Vietnam literature is a desire for purgation. Those affected by the war, in however small a way, seek closure by writing about it. What results is sometimes painfully profound and deeply moving, but in other cases wincingly sentimental and self-indulgent. The victim culture of the 1980s and 1990s has inspired a widespread desire to hop on the bandwagon of suffering. This relatively small war is unique for the flood of psychological casualties it has produced and the huge number keen to record their torment.

Before Vietnam, the architects of past American wars usually wrote triumphantly of their contribution to victory. The memoir writers of the Vietnam era found themselves in a quandary: how to explain defeat and preserve one's reputation? The task was made all the more difficult by the publication in 1972 of Halberstam's *The Best and the Brightest*, which exposed the arrogance and myopia of the supposedly gifted leaders who shaped American policy toward Vietnam. The book, which was immensely popular, meant that many Americans adopted Halberstam's antipathy toward the powerful men of the Kennedy/ Johnson era. Those men found themselves in a deep hole. Some, like George Ball (*The Past Has Another Pattern*) and Maxwell Taylor (*Swords and Plowshares*), could claim, with some justification, that their advice had gone unheeded. Others, like William Westmoreland (*A Soldier Reports*), could pass the buck, in the process reinforcing the 'stab in the back' argument promoted by Summers. Robert McNamara's response was to pen a 400-page *mea culpa*, in the hope that the public would forgive. His *In Retrospect* sheds little useful light on the machinations of decision-makers in Washington, but is an illuminating glimpse at a soul tortured by the conflict. The strident reaction to the book is also an indicator of how the wounds of war continue to fester. A man whose mistakes were so massive should not, it seems, attempt closure through such a public act of atonement.

The testimony of the more lowly participants in the war is perhaps more prosaic, but often a great deal more revealing and honest. Few welcomed the war, fewer still wanted to go to Vietnam. For most participants, therefore, the war was an imposition, a cruel and violent interruption to a time of hope, sunshine, happiness and plenty. The

1960s may seem in retrospect an era of war, protest, assassinations and race riots, but the decade also had an irrepressibly happy, often downright silly, side. Rock groups like Ohio Express ('Yummy, Yummy, Yummy'), the Kraiks ('Red Rubber Ball') and The 1910 Fruitgum Company ('Simon Says') were enormously successful with 'bubblegum music'. On television, hit shows included one about a flying nun, another about a friendly witch and a third about a delightful genie. The decade was supposed to be about moonshots, not massacres. Rather like the First World War, therefore, Vietnam was a profound cultural shock. Sacred values did not survive. Heroism, patriotism, and the belief in American moral virtue were battered in a futile and ignoble war.

The resultant malaise inspired a vast outpouring of memoirs, novels, poetry and oral history. Much of it is dime store war porn, often remarkable in making the conflict seem boring and banal. But a few examples rank with the best literature from any war. Larry Heinemann, Philip Caputo and Tim O'Brien are first-rate novelists able to penetrate to the core of the soldier's psyche and deeply sensitive to the cruel ironies of this war. W. D. Ehrhart, the former Marine, and a few other poets have demonstrated that, even in an age when television can give war savage immediacy, poetry is still essential to convey the deep vulnerability of the soldier and to strip bare his misery.

Some of the literature is crudely written, yet immensely valuable for that very reason. If not for the war, Winnie Smith would never have written a book. Her *Daughter Gone to War* is not good literature, but it is eloquent in a raw, intensely personal way. Few books, from any war, can match its harrowing descriptions of war's detritus: men literally torn apart by mines and shells and others whose blank stares betray minds ravaged by fear and suffering. The book also describes in painful detail the downward slide of a young nurse who, after volunteering for sublime patriotic reasons, eventually realizes that she is a mere cog in a death machine.

Equally unsettling, in a different sort of way, is the literature which has emerged recently from the 'other side'. Duong Thu Huong's *Novel Without a Name* and Bao Ninh's *The Sorrow of War* have destroyed the myth that the soldiers of the communist revolution were soulless automatons who fought on a bowl of rice a day. That myth has proved a handy explanation for defeat; it is easier to accept being beaten by an enemy who is neither human nor humane. In a similar fashion, oral histories which have recently been published, including David Chanoff's and Doan Van Toai's *'Vietnam' – A Portrait of Its People at War*, reveal that the revolution, for all its brutal efficiency,

11

had its draft dodgers, cowards, doubters and criminals. Soldiers could be ruthless, but they were also wracked by fear. Supporters of the revolution included those deeply committed to its ideals and those terrified of its power.

Much of the literature reinforces images of a cruel, unjust war, devoid of romance and conventional heroism. The deep reservoir of guilt and remorse within the American psyche feeds a self-hating nihilism; each new lament provides fresh evidence of a malfeasant government which waged diabolical war. American soldiers, reduced to stereotypes, are portrayed either as cruel sadists who murdered innocent civilians, or hollow wrecks destroyed by their enforced servitude to the devil. Reading war books has become a ritualized flagellation for the embarrassment and shame of Vietnam.

The politically correct image of an unjust war encourages the production of victim literature which in turn reinforces that image. Gloria Emerson's *Winners and Losers* and Myra MacPherson's *Long Time Passing* are prime examples of this genre. Both books conform to an accepted liberal interpretation of the war, and perhaps for this reason have not been subjected to serious critical examination. They are both fascinating and insightful, but also deeply flawed. Suspect sources are accepted without question if they conform to preconceived notions of an invidious America. Shocking statistics are gathered from questionable sources and sometimes simply do not tally properly. Emerson, for instance, fails to take into account Hanoi's penchant for exaggeration when adding up the cost of the war. If, as she claims, the war produced around 1.8 million civilian casualties between 1965 and 1975, that translates to nearly 500 dead and wounded *every day* for ten years.[4] The war was destructive, but probably not *that* destructive. Likewise, MacPherson writes eloquently about the psychiatric casualties of the war, but her figures for mental cases, drug addiction and suicide among American ex-servicemen have been questioned by the medical professionals who treat these casualties. Nevertheless, because both books conform to a widely accepted vision of the war, they have enjoyed healthy sales and the conclusions they contain have been incorporated without question into the accepted mythology.

Likewise, James Carroll's *American Requiem* demonstrates that one does not need to get one's evidence straight in order to win a National Book Award and climb the bestseller lists. The book is a deeply moving account of Carroll's peculiar torment as a pacifist son of a militarist father. (Joe Carroll was a US Air Force lieutenant-

---

4 Gloria Emerson, *Winners and Losers* (New York, NY, 1992), p. 357.

general who was Director of the Defence Intelligence Agency during the war.) But its admirable sensitivity cannot excuse simple (but serious) errors like his claim that 41,676 American soldiers died in Vietnam during the Nixon presidency.[5] Errors like this are important because the book is important; its popularity means that Carroll has become an accepted authority on the war, which he clearly is not.

A significant group of Americans object vehemently to the excessively negativist view of the war and its legacy prominent in the 'serious' literature. The detractors fall mainly on the political right, but not all are politically conservative. Some simply object to the unfair and one-dimensional picture of the American soldier which emerges from the literature, an image reinforced by almost all Hollywood films. As any careful study of the American force will reveal, that image is distinctly unfair. Bergerud's history of the 25th Division, *Red Thunder, Tropic Lightning*, largely based on oral testimony, reveals a group of men not unlike their fathers who fought in Korea or the Second World War. In other words, they were a reasonable cross-section of wider society, reflecting both its flaws and its strengths. Harold Moore's *We Were Soldiers Once . . . and Young*, a moving account of one battalion's experiences in the battle of Ia Drang, reinforces the Bergerud argument. The heroism of the men is revealed through a patient narration of their action, rather than through any propagandistic intent on the part of the author.

Propaganda does appear to be the underlying intent in James Webb's *Fields of Fire* and Robert Limberg's *The Nightingale's Song*, both of which attempt, not entirely successfully, to correct a perceived injustice by grafting conventional heroic imagery on to this war. What results is a rather awkward amalgam, not unlike the decision to place a traditional heroic statue next to the black granite wall of the Vietnam Memorial. That decision, not uncoincidentally, was also inspired by Webb.

The stark nature of Vietnamese communism, revealed after 1975, is ammunition assiduously exploited by those who argue that the US was right all along. Norman Podhoretz, in *Why We Were in Vietnam*, accepts that Johnson's decision for war was perhaps reckless, given the improbability of success. But he vehemently rejects the idea that the war was immoral or criminal, since its aim was to save South Vietnam from the cruel fate which did indeed befall it after 1975.

---

5 James Carroll, *An American Requiem* (Boston, MA, 1996), p. 192. The actual figure is closer to half that number. It is not entirely clear why, in Carroll's catalogue of infamy, Johnson ranks as merely misguided, while Nixon is judged a demon.

The book is interesting and certainly articulately expressed, but one has to accept that it exists only because of the anti-war, anti-America polemics of the Left. It is as belligerently subjective as the arguments it seeks to rebut. And most historians, one presumes, would object to reasoning which holds that the decision to go to war in 1965 can be justified with reference to events which occurred ten years later. The Podhoretz argument fails to take into account the possibility that the nature of the Vietnamese regime after 1975 was in part determined by the experience of a long and ugly conflict.

The Vietnam debate is often like a balloon without a string. At issue are competing visions of America, rather than conflicting explanations of the war. Antagonists engage in a self-indulgent intellectual exercise in which the war becomes an abstraction and the soldiers mere cardboard cut-outs. As in any contemporary historical debate, the postmodernists ride to the rescue, offering to unpack the historical debate and tell us what we are really thinking – and why. But their analysis instead produces even greater confusion; the balloon drifts away, buffeted by the latest intellectual whim. For example, in Eliot Gruner's *Prisoners of Culture: Representing the Vietnam POW* the war is reduced to mere stimulus for deconstructionist masturbation:

> I seek to break up what I see as a monologue, a dominant of the POW experience in American culture. I want to show the polyphony that lurks beneath the surface of popular culture. I juxtapose the representations and production to make their contradictions visible and to soften the hard objective truths that feed POW myth. I do this not so much to oppose the texts but to embrace the differences. I want to show that the array of representations I examine has rehistoricized the American POW experience in ways that channel us into certain roles and patterns of action.[6]

This sort of thing might excite fetishists who derive excitement from postmodern pillow talk, but does nothing for those who seek an understanding of the war and its effect. It is also intentionally exclusivist, designed to intimidate those who do not speak the latest jargon. Unfortunately, too many readers are impressed by that which they do not understand.

One side sees a war of perpetrators and victims, the other of heroes and villains. The war was ugly, brutal, costly and riddled with

---

6 Elliot Gruner, *Prisoners of Culture: Representing the Vietnam POW* (New Brunswick, NJ, 1993), p. 3.

perplexing moral contradictions. It did produce an extraordinary crop of casualties who still suffer the mental torment of combat and defeat. But it also saw men and women on both sides who served valiantly, acted morally and afterwards went home to lead normal lives. The literature of the war is confusing precisely because the war was (and is) confusing. It was so many different things to different people. But there is no hope in ignoring the cultural output on the assumption that a clearer contest will eventually be revealed once the haze of personal testimony is blown away.[7] Stripped of its cultural output, the Vietnam War becomes a sterile contest devoid of emotion. Tin soldiers confront each other on a cardboard battlefield and negotiators deal on diplomacy's chessboard. It was not that type of war. No war is.

SYNTHESIS

Vietnam scholarship, like much of the history produced in the United States, has been characterized by attempts to break the topic into constituent parts, each meticulously analysed. Scholars establish their reputations by stamping their ownership on a tiny territory of the war. Much of this scholarship is highly skilled and professionally presented. But the big picture is missing.

There are many books which claim to be definitive histories of the Vietnam War. But a glance at the table of contents quickly reveals the real interests of the author and the limitations of the subject matter. Phillip Davidson's *Vietnam at War*, for instance, is in truth a study of the big unit confrontations of the Johnson and Nixon years. Granted, Davidson spends quite a bit of time on the French war, but leaves the reader with few useful lessons to apply to the later conflict involving the Americans. He also never gets to grip with the role of guerrilla warfare within the revolution and therefore never really explains the American defeat. Since Davidson was chief of US military intelligence in Saigon from 1967 to 1969, his book is perhaps an allegory on the way the US conducted the war. The essentially political nature of this conflict is a characteristic Davidson still has not grasped.

In some attempts at synthesis the author's agenda is so intrusive that any attempt at balance is quickly abandoned. Marilyn Young's *The Vietnam Wars, 1945–1990* is the moral relativist's approach to the conflict: the US was evil to have entered the conflict, and the

---

7 An argument frequently presented by Joe P. Dunn, who feels that 'too much of Vietnam is presented through emotive approaches and the desired result is to evoke passion'. See his contribution to the 1996 Vietnam Conference, on the Texas Tech University Vietnam Center website.

enemy of evil is always good. American soldiers are therefore ruthless 'killers' and the revolutionaries are victims, martyrs or dedicated patriots. The book's lively, engaging style provides camouflage for the shoddy, slanted analysis. Because she does not really understand how the war was fought (violence apparently does not interest her), Young confidently concludes that the protesters were instrumental in bringing it to an end. As with the Vietnamese communists, protesters were good because their enemy was bad.

The opposite case is presented by Guenter Lewy in *America in Vietnam*. Billed as a dispassionate examination of the American conduct of the war, it attempts to cut through the hysterical propaganda about 'war crimes' evident in much of the war literature. Figures for civilian casualties are cleverly juxtaposed with statistics of communist-inspired assassinations, the effect being to show that, if this war was ugly, the ugliness was at least omnipresent. On that point, Lewy is undoubtedly correct. His book is a useful antidote to the irresponsible and exaggerrated accusations which have been hurled at the United States and which have been particularly offensive to the reputation of American ex-servicemen. But Lewy's statistics are often as suspect as those of Emerson and Young, though in the opposite direction. His evidence seems to have been carefully collected to fit a preconceived agenda.

Gabriel Kolko is even more guilty of this fault. His *Anatomy of a War*, an unashamedly Marxist analysis, offers a refreshing perspective on the nature and progress of the Vietnamese revolution. But the proof he provides for his assertions is often taken indiscriminately from the propaganda merchants who are central to his story. There are few more complete and detailed studies of the war, and the general thrust of Kolko's assessment of American defeat is clear and logical. But it is very easy for the reader to be lured in by the author's fluent analysis. Amid the intelligent commentary atrocious factual errors lurk like vicious mines on a seemingly safe jungle trail.

George Herring's *America's Longest War* and Robert Schulzinger's *A Time for War* are much more useful studies. Both are clearly written and reasonably balanced in their analysis, though Herring seems the more willing to criticize the actors in the drama. He is strong on the diplomacy of the war (his speciality) but does not cover as much ground as Schulzinger. Both books are strangely weak on the domestic struggle, the culture of the war and its legacy. Is it possible to understand, for instance, the American attitude to the Vietnam War without mentioning Bob Dylan, Merle Haggard and Sergeant Barry Sadler, each of whose songs brilliantly encapsulated a constituency of opinion?

Both also view the conflict from the wrong end of the telescope. We see the American war as it affected the Vietnamese, rather than how the Vietnamese (on both sides) shaped the war. Since the communists controlled the pace of the conflict throughout, this seems a strange failing.

Stanley Karnow's *Vietnam: A History* is the book to which most Vietnam historians return in frustration after rejecting the other flawed attempts at synthesis. It is, ironically, one of the oldest histories of the war. The author is not a historian at all, but a member of that suspicious band of war reporters whose impressionistic views historians usually find suspect. As the title implies, the book is not just about the war. For this reason, the picture it presents is detailed and complete. It is also a very eloquent narration which achieves a remarkable balance, given that it was written in 1983 when an objective view was rare and acrimony rife.

But the book is showing its age. A vast amount of detailed analysis has been completed since Karnow first published his book. A great deal more is known about the structure and conduct of the Vietnamese revolution, the effectiveness of various American tactics, and the intricacies of the conflict during the Nixon years. Personal testimonies collected from soldiers on both sides have cut through the stereotypes which once prevailed. As a result, the North Vietnamese victory and the American defeat have a shape which Karnow, for understandable reasons, never quite appreciated.

It is admittedly valuable to study aspects of the war in detail and isolation, for only by doing so can one get to grips with the very complex issues involved. But any engagement with the complexities of the war has to begin with a general overview which maps out the interconnectedness of those issues. This book represents a new attempt at synthesis. As has been shown, the literary output is massive; it is very easy to drown in a frustrating morass of contradictory assertions. Choices have to be made about what can be covered and what left alone. But the goal throughout has been to produce as complete a picture as is possible within the confines of a manageably sized book. My aim has been to convey the many fronts of a single war. It was fought in Saigon, Hanoi, Washington, Moscow, Beijing, Berkeley and Chicago, not to mention in towns and villages across America and in the tiny hamlets of South Vietnam. It was a war of guerrillas, grunts and professional soldiers, protesters, politicians and ordinary civilians. The war began before 1945 and, despite its official end in 1975, continues to plague the minds of those involved.

This book is an account of that one war.

1 'THE WHITE MAN IS FINISHED IN ASIA'

FROGS IN THE BOTTOM OF A WELL

If imperialism is an ideology of exploitation, the French were model imperialists. With typically Gallic self-assurance, they seized colonies and drained them of their riches. Unlike the British, they did not burden themselves with a great moral mission. Judgement is therefore easier: cruelty did not have its flip side – benevolence. Granted, there was talk of a *mission civilisatrice*: 'I want to give you the instrument of liberation which will gradually lead you toward those superior spheres to which you aspire', Governor-General Albert Sarraut told the Vietnamese in 1917.[1] But that instrument was in truth French domination; indigenes were fortunate to be exploited by a culture so sublime. They would prosper while their masters robbed them blind.

Prior to the French arrival, Vietnam was ruled by the tottering Nguyen dynasty. During the regime's death throes, the country became a cauldron of viperous factionalism. Sensing an opportunity, in 1858 the French sent a fleet into Da Nang harbour, supposedly to avenge the arrest of a missionary. But, meeting determined resistance, they abandoned plans to capture the imperial capital at Hué. Vietnam's lure did not, however, abate. Turning their attention to the Mekong delta, they eventually forced the Vietnamese court in 1862 to cede several provinces surrounding Saigon. This became the colony of Cochinchina.

Thereafter, the French tightened their grip. By 1884, their power extended, the country was divided into three administrative units: Cochinchina in the south, Annam in the centre and Tonkin in the north. The Vietnamese monarch retained token sovereignty, but real power rested with the French. At around the same time France extended her control over Laos and Cambodia, which joined a single Indochinese Union.

1 William J. Duiker, *Sacred War* (New York, NY, 1995), p. 11.

18

Overwhelming a weak regime was one thing, bringing stability to a divided country another. Beneath the impressive veneer of French dominion there existed a rotten state. French hegemony thrived upon Vietnamese discord; the administration did not have to be strong since its subjects were weak and quarrelsome. According to Phan Boi Chau, one of Vietnam's most revered nationalists, the Vietnamese had themselves to blame for their exploitation:

> even though the universe was shaken by American winds and European rains, our country was still in a period of dreaming in a deep sleep. Our people were still blind and resigned to their lot. We cannot blame them, for even well-known people from the higher classes like myself were like frogs in the bottom of a well or ants at the bottom of their hole. We knew nothing about life. I think that there must be no more tragic-comic people in the world than our people.[2]

The traditional order was dead, but no new ideology or system had emerged to ease their adjustment to the modern world and strengthen their resistance to Western incursion. Vietnamese torpidity would prove one of the greatest obstacles to nationalist fulfilment, and would define the limits of future rebellions.

The sector most ripe for exploitation was agriculture. Eventually, on the eve of the Second World War, in Cochinchina 6,200 landlords with estates in excess of 50 hectares owned 45 per cent of the total rice acreage. Sixty per cent of the rural population was landless.[3] Though smallholders still existed, their minuscule plots rendered them worse off than tenant farmers. This meant that power, in the form of land control, was centralized among relatively few individuals who, if not French, were at least indebted to the French system. That system caused deep disaffection among the common people. For the peasant, the land is not just a parcel of ground, but a mystical ancestral link. As the Americans would later discover, the best way to alienate the peasant is to sever that link. Thus, the cost to the French of controlling the countryside was widespread animosity among the peasants. It is no coincidence that this group would become the core of the future communist revolution.

A contemporary American economist judged the French system a 'mechanism for widespread economic exploitation and social abuse'.[4]

2 Robert J. McMahon, ed., Major Problems in the History of the Vietnam War (Lexington, MA, 1990), p. 31.
3 Gabriel Kolko, Anatomy of a War (New York, NY, 1994), p. 15.
4 Eric Bergerud, The Dynamics of Defeat (Boulder, CO, 1991), p. 16.

Tenants paid landlords 40–60 per cent of an arbitrary 'normal' yield. In abnormal years, which occurred horribly often, rent could exceed 80 per cent of yield. The tenant also had to meet *ad hoc* demands for his labour and provide 'gifts' designed to keep the landlord agreeable. Landlords tightened their hold further through loans to peasants, at interest rates of 50–70 per cent. Small loans had rates as high as 3,600 per cent.[5] Borrowing was essential in order to meet tax demands and to buy over-priced necessities (like salt) on which the French held a monopoly. Taxes had to be paid in silver, acquired from lenders or landlords at inflated rates of exchange. Whenever the price of rice fell, as during the depression of the 1930s, the need to borrow rose.

By the interwar period, Vietnam was a textbook case of nascent revolution. Thanks to the French, the peasant class had been radicalized. As for the small proletariat, employed mainly on rubber plantations and in coal mines on the Tonkin coast, French practices 'were unquestionably among the most violent and exploitative known to the twentieth century'.[6] Plantation workers were hardly distinguishable from slaves. Wages were so miserly, working conditions so abominable and penalties for petty offences so severe that the average peasant never stayed long on a job before he quit and returned to his village. This huge turnover enhanced the development of working-class consciousness. Though workers numbered hardly more than 1 per cent of the total population, those who had been radicalized by their experiences exceeded the number actually working. In other words, there were many Vietnamese who hated the French not for their land policies, but for their basic cruelty. General Tran Van Don, whose family actually thrived under French rule, nevertheless admitted that:

> Economic development always involved what benefited
> France and her French colonies, not the Vietnamese. Vietnam
> was kept as dependent on the mother country as possible, both
> as a source of raw materials and as a captive market for French
> manufactured goods. Customs regulations were designed to
> promote French products and discourage competition from
> foreign goods.[7]

Between 1918 and 1939, 62 per cent of Vietnamese imports were French.[8] Though this closed system of trade might seem impressive, in

---

5 Kolko, *Anatomy*, p. 15.
6 Ibid., p. 16.
7 Tran Van Don, *Our Endless War* (Novato, CA, 1978), p. 9.
8 Peter MacDonald, *Giap* (London, 1993), p. 49.

truth French producers drew little benefit since most Vietnamese were too poor to buy French goods.

An indigenous bourgeoisie did not develop in Vietnam. Paranoid about creating rivals to their power, the French discouraged its growth. Their fear that knowledge is power made a mockery of the *mission civilisatrice*. Education, warned the Governor-General Martial Merlin, made 'not one coolie less, but one rebel more'. Though the traditional Vietnamese village-level education continued to function, access to formal education within the French system was severely restricted. In the 1930s, only 15 per cent received any training at all, and only about 1 per cent attended school above elementary level.[9] Ironically, however, the French found that by 1940 there were not sufficient places in the colonial bureaucracy for the few Vietnamese they were educating, simply because the economy had not developed enough. Idleness bred discontent among those few who had actually benefited from a French education. Merlin's warning, it seems, had some justification.

The small industrial sector was a closed system dominated by outsiders, either Europeans, or Indians and Chinese who had traded in Vietnam for centuries. Vietnamese landlords who amassed considerable wealth via rents and usury could not invest their income in urban ventures. In one sense, the French policy worked. The urban bourgoisie provided significant energy for independence movements like the Congress Party in India and the Kuomintang in China. But in Vietnam, restrictions placed upon indigenous landlords inspired them not towards rebellion, but rather towards greater collaboration. There was money to be made in dancing the French tune. The one significant exception was the Constitutionalist Party, a group of civil servants, professionals, landlords and merchants who campaigned for a bigger say in running the country. But they were easily bought off with minor concessions. As a result, when the communists began to organize, they encountered no rival nationalist force.

VIETNAMESE COMMUNISM

The Vietnamese revolution embodied the character of Ho Chi Minh.[10] He provided leadership, direction, inspiration and stability. Ho learned his Marxism in France,[11] where he experienced at first hand the

---

9 Walter Capps, *The Unfinished War* (Boston, MA, 1990), p. 29; Duiker, *Sacred War*, p. 15.

10 The name 'Ho Chi Minh' will be used throughout the text, even though his real name was Nguyen Tat Thanh, and an earlier alias was Nguyen Ai Quoc.

11 Ho spent 30 years, from 1911 to 1941, out of Vietnam.

hypocrisy of Western liberalism. The West's liberal ideals contradicted its exploitative colonial policies. This incongruity was driven home when Ho attended the Versailles Peace Conference in 1919 and argued for the Vietnamese right of self-determination, on the basis of Woodrow Wilson's Fourteen Points. But his appeal fell on deaf ears.

The anti-colonial potential of Marxism appealed to Ho, though he despaired when Western communists turned a blind eye toward the imperialist excesses of their own countries. At the Socialist Conference in Tours in 1920, he condemned those French who 'conquered our country with bayonets. . . . we have not only been oppressed and exploited shamelessly, but also tortured and poisoned pitilessly.'[12] He was intrigued by Lenin's *Theses on the National and Colonial Questions*, which proposed that communist parties in countries under colonial rule should ally with middle-class nationalist groups in order to defeat imperialism. An enthusiastic internationalist, Ho saw the Vietnamese struggle as part of a world-wide effort to destroy colonialism. He would not have labelled himself a nationalist, preferring instead the term patriot. In the temper of the 1930s, nationalism seemed too chauvinistic, implying progress at the expense of other countries, a contradiction of Ho's internationalist outlook.

Ho realized that the chief victims of colonialism were the peasantry. Since Marxism was tailored to the proletariat, a miniscule group in Vietnam, it had to be adapted to appeal to peasants. Vietnam needed a revolution of the land which offered the peasantry a secure but relatively undisturbed life. The importance given to the peasantry distinguished Ho's communism from the Viet Nam Quoc Dan Dang (VNQDD), the militant nationalist, but vehemently anti-communist party. It consisted mainly of urban intellectuals who had little awareness of rural problems. The VNQDD wanted to evict the French forcibly, militancy which alienated the more evolutionary Constitutionalist Party. The bitter divide between non-communist nationalists benefited Ho's party, the only group both nationalist in outlook and national in scope.

Ho did not, however, wish to alienate those who did not share his ideology. He sought instead a flexible, pragmatic united front. The Vietnamese Communist Party (VCP), established in Hong Kong in February 1930, made a mockery of Comintern directives that parties should be formed only from truly radical elements. Qualifications for membership in Ho's united front were so broadly defined that potential allies were many, enemies surprisingly few. The peasantry would

12 Ho Chi Minh, *Selected Writings* (Hanoi, 1973), p. 16.

be rallied by means of a land-based revolution whose victims would be the large landlords and, of course, the imperialists. But Ho was determined that the party should not immediately alienate rich peasants, smaller landlords and the tiny urban bourgeousie, who might form a rival focus of power. Ho's Marxism also appealed to Vietnamese intellectuals who were just awakening from the 'mood of bewilderment and pessimism which had characterized their elders. . . . they possessed an infectious spirit of optimism and cultural pride.'[13]

This emphasis upon a united front was immediately denounced by the Comintern, which judged Ho's programme too unprincipled and demanded that Vietnamese communists conform more closely to the ideology of the class struggle. A meeting of the VCP in October reversed the February decisions and changed the name of the group to the Indochinese Communist Party (ICP), marginalizing Ho. Party journals censured Ho's nationalist, peasant-based plan.

The restless impetuosity of communist rivals was apparent during the Nghe Tinh uprisings which followed the May Day marches in 1930. The uprisings at first seemed promising; by autumn, soviets were established in many cantons and villages. But French reaction was ruthless. Approximately 1,300 people identified as rebels were killed, with thousands imprisoned or deported. By 1932 10,000 political prisoners were serving sentences in French jails.[14] Ho's opposition to the uprising did not prevent him from being rounded up in Hong Kong by British authorities cooperating with the French. He was imprisoned for two years. While the uprising was undoubtedly a setback, the savage French reaction did further radicalize the Vietnamese people. It also eliminated some of the more brazen elements of the ICP. The revolt demonstrated, by its failure, Ho's wisdom: the movement required the support of the rural population, which would take time to cultivate.

By 1935, a united front seemed the best response to the rising tide of fascism, even to the otherwise doctrinaire Comintern. But then, in August 1939, the Soviet non-aggression pact with Hitler sent communist parties into a spin. In Vietnam, the French reacted by cracking down on communist activity, unofficially tolerated over the previous few years. Most of the ICP officials were arrested and imprisoned, depriving the party of central control.

Nothing was more corrosive of colonialism than the Second World War. The ease with which the Japanese overturned Western power in

---

13 David G. Marr, *Vietnamese Tradition on Trial, 1920–1945* (Berkeley, CA, 1981), pp. 415–16.
14 Kolko, *Anatomy*, p. 29.

Asia contradicted the principle of white supremacy which lay at the core of colonialism. The German defeat of France in June 1940 also had profound implications in Vietnam. Vichy France, cooperating with Germany and her allies, allowed the Japanese to establish bases in Vietnam. This nefarious deal exposed France as hopelessly weak and opportunistic. Colonialism took on a fascist slant.

Recognizing an opportunity, Ho returned to Vietnam in February 1941. 'Fellow-countrymen! Rise up! . . . The hour has struck!', he declared in May. 'Raise aloft the banner of insurrection and lead the people throughout the country to overthrow the Japanese and the French.'[15] That month, he helped establish the Viet Nam Doc Lap Dong Minh (League for the Independence of Vietnam), commonly known as the Vietminh. The united front remained paramount. Land reform was to be limited to land controlled by the French or by their collaborators. This cleverly removed one important reason for collaborating: the Vietminh had postulated a future in which one could be both wealthy *and* patriotic. The Eighth Plenum of the ICP in May 1941 proclaimed that 'At this moment, sectional and class interests should be subordinated to the vital interests of the country, the nation'.[16] The class struggle had not been abandoned, merely set aside for tactical reasons. It was thought that the united front would also impress the Allied nations.

Over 2,000 Vietnamese communists were rounded up by Vichy authorities, an ironically fortuitous development since many were doctrinaire Marxists whose reckless audacity endangered the movement. Ho remained certain that the opportune moment (*thoi co*) for launching the revolution would not come until Japan was on the verge of defeat. Vichy repression also meant that members of many other diverse anti-colonial movements were arrested, executed, driven underground or persuaded to collaborate. This cleared the field for Ho; at the moment he was ready to assert his authority, he found no serious competitors. Backing him were a talented and devoted band of gifted subordinates, men like Pham Van Dong, Vo Nguyen Giap and Truong Chinh.

The key was to be prepared when *thoi co* arrived. In December 1944 Ho gave Giap command of a small band of guerrillas which would eventually evolve into the massive People's Army of Vietnam (PAVN). According to Douglas Pike, 'the Party was not preparing to

---

15 Ho, *Selected Writings*, p. 46.
16 Ken Post, *Revolution, Socialism and Nationalism in Viet Nam*, 5 vols (Aldershot, 1989), Vol. 1, p. 73.

build an army but ... to create a new militant force so unique that they would have held the word *army* technically incorrect and certainly inappropriate'.[17] The party preferred the term Armed Propaganda Team, a unit which would spend as much time proselytizing the natives as fighting the French. The team, formed by Giap in the Dinh Ca valley of Cao Bang, consisted of 34 persons, armed with two revolvers and 31 rifles, including 14 flintlocks used in the Russo-Japanese War.[18] Giap himself had no formal military training.

Contacts were established with US Office of Strategic Service (OSS) agents operating in southern China. Ho offered the Americans assistance in the war against Japan in exchange for recognition of the Vietminh. Franklin Roosevelt was sympathetic to self-determination in Asia; France, he thought, 'had done nothing to improve the natives since she had the colony'.[19] 'French Indochina must not be turned back to the French', he argued in January 1945.[20] But his British and French allies were understandably reluctant to encourage anticolonial movements. Since Roosevelt could not afford to alienate them, he ignored Ho's offer. Major Archimedes Patti did, however, liaise with Vietminh forces, and helped to train a small unit under Giap's command. 'It was a very small operation as far as war is concerned', Patti later admitted, 'but nonetheless it is true that we worked with the Vietminh against the Japanese.'[21] Though Patti liked Giap, he found the leaders of the VNQDD 'hopelessly disoriented politically', with no real ideas about what they would do if they actually seized power.[22]

Meanwhile, wartime disruption made life worse for peasants, further radicalizing them. Japanese cruelties, which the French were powerless to prevent, increased the contempt which the Vietnamese felt for their colonial masters. In 1945 the Japanese imprisonment of key French administrators who knew the system of dikes on the Day River led to widespread flooding and crop failures in northern provinces. As many as 600,000 people died in the resulting famine, which was exacerbated by the Japanese refusal to release grain surpluses. Every hunger-related death, every instance of colonial injustice, increased the communist appeal.

17 Douglas Pike, *PAVN: People's Army of Vietnam* (Novato, CA, 1986), p. 20.
18 Ibid., p. 28.
19 Gary R. Hess, 'Franklin D. Roosevelt and Indochina', *Journal of American History* 59 (1972), p. 363.
20 Walter La Feber, 'Roosevelt, Churchill and Indochina, 1942–1945', *American Historical Review* 80 (1975), p. 1292.
21 MacDonald, *Giap*, p. 35.
22 Cecil B. Currey, *Victory at Any Cost* (Washington, DC, 1997), p. 109.

REVOLUTION

In March 1945 the Japanese abolished the Vichy administration in Vietnam and granted token independence to the Vietnamese under the puppet emperor Bao Dai. Vichy officials were imprisoned, in effect dismantling the French administrative network in the countryside. Since Japanese control did not extend beyond the cities, rural Vietnam became a political vacuum which the Vietminh were determined to fill. Nationalist and communist elements now operated in relative freedom. Giap's units joined with other scattered nationalist detachments to form the Vietnamese Liberation Army. The Vietminh had hoped for a long, slow Japanese decline, which would allow time to build a legitimate alternative government. But the swift Japanese surrender after Hiroshima and Nagasaki caught the Vietminh unprepared.

At the Potsdam conference in late July, Allied leaders agreed that Chinese forces would occupy northern Vietnam and British forces the south. On 9 September 1945, 152,500 soldiers of the Nationalist Chinese Army under General Lu Han marched over the border. Their sheer number, and their rapacious attitude, worsened food shortages. Three days after the Chinese arrival, the 20th Indian Division under Major-General Douglas Gracey arrived in Saigon and took control of the South. Neither the Chinese nor the British exerted real power outside the cities. France was eager to reassert herself, but ill-prepared to do so. No other nationalist faction was prepared to step into the breach. Only the Vietminh were capable of presenting a new way forward for the country. Thus, mainly by surviving the difficult years of the 1930s and the war, the communists were poised to exploit opportunities.

On 19 August a huge crowd gathered in Hanoi to celebrate the Japanese surrender. The demonstration was organized by a nationalist committee loyal to Bao Dai. Suddenly, six armed Vietminh soldiers mounted the platform, tore down Bao Dai's imperial standard and raised the red communist flag. The crowd, suitably coached beforehand, began waving Vietminh flags. 'With inconceivable strength', wrote Truong Chinh, 'the whole Vietnamese people rose up and did their utmost to break the yoke imposed by the French and Japanese fascists, and resolutely went forward . . . in the vanguard of the Far-East peoples' liberation movement.'[23] Though the demonstration was by no means as spontaneous as subsequent myth proudly proclaimed, it left Vietminh leaders convinced of the popularity of their movement.

23 Truong Chinh, *Primer for Revolt* (New York, NY, 1963), p. 16.

As the Vietminh swept through the North they encountered little resistance. In late August Vietminh units arrived in Hué where they confronted Bao Dai. Given the choice between abdication and execution, he chose the former. On 2 September President Ho proclaimed the new Republic of Vietnam. His carefully chosen words were calculated to impress both his audience and, beyond them, the Americans – whose support he desperately needed. The 'Star Spangled Banner' was played and Ho praised the 'particularly intimate relationship with the United States'.[24] His Declaration of Independence had a familiar ring:

> 'All men are created equal. They are endowed by their Creator with certain inalienable Rights; among these are Life, Liberty and the pursuit of Happiness.' This immortal statement appeared in the Declaration of Independence of the United States of America in 1776. In a broader sense, it means: All the peoples on the earth are equal from birth, all the peoples have a right to live and to be happy and free.[25]

The revolution was not a military victory, but a general uprising. It was

> the sort of mass voluntarist surge of power that anticolonialists had dreamt of for decades. . . . for those who were in their teens or early twenties, it represented the formative experience of their lives, fostering a deep sense of soldiarity and readiness to sacrifice; older Vietnamese saw the August Revolution as justification for the previous agonies, capping three generations of struggle against unbelievable odds.[26]

The people brought Ho to power. He and his followers would never forget this fact. The general uprising was henceforth enshrined as an article of faith in Vietnamese communist mythology: it was confidently assumed that the people, having risen once, could be persuaded to rise again.[27]

Impressive as the victory seemed, it was incomplete. In Cochinchina, two powerful religious sects, the Cao Dai and the Hoa Hao, siphoned off nationalist support. The Vietminh failure to consolidate power left the door ajar for a French return. Admiral Lord Louis Mountbatten, supreme commander of British forces in Southeast Asia,

---

24 Capps, *Unfinished War*, p. 31.
25 Ho, *Selected Writings*, p. 53.
26 Marr, *Vietnamese Tradition*, p. 416.
27 The 1968 Tet Offensive was another attempt to organize a mass uprising. On that occasion, the masses decided to stay on the fence.

instructed Gracey to remain neutral and not to hand power back to the French. But Gracey, under the influence of Colonel Jean Cedile, French commissioner for Cochinchina, ignored these orders. As Tran Van Don indicates, nationalists of all persuasions expected a more even-handed approach:

> The British cooperated beautifully, not only rearming the French who had remained in the area, but using armed Japanese in conjunction with their own troops to suppress Vietminh soldiers who were attempting to maintain their authority [in the South]. Although the British found a functioning Vietnamese government operating in Saigon, they refused to enter into any kind of negotiations, declared martial rule, and by force of arms gradually overwhelmed the Vietminh.[28]

Though Gracey cooperated with the French, he was appalled by their 'unnecessary brutality'. 'The French troops are leaving a pretty good trail of destruction behind them', he commented, fearing that this would lead to 'guerilla warfare, increased sabotage and arson as soon as we leave the country'.[29] A *Daily Telegraph* correspondent remarked: 'the solution of the problem of rule in Indo-China will depend primarily upon French ability to exercise tact and conciliation'.[30] Few considered the French capable of such tact.

Ho expected the Americans to restrain the French. But they had a different agenda. Roosevelt had initially preferred a brief period of United Nations (UN) trusteeship, prior to full independence. But at Yalta in February 1945, under pressure from the British, French and his own State Department, he reluctantly backed down. By October, a State Department document declared that 'with regard to the situation in French Indochina, this Goverment does not question French sovereignty'.[31] Roosevelt nevertheless hoped to pressure the French to grant independence quickly. But he was not prepared to risk instability in Europe for the sake of self-determination in Asia.

His successor, Harry Truman, unashamedly placed European security before decolonization, and was therefore more openly tolerant of French excesses. In a 1948 statement of policy, the Americans

---

28 Don, *Endless War*, p. 28.

29 Peter M. Dunn, *The First Vietnam War* (London, 1985), p. 293.

30 Anthony Short, 'France and Vietnam: the inevitable war', in Phil Melling and Jon Roper, eds, *America, France and Vietnam: Cultural History and Ideas of Conflict* (Swansea, 1991), p. 42.

31 William Appleman Williams *et al.*, eds, *America in Vietnam: A Documentary History* (New York, NY, 1975), p. 39.

categorically stated that they sought the 'establishment of a truly nationalist government in Indochina'.[32] But, in the Vietnamese case, nationalist meant communist. Truman's Secretary of State George C. Marshall announced that the US was 'unwilling to see colonial empires and administrations supplanted by philosophies and political organizations emanating from the Kremlin'. Dean Acheson, who succeeded Marshall, argued that the 'question whether Ho [is] as much nationalist as Commie is irrelevant. All Stalinists in colonial areas are nationalists.' He predicted that if Ho was allowed to consolidate power, he would inevitably resort to 'subordination [of the] state to Commie purposes and ruthless extermination [of] . . . opposition groups'.[33] He instead wanted the US to

> help toward solving the colonial-nationalist conflict in a way that would satisfy nationalist aims and minimize the strain on our Western European allies. This meant supporting the French 'presence' in the area as a guide and help to the three states in moving toward genuine independence within . . . the French Union.[34]

And pigs might fly. There was no way to satisfy nationalist aims, defeat communism *and* minimize the strain on France. As William Fulbright aptly described it, the American reaction to Ho's revolution reflected a fundamental contradiction:

> The American view of revolution, is . . . shaped by a simple but so far insuperable dilemma: we are simultaneously hostile to communism and sympathetic to nationalism, and when the two become closely associated, we become agitated, frustrated, angry, precipitate, and inconstant. Or, to make the point by a simple metaphor: loving corn and hating lima beans, we simply cannot make up our minds about succotash.[35]

THE FIRST VIETNAM WAR: PHASE ONE

The return of the French to the South challenged Ho's legitimacy, especially since France refused to recognize his right to govern in the North. Keen to resolve this problem, Ho initiated talks with Jean

32 McMahon, *Major Problems*, p. 74.
33 Williams *et al.*, eds, *America in Vietnam*, pp. 95–6.
34 Capps, *Unfinished War*, pp. 37, 39.
35 William Fulbright, *The Arrogance of Power* (London, 1967), p. 77. Succotash is a mixture of lima beans and corn, peculiar to North American diets.

Sainteny, the representative of Charles de Gaulle, in autumn 1945. After lengthy discussions, the French agreed to recognize North Vietnam as a 'free state', with its own army, parliament and finances – an advanced form of home rule. Ho in turn granted the French the right to station 15,000 troops in the North and to maintain a cultural and economic presence. It was further agreed that the southern population would eventually decide by plebiscite whether to affiliate with the free state or to make a separate arrangement with France.[36] Militants derided the apparent sell-out, but it is difficult to see how Ho could have persuaded the French to be more generous, given the American attitude and the weakness of his own regime. The important issue for him was that the deal had insured the departure of the Chinese. He chided his detractors:

> You fools! Don't you realize what it means if the Chinese remain? Don't you remember your history? The last time the Chinese came, they stayed a thousand years. The French are foreigners. They are weak. Colonialism is dying. The white man is finished in Asia. But if the Chinese stay now, they will never go. As for me, I prefer to sniff French shit for five years than eat Chinese shit for the rest of my life.[37]

For Ho, the agreement was a pragmatic short-term solution which would provide the respite he needed to consolidate power in the North and to prepare for the next stage of revolution.

But the agreement proved a false dawn. In Cochinchina, French colonials and their Vietnamese collaborators blocked the plebiscite. They were backed by the new French high commissioner, Georges Thierry d'Argenlieu, who staunchly defended the French right to govern. Dr Nguyen Van Thinh was chosen, with French approval, as head of the provisional government of Cochinchina, but his government was a sham. Beneath the veneer of Vietnamese rule, the power structure resembled pre-war days. Thinh was a mere puppet. 'They did give him an official car, but the license plate was marked with five zeros in order to make him an object of ridicule', Don recalled. Being constantly humiliated by the French and vilified by the Vietminh was agony for an otherwise principled man. 'France is not fair', he told Don in November 1946, 'I have not been enough of a puppet for them, so they are trying to replace me.'[38] The next day he hanged himself in protest.

36 Duiker, *Sacred War*, p. 57.
37 Stanley Karnow, *Vietnam: A History* (Harmondsworth, 1993), p. 169.
38 Don, *Endless War*, pp. 34–5.

By autumn 1946 armed clashes between French and autonomous Vietminh units were frequent. But Ho was not ready for war. His own troops were ill-prepared, and the possibility of outside aid was minimal given that Chinese communists were preoccupied with their own civil war and the Soviets with events in Europe. Keen to delay the inevitable clash, Ho proposed further negotations. But then, in late November, the French attempted to seize Haiphong harbour, used by the Vietminh to import Chinese arms. The confrontation quickly escalated, with the French eventually shelling the town, killing thousands.[39] Ho, under severe pressure from his colleagues, finally accepted that further negotiations were pointless.

On 19 December Vietminh detachments attacked various French strongpoints throughout Saigon. In the North, regular army units retreated to prepared positions in the Red River Delta. Giap discussed prospects with Ho:

> Uncle Ho asked me how long Hanoi could be held if the enemy widened the war in the north. I told him, 'Possibly for a month.' He then asked, 'What about the other towns?' I replied, 'We can hold them more easily.' 'And the countryside?' I said immediately, 'We can surely hold the countryside.' He pondered for awhile and then said, 'We shall return to the Viet Bac.'[40]

On 27 November the Vietminh withdrew from Hanoi and regrouped in the Viet Bac. A liberated zone was created in the area around Bac Can, 80 miles north of Hanoi. The zone was too remote and well-defended for the French to eliminate and too big for them to cordon.

The Vietminh set in motion a three-stage Maoist revolutionary strategy.[41] In the first phase, that of 'contention', small guerrilla units would harass French troops, while avoiding pitched battles. The troops would spend most of their time as propaganda agents indoctrinating the local peasantry. 'It was ... necessary', Giap explained, 'to bring everything into play to enlighten the masses of the people, educate and encourage them, organize them in fighting for national salvation.' He added: 'The Vietnamese people's war of liberation brought out the importance of building resistance bases in the countryside and the close and indissoluble relationships between the anti-imperialist revolution and

---

39 Or so the communists claimed. Exaggerating losses had clear propaganda value.
40 MacDonald, *Giap*, p. 76. The Viet Bac was the term Giap and others used for the provinces of Bac Thai, Cao Bang, Ha Giang, Lang Son and Tuyen Quang.
41 This is discussed in greater detail in Chapter 4.

the antifeudal revolution'.[42] In other words, the life of the peasantry had to be improved at the same time that French rule was undermined. 'We had to mobilize the masses for the resistance while trying to satisfy their immediate interest in improving their living conditions.'[43]

During phase two, that of equilibrium, battles would become more frequent and larger, but would be carefully chosen to ensure maximum attrition of the enemy. In phase three, the counter-offensive, the Vietminh would mobilize in division strength and aim for a decisive battle. The movement into a new phase did not imply the abandonment of previous tactics. Small guerrilla engagements, designed to wear down French morale, would continue throughout the war.

The first phase proceeded according to plan. French attempts to reassert control over the countryside were frustrated by Vietminh elusiveness. Truong Chinh described this quality:

> If the enemy attacks us from above, we will attack him from below. If he attacks us in the North, we will respond in Central or South Vietnam, or in Cambodia and Laos. If the enemy penetrates one of our territorial bases, we will immediately strike hard at his belly and back, . . . cut off his legs [and] destroy his roads.[44]

French pacification strategy entailed building concrete fortresses throughout the North, from which search and destroy operations were conducted. These also provided protective screens around important cities like Hanoi and Haiphong. But the strategy encouraged a defensive psychosis, further alienating the French from the peasantry. And, as time passed, the forts grew less secure, eroding the morale of French Union troops. Giap recognized that the fortresses revealed a French weakness:

> The main cause of their difficulties lay in the very nature of their unjust war of aggression. The ultimate goal of the French colonialists was to grab our land; faced with our opposition, they had to scatter their forces and set up thousands of military posts, big and small, to protect what they had seized . . . The more it was scattered the better were the opportunities we had to destroy it bit by bit.[45]

---

42 Vo Nguen Giap, *The Military Art of People's War*, ed. Russell Stetler (New York, NY, 1970), p. 96.
43 Ibid., p. 103.
44 Duiker, *Sacred War*, p. 67
45 MacDonald, *Giap*, p. 84.

The French could not tolerate a protracted war. The Vietminh, for whom patience was a weapon, could. 'It was only by a long hard resistance that we could wear out the enemy little by little while strengthening ours, progressively turn the balance of forces in our favor and finally win victory', Giap explained. 'We did not have any other way.'[46] The progressive deterioration of French will and the inexorable expansion of Vietminh forces would eventually produce *thoi co*, at which the decisive blow could be struck.

As time passed, the revolution spread and Vietminh numbers increased. 'This people's war for freedom is very hard and long', Truong Chinh wrote. 'To win victory, the whole people must participate in it, shoulder their responsibilities, be courageous and make sacrifices. Therefore, the entire people must be mobilized.'[47] But, according to one contemporary observer, the revolution had its sinister side:

> The Vietminh . . . subjected the people to an extremely painful strain, practically a permanent mobilization, with its unending meetings, mass demonstrations, and the like, with its requisitions, with its control of thoughts and acts, with its atmosphere of suspicion and its informers, with the arrogance – and often the arbitrariness – of its officials . . . and with the arrests, the abductions or assassination of its opponents and even of those considered lukewarm or suspect. If the Vietminh still seemed to be the only movement capable of achieving the fulfilment of the people's aspiration to national independence and to social justice, it nevertheless ruled with the aid of physical terror and moral constraint. As under the old régime, the political police . . . was the main buttress.[48]

One should not be led astray by noble rhetoric. The revolution succeeded because it was ruthless, not necessarily because it was good.

In early 1949 the French signed an agreement with Bao Dai at the Elysée Palace in Paris. The Elysée Accords established the Associated State of Vietnam (ASV), which granted some home rule but left foreign policy and defence, not to mention crucial economic and political decisions, the domain of the French. 'We could not truly call ourselves "independent" if we could not make foreign policy', Don argued. 'Had [the French] granted this concession, the Vietminh position would have been greatly undermined.'[49] The Accords were an attempt to

---

46 Giap, *Military Art*, pp. 103–4.
47 Truong Chinh, *Primer*, p. 205.
48 Anthony Short, *The Origins of the Vietnam War* (London, 1989), pp. 53–4.
49 Don, *Endless War*, p. 40.

establish a new focus for nationalist allegiance. But Bao Dai commanded little support. A man of dubious morals and mercurial temperament, he could be trusted only to look after himself. The Catholics, Hoa Hao and Cao Dai, who could not bring themselves to support the communists, backed him, but unenthusiastically. Others saw the Accords as proof of French perfidy, as did Bao Dai himself: 'What they call a Bao Dai solution turns out to be just a French solution'.[50]

Granted, the number who were 'pro French' was extremely small. But the 1945 revolution did encourage the growth of anti-communism. The fact that the French were able to fight a war at all was due to the fact that the party had its enemies among the Vietnamese people. A significant group of anti-communists looked to the French Union as a temporary solution; they had no love of France but they were scared of Ho. The bourgeoisie, those who possessed small parcels of land, the Catholics, the sects, and the Chinese together constituted a significant percentage of the population who feared the revolution. Significant, but not monolithic. As the more perceptive anti-communists would eventually discover, mobilizing the people to fight against a threatening ideology was infinitely more difficult than encouraging them to fight for land redistribution and independence. The party, like the devil, played the best tunes. But a legitimate and sizeable (if fragmented) opposition to Ho arose quickly, always existed and could not be imagined away.

The French hoped that the Accords would pave the way for a Vietnamese National Army (VNA) which would lighten their military burden. Put more bluntly, they wanted to downplay the imperial war and highlight those aspects of the conflict which resembled a civil war. It was also hoped that the Accords would impress the Americans who would commit themselves more wholeheartedly to the war. Though the Truman government felt deep unease about Bao Dai, it praised the new arrangement as 'the basis for the progressive realization of the legitimate aspirations of the Vietnamese people'[51] and gave official recognition to the ASV in February 1950. As the Americans would soon learn, it was a short step from recognizing the ASV to supporting it financially and militarily.[52]

Three events around this time inspired an abrupt shift in American policy toward Vietnam. The first was the victory of Mao Zedong's

50 *The Guardian*, 5 August 1997.

51 McMahon, *Major Problems*, p. 76.

52 See Gary R. Hess, 'The first American commitment in Indochina: the acceptance of the "Bao Dai Solution"', *Diplomatic History* 2 (1978), p. 337.

communists over Chiang Kai-shek's nationalist forces in China in the autumn of 1949. The spectre of communism, which hitherto had seemed a Soviet threat largely confined to Europe, had suddenly become global. Within the United States, argument raged over who to blame for 'losing' China. Further 'surrenders' would not be tolerated by the increasingly strident anti-communist lobby.

Since the Second World War, the Americans had assumed that their nuclear monopoly was sufficient to deter Soviet expansionism. All that changed with the second event, the explosion of the first Soviet atomic device in late 1949. Suddenly, it was no longer possible to keep the communists in check by threatening unilateral nuclear annihilation. America responded by approving the building of the largest peacetime military force in US history, and by encouraging rearmament among those countries which had joined the North Atlantic Treaty Organization the previous April.

The third defining event was the attack by North Korea upon South Korea in June 1950. Since it was assumed that the North Koreans would not have attacked without Soviet approval, the event seemed to presage a more aggressive Soviet strategy in Asia, and perhaps in the rest of the world. This threat was made all the more frightening by China's intervention in late November. The Korean situation seemed to demonstrate that there was indeed a Sino-Soviet bloc, bent on world domination. This meant that the American strategy of containment, first set out by George Kennan in early 1947 and described by him as 'long-term, patient, firm and vigilant', suddenly became a great deal more urgent. Kennan had postulated that 'the Kremlin is under no ideological compulsion to accomplish its purposes in a hurry', but recent events suggested otherwise.[53] The confident composure which characterized late-1940s foreign policy gave way to the fear and panic of the 1950s. This fear drew the Americans toward Indochina. Containing communism meant taking a stand in Vietnam. But painful memories of hordes of Chinese troops crossing the Yalu in 1950 would henceforth render the Americans rather cautious about the way they asserted themselves in Southeast Asia.

Mao's victory meant that China would now be better able to provide aid to the Vietminh. It is no coincidence that Giap's first great victories over the French were in the area of northern Vietnam which opened a route on which Chinese aid could flow relatively freely. The

53 John Spanier, *American Foreign Policy Since World War II* (New York, NY, 1965), pp. 31–2.

Chinese refused to entrench themselves as deeply in Vietnam as in Korea and were determined to avoid large losses of Chinese lives. Thus they moderated their largesse to the situation on the battlefield, seeking to tip the balance, not to overwhelm. The amount of aid was determined by how well the French performed. Supplies also came at a price. The Vietminh had to tone down anti-Chinese rhetoric and, superficially at least, had to tailor their own revolution more closely to Maoist designs. Ho's rhetoric became less anti-imperialist and more pro-communist.

The panic which Mao's success inspired in Washington was cleverly exploited by the French, who demanded a steadily increasing supply of military aid. In August 1950 Truman established the Military Assistance Advisory Group (MAAG), which was to counsel the French on the use of American hardware. In March 1952 the State Department announced categorically that 'The strategic importance of Indochina derives from its geographical position as a key to the defense of mainland Southeast Asia; its economic value as a potential large exporter of rice; and its political importance as an example of Western resistance to Communist expansion'.[54] But, like the Chinese, the Americans were determined to limit their aid to money and munitions, not men. They eventually financed 78 per cent of the war's total cost, or well over $1 billion by 1954.[55] But this aid did not buy a real say in the war. The US desperately wanted the French to make a categoric commitment to eventual independence for all her Indochinese possessions, otherwise the Bao Dai solution would be exposed for the sham that it was. The French responded by arguing (with some justification) that to do so would remove any remaining reason for the French public to support the war. The US realized that, if pushed too hard to reform, the French might pull out entirely. Thus, Americans were inextricably linked to an unpopular ideology and an even more unpopular administration. To the Vietnamese peasant they were the brokers of colonialism. Ho's speeches increasingly pointed to the Americans, not the French, as the real enemy. 'The US imperialists are intensifying their plot to discard the French colonialists so as to gain complete control over Indochina', he told supporters in 1950.[56] As would be demonstrated time and again, the Americans had a disturbing tendency to bring themselves into disrepute in their righteous war against communism.

54 Williams *et al.*, eds, *America in Vietnam*, p. 122.
55 Melvin Gurtov, *The First Vietnam Crisis* (New York, NY, 1967), p. 25.
56 McMahon, *Major Problems*, p. 82.

THE WAR ENTERS A NEW PHASE

By 1951, the Vietminh were feeling confident. They controlled two-thirds of the country by day, three-quarters by night.[57] Victories along the Chinese border during 1950 had shattered French morale. *Thoi co* seemed to have arrived. In January an attack was launched upon Vinh Yen, the last major French outpost north of Hanoi, by two Vietminh divisions, or around 20,000 men. But skilful use of his limited resources enabled the new French commander, Jean de Lattre de Tassigny, to blunt Giap's ambitions. The Vietminh proved particularly susceptible to aerial bombardments. Giap was dealt a severe repulse which left over 6,000 Vietminh dead.[58] He nevertheless remained confident that an offensive along the Day River in June 1951 would allow Ho a triumphant entry into Hanoi within six months. But after three weeks of heavy fighting, no significant progress was made. The two campaigns had cruelly exposed Vietminh logistical inadequacies. Giap had yet to figure out how to keep a large mobile force supplied.

When the monsoon ceased in late September, Giap attacked in the Red River valley, east of Hanoi. Anticipating this, de Lattre seized the town of Hao Binh, an important Vietminh communication centre, hoping to entice a counter-attack. Giap complied. Copying Chinese communist tactics, he launched human wave assaults upon French positions on 9 December 1951. Vietminh infantrymen were stacked like cordwood in front of French machine gunners. Ho was disappointed but did not censure his commander. His chagrin arose because the campaign had failed, not because losses were severe.

De Lattre died of cancer on 11 January 1952 and was replaced by Raoul Salan. He abandoned Hao Binh, which had served its purpose as a meatgrinder. In October, Giap launched his Black River valley offensive, the prelude to an invasion of Laos – designed to hearten the Pathet Lao communist guerrillas and open up a rich source of supplies. Central to Giap's Laotian strategy was the border town of Dien Bien Phu, seized on 30 November. The French at first claimed that it was not strategically important, but there was no escaping the fact that the Vietminh now controlled the vital northwestern corner of Vietnam. In early January 1953 came a *volte face* from Salan; he demanded that Dien Bien Phu be recaptured.

57 When darkness fell, villages became more dangerous for local French officials, who often retreated to their fortresses. The Vietminh would move in, and proceed with the task of indoctrinating the villagers.

58 Phillip B. Davidson, *Vietnam at War* (Oxford, 1988), pp. 109–12.

Salan put his faith in the *Base Aéro-Terrestre*, a tactic designed to exploit superior French weaponry in order to repulse human wave assaults and attrite the Vietminh. The base was comprised of an outer perimeter of gun posts and forts with interlocking fields of fire. These protected an airstrip, the link with the outside. In theory, the base could be surrounded without being cut off. The tactic was applied with significant success at Na San, adjacent to Provincial Road 41, in mid-October 1952. With deadly inevitability, a trap was set, the Vietminh charged and French machine gunners annihilated them. French casualties were negligible.

Success at Na San convinced the French that they could establish a large fortified camp deep within enemy territory, supply it by air and make it invulnerable to attack. They further surmised that if such a camp could be positioned somewhere immensely important to Giap, he would be forced to accept battle and would waste his main force in futile attacks. Thus, during 1953 the French concentrated upon re-creating Na San on a much larger scale at Dien Bien Phu. The Vietminh in turn concentrated upon exploiting their Black River success by moving into Laos. A collision became inevitable.

In May 1953 General Henri Navarre succeeded Salan. He promised an honorable end to the war, if given more troops. Though escalation ran counter to Prime Minister Joseph Laniel's intentions, he increased French forces to 250,000. At the same time, a further US$385 million in military aid was secured from the United States.[59] Stung by their Korean experience, and the 'loss' of China, the Americans sought to avoid another embarrassing concession to the communists. They were also keen for France to assume her rightful place in the European Defence Community (EDC). Germany could not join the EDC until France did, but France could not join until the Vietnam problem was settled. In concrete terms, this meant that the US supplied 554 aircraft, 347 naval vessels, 182 tanks, 1,498 combat vehicles, 20,593 trucks, 280,349 small arms and machine guns, 4,753 artillery pieces, 442,360,000 small arms ammunition, and 8,212,000 artillery rounds during the course of the war.[60]

Navarre's plan called for the French to assume a strategic defence in the North throughout the 1953–54 campaigning season. During this period, French forces would be increased and the VNA would be equipped for a larger role. Major operations in Annam and in the Central Highlands would cut Vietnam in two. Navarre would then

59 Gurtov, *First Vietnam Crisis*, p. 24.
60 Williams *et al.*, eds, *America in Vietnam*, p. 135.

concentrate on defeating the Vietminh in the North during the following year. 'A year ago none of us could see victory', one of his subordinates told *Time* magazine. 'There wasn't a prayer. Now we can see it clearly – like light at the end of the tunnel.'[61] These plans contradicted Laniel's goals. When he and Navarre met in Paris in July 1953, Laniel never let on that he was hoping for a Korea-style truce, dividing Vietnam between a communist North and a non-communist South. Nor did he explain that he was prepared to abandon Laos if the cost of protecting it rose too high. This was enormously significant, since Navarre's plans for retaking Dien Bien Phu were based on the presumed need to protect Laos. Thus, while Navarre envisaged employing his extra troops to defeat the Vietminh, Laniel saw them merely as a way to ensure success at a future peace conference.

Navarre's plan complemented the foreign policy of the new American President, Dwight Eisenhower, whose Secretary of State, John Foster Dulles, confidently predicted that the commander could end the war within a year.[62] Eisenhower was keen to avoid protracted, indecisive engagements like Korea. China's role in that war, when combined with the development of a Soviet nuclear arsenal and the escalating Cold War in Europe, made the dangers facing the US seem more threatening. Fear of communist expansionism inspired a more robust foreign policy. But the apparent ubiquity of the communist threat necessarily limited American assertiveness.

Eisenhower's solution was the 'New Look', a strategy which would rely more heavily upon nuclear weapons, either for deterrence or actual combat, instead of ground troops. As he explained to a reporter:

> I have said time and again that I can conceive of no greater disadvantage to America than to be employing its own ground forces, or any other kind of forces, in great numbers around the world . . .
> What we are trying to do is make our friends strong enough to take care of local situations by themselves, with the financial, the moral, the political and, certainly, only where our own vital interests demand, any military help.[63]

The New Look was formally unveiled in a speech by Dulles on 12 January 1954. 'It is not sound policy', he argued, 'permanently to

---

61 *Time*, 28 September 1953.
62 He was right, but it was not the end he had in mind!
63 Melanie Billings-Yun, *Decision Against War: Eisenhower and Dien Bien Phu, 1954* (New York, NY, 1988), p. 78.

commit United States land forces to Asia to a degree that gives us no strategic reserve.' But America, he claimed, was prepared to use her nuclear weaponry. It was not clear whether the US considered Vietnam worthy of the ultimate sanction, since Dulles also admitted that 'setbacks to the cause of freedom' would occur. 'Massive atomic and thermonuclear retaliation is not the kind of power which could most usefully be evoked under all circumstances.'[64] This deliberate uncertainty was (according to its exponents) the strength of the policy: adversaries would be kept in line because they could never be certain when and where the bomb might be deployed.

In November 1953 Ho learned that French, British, American and Soviet delegates would meet in Geneva in late April 1954 to discuss Vietnam, among other topics. Ho decided that the best way to expel the French was to inflict upon them a heavy defeat just before the conference. Giap felt the sharp end of these ambitions. Aware that the patience of his troops and of Ho was not limitless, he knew that further heavy losses would only be tolerable if they produced decisive victory. Giap realized that if the Vietminh did not win in 1954, and the war continued, he would henceforth face a French army fortified by ever more American money and bolstered by an improved VNA.

Laniel hoped that the conference would allow French troops to leave Vietnam with dignity intact. Like Ho, he felt that a favourable settlement was more likely if it coincided with success on the battlefield. By December 1953, French casualties in the war exceeded 100,000, and the peace faction at home was increasingly restless. Thus, for both sides, an honourable settlement seemed attractive, and a final bloody battle the necessary prerequisite.

DIEN BIEN PHU: THE PRELUDE

At 1035 hours on 20 November, two French paratroop battalions dropped in the vicinity of Dien Bien Phu. A fierce, hut-to-hut contest ensued with the Vietminh troops garrisoned there. At 1215, a French airstrike broke the Vietminh resistance. They withdrew, leaving 115 dead behind. The French suffered 11 dead and 52 wounded, a small price to pay for the valley.[65]

It was not clear what the French intended to do next. Was Dien Bien Phu to provide a mooring point for small-scale search and destroy

64 Gurtov, *First Vietnam Crisis*, pp. 57–8.
65 Bernard Fall, *Hell in a Very Small Place* (New York, NY, 1967), p. 15; Howard R. Simpson, *Dien Bien Phu: The Epic Battle America Forgot* (Washington, DC, 1994), p. 12.

operations, or would it be a *Base Aéro-Terrestre*, as Navarre envisaged? A mooring point implied a small, mobile and lightly armed force capable of quick evacuation. A fortified airhead, in contrast, involved a large contingent of heavily-armed troops equipped for a long siege and backed by massive air support. Since Dien Bien Phu was not supposed to be the main French offensive of the 1953–54 season, it was never likely to receive these essentials. Furthermore, troops used in search and destroy operations could not at the same time build fortifications.

As late as 11 November, General Rene Cogny, commander of French forces in the Tonkin, was under the assumption that Dien Bien Phu would be a mooring point. In other words, just nine days before the assault, he and Navarre disagreed fundamentally about the operation's objectives. Cogny was deeply worried 'that Dien Bien Phu shall become, whether we like it or not, a battalion meat grinder'.[66] Navarre, in contrast, was totally confident of success, even though he realized that, since the campaign further south (code-named Atlante) would take precedence, no more than eleven battalions could initially be spared for Dien Bien Phu. He optimistically assumed that the Vietminh would be unable to concentrate more than one division around Dien Bien Phu within one month of the French landing and that French bombardment of the Vietminh line of communication would prevent Giap from ever deploying a siege force of more than two divisions.

Navarre, of course, wanted a big battle. Giap obliged. For him, the strategic value of Dien Bien Phu was self-evident. As a link to Laos it was vital. The valley also produced 2,000 tons of rice per year and was the centre of the opium trade in northwestern Vietnam. Raw opium to the value of US$1 million was collected every year, and used by the Vietminh to buy arms.[67] For all these reasons, it had to be held. But Giap initially had no plans for a decisive battle there. He originally intended instead a major offensive to isolate Hanoi and Haiphong. But by mid-November he had turned his attention to Dien Bien Phu, alerted by press reports which discussed French plans with surprising candour.[68]

Giap's strategy was therefore reactive; the sudden French occupation of the valley dictated his response. He could not help but notice

66 Fall, *Hell*, pp. 35–6. The words were actually those of Cogny's staff, contained in a memorandum of points which it was suggested should be made to Navarre. In *Agonie de l'Indochine* (Paris, 1956), p. 197, Henri Navarre claimed that 'none of my subordinates, neither from the Army nor the Air Force . . . had raised the least objection'.

67 Fall, *Hell*, p. 9.

68 Anthony Clayton, *The Wars of French Decolonization* (London, 1994), p. 68.

that the French troops that landed on 20 November were lightly armed and were at the extreme range of their combat aircraft. Dien Bien Phu suddenly became a very attractive site for a decisive battle. On news of the French landing, he ordered an immediate attack upon the nearby French base of Lai Chau. This would force the French to abandon the small garrison and place all their eggs in the Dien Bien Phu basket.

Meanwhile, the French reinforced their position. A stream of transport planes brought men and material. With bulldozers dropped from C-119 Flying Boxcars, engineers paved the grass airstrip with prefabricated pierced steel plates. By nightfall on the 22nd, the garrison numbered 4,560 men.[69] They were deployed according to a classical pattern of interlocking fortified positions. Surrounding the airstrip were four strongpoints: Dominique, Huguette, Eliane and Claudine. Four subsidiary positions were also constructed. Three of these, Anne-Marie, Gabrielle and Beatrice, were positioned to the north in the line of the expected Vietminh attack. The fourth, Isabelle, stood 7km to the south. Its purpose was to provide artillery support to the main position.

Experience in Indochina had revealed that a 700-strong battalion could defend no more than one mile of line. Dien Bien Phu had a defensive perimeter of 31 miles. That meant 31 battalions, or 21,700 men. Fewer than 5,000 men initially landed. But even this small force required 150 tons of supplies every day, all of which had to arrive by air. If the force grew, so did the supply problem. Furthermore, since French troops were not originally intended to be a siege force, they were relatively lightly armed. Orders to build bunkers capable of resisting 105 mm artillery shells were not issued until 26 December, one month after the landing. A severe shortage of wood and other fortification material in the valley hindered construction. The collection of building materials denuded the valley floor of almost all natural cover, thus leaving positions dangerously exposed. Woodcutting parties sent into the surrounding hills were easily driven back by the Vietminh. The only solution was to dig deep shelters, but the soil was ill-suited to this purpose.

French engineering manuals stipulated that to protect one battalion required 2,550 tons of construction materials and 500 tons of barbed wire. In order to build these fortifications, a battalion would have to work at nothing else for two months. To protect the entire garrison of ten infantry and two artillery battalions therefore required

69 Fall, *Hell*, p. 18; Simpson, *Dien Bien Phu*, p. 16.

36,000 tons of material. After taking local supplies into account, the garrison was 34,000 tons short. To transport that amount into the valley would have required 12,000 flights of C-47 aircraft. Since about 80 aircraft were available, it would have taken five months to transport the material, assuming that the airplanes carried no other cargo.[70]

Some of France's best soldiers landed at Dien Bien Phu. The infantry was well-trained, equipped with modern equipment, and hardened by long experience of jungle combat. The force was a cross-section of the French empire,[71] but morale was a problem among non-French troops. For many Vietnamese, loyalty to France was contingent upon the war going well. The Algerians and Moroccans were sometimes susceptible to Vietminh propaganda which played upon the irony of colonial troops fighting for colonialism in a colony. The French were also supported by indigenous units like the Laotian Autonomous Artillery Battery and by T'ai tribesmen eager to fight the despised Vietminh. But these were of suspect quality, the Laotians because they were uncomfortable fighting far from home, and the T'ai because their training was poor and their commitment somewhat capricious.

Command of the garrison went to Colonel Christian de la Croix de Castries. Several more senior colonels turned down the assignment, one predicting that it would lead inevitably to disaster. An aristocrat, reckless gambler and inveterate womanizer, de Castries was highly respected – at least within his profession. During the Second World War he earned a reputation for aggression. Having earlier commanded a mobile group on the Red River, he was no stranger to Vietnam. But his cavalry background and his passionate character rendered him ill-suited to this operation. After the war, he confessed that proximity to pain or death made him uncomfortable. He lacked the patience and fortitude necessary to endure a long siege.

On the Vietminh side, morale was solid, but not indestructible. Evidence suggests that Ho welcomed the Geneva talks in part because he feared that war weariness was reaching dangerous levels. On the other hand, morale was boosted by the fact that supplies had never been more plentiful. The flow of Chinese weapons into Vietnam had increased significantly since the end of the Korean War, rising to 10,000 tons per month by July 1953. The Soviets also supplied a significant

---

70 Fall, *Hell*, pp. 89–91.

71 The French effort was *not* spear-headed by the Second World War veterans of the German SS who joined the French Foreign Legion, as many believe. The Foreign Legion formed only a fraction of French forces and the number of Germans within it was not high.

number of heavy trucks.[72] But everything the Vietminh needed for the battle had to come from depots along the Chinese border. By a direct route, the journey totaled 295 miles, but detours could add another 200 miles. The route was not originally suited to heavy transport traffic, being little more than a dirt track in places. Bombing totally destroyed the last 50 miles into Dien Bien Phu. Twenty thousand coolies impressed from nearby villages slaved for three months so the road could accommodate heavy trucks and artillery.

When French interdiction efforts prevented motorized transport, Giap switched to human carriers. According to the Vietminh, human columns carried 8,286 tons of supply to Dien Bien Phu. Bicycles were adapted to carry up to 220 kilos, with the bearer steering from behind.[73] The Vietminh were masters of camouflage. Each soldier would pick foliage as he marched and attach it to his comrade in front, thus insuring that the camouflage matched the vegetation through which the column marched. Bridges were built underneath the surface of streams, rendering them nearly undetectable from the air. The jungle canopy was sometimes tied together to provide a secure transport tunnel.

The Vietminh strategy sought first to deny the French the use of the base as a mooring point for raids into the jungle by rendering those raids too costly. Then, if the garrison evolved into a fortified base, the key was to envelop it with superior forces and firepower. Vietminh anti-aircraft units would deny the French their vital air link, while the artillery pounded the garrison into submission. Na San had convinced the French that they could supply a besieged force by air and evacuate it if necessary. Vietminh strategy aimed at denying both these possibilities.

On 24 November three Vietminh divisions, stationed in the Viet Bac, began a forced march toward Dien Bien Phu. Navarre, aware of this movement, concluded that the units could not possibly be full divisions since the available roads would not support a deployment of that magnitude. When he visited the valley on 29 November he judged the defences strong enough to resist anything Giap could throw at them. This confidence was based upon his belief that his forces would

72 The Russians were keen to disrupt relations between the French and the Americans and, in so doing, wreck American plans for an early French entry into the European Defence Community. The Soviets, fearful as always of a French/German rapprochement, were determined to keep the French occupied in Vietnam and confident that the longer they were occupied the more corrosive that conflict would be to French/American relations.

73 See Fall, *Hell*, pp. 125–8.

enjoy artillery superiority since the surrounding hills were too steep to allow deployment of heavy guns. After the war, an inquiry into the battle by the French War College censured commanders for giving greater weight to their preconceptions than to the actual facts provided by intelligence.

THE DECISIVE BATTLE

During the four months which followed the their landing, French interdiction efforts failed miserably. The Vietminh were allowed to build up their supplies, without being forced to expend huge quantities of ammunition. The French had around 120 aircraft available for interdiction, but the most effective were the Navy's Privateer Heavy Bombers, of which there were only six.[74] Since maintenance crews were chronically under-strength, only 75 per cent of aircraft were operational at any given time. Damage inflicted by Vietminh anti-aircraft (AA) batteries protecting the line of communication was prodigious. The interdiction effort also cut into the transport of supplies to the garrison, since most planes performed both functions.

On 5 December Cogny evacuated Lai Chau. Local T'ai guerrillas, left behind to cover the evacuation and destroy ammunition, were instructed to make their way overland to Dien Bien Phu. Three French officers, 34 non-commissioned officers (NCOs), and over 2,000 tribesmen left Lai Chau on 9 December. One officer, nine NCOs, and only 175 tribesmen reached their destination thirteen days later.[75] As the noose tightened around Dien Bien Phu, French search and destroy missions either failed to locate the Vietminh or were badly mauled by them. The garrison could no longer sensibly fulfil its mission as a mooring point. But it was hardly ready to assume the role of a fortress.

Meanwhile, the main French offensive, codenamed Atlante, was launched further south, with the aim of cutting the country in two. On 20 January fifteen French battalions advanced from Nha Trang northwards, while an amphibious force simultaneously went ashore at Tuy Hoa, behind Vietminh lines. Giap decided not to give battle but instructed his troops merely to harass the French. Their attack soon bogged down, causing rampant desertion among VNA units. Meanwhile Giap launched his own counter-offensive, striking in the Central Highlands and northern Laos. In panic, Navarre rushed troops to Kontum, but could not prevent its fall. In a similar fashion, Giap's

---

74 Ibid., pp. 129–31.
75 Simpson, *Dien Bien Phu*, p. 27.

drive into Laos forced Navarre to airlift five battalions to Louang Phrabang, but not before the Vietminh had seized the opium crop. Clearly, Atlante was a costly failure. Giap had completely blunted Navarre's ambitions and inflicted heavy losses. More importantly, he had forced Navarre to disperse his mobile reserve and to use his limited air transport to support distant fronts, when both would have been more useful around Dien Bien Phu.

On 26 January Vietminh guns began a desultory bombardment of the garrison, apparently designed to lull the French into a false sense of security. If so, it succeeded. Colonel Charles Piroth, the French artillery commander, boasted that his counter-battery operations would quickly destroy all Vietminh guns. Seldom has confidence been so unjustified. Though the Vietminh guns were positioned on the forward slopes of the hills (ordinarily rendering them highly vulnerable to counter-battery fire), each was placed in pre-constructed shell-proof gun pits which were virtually undetectable from the valley below. Tunnels were sometimes dug through the summit of a mountain, rendering the gun virtually invulnerable, and allowing ammunition to be transported from the side opposite the French garrison. Dummy pits, with explosive charges timed to coincide with actual firing, sowed confusion among the French. Guns were also fired just before dusk, when there was still enough light to register targets but not enough left to allow French batteries to strike back accurately.

For the next six weeks, Vietminh batteries methodically shelled the French position, turning the airstrip into a mass of shell craters. Their accuracy was greatly aided by the capture of a French aerial map soon after the siege began and by the fact that French targets were neither well camouflaged nor very mobile. Men sent to repair the damage were driven away and exposed aircraft were mercilessly picked off like fish in a barrel. By the beginning of March, the Vietminh had all their men and material in place. The French could do little but wait for the attack. De Castries realized that his situation was desperate, but withdrawal was no longer an option since the airstrip had become too exposed.

Giap had at his disposal 49,000 combat troops, plus 10,000–15,000 logistical personnel. He had at least twenty-four 105 mm field howitzers, eighteen 75 mm pack howitzers, twenty 120 mm heavy mortars, forty 82 mm mortars and probably more than fifty 75 mm recoilless rifles, in addition to 36 heavy flak guns and 80 AA machine guns.[76] In contrast, the French had 10,800 men in the various

---

76 Fall, *Hell*, pp. 126–7.

strongpoints on the valley floor, only 7,000 of whom were combat personnel. They were supported by twenty-four 105 mm howitzers, four 155 mm howitzers and four 120 mm mortars. Six fighters, one helicopter and six observation planes were on permanent station. The fortress also had ten light tanks.[77]

The Vietminh assault began on 13 March. The artillery barrage quickly neutralized French batteries within the main fortress, smashed trenches and destroyed aircraft on the runway. As planes took off, either to attack the Vietminh or to evacuate the runway, they came under fire from AA guns in positions previously unknown to the French.

Strongpoint Beatrice was the first target. Devastatingly accurate artillery fire immediately destroyed two important command posts, killing senior commanders and leaving defenders in chaos.[78] At 1700 hours six Vietminh battalions went forward from assault trenches located just 200 yards away. The flaws in de Castries's deployment were laid bare. Batteries located at Isabelle were too far distant to provide adequate protection. In addition, the distance from the central position, where the reserves were situated, ruled out an effective counter-attack. Just after midnight Beatrice fell. The French lost perhaps 400 of the 500 men positioned there, while the Vietminh lost 600 dead and another 1,200 wounded.[79]

On the 14th, the relentless bombardment of the airstrip continued. French fighters and observation aircraft were destroyed. Direct hits demolished the radio beacon and control tower. The airstrip itself was rendered unusable by combat aircraft. Thus, the garrison's vital link with the outside world was cut on only the second day of the battle. Colonel Piroth could not bear the humiliation. He retired to his dugout, pulled the pin out of a grenade and held it to his chest.

Gabrielle was next. Two Vietminh regiments went forward at 2000 hours on the 14th. Again, a deadly artillery round destroyed the command post, cutting off radio contact with the rest of the strongpoint and leaving defenders in turmoil. De Castries ordered a tank-led counter-attack, mainly by the 5th Vietnamese Parachute Battalion. The paratroopers were still recovering from their harrowing arrival through thick gunfire the previous day and were totally unfamiliar with conditions on the valley floor. Perhaps inevitably, they immediately cracked

---

77 See ibid., chap. 4.

78 The Vietminh ability to hit the command posts early in an action is easily explained. These posts were clearly identified by their tall radio antennae, which were easily spotted in a landscape denuded of vegetation.

79 Davidson, *Vietnam at War*, p. 236.

and the counter-attack disintegrated. By 0800 hours the following day, Gabrielle was in Vietminh hands. The French lost around 1,000 men, the Vietminh perhaps twice that number.[80]

That left Anne-Marie, held by the 3rd T'ai Battalion. Over the preceding weeks, they had been inundated with Vietminh propaganda leaflets inviting them to switch sides. The annihilation of Beatrice and Gabrielle finally broke their resolve. On the night of the 17th, under cover of a thick fog, they defected *en masse* to the Vietminh or simply melted into the wilderness. Anne-Marie fell without a shot fired.

AA guns were immediately dragged into position on the captured strongpoints of Gabrielle and Anne-Marie, rendering French air drops ever more precarious. During the battle, the Vietminh shot down 48 aircraft, destroyed another 14 on the ground and damaged 167 others.[81] The increasing volume and accuracy of flak forced French parachute drops to ever higher altitudes, decreasing their accuracy. Efforts to neutralize the flak proved futile. Flying Boxcars dropped napalm on Vietminh positions, but this reduced the transport role of the airplanes at a time when the garrison was literally starving. In any case, the deep Vietminh tunnels and thick jungle cover severely limited the effectiveness of napalm.

The garrison's survival now depended upon the ability of French pilots to negotiate an increasingly dense torrent of flak while dropping supplies and reinforcements onto an area of less than three square miles. During the battle, 82,296 parachutes were dropped.[82] Difficult as it is to imagine, this was not nearly enough. US Army logistics experts calculated that the French needed at least 200 tons of supplies per day. From 13 March to 7 May, deliveries averaged 120 tons per day, but seldom more than 100 tons actually landed on the garrison.[83] Stray drops were picked up by the Vietminh – one-tenth of their shells came courtesy of the French.

The quick demise of Beatrice, Anne-Marie and Gabrielle underscored de Castries's unsuitability for a siege operation. He was effectively replaced by Colonel Pierre Langlais and, as the battle wore on, retreated to his bunker. Morale in the garrison steadily deteriorated. On 7 April all food reserves were used up. Efforts to replenish stocks over the next few days resulted in dangerously low ammunition supplies. This depressing sequence continued for the rest of the battle.

---

80 Ibid., p. 238.
81 Fall, *Hell*, p. 455.
82 James P. Harrison, *The Endless War* (New York, NY, 1989), p. 123.
83 Davidson, *Vietnam at War*, p. 219.

Medical care became desperate. In an effort to increase the strain upon the French, the Vietminh refused to allow mercy flights to evacuate the wounded, and even rejected offers to collect their own wounded. Clearly marked medevac helicopters and planes were fired upon, in violation of the Geneva Convention. The fortress hospital was a Stygian labyrinth, with tunnels continually extended to accommodate a relentless flow of wounded. Originally designed for 44 beds, it would eventually care for 3,000 wounded. Floors were covered in blood, faeces and urine; walls crawled with maggots. Doctors were powerless to prevent the spread of gangrene.[84]

By the end of March, the main position around the airport was completely encircled by Vietminh attackers. To the south, Isabelle was totally cut off. The Vietminh attacked on the night of 30th, but encountered stiff resistance. Human wave assaults were torn apart by machine guns, mortars, mines, and by the vicious fire of Quad-50s[85] situated within Dominique and Huguette. The French fought with unexpected stubbornness from a situation which was, by any reckoning, hopeless. But while they could slow the assault, they could not stop it. For three weeks, a bitter struggle was waged over each scrap of land. Giap's tactics were successful, but the costs were atrocious. By 13 April, his losses totaled about 6,000 killed, 8,000 wounded, and 2,000 taken prisoner.[86]

Mud, filth and incessant rain eroded the seemingly indomitable Vietminh spirit. On 12 April, during an attack on Eliane, morale broke. Reluctant soldiers were forced to advance at gunpoint by officers and NCOs. Suicidal human wave assaults had taken their toll. Appallingly poor medical care – the Vietminh army had one surgeon and six ill-trained assistants – added to the strain. In his usual hardbitten way, Giap wrote:

> the battle having lasted a very long time, more troops became fatigued and are worn and are faced with great nervous tension ... there appear negative rightest tendencies, whose manifestations are the fear of having many killed, the fear of suffering casualties, of facing up to fatigue, difficulties, privations.[87]

84 Simpson, *Dien Bien Phu*, pp. 154–5; Fall, *Hell*, p. 121.

85 Americans in Korea discovered that .50 calibre anti-aircraft guns could be used effectively against human wave assaults. This experience was passed on to the French.

86 Davidson, *Vietnam at War*, p. 257.

87 Currey, *Victory*, p. 202.

'At all levels the Party worked to eradicate these attitudes and heighten a sense of responsibility. We had to win the battle.'[88] Fresh reinforcements were immediately brought forward. Political cadres conducted a sweeping campaign of ideological education among the troops. 'This ideological struggle was very successful', Giap later claimed. It was 'one of the greatest achievements in political work in our army's history'.[89] In truth, the improvement in morale was due largely to a change in tactics. There were no more human wave assaults. Instead, troops were instructed to dig their way to the French periphery. The new slogan was 'Dig Now – Fight Later'. A highly sophisticated trench system was developed, with attack trenches dug to within 15 yards of the French line. The First World War had been recreated in a Vietnamese valley. Vietminh attackers advanced in front of a creeping barrage, often with specially selected storm troops. Defenders relied upon concentrated machine gun fire, artillery, mine fields and barbed wire to prevent attackers from crossing No Man's Land.

Meanwhile, Langlais reorganized his defences. French forces were concentrated into an area little more than a mile in diameter, taking in Claudine, Eliane, and parts of Dominique and Huguette. Two new strongpoints, Sparrowhawk to the north of the command bunker and Juno to the south, completed the perimeter. Strongpoint Isabelle was still intact, but its value was dubious since there was no land link to the rest of the fortress. Supplying it by air had become extremely difficult. The French predicament was made infinitely worse by the arrival of the monsoon on 29 March. On average, 5 feet of rain falls on the valley between March and August. Both sides had to fight in mud and water which was sometimes waist deep, but the Vietminh could at least escape to high ground.

The desperate situation inspired three rescue proposals. Operation Condor called for a relief column to advance on the beleaguered garrison from Laos. By the time it was launched, there were insufficient reserves to give it any chance of success. Operation Albatross, a breakout from Dien Bien Phu, was even more fantastically ill-conceived and was fortunately never attempted. Operation Vulture seemed to offer greater promise. On 25 March 1954, Admiral Arthur Radford, chairman of the US Joint Chiefs of Staff (JCS), suggested to General Ely, the French Chief of Staff, that a force of 75 to 100 American B-29 bombers might be able to destroy Vietminh positions around Dien Bien Phu. In order to avoid annoying the Chinese, the B-29s would be

---

88 MacDonald, *Giap*, p. 150.
89 Currey, *Victory*, p. 203.

repainted with French colours, and US pilots would resign their commissions and join the French Foreign Legion. The idea of using three tactical nuclear weapons was briefly floated. It had the backing of Richard Nixon, the Vice-President.[90]

There was no guarantee that bombing, even if accurate, would destroy Giap's troops, dug so deeply into the hills. And then what? 'One cannot go over Niagara Falls in a barrel only slightly', a Defense Department analyst warned.[91] Nixon and Dulles supported the bombing idea.[92] Eisenhower's position is somewhat obscure. On 24 March he confessed to Dulles that he would not 'wholly exclude the possibility of a single strike, it it were almost certain that this would produce decisive results', but American action would have to be suitably camouflaged – 'we would have to deny it forever'.[93] It is perhaps because he realized that a single strike could not be decisive that he eventually lost enthusiasm for the idea:

> I couldn't think of anything probably less effective than in a great big jungle area and with a besieged fortress, trying to relieve it with air force. I just can't see how this could have been done unless you were willing to use weapons that could have destroyed the jungles all around the area for miles and that would probably have destroyed Dien Bien Phu itself, and that would have been that.[94]

On 3 April he met Congressional leaders to discuss the plan. Senator Lyndon Johnson indicated that Congress would withhold approval unless America's allies, in particular Great Britain, provided active support. He personally abhorred the idea of 'sending American GIs into the mud and muck of Indochina on a bloodletting spree to perpetuate colonialism and white man's exploitation in Asia'.[95]

British Prime Minister Winston Churchill thought that Dulles was 'the only case of a bull ... who carries his china closet with him'.[96] His Foreign Secretary Anthony Eden commented, with considerable prescience, 'I am beginning to think Americans are quite ready to

90 Richard Nixon, *RN: The Memoirs of Richard Nixon* (New York, NY, 1978), p. 154.

91 George C. Herring, *America's Longest War* (New York, NY, 1986), p. 32.

92 There remains some dispute about where Dulles stood. See Billings-Yun, *Decision Against War*, chap. 4.

93 McMahon, *Major Problems*, p. 138.

94 Gurtov, *First Vietnam Crisis*, p. 136.

95 Alexander Kendrick, *The Wound Within* (Boston, MA, 1974), p. 67.

96 Fawn M. Brodie, *Richard Nixon: The Shaping of his Character* (Cambridge, MA, 1983), pp. 323–4.

supplant French and see themselves in the role of liberators of Vietnamese patriotism and expulsers or redeemers of Communist insurgency in Indo-China. If so they are in for a painful awakening.'[97] When Churchill and Eden vetoed British involvement, Vulture was abandoned.

POSTSCRIPT

On the morning of 7 April 1954, Giap ordered a general advance. Vietminh infantry poured forward, sweeping aside bedraggled French defenders. At 1730, a forward unit entered the command bunker and raised the Vietminh flag. Isabelle survived a further 24 hours.

Vietminh losses are difficult to ascertain. Perhaps 8,000 lost their lives in the action, with countless others dying as a result of French interdiction efforts. The French suffered 8,200 casualties, with around 2,000 killed. Seventy-five per cent of all French casualties resulted from artillery fire, a grim testimony to the folly of underestimating Vietminh gunners. Of the 9,500 French prisoners who were forced to march nearly 500 miles to prisoner of war (POW) camps, only a third were alive when the war ended.[98]

'There is . . . no military or logical reason why loss of Dien Bien Phu should lead to a collapse of French will', Dulles argued. That was true, but even he understood that logic did not apply; Dien Bien Phu was 'a symbol out of all proportion to its military importance'.[99] The French people could not tolerate a humiliation of this magnitude. It transformed the peace faction at home into an insurmountable force. Nixon remained certain that, if not for the British reluctance to intervene, disaster could have been averted. 'The British haven't got it anymore', he concluded. 'The Asian mess is significant of dire future events; i.e. eventual confrontation of white- vs. dark-skinned races, unless we can align ourselves on the side of freedom for these downtrodden colonies.' Eisenhower, in contrast, concluded: 'the sun's still shining. . . . Dien Bien Phu isn't the end of the world; it's not that important.'[100]

---

97 Lloyd Gardner, *Approaching Vietnam: From World War II through Dien Bien Phu* (New York, NY, 1988), p. 256.

98 Simpson, *Dien Bien Phu*, pp. 169, 176; Fall, *Hell*, p. 267.

99 Gurtov, *First Vietnam Crisis*, 106.

100 Brodie, *Nixon*, pp. 322–6. Though Eisenhower suggested otherwise, it appears that he never intended intervening and that the Churchill decision merely allowed him to blame the British for abandoning the French. See Billings-Yun, *Decision Against War*, pp. 143–4.

2 'ASK NOT . . .'

GENEVA

In 1959 Giap confessed that Dien Bien Phu 'was the last desperate exertion of the Vietminh army. [It was] on the verge of complete exhaustion. . . . Years of jungle warfare had sent morale in the fighting units to the depths.' While there was probably more than a bit of heroic hyperbole in this statement, the condition of Vietminh forces does perhaps explain why the Vietminh decided not to follow up their victory by driving toward Hanoi. Instead, they put their trust in negotiations. 'The situation was very grave', Khrushchev confirmed, 'The partisans were counting on the Geneva Conference to produce a cease-fire agreement which would enable them to hold on to the conquests . . . they had won.'[1]

By agreeing to talks before Dien Bien Phu, the French gave the Chinese extra incentive to help the Vietminh to a major victory. That victory made the Chinese the most influential of the great powers gathered at Geneva. This prospect appealed to the Chinese, not because it would benefit the Vietminh, but rather because it would allow them to strut triumphantly on the world stage, so soon after their own revolution. The French allowed the Chinese an important role, since they alone could force the Vietminh to cooperate. The Americans, still smarting from their Korean experience, found this prospect distasteful, but their hands were tied since the French made participation in the EDC contingent upon a suitable agreement.

The Democratic Republic of Vietnam (DRV) was man-handled into accepting a settlement which did not reflect the balance of forces in Vietnam. The Chinese were keen to advance communism in Asia, but could not bankroll the Vietminh forever. Thus, they sought a settlement which would end the war, but also one calculated to mollify the Americans. The Soviet Union was likewise more interested in peace

---

1 Carlyle Thayer, *War by Other Means* (Sydney, 1989), p. 3.

than in a solidly communist Indochina, especially since the latter would merely enhance Chinese influence. Thus, by the summer of 1953, both China and the USSR favoured a Korean-style division of Vietnam. Once it became clear that the United States would not block such a settlement, the Chinese, through direct negotiation with the French, traded their ability to constrain the Vietminh for diplomatic and commercial concessions. In persuading their ally, the Chinese and Soviets made much of the American bogey, and both made it clear that aid would be withdrawn if the DRV took an uncooperative line. The Vietminh had virtually no influence upon the settlement, which was merely a manifestation of Cold War power politics. It was, Tran Van Don remarked, 'absolutely impossible to surmount the hostility of our enemies and the perfidy of false friends'.[2]

The settlement divided Vietnam at the 17th parallel, the North to be controlled by the Vietminh, the South by the Bao Dai government. An International Control Commission would police the settlement until elections, to be held in July 1956, brought a single national government. Since Bao Dai commanded little influence in the South, the deal seemed to offer the communists a reasonable prospect of quick unification. In any case, a cease-fire (which is in truth the way the party saw the agreement) would allow time to consolidate government in the North and plan the extension of the revolution to the South. A respite was welcome since, to the extent that the party was weak, it was weak in the South. An internal party document admitted that 'peace is concluded to procure advantages for us, not for the purpose of ceasing the struggle'.[3]

Though the US loudly opposed the agreements and refused to ratify them, it did promise to 'refrain from the threat or use of force to disturb them' and 'would view any . . . violation . . . with grave concern'.[4] In truth the Americans felt the deal was better than the military situation warranted. 'We got more than I expected', Walter Bedell Smith, the chief US negotiator, told Eisenhower.[5] For Dulles, the next priority was to see 'whether we could salvage what the Communists had ostensibly left out of their grasp in Indochina'.[6] The US hoped to

2 Lloyd C. Gardner, *Approaching Vietnam: From World War II through Dien Bien Phu* (New York, NY, 1988), p. 281.

3 Thayer, *Other Means*, p. 7.

4 William Appleman Williams *et al.*, eds, *America in Vietnam: A Documentary History* (New York, NY, 1975), p. 171.

5 Gardner, *Approaching Vietnam*, p. 281.

6 Gabriel Kolko, *Anatomy of a War* (New York, NY, 1994), p. 82.

encourage the emergence of a credible non-communist nation in South Vietnam, as had been achieved in Korea. 'Dien Bien Phu was a blessing in disguise', Dulles candidly argued. 'We have a clean base there now without a taint of colonialism.'[7] Unfortunately, because the Americans had aligned themselves rather too closely with the French, it would be difficult to wash that taint out of their clothes.

A NEW NATION

The Geneva settlement, though somewhat disappointing for Ho, did provide the context in which his government could address urgent domestic issues. For most of the war, expenses had been met by printing money; inflation threatened by itself to defeat the Vietminh. In early March 1955 the Politburo resolved to 'achieve agrarian reform, restore and increase production and strengthen the people's army so as to consolidate northern Vietnam'.[8]

The prospect of a communist administration frightened the bourgeoisie in the North. Some 880,000 civilians and 190,000 soldiers immediately fled south, many from the educated and professional classes whose capital and expertise were essential to reconstruction.[9] Factories and shops consequently closed; of the 30 French-owned factories in Haiphong, 29 shut. Fuel was scarce, the irrigation network was in disrepair, and 10 per cent of previously cultivated land in the Red River Delta was abandoned, the farmers having fled to the cities.[10] Floods in December 1954 threatened another disastrous famine.

Peasants whose loyalty had been bought with promises of land had to be satisfied, even if doing so contradicted collectivist ideals. Until 1954 the united front protected most landowners. As long as they did not actively oppose the revolution, they were usually able to keep their land. With the war over, the time seemed ripe for further redistribution. But in the North two immediate complications arose: insufficient land and an impatient peasantry. For both ideological and sentimental reasons, the land reform campaign was escalated, so much so that in many areas vindictive peasant courts engaged in an orgy of land seizure. Perhaps as many as 100,000 were executed, not all of

7 Melvin Gurtov, *The First Vietnam Crisis* (New York, NY, 1967), p. 130.
8 Thayer, *Other Means*, p. 13.
9 Ken Post, *Revolution, Socialism and Nationalism in Viet Nam*, 5 vols (Aldershot, 1989), Vol. 1, pp. 232–3.
10 William J. Duiker, *Sacred War* (New York, NY, 1995), p. 97.

whom actually owned land.[11] The system promised great rewards to those willing to finger a neighbour as a reactionary, a landlord, a traitor, or social deviant. A daughter might be persuaded to accuse her otherwise virtuous father of incest and a wife might suddenly claim that her husband had spied for the French.[12] Many innocent people were denounced, with perhaps 30,000 peasant households wrongly classified. In an atmosphere of deep paranoia, few had the courage to come to a persecuted neighbour's defence.[13] Fearful of arousing suspicions regarding their wealth, peasants produced only enough to feed themselves, causing agricultural production to plummet.

By the summer of 1956 the party began to reassert itself. Ho took the extraordinary step of publicly apologizing for the programme's excesses. Land reform, he admitted, had 'caused deficiencies and errors in the tasks of achieving rural unity', though the 'opposing enemy' who had 'carried out insane sabotage' was partly to blame.[14] In October, Giap, upon whom a great deal of blame must rest, admitted:

> We indiscriminately attacked all families owning land. Many honest people were executed. We saw enemies everywhere and resorted to widespread violence and the use of terror. . . . We placed too much emphasis upon class origins rather than political attitudes. We resorted to disciplinary punishment, to expulsion, to execution. . . . torture came to be regarded as a normal part of the party organization. There were grave errors.[15]

The party had only itself to blame. Land reform, desired by the peasants, was a far cry from collectivism, desired by the party. The inherent contradiction caused terrible suffering.

Other aspects of reconstruction were handled only marginally better than land reform. The Marxist historian Gabriel Kolko is apparently quite impressed with Vietnam's progress during this period. According to his figures, between 1958 and 1960 the number

---

11 Cecil B. Currey, *Victory at Any Cost* (Washington, DC, 1997), p. 221. The number executed varies widely. Kolko (*Anatomy*, pp. 66–7) says that 15,000 landowners were executed, with another 20,000 imprisoned. At the time, Richard Nixon stated that 500,000 were killed. Others have since suggested *only* 5,000. See John M. Del Vecchio, 'The importance of story', 1996 Vietnam Symposium, Texas Tech University Vietnam Center website.

12 Currey, *Victory*, p. 221.

13 Edwin Moïse, 'Land reform and land reform errors in North Vietnam', *Pacific Affairs* 49 (1976), p. 83.

14 Post, *Revolution*, Vol. 1, p. 274.

15 Peter MacDonald, *Giap* (London, 1993), p. 174.

of industrial workers doubled, rising to 43,000. Industrial growth stood at around 50 per cent per annum between 1957 and 1960. Industry and handicraft constituted 42 per cent of gross national product by 1960, up 11 per cent from 1957.[16] But even if these figures are correct, they are only impressive in the sense that any movement from rock bottom always seems significant. In comparison to other former colonies in Southeast Asia, Vietnam's growth was stunted. Ho boasted in July 1956 that the party had created the conditions for extending the revolution to the South. 'To build a good house we must build a strong foundation. The North is the foundation, the root of the struggle for complete national liberation and the reunification of the country.'[17] While that may have been true politically, in economic terms it was mere bluster. Ho's confidence that he could soon extend the revolution to the South was founded mainly on Soviet and Chinese assurances of massive aid. Had the DRV been forced to wage the coming war by relying on its economic resources alone, it genuinely would have mobilized an army of 'barefoot guerrillas' because it would not have been able to afford shoes for its soldiers.

THE COMMUNIST THREAT

After 1945 the battle against communism become a foreign policy priority for the United States. The emergence of the USSR as a formidable power and the extension of its hegemony over Eastern Europe frightened the US, which assigned itself the task of stopping the relentless communist tide. Shortly after the war, two policies converged to form the anti-communist strategy Americans would pursue for the next 40 years. The first was containment: the idea that, while the US could not destroy communism, it should prevent its expansion. The second was the domino theory. 'You have a row of dominoes set up, you knock the first one, and what will happen to the last one is the certainty that it will go over very quickly', Eisenhower explained to a journalist on 7 April 1954. 'So you could have a beginning of a disintegration that would have the most profound influences.'[18] The key to containment was to prevent dominoes from falling. This meant that, contrary to customary foreign policy dynamics, problems could not be prioritized. In theory, there was no such thing as a minor problem of communist insurgency. The Vietnam problem was not at this stage

16 Kolko, *Anatomy*, p. 70.
17 Thayer, *Other Means*, p. 76.
18 Jeffrey P. Kimball, ed., *To Reason Why* (New York, NY, 1990), p. 31.

unique; the money spent there between 1953 and 1962 was less than went to Turkey, South Korea and Taiwan, and about the same as was expended on Pakistan. Greece and Spain received slightly less.[19]

The domino theory distorted foreign policy perceptions. A country like Vietnam might not have been important to the world order *per se*, but once the Americans made a blanket pledge to resist the spread of communism, it became important. As Dulles argued in 1950, American prestige was at stake. A French defeat 'would have further serious repercussions on the whole situation in Asia and the Pacific. It would make even more people in the East feel that friendship with the United States is a liability rather than an asset.'[20] But Dien Bien Phu underlined the limits of American power. Massive American aid could not buy a French victory. More active intervention might have resulted in a confrontation with the Chinese. American reluctance to become more deeply involved cannot, however, be explained entirely by fears of confrontation with China. Some credit for restraint must go to Eisenhower, who understood the dangers of intervention. 'I'm convinced that no military victory is possible in that kind of theater', he wrote in 1951.[21] He realized that US forces had not been trained to fight a Vietnam-type conflict and was respectful of the military prowess of the Vietminh. In 1963, while writing his memoirs, he concluded (rather prophetically) that 'the jungles of Indochina . . . would have swallowed up division after division of United States troops, who, unaccustomed to this kind of warfare, would have sustained heavy casualties'.[22] He also feared the cost of direct intervention – in money and lives. The Korean War had increased American military spending to 13.8 per cent of gross domestic product, causing serious inflation and budget deficits.[23] But, though Eisenhower ruled out direct intervention, he did not give up on the idea of saving South Vietnam from communism.

The costs of containment inspired the New Look strategy.[24] The US took refuge under the nuclear umbrella, putting the USSR and China on notice that meddling in the affairs of a third country might trigger atomic annihilation. Defence spending consequently fell. At the same time, greater emphasis was given to covert warfare waged by the CIA – a cheap and inconspicuous way to confront communists.

19 Kolko, *Anatomy*, p. 75.

20 Gurtov, *First Vietnam Crisis*, p. 25.

21 Melanie Billings-Yun, *Decision Against War: Eisenhower and Dien Bien Phu, 1954* (New York, NY, 1988), p. 76.

22 Stephen E. Ambrose, *Eisenhower: The President* (London, 1984), p. 176.

23 Kolko, *Anatomy*, p. 78.

24 See Chapter 1, pp. 39–40.

The apparent success of covert operations in Iran and Guatemala seemed to imply that the strategy had wider applications. But the great problem with the 'New Look' was that it relied heavily upon bluff. American credibility declined with every confrontation she shunned. The strategy would only work if at some stage the Americans committed themselves to keeping a domino upright. Mere threats were not sufficient to demonstrate this commitment.

The domino principle was not invented by Dulles, but by Lenin. Dulles and Eisenhower simply presented an oft-repeated communist goal in terms every American could understand. Communists around the world salivated over the opportunities which the collapse of European empires seemed to offer. In the 1950s, virtually every country in Asia and Latin America experienced an indigenous communist insurgency of some sort. The countries gaining independence were all poor, had badly developed civic structures, weak political systems and appeared every bit as receptive to the 'wave of history' as had China and Vietnam. The revolutionaries, in common with the Vietminh, reassured themselves that they were armed with a strategic concept – 'people's war' or 'protracted war' – that would guarantee victory. If Dulles needed evidence for the validity of the Domino Theory, he could have found it easily at a hamlet propaganda session in rural Vietnam. In tiny hamlets, eighteen-year-old peasants were taught to see themselves as standard-bearers of a new world order, a heady brew which undoubtedly contributed to their tremendous morale. In other words, American fears had justification. The domino principle may have been simplistic, but it was not illogical.

The strength of the principle was its simplicity. Country Western artist Tom T. Hall had no difficulty explaining it in his eminently forgettable 'Hello Vietnam': Americans had to 'save freedom . . . at any cost' – or 'someday our own freedom will be lost'. But simplicity was also the principle's greatest fault. Falling dominoes presented an image easily understood by an American public not given to deep contemplation of foreign policy. The communist threat was reduced to a simple metaphor of wooden blocks toppling with gathering momentum. But foreign policy is never simple; to suggest otherwise was dangerously irresponsible. Dominos are uniform, yet there was no uniformity in the culture, religion, economy or political perceptions of the disparate countries at risk of insurgency. To reduce international affairs to a metaphor which a child could understand encouraged childish reactions.

The big problem with the domino principle was that friends and enemies were chosen according to the most superficial criterion.

Danger was painted red, with no shading or subtlety of hue. This guaranteed that the US would support some very nasty regimes (which was bad for morale) but also some very weak ones (which was strategically unsound). South Vietnam was both nasty and weak. Yet when the US needed to justify intervention to save a 'free' RVN, the metaphor worked its magic on a gullible public. As a result, the US found herself tied to an unpopular ally and a losing cause for the sake of an elusive goal and a simplistic principle.

'SINK OR SWIM WITH NGO DINH DIEM'

In order to ensure a positive outcome in the plebiscite, the DRV kept some 10,000 activists in the South, who now concentrated on political insurgency.[25] Trinh Duc, who was ordered to stay in the South, recalled:

> Aside from keeping our basic networks alive, we also cached weapons, buried for the most part in tombs and graves. . . . we had to continue the movement, keep people warmed up and keep organizations going. If there really were elections, then we would be able to capitalize on the situation more quickly if the networks were in place. And if there weren't, we would be better prepared to resume the struggle.[26]

In February 1955 a State Department research unit concluded that 'Almost any type of election that could conceivably be held in Vietnam in 1956 would, on the basis of present trends, give the Communists a very significant if not decisive advantage'.[27] This naturally caused considerable alarm in Washington. The Eisenhower administration wanted to establish a non-communist alternative in the South, but there was no credible nationalist force to rival the communists. South Vietnam was a diplomatic contrivance; there was no such thing as South Vietnamese nationalism. Most potential leaders were tainted by past associations with the French. Granted, southern peasants were not overwhelmingly enamoured of the Vietminh, but their unease could not easily be converted into a positive, non-communist movement.

Into this breach strode Ngo Dinh Diem, who was conveniently both anti-communist and anti-French. During the ASV period, he had steered clear of the puppet government. Bao Dai nevertheless appointed

25 Douglas Pike, *PAVN: People's Army of Vietnam* (Novato, CA, 1986), p. 41.

26 David Chanoff and Doan Van Toai, *'Vietnam' – A Portrait of its People at War* (London, 1996), p. 27.

27 George McT. Kahin, *Intervention* (New York, NY, 1986), p. 89.

him Prime Minister after the French defeat, in part to impress the United States. American officials were at first decidedly lukewarm. Robert McClintock, the *chargé d'affairs* in Saigon, noted that 'Diem is a messiah without a message. His only formulated policy is to ask for immediate American assistance in every form . . . His only present emotion, other than a lively appreciation of himself, is a blind hatred for the French.'[28] Joseph Buttinger, who worked closely with him, described his chief fault: 'Diem's temperament, social philosophy and political comportment seemed to preclude all prospects of him ever becoming a popular hero. His stiff demeanor would have doomed any attempt to stir the masses . . . had he ever been persuaded of the necessity to make himself admired and loved.'[29] The American Chief of Mission, Donald Heath, felt that Diem was out of touch with the peasantry, unsympathetic to reform, hostile to the religious sects, and plain inept. But he still advised that Diem should be supported because there was 'no one else'.[30]

In April 1955 the US National Security Council (NSC) explored 'ways and means of replacing Diem and his government', not all of them above board.[31] Part of the problem was that Diem refused to be a puppet. His unsubtle liquidation of his enemies frightened sensitive Americans. The US eventually committed itself to him, but, as Dulles confessed, 'only to buy time'.[32] The Americans henceforth sought to save South Vietnam from the communists, but also from itself. 'Can we make a synthetic strong man of [Diem]?', Smith asked on 28 September 1954. 'Can we associate with him competent people who may compensate for his deficiencies in administrative ability and governing capacity?'[33] It was hoped that the CIA's Colonel Edward Lansdale, who had been so successful in helping to bring into power the pro-American government of Ramon Magsaysay in the Philippines, could work similar magic with Diem. Dulles told Lansdale: 'Do what you did in the Philippines'.[34]

Eisenhower replied cautiously to Diem's initial requests for aid: 'An intelligent program of . . . aid' would be instituted, provided that it was 'met by . . . needed reforms'.[35] But quite soon all conditions

---

28 Ibid., p. 78.

29 Joseph Buttinger, *Dragon Embattled*, 2 vols (Newton Abbot, 1973), Vol. II, p. 846.

30 Duiker, *Sacred War*, p. 103.

31 Robert J. McMahon, *Major Problems in the History of the Vietnam War* (Lexington, MA, 1990), p. 128.

32 Stanley Karnow, *Vietnam: A History* (Harmondsworth, 1993), p. 236.

33 Gardner, *Approaching Vietnam*, p. 315.

34 Kahin, *Intervention*, p. 81.

35 Eisenhower to Diem, 23 October 1954. Internet document.

were removed and the money began to flow without impediment. The US policy, as one journalist described, was to 'sink or swim with Ngo Dinh Diem'.[36] In anticipation of the Premier's 1957 visit to the US, the administration carefully sought to turn an incompetent into a hero. Suitably coached, New York mayor Robert Wagner described him as 'a man history may yet adjudge as one of the great figures of the twentieth century'. The *Saturday Evening Post* dutifully chipped in with 'the mandarin in a sharkskin suit who's upsetting the Red timetable'.[37]

A State Department official admitted that the Diem government had to campaign 'against the knowledge, shared even by illiterate coolies, that there would be no . . . independence as now exists had it not been for the Vietminh'.[38] In view of this fact, the plebiscite had to be avoided; Ho could not be allowed an easy victory via the ballot box. Diem solved this problem by stating outright that, since his government had not been represented at Geneva, he was not bound by its terms. There would be no elections. Hanoi complained to Great Britain, but the British were not prepared to pursue a line different from their American allies. China demanded a reopening of the Geneva Conference, but did not press this claim. The Soviets were conspicuously silent.

Bolstered by American support, Diem quickly moved to consolidate power. He ruthlessly excised the remaining pro-French elements from the government, emasculated the sects, and rooted out communists. At the urging of Lansdale, he engineered a referendum in October 1955 which asked: 'Do the people wish to depose Bao Dai and recognize Ngo Dinh Diem as the Chief of State . . . with the mission to install a democratic regime?' Bao Dai, out of the country at the time, could do little to influence the result. The outcome was predictable, but the margin of victory obscene: 98 per cent supposedly supported Diem. (Lansdale had suggested that 60 per cent would be respectable.) In many areas, ballots supporting Diem outnumbered legal voters.[39] American officials were left regretting that if they had to back a corrupt leader, they could not at least have found one who cheated with a bit of subtlety.

36 Buttinger, *Dragon*, Vol. II, p. 938.

37 Ronald H. Spector, *Advice and Support* (New York, NY, 1985), p. 304.

38 Ibid., p. 303.

39 He collected 605,025 votes in Saigon, where only 450,000 voters resided. David L. Anderson, *Trapped by Success: The Eisenhower Administration and Vietnam, 1953–1961* (New York, NY, 1991), p. 128; Cecil B. Currey, *Edward Lansdale: The Unquiet American* (Boston, MA, 1988), p. 180.

Following the referendum, the Republic of Vietnam (RVN) was formally established. The new government had a constitution and parliament, but in truth, real power was centralized in the executive, with Diem as President. The National Assembly was packed with hand-picked sympathizers of the new regime, who formed themselves into the Personalist Labor, or Can Lao Party. It was headed by Diem's younger brother, the corrupt Ngo Dinh Nhu, who also served as Minister of the Interior. Opposition parties were outlawed.

For most southerners, the Diem government was an alien force. He drew his support from 1 million Catholics, just 7 per cent of the population. They were by nature more rabidly anti-communist than the Buddhists or animists, and many were northerners who had fled south after Geneva, encouraged to do so by Lansdale and his CIA cronies. Operation Exodus brought 544,000 northern Catholics (65 per cent of the total of northern emigrés) to South Vietnam. The US funded their resettlement to the tune of US$93 million.[40] Diem's first Cabinet had no southerners in it, a fact of great importance to a people profoundly distrustful of 'strangers'.

'Since he firmly believed that he was divinely inspired and, being by nature obstinate, [Diem] did not willingly accept advice . . . particularly when [it] came from independent personalities who were not inclined to flatter him', Tran Van Don wrote. 'He liked to hear only good news . . . On those rare occasions when he left the presidential palace and visited the provinces, he never saw . . . the wretched condition of his people.' Don recalls one occasion when Diem went to inspect a model village in Binh Tuy. 'The province chief simulated fruit tree plantings along the road on which the presidential cortege passed. . . . As soon as the party had passed, the rootless trees immediately taken to the dump. They had served their purpose.'[41]

Copying Vietminh techniques, Diem sent Civic Action cadre teams into the villages to live with the people, set up self-help projects and spread propaganda. Meetings, which all male villagers were expected to attend, turned into ritualized denounciations of communists. According to one cadre leader:

We were supposed to explain why the Communists were bad and why the people must follow the government. But during the Resistance the communists had been the only ones in the village to fight against the French, so when we tried to explain

---

40 Post, *Revolution*, Vol. 1, p. 232; Neil Sheehan, *A Bright Shining Lie* (London, 1990), p. 137.
41 Tran Van Don, *Our Endless War* (Novato, CA, 1978), pp. 50–1.

that the communists were evil people, the villagers just didn't listen to us.[42]

The Civic Action teams had little positive effect. For many an ambitious young man, the appointment was a coveted step up the greasy pole of corrupt Saigon politics. Most of the cadres came from northern Vietnam, which created language problems and much distrust among the peasantry. Opportunities for graft were enormous, especially since the United States, eager to make the programme work, freely provided financial backing.

Diem's dependence upon wealthy landlords made him reluctant to resolve the iniquitous land distribution problem. Over half of the cultivable land in the South was owned by less than 1 per cent of the population, much to the annoyance of the Americans, who understood the need for progressive reform. Diem's Ordinance 57 of 22 October 1956 established a redistribution system, but after several years and mountains of paper, less than 10 per cent of the land set aside for transfer actually changed hands. In Long An province, only 5 per cent of the 35,000 families renting land benefited. Though rents had declined since the terrible days of French rule, in a typical village they still amounted to 25–30 per cent of the main crop. Two-thirds of farmers were in debt.[43] Reforms which were implemented, such as rent restrictions and maximum allowable acreage limits, might once have impressed peasants accustomed to French exploitation, but paled in comparison to Vietminh programmes. In some provinces, peasants were required to purchase land they had been given by the Vietminh. Some did so, in the process borrowing money at extortionate rates. In Kien Phong province, one farmer was imprisoned 'in a cage too small to stand up in' while his wife sold their oxen to pay the loan.[44] Nguyen Van Thanh recalled:

> In my village there were about 4,300 people. Of these, maybe ten were landlords. . . . The rest of the people were tenants or honest poor farmers. I knew that the rich oppressed the poor. The poor had nothing to eat, and they also had no freedom. We had to get rid of the regime that allowed a few people to use their money and authority to oppress the others.[45]

42 Jeffrey Race, *War Comes to Long An* (Berkeley, CA, 1972), p. 26.
43 Eric Bergerud, *Dynamics of Defeat* (Boulder, CO, 1991), p. 17; Race, *Long An*, p. 60; Duiker, *Sacred War*, p. 109; Buttinger, *Dragon*, Vol. II, p. 933.
44 Spector, *Advice*, p. 309.
45 Chanoff and Toai, *Portrait*, p. 43.

Despite all the iniquities of land distribution, Elbridge Durbrow, ambassador to the RVN, somehow managed to praise 'the largest land reform program in Asia'.[46]

In 1958 Diem began building *agrovilles*, designed to reduce the susceptibility of rural areas to communist infiltration. Peasants were moved into fortified compounds and provided with the means to protect themselves against attack. 'The purpose of the *agroville* was to gather . . . people together, to urbanize them, to bring the light of civilization to them', one enthusiast described. 'In this way they would understand that the government cared for them and wanted to help them, so they would not follow the communists.'[47] Most peasants did not welcome the 'protection' offered. Ties to the land (both economic and ancestral) were so deeply rooted that they resented being forced to move into inhospitable and unfamiliar compounds. One province chief felt that they 'forced many noncommunists into the underground, where they joined the communists'.[48]

In his battle against communism, Diem chose to target suspected infiltrators rather than trying to improve the living standards of those susceptible to infiltration. A 'Denounce the Communists' campaign, launched in the summer of 1955, encouraged reporting of suspects, who were then arrested, detained without trial, often tortured, and sometimes executed. Many encountered that great French tool of counter-revolution, the guillotine. The scheme was designed as much to frighten ordinary citizens as to root out infiltrators. The US Defense Department expressed concern at the 'innumerable crimes and absolutely senseless acts of suppression against both real and suspected Communists'.[49] One Long An resident recalled:

> anybody who had a relative with the Vietminh was arrested and beaten up. . . . Look what happened to me. . . . they poured water in my nose, and then later hooked up a generator to my fingers and toes and cranked so hard I collapsed and wanted to die. . . . I told them, 'Stop, stop, I confess, I haven't done anything but I confess anyway'.[50]

Despite its cruelties, Diem's campaign undoubtedly reaped benefits. The communist infrastructure suffered heavily. 'Our lives were counted

---

46 Spector, *Advice*, p. 309.
47 Race, *Long An*, p. 54.
48 Ibid., p. 19.
49 Bergerud, *Dynamics*, p. 14.
50 Race, *Long An*, p. 27.

in days and hours', one lucky survivor recalled.[51] By early 1959, Communist Party membership in the South had declined to around 5,000. In the Saigon suburbs of Go Vap and Tan Binh, where more than 1,000 members had resided in 1954, arrests, imprisonments and executions depleted the ranks to just one active member by mid-1959.[52] This was, the National Liberation Front (NLF) admitted, the 'darkest period' of the struggle; Diem's forces 'truly and efficiently destroyed our party'.[53] Dulles, suitably impressed, warned Durbrow that reforms should be encouraged only 'to the extent that they do not weaken central authority'.[54]

American officials felt some unease about Diem's tactics, but congratulated themselves on establishing, from virtually nothing, what appeared to be a solid non-communist government in the South. 'US actions . . . were largely responsible for the survival of a government in Free Vietnam with a will and capability to resist accommodation to the Vietminh', a NSC report concluded.[55] But the US seems to have decided that the secret to creating a nationalist alternative to Ho lay in the creation of a strong southern bourgeoisie who would owe their wealth to Diem and to the US. 'An enormous umbilical cord, tapping into an American economy 6,000 miles away, carried the lifeblood of a new "middle class" that South Vietnam's indigenous economic base could never have begun to support on its own.' Between 1955 and 1961, the US gave Diem US$1,447 million in grant aid.[56] Each dollar strengthened the chains of commitment.[57]

THE NATIONAL LIBERATION FRONT

The revolution could only be squeezed so far. Its moment of greatest despair was also the beginning of its resurgence. Diem's cruelty and his iniquitous policies eventually reached a point of diminishing return: greater ruthlessness was needed to eradicate the remaining cadres, yet that ruthlessness spread alienation and support for the revolution. Furthermore, the purge had eliminated the most vulnerable; those activists who remained were able individuals deeply embedded in the communities from which they derived support. The fittest were surviving.

51 Neil Sheehan, *Two Cities: Hanoi and Saigon* (London, 1992), p. 77.
52 Duiker, *Sacred War*, p. 118.
53 Spector, *Advice*, p. 326.
54 Duiker, *Sacred War*, pp. 107–8.
55 Kahin, *Intervention*, p. 164.
56 Ibid., pp. 84–5
57 As is convincingly argued in Anderson's *Trapped by Success*.

In 1957 the British journalist David Hotham opined that 'It is not that the communists have done nothing because Diem is in power, rather Diem has remained in power because the communists have done nothing'.[58] It is certainly true that official NLF policy was to turn the other cheek. By adopting a defensive role during this period the party cast itself as the victim of government repression, thus impressing the peasantry with its stoicism. The costs were very high, but, according to Jeffrey Race, 'by suffering these . . . costs, the Party created the conditions without which the advance to the stage of violence would not have been possible'.[59]

Hanoi's official line during this period was to support a peaceful revolution, firstly because the time was not ripe for war and secondly because it did not wish to aggravate the Americans. But Le Duan, the combative director of communist operations in the South, favoured a more aggressive strategy which would allow cadres to protect themselves and hasten the revolution. His ideas, formally presented in *Duong Loi Cach Mang Mien Nam* (*The Line of Revolution in the South*), were given party approval in December 1956, when it was announced that

> Due to the needs of the revolutionary movement in the South, to a certain extent it is necessary to have self-defense and armed propaganda forces to support the political struggle and eventually use those armed forces to carry out a revolution to overthrow US–Diem . . . The path of advance of the revolution in the South is to use a violent general uprising to win political power.[60]

Initially, the violence was not directed against RVN forces, but rather against the administrative network. A policy of *tru gian* – extermination of traitors – began. 'Anyone who worked for the government at that time was considered a traitor', a former activist explained:

> The principal purpose . . . was to protect the very existence of the Party. Without exterminating the [government] hard-core elements, the party apparatus could not have survived. A second purpose was to aid in the development of the Party by creating fear in the enemy ranks and by creating faith among the masses in the skilled leadership of the revolution.[61]

58 Spector, *Advice*, p. 305.
59 Race, *Long An*, p. 184.
60 Thayer, *Other Means*, p. 105. In early 1957 Le Duan was transferred to Hanoi, becoming acting General Secretary of the Vietnam Workers' Party, effectively in charge of the Politburo.
61 Race, *Long An*, p. 83.

According to American Embassy calculations, there were 193 assassinations and 236 abductions in 1958, rising to 233 and 343, respectively, in 1959.[62] Ironically, the corrupt were most likely to survive. 'In principle, the party tried to kill any [government] official who enjoyed the people's sympathy and left the bad officials unharmed in order to wage propaganda and sow hatred against the government', a former party leader admitted.[63]

Meanwhile, preparations were made for military action. In 1958 a regional command was formed in Tay Ninh for the purpose of directing self-defence operations. Four companies of resistance forces created two liberated base areas northeast and northwest of Saigon.[64] From these strongholds, increasingly frequent guerrilla attacks were launched, including an assault upon the US military base at Bien Hoa in October. These attacks did not weaken the Diem regime, but they did have an enormous moral effect in demonstrating that the revolution was still alive.

When the Fifteenth Plenum met in Hanoi in January 1959, it was decided that 'The fundamental path of development for the revolution in South Vietnam is that of violent struggle'.[65] This momentous decision did not lead immediately to war. In subsequent months, attention was instead directed towards strategic and logistical preparation. In March 1959 work was begun on a revolutionary base in the Central Highlands, designed to capitalize on discontent with the Diem regime among ethnic minorities. Two months later, the secret Group 559[66] began building a network of trails for transporting troops, supplies and weaponry to southern revolutionaries through Laos, bypassing the demilitarized zone (DMZ). It would eventually become known as the Ho Chi Minh Trail. Most of the new troops were highly motivated 'regroupees' – southerners who had gone north for training after Geneva.[67]

The Hanoi leadership theoretically supported the shift to violence, but was actually bitterly divided. Le Duan welcomed the decision, but the notoriously cautious Truong Chinh, recently demoted from the position of General Secretary, attacked his colleague's

---

62 Thayer, *Other Means*, p. 145.

63 William R. Andrews, *The Village War: Vietnam Communist Activities in Dinh Tuong Province, 1960–1964* (Colombus, MO, 1973), p. 59.

64 These would become War Zones C and D, scene of heavy combat during the war with the Americans.

65 Duiker, *Sacred War*, pp. 119–20.

66 So called for the date of its formation.

67 Perhaps 90,000 Vietminh troops were recalled after Geneva. Pike, *PAVN*, p. 41.

impatience. But then, in November 1960, the Kremlin signalled its support for the 'non-peaceful transition to socialism' in areas where the 'exploiting classes' have already resorted to force. In early 1961, Khrushchev, with specific reference to Vietnam, promised to support communist struggles 'whole-heartedly and without reservation'.[68]

Meanwhile, in Vietnam, the NLF was formally established at a secret meeting in Tay Ninh province on 20 December 1960. It was not by definition a communist organization, though communists were undoubtedly influential. Truong Nhu Tang, one of the founders of the NLF, sincerely believed that

> Had Ngo Dinh Diem proved a man of breadth and vision, the core of people who filled the NLF would have rallied to him. As it was, the South Vietnamese nationalists were driven to action by his contempt for the principles of independence and social progress in which they believed. In this sense, the Southern revolution was generated of itself, out of the emotions, conscience and aspirations of the Southern people.[69]

The two main enemies of the South Vietnamese people, according to the NLF, were imperialism (represented by the US) and feudalism (namely the Diem regime). But, in order to widen the NLF's appeal, the former enemy was stressed. The struggle was presented as a nationalist, not socialist revolution, and the link with Hanoi was prudently camouflaged, so much so that the number of communists allowed to hold leadership positions was carefully controlled.[70]

The formation of the NLF paved the way for the Second Vietnam War. Controversy continues to rage over who started it. George McT. Kahin and others have argued that Diem's violent repression of otherwise peaceful southern communists forced them to take up arms in self-defence.[71] The reluctance of Hanoi to abandon the strategy of peaceful political revolution is cited as evidence of its lack of culpability. On the other hand, though Diem was hardly innocent, it requires a deep naiveté to believe that the war started because embattled communists in the South were forced to defend themselves. Most of those who would eventually fight in the South were trained, armed and indoctrinated in the North. 'Our Party', Le Duan boasted in his 1975 victory speech, 'is the unique and single leader that organized,

---

68 Duiker, *Sacred War*, pp. 129–30.

69 Truong Nhu Tang, *A Vietcong Memoir* (San Diego, CA, 1985), p. 68.

70 Douglas Pike, *Viet Cong: The Organization and Techniques of the National Liberation Front of South Vietnam* (Cambridge, MA, 1966), p. 81.

71 See Kahin, *Intervention*, pp. 113–14.

controlled and governed the entire struggle of the Vietnamese people from the first day of the revolution.'[72] The war began when Hanoi was ready and was, as Douglas Pike has argued, 'premeditated, planned, organized at length and in detail and then pushed and driven into existence' by the Politburo.[73] Hanoi played a clever political game, designed not only to capitalize on the opportune moment for shifting to a war footing, but also to win the propaganda argument over blame for starting the war.

The debate over culpability derives from the struggle by the American people to make sense of the war. The debate exists because most Americans persist in seeing Vietnam as two nations, while those in Hanoi always insisted that it was just one. The American view reflected opinion in Saigon, where few thought seriously about unification. Granted, the RVN flag had a stripe for Annam, Cochin and Tonkin, yet for non-communists the best hope lay in permanent partition, for which Germany and Korea provided useful precedents. Those who fought for the Saigon regime (and one should never forget that many people fought for a long time) were not fighting to unify the country, but to gain some acceptance that they deserved to exist outside the communist sphere. The Geneva negotiators tried to establish a process by which two antagonistic visions of Vietnam might be resolved. But there was no middle ground between those who wanted one nation and those who hoped for two. By 1958, it was clear to Hanoi that Geneva had failed. The time had come to pursue reunification by other means.[74]

ENTER KENNEDY

In 1961 came a new American President with a different foreign policy. John Kennedy was a determined Cold Warrior. Vietnam was 'a proving ground for democracy . . . a test of American responsibility and determination', he argued in 1956. It was 'the cornerstone of the Free World in southeast Asia, the keystone in the arch, the finger in the dike'.[75] In common with his contemporaries, he willed himself to think good thoughts about Ngo Dinh Diem – 'one of the true statesmen of the new Asia'.[76]

72 McMahon, *Major Problems*, p. 435.
73 Pike, *Viet Cong*, p. 80.
74 Duiker, *Sacred War*, p. 137.
75 Kim McQuaid, *The Anxious Years* (New York, NY, 1989), pp. 54–5.
76 Walter Capps, *The Unfinished War* (Boston, MA, 1990), p. 46.

'In the long history of the world, only a few generations have been granted the role of defending freedom in its hour of maximum danger', announced Kennedy in his inaugural address on 20 January. 'I do not shrink from that responsibility, I welcome it.'[77] He was nevertheless plagued by dilemmas which had not bothered Eisenhower. His expertise in foreign policy was unproven and the respect he could command hardly unanimous. As a Democrat, and a liberal, he was naturally more suspect within the anti-communist lobby. He had therefore to seem a great deal tougher than his predecessor. Furthermore, Kennedy and his team felt that they had inherited a number of thorny problems, in Germany, Cuba and Southeast Asia, which had been worsened by Eisenhower's failure to take a stand.

Kennedy made an aggressive foreign policy seem noble and heroic. Though there were many who were sceptical of the new President, the American people did not need much convincing about the morality of their cause or their right to pursue it. The Second World War, the 'good war', inspired a deep confidence in the American people and a belief that the military could be relied upon to provide solutions to international crises. Korea did not destroy that confidence. It still seemed right and proper to shape the world in the American image, by force if necessary. Thus, Kennedy inherited what Michael Sherry feels was a militarized society in which war penetrated to almost every aspect of daily life, from the mundane to the deadly serious.[78] Given the extent of militarization, intervention in Vietnam seemed both possible and logical.

Within this context, the New Look seemed old-fashioned. Since even the smallest problem threatened nuclear holocaust, atomic weapons bred impotence. Kennedy instead formulated a policy of 'flexible response' which tailored American action to each specific problem. This necessitated creating a military which could fight a massive war on the plains of Eastern Europe *and* eradicate guerrillas in the jungles of Southeast Asia:

> Too long we have fixed our eyes on traditional military needs, on armies prepared to cross borders, on missiles posed for

---

77 McQuaid, *Anxious Years*, p. 328.

78 See Michael Sherry, *In the Shadow of War* (New Haven, CT, 1995). Sherry provides a fascinating analysis of the preoccupation of the American people with the military and war. Some of it is overblown (is it really significant that Johnson declared a *war* on poverty, or that American football players regularly 'blitz'?) and much of it lacks perspective (comparison with the 'war cultures' of Germany and Great Britain at the height of their empires would have been illuminating). But Sherry does demonstrate that, in a cultural sense, Vietnam was a war which Americans were mentally prepared to fight.

71

flight. Now it should be clear that this is no longer enough –
that our security may be lost piece by piece, country by country,
without the firing of a single missile or the crossing of a single
border.[79]

This was basically the domino principle restated with Kennedy eloquence. But the new President also believed that, in Vietnam, military
action had to coincide with political reform designed to win hearts
and minds. Americans relished such a challenge in part because it
played upon their perceived virtues: a contest calling for strength,
ingenuity and compassion seemed attractive in comparison to the soulless and potentially catastrophic nuclear posturing which the New
Look implied.[80]

At first, the Laotian situation seemed more serious than Vietnam.
In the late 1950s, fighting broke out between units of the Pathet Lao
and the Royal Lao Army. Since Congressional leaders were reluctant
to make a military commitment to Laos, Kennedy had to bluff his
way to a diplomatic solution. US troops were placed on alert while
Moscow and Beijing were invited to talks. During the summer of
1961, the US agreed to a settlement which established a tripartite
government consisting of rightists, neutrals and the Pathet Lao, held
together by the neutralist Prime Minister Souvanna Phouma. The agreement was ratified the following year. The Pathet Lao were allowed a
permanent sanctuary in the mountains of eastern Laos, where they
were dominant. W. Averell Harriman, chief US negotiator, admitted
that it was 'a good bad deal'[81] – the best the US could expect. The
settlement nevertheless failed to impress hardline anti-communists,
who judged it another sell-out to Moscow. Despite the eloquent promises in his inaugural address, Kennedy seemed reluctant to 'bear any
cost and pay any price' for the defence of freedom. Thus, compromise
over Laos made a determined stand in Vietnam more likely. The Bay
of Pigs fiasco and the building of the Berlin Wall, which both occurred in the autumn of 1961, made such a stand likelier still.

In the summer of 1961, US officials met briefly with DRV representatives to explore the possibility of a peaceful settlement. But by
this stage a steady stream of supplies and troops was being transported down the Ho Chi Minh Trail. Kennedy concluded that Hanoi
could not be trusted. Just prior to the election, the CIA had reported
that 'travel on public roads more than 15 miles outside of Saigon has

79 Williams *et al.*, eds, *America in Vietnam*, p. 191.
80 See Sherry, *Shadow*, pp. 241–54.
81 Duiker, *Sacred War* p. 154.

become hazardous'.[82] South Vietnam seemed on the verge of complete disintegration. In order to shift from 'the defense to the offense', Kennedy added US$42 million to an aid programme already costing US$220 million per year.[83] General Maxwell Taylor and Walt Rostow (Special Assistant for National Security Affairs) were sent on a fact-finding tour of Vietnam. On 1 November they suggested a shift to a 'limited partnership' with the RVN and called for the deployment of 8,000 combat troops who would 'provide the military presence necessary to produce the desired effect on national morale in SVN [South Vietnam] and on international opinion'. The report also maintained that 'NVN [North Vietnam] is extremely vulnerable to conventional bombing, a weakness which should be exploited diplomatically in convincing Hanoi to lay off SVN'.[84]

Secretary of State Dean Rusk and Defense Secretary Robert McNamara echoed these sentiments. 'The United States should commit itself to the clear objective of preventing the fall of South Viet-Nam to the Communist[s]', they wrote on 11 November. 'We should be prepared to introduce United States combat forces if that should become necessary for success. Dependent upon circumstances, it may also be necessary for United States forces to strike at the source of the aggression in North Viet-Nam.'[85] This alarmed Under-Secretary of State George Ball, who warned Kennedy that if he acted on the recommendations, in five years the US would have 300,000 men in 'the paddies and jungles and never find them again'. Americans would find themselves 'in a protracted conflict far more serious than Korea'. 'George, you're just crazier than hell', Kennedy replied. 'That just isn't going to happen.'[86]

Kennedy rejected Taylor's advice, but did approve a changed role for American military advisers. Previously assigned to division level, they now liaised directly with infantry battalions and lower echelon combat units. Over the next twelve months, an additional 10,000 special forces and logistical troops were deployed, not to mention 120 helicopters and 300 aircraft.[87] The Military Assistance Command,

82 Ibid., p. 126.

83 Lawrence Basset and Stephen Pelz, 'The failed search for victory: Vietnam and the politics of war', in Thomas G. Paterson, ed., *Kennedy's Quest for Victory* (New York, NY, 1989), p. 231.

84 George Herring, ed., *The Pentagon Papers*, abridged edn (New York, NY, 1993), p. 57.

85 Williams *et al.*, eds, *America in Vietnam*, pp. 195–6.

86 George Ball, *The Past Has Another Pattern* (New York, NY, 1982), p. 366.

87 R.B. Smith, *An International History of the Vietnam War*, 3 vols (London, 1983) Vol. 1, p. 260.

Vietnam (MACV) was formed in February 1962 to oversee the steadily expanding American commitment. Kennedy was reasonably confident about taking a stand in South Vietnam, since, unlike Laos, it did not share a border with China. Unfortunately, the Laotian settlement made success in Vietnam less likely, since the legitimacy granted the Pathet Lao made it easier for the DRV to move traffic along the Ho Chi Minh Trail.

By early 1961, insurgent forces in War Zone D, north of Saigon, numbered around 10,000, a five-fold increase on two years earlier. US intelligence reported that by late 1961, the NLF could call upon the support of 20,000 active members, up 12,000 from July. Saigon estimated that the NLF had 200,000 loyal followers throughout the South.[88] Disparate military forces were unified into a single integrated command, called the Quan Doi Nhan Dan Giai Phong, or People's Liberation Armed Forces (PLAF), known to its enemies as the Viet Cong (VC). Command was assigned to the revived Central Office of South Vietnam (COSVN), staffed with senior officers from the North. The stream of ordinary soldiers infiltrating southward steadily gathered pace.

Though these developments are the best indication of a shift to armed struggle, it was not presumed that the war would be won by military means alone. Violence still played a relatively small part in revolutionary strategy. Grass-roots political indoctrination still seemed the best way to topple Diem. Hanoi feared that premature or excessive use of force might convince the Americans to intervene militarily. As he confessed to a Polish diplomat, Ho thought that the Americans

> are more practical and clear-sighted than other capitalist nations. They will not pour their resources into Vietnam endlessly. One day they will take pencil in hand and start figuring. Once they really begin to analyse our ideas seriously, they will come to the conclusion that it is possible and even worthwhile to live in peace with us. Weariness, disappointment, the knowledge that they cannot achieve the goal which the French pursued to their own discredit will lead to a new sobriety.[89]

Hanoi hoped that eventually the US would accept a Laotian-type settlement for South Vietnam, thus allowing the NLF legitimate entry to the government of South Vietnam. Diem could be undermined from

---

88 Duiker, *Sacred War*, pp. 146–7.
89 Sheehan, *Two Cities*, p. 59.

within and communist unification would follow quickly. But this scenario would be much less likely to occur if American soldiers were fighting and dying in South Vietnam.[90]

Kennedy's political response to communist insurgency involved the revival of the discredited *agrovilles*, now called strategic hamlets. The new version was supposed to be more formidable but less distasteful than the old. Peasants would not be removed from villages, but would instead construct their own fortified compounds where they lived, after insurgents were identified and removed. Improved living standards, better services, financial assistance and greater security would ensure peasant loyalty.

Encouraged and funded by the Americans, Diem began an ambitious programme of strategic hamlet construction in early 1962. His goal was 14,000 hamlets in fourteen months, a task assigned to the devious and unscrupulous Nhu. The programme was doomed from the start, if for no other reason than that Nhu was a psychopath who saw a golden opportunity to massacre enemies and suspected enemies. Washington, worried about hasty implementation, encouraged caution, but Diem surged ahead. By October, he was claiming that 7,267,517 people were protected in fortified hamlets. In truth, a province chief had only to erect a fence and claim that his people were inside it for the hamlet to be deemed pacified. The Agency for International Development noted:

> From the very inception of the Strategic Hamlet Program it was apparent that many . . . (provincial Vietnamese) officials did not fully understand the concept, and were so frightened by the pressures from . . . Diem and his brother that they would employ any measures from forced labor and confiscation to achieve the quantitative goals set.[91]

Strategic hamlets did hinder communist infiltration. But, according to Don, they

> had a hidden motive of destroying opposing nationalist elements and consolidating [Diem's] own position by placing loyal Can Lao party members in command positions from the village to the province level. This program gave unscrupulous officials in rural areas the opportunity to perpetrate reprisals,

90 Given this logic, it seems bizarre that the PLAF launched attacks on US bases in 1964 (see p. 127). Hanoi has not, subsequently, provided an explanation for why it suddenly seemed sensible to anger the Americans.

91 Anthony Short, *The Origins of the Vietnam War* (London, 1989), p. 259.

embezzle funds, and oppress the people by forcing them to perform compulsory labor without pay.[92]

American construction materials were sold to peasants at extortionate prices by corrupt officials.[93] Because life within the hamlet was not better, the peasant found little incentive to defend it from PLAF insurgents. By spring 1963, only 1,500 of the 8,500 strategic hamlets actually constructed were still viable. At the same time, the NLF was levying taxes in 42 of the 44 provinces supposedly under Diem's control.[94]

'It is certainly a fact', wrote Truong Nhu Tang, 'that . . . the strategic hamlets created even more hostility among the peasants than had the Agrovilles before them.'[95] Kennedy failed to appreciate that mere programmes, no matter how well intentioned or heavily funded, could not by themselves win over the people. Equally important were brave, committed administrators, drawn from the rural areas, who were willing to risk their lives. Such people were in short supply. Evidence collected by the Bureau of Intelligence and Research (INR) in the early 1960s suggested that American aid did little to improve the quality of governance or increase peasant loyalty. If anything, aid corrupted more than it purified. But this evidence was ignored because its implications were intolerable: if money could not save the RVN, what could?[96]

AP BAC

On 2 January 1963, units of the Army of the Republic of Vietnam (ARVN) fought PLAF forces at Ap Bac, in the Mekong Delta. The battle assumed an importance which far exceeded the strategic value of the village. For the ARVN, it offered a chance to impress upon the peasant population the strength and resolution of the Saigon regime and the futility of supporting the NLF. For the NLF, it provided an

92 Don, *Endless War*, p. 82.

93 In contrast, the NLF protected the peasant from the ARVN by building bunkers at no cost.

94 Bassett and Pelz, 'Failed search', p. 242. It did not help that one of the senior officials in charge of the strategic hamlet programme, Pham Ngoc Thao, was an NLF agent who worked to undermine the programme. See Truong Nhu Tang, *Vietcong Memoir*, pp. 46–7, and Duiker, *Sacred War*, p. 154.

95 Truong Nhu Tang, *Vietcong Memoir*, p. 47.

96 James Clay Thompson, *Rolling Thunder: Understanding Policy and Program Failure* (Chapel Hill, NC, 1980), pp. 9–10. When the Defense Department complained about the INR's pessimistic reports, Rusk apologized profusely and directed the INR to refrain from criticizing the DOD's appraisals without its prior approval.

opportunity to demonstrate that American weaponry did not render the ARVN invincible.

In late December, three PLAF companies took up positions on a battlefield carefully chosen to provide greatest tactical advantage. They were lightly armed, but well-trained, supremely disciplined and deeply committed. By the time the ARVN arrived, they were dug into fox-holes on high ground. They had in mind a classic guerrilla strategy: lure the enemy into a trap, strike hard and fast, then escape before superior numbers and equipment begin to tell.

The ARVN enjoyed a four-to-one advantage in personnel and an impressive array of American weaponry, including H-21 and Huey helicopters, Birddog observation planes, M-113 armoured personnel carriers (APC), and Skyraider fighter bombers equipped with napalm. But the local commander, Colonel Bui Dinh Dam, was chosen more for his loyalty to Diem than for his competence. He applied classic search and destroy tactics with consummate idiocy. His troops arrived in fifteen helicopters in the middle of a rice paddy, offering the PLAF an opportunity not unlike a carnival duck shoot. As the helicopters landed, all came under highly accurate fire. Four were destroyed, with seventeen soldiers (including three Americans) killed almost immediately. The ARVN reserves in the APCs should at this point have responded, but for their commander's reluctance to commit them. In an attempt to relieve the situation, Skyraiders dropped napalm on PLAF positions, but without effect. When the APCs finally arrived, they were beaten back by pinpoint machine gun fire. ARVN troops were pinned down in the paddy unable to move against troops they could not even see. An airstrike against PLAF positions was futile.

When night fell, the PLAF disappeared into the darkness, satisfied that they had demonstrated their prowess. The much-touted mobility of helicopter-borne ARVN had proved a sham. NLF recruitment subsequently increased, which suggests that the propaganda aims of the battle had been brilliantly achieved.[97] On the American side, argument raged regarding how to interpret the fight. Colonel John Paul Vann, the senior American adviser on the scene, and one of the most perceptive American soldiers to serve in Vietnam, concluded that ARVN troops were cowards who had no hope of defeating the PLAF. This implied that greater American involvement was needed, though Vann was not optimistic that American troops could be successful.

Nor was Senate Majority Leader Mike Mansfield, who visited Saigon around the same time. On his return to Washington, he warned

97 Sheehan, *Bright Shining Lie*, p. 311.

Congress that, after eight years of effort and $2 billion spent, American efforts to establish an independent non-communist Vietnam were 'not even at the beginning of a beginning'.[98] 'It is difficult to conceive of the alternatives', he concluded, 'with the possible exception of a truly massive commitment of American military personnel . . . and the establishment of some form of neocolonial rule in South Vietnam.'[99] But, in truth, the battle caused less consternation than might have been expected. Some analysts displayed their ignorance of guerrilla warfare by arguing that the ARVN had won, since the PLAF had eventually abandoned their positions. The congenitally optimistic General Paul Harkins, head of MACV, warned Kennedy not to believe press reports: '[We] are winning lowly on the present thrust'. General Earle Wheeler, Army Chief of Staff, argued that it was important to focus on the wider picture. Ap Bac was a miniscule setback amidst unbridled success; 'improvement is a daily fact'.[100]

American commitment to Vietnam had taken on a force of its own. According to Arthur Schlesinger, at one turbulent Cabinet meeting, Robert Kennedy, the Attorney General, asked why, if the situation was indeed so dire, the US did not simply withdraw forthwith. The 'question hovered for a moment, then died away'. It was 'a hopelessly alien thought in a field of unexplored assumptions and entrenched convictions'.[101]

CONSPIRACIES AND CULPABILITY

Thanks to Oliver Stone, many believe that Lyndon Johnson had Kennedy killed in order to escalate the Vietnam War. Stone's film *JFK* drew inspiration from John Newman's book *JFK and Vietnam*. Newman argues that Kennedy's National Security Action Memorandum (NSAM) 263, his last policy document to deal with Vietnam, ordered the immediate withdrawal of 1,000 soldiers, preparatory to complete disengagement by 1965. Then, on 22 November, Kennedy was assassinated. Four days later, Johnson issued NSAM 273, cancelling the withdrawal and initiating covert action in North Vietnam and Laos.[102]

98 Dennis J. Duncanson, *Government and Revolution in Vietnam* (New York, NY, 1968), p. 325.

99 McMahon, *Major Problems*, p. 185.

100 Bassett and Pelz, 'Failed search', p. 243.

101 Arthur Schlesinger, *Robert Kennedy and His Times* (New York, NY, 1979), p. 770.

102 See John Newman, *JFK and Vietnam* (New York, NY, 1992), esp. pp. 407–11, 438–42, 445–9, 451–60.

With Johnson as President, the year 1965 brought escalation, not disengagement.[103]

It only requires a conspiracy theorist like Stone to knit evidence and innuendo into an enthralling plot: Kennedy was assassinated in order to bring about a war which would be lucrative for American arms manufacturers. And it only requires a public still besotted with Kennedy to imagine what might have been: no Vietnam, no defeat, no budget deficit, better social programmes, better race relations. A more confident, harmonious America. Camelot realized.

The evidence that Kennedy wanted withdrawal *is* striking. He supposedly told Mansfield that 'he had changed his mind and wanted to begin withdrawing troops beginning ... January 1964'. Complete withdrawal would be delayed 'until 1965 – after I'm reelected'.[104] Robert McNamara, his Secretary of Defense, claims JFK planned to 'close out Vietnam by 'sixty-five, whether it was in good shape or bad'.[105] Shortly before his assassination Kennedy supposedly told Senator Wayne Morse, the earliest critic of American policy: 'Wayne, I want you to know you're absolutely right ... I'm in the midst of an intensive study which substantiates your position on Vietnam'.[106]

But evidence for Kennedy the hawk is equally impressive. In September 1963 Kennedy told Walter Cronkite: 'I don't agree with those who say we should withdraw. That would be a great mistake.'[107] On the day of his death he planned to tell Dallas citizens: 'We in this country in this generation, are – by destiny rather than choice – the watchmen on the walls of freedom. .... Our assistance ... to nations can be painful, risky and costly, as is true in Southeast Asia today. But we dare not weary of the task.'[108] On 18 February 1962 Robert Kennedy publicly proclaimed: 'We are going to win in Vietnam. We will remain ... until we do win.'[109]

---

103 The argument is echoed in Peter Dale Scott, *Deep Politics and the Death of JFK* (Chicago, IL, 1996), p. 24. It is effectively demolished by Larry Berman in 'NSAM 263 and NSAM 273: Manipulating history', in Lloyd C. Gardner and Ted Gittinger, eds, *Vietnam: The Early Decisions* (Austin, TX, 1997).

104 Kenneth P. O'Donnell and David F. Powers, *'Johnny, We Hardly Knew Ye'*, (Boston, MA, 1970), p. 16; Michael Charlton and Anthony Moncrieff, *Many Reasons Why* (New York, NY, 1978), p. 81.

105 Deborah Shapley, *Promise and Power* (Boston, MA, 1993), p. 262.

106 Newman, *JFK and Vietnam*, pp. 423–4.

107 Williams *et al.*, eds, *America in Vietnam*, p. 187.

108 Bassett and Pelz, 'Failed search', p. 249.

109 Ibid., p. 239. When asked in 1967 if JFK intended to pull out of Vietnam, Robert Kennedy, his brother's most intimate confidant, replied 'No'. See Larry Berman, 'Counterfactual historical reasoning: NSAM 263 and NSAM 273', University of Texas Vietnam Conference, 1993, p. 20.

Clearly, JFK was extraordinarily skilled at telling people what they wanted to hear. Or, as Dean Rusk argued, 'Kennedy's attitude on Vietnam should be derived from what he said and did while president, not what he may have said at tea table conversations or walks around the Rose Garden'.[110] What he did was increase the number of soldiers in Vietnam from 700 to over 16,000, and initiate the nefarious strategic hamlets, covert terror, sabotage, and clandestine incursions into the North. These are not the actions of a man who had a half-hearted commitment to the struggle. There is little hard evidence to suggest that Kennedy's assassination was a turning point in US policy, as Newman suggests. Had he lived, he would have faced virtually the same set of circumstances in Vietnam as Johnson eventually faced. Logic suggests that he would have reacted in the same way, by escalating.

Kennedy had embarked on the road to escalation before he died, though he perhaps did not realize he was on that road. If there was a pivotal event in the war it was not his assassination but that of Diem exactly three weeks earlier. The coup on 1 November 1963 which toppled Diem was planned and implemented by South Vietnamese Air Force officers, but carried out with the encouragement of US ambassador Henry Cabot Lodge. When Kennedy heard of Diem's assassination during a meeting with General Taylor, he 'rushed from the room with a look of shock and dismay on his face which I had never seen before'.[111] One suspects his reaction arose from guilt as much as horror. The administration had for some time been liaising with General Don, one of the main conspirators, through Lucien Conein, a CIA operative in Saigon. On 25 October Lodge advised McGeorge Bundy (Special Assistant to the President for National Security Affairs) that 'We should not thwart a coup' since 'it seems at least an even bet that the next government would not bungle and stumble as much as the present one has'. He reassured Bundy that 'our involvement to date through Conein is still within the realm of plausible denial' – one of the administration's prime requirements. In his last cable to Lodge before the coup, dated 30 October, Bundy relayed the administration's deep concerns but concluded that 'once a coup under responsible leadership has begun . . . it is in the interest of the US Government that it should succeed'.[112]

Diem had become inconvenient to American goals. The Kennedy administration doubted his ability to hold his country together. His

110 Dean Rusk, *As I Saw It* (New York, NY, 1990), p. 442.
111 Maxwell Taylor, *Swords and Plowshares* (New York, NY, 1972), p. 301.
112 Herring, *Pentagon Papers*, pp. 73–4, 79–81.

increasingly erratic and authoritarian rule, especially his persecution of Buddhists, was embarrassing. In early May 1963 Buddhists in Hué had rallied to protest against government harassment. RVN forces sent to suppress the rally over-reacted, killing a number of protestors. During a sympathetic demonstration by Saigon Buddhists on 11 June, the Venerable Thich Quang Duc quietly sat down in a public inter-section, doused himself with gasoline, and set himself alight. The incident, televized around the world, called into question America's choice of allies. Matters worsened when Madame Nhu, Diem's sister-in-law, referred to the episode as a 'barbecue' and promised that the next time she would supply the matches. On 21 August raids on pagodas in Saigon, Hué and other cities resulted in more than 1,400 Buddhists being arrested and sent to concentration camps.

Diem was no stranger to coups, but earlier unsuccessful attempts had no effect upon him. He 'attributed his delivery from danger to the workings of the divine providence and became more intransigent than ever', writes Don. 'We, therefore, became more convinced than ever that only a well planned coup d'état, a real revolution, could solve our country's problems.'[113] Discontent within Saigon ruling circles coincided with an uneasy feeling in the Oval Office. Kennedy became increasingly convinced that, if the war was to be won, Diem had to go. American action in Vietnam, he was certain, was nearing success, a belief encouraged by the Pentagon. Diem could not be allowed to jeopardize this success. Kennedy's anxiety increased when intelligence sources informed him that Diem's brother Nhu was engaged in secret talks with the NLF.

NSAM 263, the proposed withdrawal of 1,000 troops, was in keep-ing with Kennedy's belief that the war was being won – rather than the opposite, as argued by Newman. The British counter-insurgency expert Robert Thompson, convinced that the strategic hamlet programme was destroying the PLAF, suggested to Kennedy in March 1963 that the US should withdraw 1,000 advisers from Vietnam as a gesture of confidence.[114] Rusk recalled 'a period of optimism in the summer of 1963 when we thought the war was going well and we could begin to think of withdrawing American advisors'.[115] A report on the war by McNamara and Taylor in October 1963 concluded that 'The military campaign has made great progress and continues to progress'. The authors expected that, with the steady improvement of ARVN forces,

---

113 Don, *Endless War*, p. 81.
114 Duiker, *Sacred War*, p. 158.
115 Berman, 'NSAM 263 and NSAM 273', p. 187.

tasks performed by American military personnel 'can be carried out by Vietnamese by the end of 1965. It should be possible to withdraw the bulk of US personnel by that time.'[116] American soldiers would leave Vietnam not with tails between their legs, but with heads held high.

A few days after the Diem assassination, Lodge told Kennedy: 'I believe prospects of victory are much improved'.[117] It is perhaps understandable that Kennedy and Lodge should have thought that Diem was the only obstacle to victory. In truth, his ruthlessness was the only thing holding his country together. According to Taylor, the coup lifted 'the lid from the Pandora's box in which Diem had confined the genies of political turbulence. When freed, these forces tore South Vietnam apart.'[118] In the eighteen months that followed, Saigon went through five different Prime Ministers, all of them more ineffectual than Diem, and most of them more corrupt. But because of its complicity in the coup, the US was locked into supporting each new regime. Kennedy as much as recognized this when he noted that, since his administration had done much to 'encourage' the coup, 'We thus have a responsibility to help this new government to be effective in every way that we can'.[119] As Saigon grew weaker and more chaotic, US involvement deepened.

Kennedy and Johnson shared the same basic goals in Southeast Asia – both were fiercely determined to defeat the communists. It could be argued, in fact, that Kennedy's escalation was more significant than Johnson's, since Kennedy squandered the last chance to withdraw from Vietnam gracefully. Thanks to him, the problem was substantially more awkward at the end of 1963 than it had been in 1961. Diem's assassination brought about a tragic inevitability which Johnson recognized soon after he entered the White House. In his inimitable way, he confessed that he felt like 'one of those catfish down in Lady Bird's country . . . I feel like I just grabbed a big juicy worm with a right sharp hook in it'.[120] Harvard-educated Kennedy might have described the predicament differently, but, if he had survived into a second term, he would have been similarly hooked.

116 Berman, 'Counterfactual historical reasoning', p. 8. See also Phillip B. Davidson, *Vietnam at War* (Oxford, 1988), p. 302.

117 Newman, *JFK and Vietnam*, p. 422.

118 Taylor, *Swords*, p. 401.

119 Short, *Origins*, p. 271.

120 *Newsweek*, 2 October 1975.

3 THE VIETNAMESE ALLY

In 1961 Lieutenant-Colonel George Eblen arrived in Vietnam as Staff Judge Advocate to MAAG. Eblen worked closely with Colonel Nguyen Van Mau, ARVN Director of Military Justice, on legal issues arising from the escalating war. One day, Mau asked Eblen why the Americans were in Vietnam. After some thought, Eblen answered that the US wanted to help the Vietnamese fight communism, and wished to show them how American-style democracy would bring economic prosperity and happiness to the Vietnamese people. Mau paused for a moment, then replied:

> 'Yes, I understand what you are saying, but why are you Americans REALLY here?'
> 'It's as I said, we are here to help you.'
> 'No, be honest, why are you REALLY here?'

The gulf was never breached. Mau's frame of reference was French imperialism; he could understand an exploitative mentality, but not an altruistic one. He probably felt more comfortable with the French, whose mission was more transparent. Since he could not accept that the Americans merely wanted to help, he concluded that they must be even more sinister and devious than the French.[1]

Just as 'loyal' Vietnamese did not understand their allies, so too Americans did not understand the Vietnamese. Nor did they try. Very few American advisers, at any stage in the war, spoke Vietnamese. Ignorance was almost wilful. America's universities usually transform themselves into strategic think-tanks to aid a war effort. Yet between 1954 and 1968, of the 7,615 graduate dissertations in modern history, political science or international relations, only 22 dealt with Vietnamese issues. Only two tenured professors spoke Vietnamese.[2]

---

1 Eblen, interview with Frederic Borch, August–September 1996, retold in Borch to the author, 18 July 1997.
2 Kim McQuaid, *The Anxious Years* (New York, NY, 1989), p. 80.

When, in 1970, the Agency for International Development (AID) offered US$1 million to create a Vietnam Study Center, only one university applied for the funding.[3] 'We didn't understand their culture', Shad Meshad, a psychological operations officer, admitted. 'We just went in there like superstars. We're red, white and blue! We're John Wayne! We do it!'[4] When Robert McNamara toured South Vietnam in 1964, he was carefully coached beforehand to shout '*Viet Nam Muon Nam*' to the assembled crowds. Blissfully unaware that Vietnamese is a tonal language, he thought he was saying 'Long Live South Vietnam!'. The crowds heard: 'The southern duck wants to lie down'.[5]

A SOUTH VIETNAMESE NATION?

The Republic of Vietnam, the product of a compromise between great powers gathered at Geneva, should not have existed in the first place and, like a fledgling which has fallen from the nest, should not have survived long. Had the Geneva terms been observed, the South would have been quickly absorbed into one, communist Vietnam. Instead, thanks largely to the American anti-communist obsession, this synthetic nation was artificially sustained by American money, advice and support. Weakened by insurgency and corruption, it should have died in 1965. But the Americans then sent combat troops to rescue it. It is perhaps no wonder that the RVN's relationship with the US was so difficult. South Vietnam could not envisage a world without the Americans because without them it would never have existed. Yet the American presence made any assumption of nationhood a sham.

The nation may have been synthetic, but the non-communist movement was not. It is easy to dismiss the Republic of Vietnam as a right-wing tin-pot dictatorship – corrupt, ineffectual and non-representative. Yet no amount of American money and military support could have sustained a struggle until 1975 had there not existed, on the ground in South Vietnam, a huge opposition to communist rule. The war, it must be remembered, existed before the Americans arrived in force, and continued after they left. Granted, that opposition was united only by its hatred of the communists; no other positive unifying factor existed. Those who opposed Hanoi were not well-served by their government in Saigon. But it is a measure of the strength

3 Allan E. Goodman, 'The dynamics of the United States–South Vietnamese alliance: what went wrong', in Peter Braestrup, ed., *Vietnam as History: Ten Years After the Paris Peace Accords* (Washington, DC, 1984), p. 91.

4 Walter Capps, *The Unfinished War* (Boston, MA, 1990), p. 93.

5 McQuaid, *Anxious Years*, p. 80.

of their commitment that their movement survived in spite of the inadequacies of the RVN government and the aggression of North Vietnam – the most strongly armed communist client state in the history of the Cold War.

'We were not puppets, yet we never achieved the standing or appearance of an independent, self-governing country', Nguyen Cao Ky once reflected.[6] There were few more fierce nationalists than Ngo Dinh Diem, yet he had to suffer allegations that he was tainted by French Catholicism and American capitalism. His subordinate and later adversary Tran Van Don reflected on the difficulty non-communist nationalists had in proving their credibility: 'To the French, and later the Americans, if we failed to agree with them we were either Communists or neutralists, while to the other side, by cooperating, we became puppets'.[7] Ky thought that strong leadership might have solved this problem: 'We never produced a leader to unite the country with its many religious and political factions. Neither Diem, nor [Nguyen Van] Thieu – both backed by the Americans – won the hearts of even the South Vietnamese.'[8] But poor leadership was probably a symptom of disunity, not its cause. No leader could have inspired unified support for a nation formed predominantly out of opposition to communism, and which lacked an embracing ideology of its own. For many in South Vietnam nationalism meant one Vietnam, led by Ho. Among non-communist nationalists, there was no positive platform around which to unite.

The importance of nationalism can be exaggerated. Ordinary peasants objected to a government which was pro-French or pro-American, because they associated the French and the Americans with poverty, inequality, imperialism and misrule. But an identifiably Vietnamese government was not by definition appealing, unless it also improved the life of the peasant. Loyalty was formed not because of abstract national identity, but because of the way the government affected life at the communal level. Colonel Nguyen Be, one of the few humane and perceptive RVN officials, recognized that

> The important thing is not to make the people feel that they are fighting for 'the nation' or 'the central government' but rather that they are fighting for things of immediate and practical significance for themselves. . . . the most important thing is to eliminate the contradictions within society, to reduce the

6 Nguyen Cao Ky, *Twenty Years and Twenty Days* (New York, NY, 1976), p. 137.
7 Tran Van Don, *Our Endless War* (Novato, CA, 1978), p. 10.
8 Ky, *Twenty Years*, p. 137.

extreme differences among people in their daily life. . . . If we want to bring about true unity in order to rebuild our country . . . then we must bring about social justice.[9]

The Saigon government was weak because it could not generate loyalties at the village level. It could not do so because the price of peasant fidelity implied too many sacrifices for the landlords, mandarins and other elites who benefited from RVN power.

The role of the US in 'nation-building' was fraught with difficulty. If the Americans exerted too much pressure, they were labelled imperialists; if they failed to assert themselves, they encouraged rogues, demagogues and criminals. Bui Diem, the former RVN ambassador to the United States, felt that the Americans were too autocratic: 'In a mood that seemed mixed of idealism and naiveté, impatience and over-confidence, the Americans simply came in and took over. . . . The message seemed to be that this was an American war, and the best the South Vietnamese could do was to keep from rocking the boat.'[10] But Diem also felt that 'For all the rhetoric, the American commitment to democracy in Vietnam was a timid and wavering and sometime thing'.[11] This raises the question: how could the US have played a larger role in nation-building without becoming even more intrusive? What is clear is that the US invested more effort toward defeating the revolutionaries militarily than toward addressing why the revolution existed in the first place. Pacification became a mainly military programme, not a social or economic one. It was Maxwell Taylor who reassured Johnson that 'as long as the armed forces are solid, the real power is secure'.[12] Deputy Ambassador Charles Whitehouse, when asked in 1973 whether the US government might help the Vietnamese set up model farms, replied: 'The United States helps the Vietnamese Army fight the Communists. It does not help you till the fields and milk the cows.'[13] One American official admitted in 1968 that 'The basic reason land reform was not pursued was that US officials did not believe that land-based grievances were important'.[14] The solution to the revolution seemed to be power, not justice. As the popular aphorism maintained: 'Just grab the Gooks by the balls and their hearts and minds will follow'. By backing tyrants and by acting tyrannically, the US

9 Jeffrey Race, *War Comes to Long An* (Berkeley, CA, 1972), pp. 244–6.

10 Robert J. McMahon, *Major Problems in the History of the Vietnam War* (Lexington, MA, 1990), p. 436.

11 Ibid., p. 437.

12 Anthony Short, *The Origins of the Vietnam War* (London, 1989), p. 304.

13 Don, *Endless War*, 161.

14 Gabriel Kolko, *Anatomy of a War* (New York, NY, 1994), p. 131.

sullied its moral mission, spreading disillusionment at home and alienation in Vietnam.

But the American mission was immensely complex. The great dilemma was that pacification and nation-building so often worked against each other. Winning the support of the population required removing the competing influence of the NLF. Yet its removal often alienated the population. The NLF was like a virulent, deadly cancer. If the patient is to survive, the cancer must be excised, but doing so kills the patient.

WAR AND SOCIAL CHANGE

The US recognized that creating a viable nation required establishing a stable economy. It addressed this prerequisite with massive aid. During the Eisenhower presidency, well over US$1 billion was funnelled through the Commercial Import Program (CIP), a sort of Marshall Plan for Vietnam, which one of its administrators called 'the greatest invention since the wheel'.[15] The system was designed to provide funds for the purchase of American imports, while controlling inflation by making sure that American dollars did not circulate freely. Inflation was controlled, but, according to David Anderson,

> Unlike Europe's economic progress under the Marshall
> Plan, the RVN's progress was phony. Instead of purchasing
> manufacturing equipment and industrial raw material, millions
> of counterpart dollars went into the acquisition of luxury items
> like Japanese motorcycles and American refrigerators. . . . the
> result was an artificial urban vitality while the countryside
> languished and industry remained virtually non-existent.

By 1961, the RVN had a balance of payments deficit which exceeded US$1 billion. Imports exceeded exports by as much as 200 per cent in a given year.[16] This situation naturally worsened with the American military build-up. In 1969–71 imports were over 50 times higher (in monetary value) than exports.[17] A few Vietnamese importers grew obscenely wealthy supplying American consumers. Native industries withered. The ramshackle economy was built on the shaky foundation of the American military mission. At one point in the war, there were

15 Ken Post, *Revolution, Socialism and Nationalism in Viet Nam*, 5 vols (Aldershot, 1989), Vol. I, p. 245.

16 David Anderson, *Trapped by Success: The Eisenhower Administration and Vietnam, 1953–1961* (New York, NY, 1991), pp. 155–7.

17 Kolko, *Anatomy*, p. 224.

56,000 *registered* prostitutes in Saigon, whose consumption of American cosmetics and hairspray was voracious. Through silicone injections and other cosmetic surgery, these women transformed themselves to suit American tastes.[18] A service economy developed in which there was little regard for the fact that those being served would not remain forever. Entrepreneurs who understood that the American presence was merely temporary tried to make as much money as possible while the opportunities remained golden.

American farm surpluses totalling US$1.3 billion flowed into Vietnam between 1958 and 1975. Domestic agricultural production consequently fell drastically.[19] In order to prevent food shortages in the cities, US-imported rice was sold at well below world prices. This upset the domestic rice market, giving the peasant producer little incentive. In 1940 Vietnam exported a million tons of rice. In 1965, despite more fertilizers and better strains, she became a net importer, to the tune of 130,000 tons, rising to 750,000 tons in 1967.[20] This spurred an exodus to the cities, which further decreased agricultural production, completing a vicious circle. Economic independence is important to the development of national identity, yet American-style nation-building destroyed the RVN economy, encouraging an addiction to aid and subsidies.

According to conservative estimates, one half of the South Vietnamese peasantry became refugees at least once during the war. Most ended up in the cities. In 1960, 20 per cent of the population lived in urban areas. By 1971, the figure had risen to 43 per cent, a rate of increase five times higher than similar countries during the same period.[21] Many Americans blithely assumed that refugees were voting with their feet against communism. In fact, migration was motivated by survival, not economic opportunity or political choice. The damage done to Vietnamese society often went unnoticed since, in the American world-view, urbanization implied progress. James May, a civilian adviser to the US pacification programme in Quang Ngai province, argued that, in the refugee camps outside major cities,

> There's always plenty to eat and a roof over their head . . . the refugees have a better standard of living than they did in the villages. Look at the tin on their roofs. It's better than the old thatched roofs – it doesn't leak. And the refugee camps bring

18 Neil Sheehan, *A Bright Shining Lie* (London, 1990), p. 625.
19 Kolko, *Anatomy*, p. 226.
20 George McT. Kahin, *Intervention* (New York, NY, 1986), p. 410.
21 Kolko, *Anatomy*, pp. 201–2.

the people in closer to the urban centers, where they can have modern experiences and learn modern practices. It's a modernizing experience.[22]

The cities were safer, but they were not paved with gold. Vietnam did not undergo the industrial transformation which inspired urbanization elsewhere in the world. Poverty within Saigon, Qui Nhon, Da Nang and other cities was dire. No wonder, then, that people resorted to crime, corruption and prostitution to feed themselves. Mental suffering, resulting from the complete destruction of the only world the peasant knew, was profound. 'Looked at objectively', Kolko concludes, 'the United States in less than a decade did more damage to an entire society than other colonial nations or the urbanization process elsewhere accomplished over generations.'[23]

The refugees were very often people who did not support the NLF. Removing them from an area meant surrendering that area to the NLF. But one of the most damaging effects of urbanization was also the least obvious. Vietnam had been a rural country, which followed an agrarian ethos. Ancestral ties held society together and gave the people a sense of identity, an essential component of nationalism. The transformation of South Vietnam into an urban society destroyed that identity, leaving the people rudderless. It was difficult to motivate refugees to defend a past which no longer existed and a future which seemed threatening. The NLF, because of its ties to the land and its promise to protect the peasant livelihood, grew more popular as the agrarian ethos came under increasing threat. The peasants had no doubt who was responsible for the destruction of old Vietnam. The Americans, in the interest of supporting a nationalist alternative to the NLF, destroyed the very essence of nationhood.

A CULTURE OF CORRUPTION

In the late 1960s, in response to looting by an ARVN Ranger Battalion, high school students in one particular province decided *en masse* to join the local branch of the Anti-Corruption League, set up with much fanfare by Ky. Their action received great publicity, as their commitment to honest government seemed to suggest that there was hope for the RVN. A few months later the group was disbanded after its leader absconded with its funds.[24]

22 Kahin, *Intervention*, p. 408.
23 Kolko, *Anatomy*, p. 204.
24 Samuel L. Popkin, 'Pacification: politics and the village', *Asian Survey* 10 (August 1970), p. 669.

'Just about any way to make a dishonest piaster was tried at one time or another', recalls Don. 'Virtually everyone who was able took advantage of his position and engaged in profiteering.'[25] At the village level, Cong An agents, whose duty it was to root out communists, 'were just out to have a good time and get money out of the people. By the tenth of the month their salary would be gone and they would ask to "borrow" some money from . . . the people . . . [Those who] didn't "lend" it, . . . would be arrested.'[26] Ky admitted that 'Most of the senior officials in the provinces are corrupt'.[27] Loyalty followed the flow of money. By granting concessions in the import sector, the opium trade, or elsewhere, Thieu tied perhaps 100,000 of South Vietnam's most powerful individuals closely to him.

Extorted money was not reinvested in the domestic economy but salted away in Swiss or French accounts. Embezzlers were keenly aware of the short term and the long; they sought to extort as much as possible before the inevitable communist victory. The US turned a blind eye because it preferred power to rectitude. In December 1963 a CIA report concluded that 'however desirable and perhaps even necessary' a purge of corrupt elements might be in the long term, it could nevertheless have, in the short term, 'a disruptive effect upon the solidarity of the military establishment'.[28]

The atmosphere of corruption eroded the morale of American troops. Told that they were in Vietnam to defend something good, they quickly became disenchanted. 'We all wondered: why do we want those guys in there?' one former officer reflected. 'Are they any better than the guys we are fighting?'[29] Little could be done about an ARVN officer on the take, since protocol impeded redress. According to Don, corrupt Vietnamese commanders would usually ask for an excessively scrupulous American adviser to be transferred, on grounds of a 'personality clash'. 'Generally, the American high command complied, and many really effective officers were removed from their jobs to the detriment of their careers.'[30]

Few Americans admitted the extent to which they colluded in corruption. Fraud and petty pilfering were easy since American largesse seemed unlimited. The Judge Advocate General (JAG) Corps lawyers spent a vast amount of of time prosecuting American soldiers

25 Don, *Endless War*, pp. 169–70.
26 Race, *Long An*, pp. 66–7.
27 George Herring, *America's Longest War* (New York, NY, 1986), p. 162.
28 Kahin, *Intervention*, p. 195.
29 Eric Bergerud, *Red Thunder, Tropic Lightning* (New York, NY, 1994), p. 258.
30 Don, *Endless War*, p. 158.

for black marketeering, currency manipulation and related misconduct.[31] Goods destined for base exchanges often disappeared *en route*. For most of the war, loss of fuel to pilferage hovered around 25 per cent.[32] 'Americans have told me that whenever they couldn't find an item in the PX [post exchange], they could purchase it openly on the streets of Saigon or Qui Nhon',[33] Don recalled. Some enterprising Vietnamese even produced catalogues of goods which never quite made it to the PX.

One final point needs emphasis: it was not corruption which made the RVN bad, but rather the nature of the government, the lack of an organic link to the governed, which inspired corruption. Honest administrators could not have saved the system because the system had no logic. As Jeffrey Race has argued, 'even with a government of saints, the situation . . . would have moved in the same direction, although perhaps not as fast'.[34]

ALLIES?

In November 1954 Don and other senior ARVN commanders attended a joint planning session with the new MAAG, headed by General John O'Daniel. The Vietnamese, drawing upon their experience fighting beside the French against the Vietminh, made a number of pertinent suggestions designed to promote mobility. It was suggested that battalions be formed into mobile groups, with only light artillery, and that infantry units should fight in the locale from which they were recruited. Underground guerrilla forces should be formed to prevent infiltration from Laos and Cambodia. According to Don, these arguments

> fell on deaf ears. The Americans evidently put us in the same mold as the Koreans whose army they had organized and trained, and they seemed to think our country was similar to the Korean peninsula. They believed, I suppose, that what would work for Korea would certainly work for Vietnam. . . . The Americans were organized to fight a war in which there are well-defined front lines with relatively secure rear areas . . . and where the overwhelming fire superiority of American weapons could bring decisive results.

31 Frederic Borch, 'Judge advocates in combat', unpublished manuscript, chap. 2, pp. 17–20.
32 Kolko, *Anatomy*, p. 357.
33 Don, *Endless War*, p. 171.
34 Race, *Long An*, p. 204.

Don felt that the major threat to the RVN came from guerrilla units operating at village level. Large, immobile conventional units seemed inappropriate to such a challenge. 'The French had already proved this to us. We wondered why we had to repeat the mistake for the Americans.'[35] But the Americans were convinced that the communists would attempt to conquer South Vietnam through a conventional invasion from the North. The ARVN was therefore equipped, organized and trained to meet this threat. It seemed wiser to tailor the Vietnamese force to its benefactor's strengths, rather than to the danger it actually faced. Despite Don's retrospective protestations, most ARVN officers willingly conformed to American wishes. By 1966, Colonel Nguyen Van Nuu, province chief in Long An, was confidently claiming that 'the reason that the Vietcong use guerrillas is because they are weak and do not have enough strength to attack us directly'. There was no reason to imitate PLAF techniques since, if ARVN soldiers were to fight in civilian clothes like the PLAF, 'we will not be able to distinguish our men from the enemy and . . . might mistakenly shoot each other'.[36]

Diem was a willing partner in the conversion of the ARVN into a conventional force. He believed, with some justification, that rural insurgents could be adequately handled by local defence forces. The ARVN would instead take on PLAF or PAVN main force units, action which necessitated large conventional forces, massive firepower, and heavy armour. Don's complaint is in keeping with the tendency to seek an American explanation for everything that went wrong in Vietnam. In fact, the 'ARVN was an ineffective instrument because many of its officers were poor and many of its soldiers sullen', Bergerud argues. 'Organizational change would not have altered this basic situation . . . If a "heavy" ARVN failed against the insurgents because of a lack of will to fight, it is reasonable to conclude that a "light" ARVN would have failed for exactly the same reason.'[37]

Nevertheless, the deficiencies of the American military machine, in particular its reliance on unlimited firepower, were magnified by its ally. The ARVN, in common with the Americans, required a huge and highly vulnerable logistical network to supply its armament-hungry soldiers. Those soldiers were reluctant to attack without a preliminary artillery barrage or airstrike, and were not overly conscious of the need to conserve ammunition (for instance through accurate

---

35 Don, *Endless War*, pp. 149–50.
36 Race, *Long An*, p. 241.
37 Bergerud, *The Dynamics of Defeat* (Boulder, CO, 1991), p. 26.

firing). The greatest problem with this method of warfare was that it could not be sustained after the Americans withdrew.

It was unfortunate that the first priority of the American soldier was his own survival, but disastrous that the same was true of the ARVN soldier. To the peasant in a beleaguered hamlet, the ARVN fought a coward's war. They never demonstrated a willingness to make sacrifices on the peasants' behalf. Colonel James Herbert, an adviser in Long An, regretted the way ARVN commanders failed to deploy their forces 'so as to protect people and not just to . . . protect themselves'. But he understood the reason for this deficiency: 'American forces . . . go into bigger outposts and bigger bases, and do not deploy their forces so as to provide security for the people in the hamlets. . . . it is very difficult to get the Vietnamese to do what the US doesn't do.'[38] Samuel Popkin, who spent several years in Vietnam villages, 'studying the war from the bottom up', concluded that 'If America had fought the war as if defending peasants was as important as killing Communists, we would have done better at both'.[39]

The Americans expected the South Vietnamese to conform to their military dogma, but they would not entertain the idea of unified command. Westmoreland decided, probably quite rightly, that Americans could not be expected to fight under ARVN commanders, and that, for the South Vietnamese, unified command would evoke bitter memories of the French war. But, though unity was not perhaps the answer, the status quo was hardly adequate. The gulf of understanding mentioned at the beginning of this chapter was never bridged. As a result, according to Bui Diem, 'there were two separate wars, one fought by the Americans and another fought by the South Vietnamese. . . . that was one of the main reasons for the tragic outcome in Vietnam.'[40]

RVN FORCES

With the ARVN trained to perform a conventional military function, village protection went to the Regional and Popular Forces (RF/PF), recruited from their own locale. As the war progressed, their proportionate strength within the RVN armed forces increased, exceeding

---

38 Race, *Long An*, p. 232.

39 Samuel L. Popkin, 'Commentary: the village war', in Braestrup, *Vietnam as History*, p. 103.

40 Bui Diem, 'Reflections on the Vietnam War: the views of a Vietnamese on Vietnamese-American Misconception', in William Head and Lawrence Grinter, eds, *Looking Back on the Vietnam War* (Westport, CT, 1993), p. 243.

50 per cent by 1971. They were not as heavily armed as the ARVN, had low priority for air and logistical support and were the last to receive sophisticated weaponry. But, because they were tied to their native villages, they were often more dependable than the ARVN and fought with greater vigour. They cost less to maintain, achieved a higher kill ratio and experienced far fewer cases of desertion.[41]

The ARVN, one American soldier commented, 'was a joke. . . . Every, every, every, *every* firefight that we got into, the ARVN broke, the ARVN fucking ran.'[42] 'They were very poor fighters', another remarked, 'The majority of the armed forces could more easily have been termed armed farces!' 'I despised the whole lot of them', Dan Vandenberg recalled.

> They were all cowards. In the morning their uniforms were spotless and their weapons clean. They'd look the same at the end of the day. We did all the work. We looked like tramps. For us to get new gear would take an act of Congress. The South Vietnamese always seemed to have a lot. We would rather go it alone: At least you had only to fight one enemy.[43]

Search and destroy operations conducted by the ARVN often turned into 'search and avoid'. By the end of 1967 the ARVN outnumbered the American force, yet the Americans killed twice as many enemy per week. Only 46 per cent of large ARVN operations (battalion or bigger) resulted in contact with the enemy, while the corresponding figure for the Americans was 90 per cent.[44] During one five-day period in December 1966, the 18th ARVN Division at Xuan Loc supposedly conducted 5,237 patrols, but only made contact with the enemy thirteen times.[45] ARVN artillery strikes were often intentionally inaccurate, so as to warn the enemy and provide opportunity for escape. Quite often, informal truces were struck.

The explanation for ARVN deficiencies is not clear. PLAF soldiers, drawn from the same population pool, were usually professional, deeply committed and capable of great acts of heroism. 'The enemy was a tough, hard, dedicated fucking guy, and the ARVN didn't want to hear about fighting', a GI remarked.[46] But, since South Vietnam had little

41 See Race, *Long An*, pp. 231–2.

42 Albert Santoli, *Everything We Had: An Oral History of the Vietnam War by Thirty-Three American Soldiers Who Fought It* (New York, NY, 1981), p. 112.

43 Bergerud, *Red Thunder*, pp. 246–8.

44 Guenter Lewy, *America in Vietnam* (Oxford, 1978), p. 163.

45 Sheehan, *Bright Shining Lie*, p. 628.

46 Santoli, *Everything*, p. 112.

sense of identity as a nation, nationalism provided little inspiration. In 1959 draft evasion in Long An province ranged between 16 and 35 per cent per month.[47] In South Vietnam as a whole, there were an estimated 250,000 draft evaders by the end of 1965. Those who did enlist assumed a pragmatic approach to service. When danger outweighed profit, many deserted. In 1967 desertions totalled 78,000, a figure which then rose steadily, exceeding 140,000 in 1971.[48] Soldiers almost always left for personal reasons; most were desperate to get back to families. Because a soldier's pay was seldom sufficient to support his family, he often felt a need to desert and take more lucrative employment. Only very rarely did the deserter defect to the other side.[49]

Both Diem and Thieu were more interested in a loyal army than an effective one. Thieu in particular tried to deflect the political ambitions of his military rivals by granting them lucrative opportunities for graft. 'We would be left with practically no one to fight the war', his Vice-President Tan Van Huong admitted, 'if all corrupt commanders were to be prosecuted and relieved.'[50] But lucre was only a partially effective solution to the rivalries that corroded the ARVN. As Jeffrey Clarke has argued, the various units were 'a greater threat to each other than to the local insurgents and the growing number of North Vietnamese troops who were moving south . . . the leading South Vietnamese commanders were often little more than medieval warlords whose power and position depended on the number of troops loyal to them'.[51] Thieu drastically expanded the number of junior officers in the ARVN, thus increasing the number beholden to him. Between 1968 and 1970, the number of first lieutenants and captains more than doubled, while the army itself grew by just 20 per cent. In order to ensure their loyalty, these men were assigned small racketeering concessions, such as the collection of rice rations, selling of blackmarket petrol or supplies, loan sharking, or the embezzlement of salaries of 'phantom' soldiers who had died or deserted.[52]

Since officer candidates required a high school diploma, they came mainly from the middle and upper urban classes. Catholics were

47 Race, *Long An*, p. 72.

48 Lewy, *America in Vietnam*, p. 174.

49 See Anthony James Joes, *The War for South Viet Nam* (New York, NY, 1989), pp. 86–7; Goodman, 'The dynamics of the United States – South Vietnamese alliance', pp. 90–1.

50 Kolko, *Anatomy*, pp. 214–15.

51 Jeffrey Clarke, 'Civil–military relations in South Vietnam and the American advisory effort', in Jayne S. Werner and Luu Doan Huynh, eds, *The Vietnam War: Vietnamese and American Perspectives* (Armonk, NY, 1993), pp. 188–9.

52 Kolko, *Anatomy*, p. 214.

disproportionately represented, and favoured for high promotion.[53] There was no promotion from the ranks. While a gulf between officers and men is not necessarily an impediment to effective command, there was no overriding sense of *noblesse oblige* among officers to compensate for the class divide. It was not unusual for an officer to sell supplies to the enemy, leaving his own troops hungry and poorly armed. 'The greatest obstacle in improving and training the armed forces was the lack of qualified leadership at all levels', General James Collins argued. 'US advisers continually cited poor leadership as the foremost reason for unit ineffectiveness. But with the lack of replacements, unsatisfactory commanders were seldom relieved.'[54] Performance in combat very seldom influenced promotion – either positively or adversely.

'The lives of the soldiers and low-ranking officers were terrible, simply because they could not make enough to live any kind of dignified existence', Don admitted. 'Little towns of wretched hovels sprang up around the various posts where the troops were stationed, because a soldier did not get enough money to allow him to maintain a house for his family in a village away from his post.'[55] Married soldiers had an average of 3.9 children and poverty forced nearly 50 per cent of them to keep their families close to the base where they were stationed.[56] The ARVN could do little about this problem; if soldiers were moved from their families, desertions rose. It was difficult for the ARVN to fulfil a mobile function since, whenever it moved, families moved with it.

Corruption and embezzlement were rife for the simple reason that pay was desperately low, if it arrived at all. The cost of field rations was, until 1967, deducted from a soldier's pay. Ordinary soldiers were forced to live off the land by looting from the peasants. One-third reported being in debt, nearly 40 per cent experienced food shortages, and nearly 25 per cent took part-time employment outside the army.[57] Soldiers had to bear the indignity of seeing wives and daughters go into prostitution to fend off starvation. Yet when improvements in pay and conditions occurred later in the war, corruption – by this stage a habit – did not abate. In 1969 an NSC study found that 42 per cent of all hamlets reported crimes committed by RVNAF personnel, ranging from minor incidents like chicken

53 Joes, *War for South Vietnam*, pp. 79–80.
54 Lewy, *America in Vietnam*, p. 170.
55 Don, *Endless War*, p. 77.
56 Kolko, *Anatomy*, p. 256.
57 Ibid., p. 261.

stealing to rape and murder. Officers often felt that looting made soldiers fierce, uniting them 'with a tradition of soldiering associated with the legendary and successful armies of Vietnam's past'.[58]

PEASANTS, POLITICS AND WAR

ARVN officers came almost invariably from the cities, while ordinary soldiers were drawn increasingly from the refugees who migrated there. In contrast, the revolution drew its strength predominantly from the rural areas it controlled. This meant that, as urbanization proceeded, it undercut the revolution, depriving it of the manpower and economic base upon which it depended. For the US, this seemed an attractive prospect. In 1968 Harvard Professor Samuel Huntington remarked that the rural exodus 'struck directly at the strength and potential appeal of the Viet Cong'. Urbanization 'on such a massive scale' would undermine 'the basic assumptions underlying ... Maoist doctrine of revolutionary war ... The Maoist-inspired rural revolution is undercut by the American sponsored urban revolution.'[59] But this was delusion on a grand scale. Rapid urbanization was hardly a long-term solution, since it also implied increased dependency upon US aid. Furthermore, an army which was considered alien could not win the hearts and minds of the peasant population.

Early in the war, many peasants preferred to live in NLF-controlled areas where cruel landlords were eliminated, land was redistributed, taxes were lower and food more plentiful. The NLF also imposed a strict moral code, eliminating gambling, extortion and prostitution. If the NLF hold was quite secure, the area tended to be peaceful. Peasant support was therefore often pragmatic; no ideological conversion was required. What mattered was survival. Peasants found it difficult to welcome Americans or ARVN, who brought with them a destructive firepower which the NLF did not possess. Nor did they appreciate being persuaded to move into 'safer' areas with artillery, airstrikes or defoliants.

Later in the war, living in an NLF area became dangerous: inhabitants endured frequent battles and bombing, not to mention increased taxes charged by the NLF to fund the rising cost of defence. A PLAF defector remarked that, after 1967

---

58 Lewy, *America in Vietnam*, p. 178.
59 Samuel Huntington, 'The bases of accommodation', *Foreign Affairs* 46 (June 1968), p. 650.

> The villagers began to hate the VC after so many of them were innocently killed and their standard of living became increasingly difficult. In addition, the VC promised to liberate the villagers, but all the villagers saw around them was killing and starvation. They had to go find freedom for themselves and their families. They started to move out of their native villages . . .[60]

The greater the pressure upon the NLF, the greater the commitment and sacrifice it demanded from the population and the greater the hardships endured. Thus, many peasants found it safer to live under the protection of the RVN. The Hamlet Evaluation Survey (HES) conducted by US authorities showed a marked decline in the number of NLF-controlled villages in the late 1960s. But the HES measured control, not support. Pacifying a village did not mean that the inhabitants automatically switched sides and began backing the government. A peasant interviewed in 1967 described how the war affected loyalties:

> The Viet Cong collect higher taxes but they know how to please the people; they behave politely so people feel that they are more favored. . . . They do not thunder at the people like the government soldiers.
>
> People like the government because of freedom, but there is no equality even though the taxes are lower than the Viet Cong's. The thing the people don't like in the government is their behavior. . . . the soldiers often arrest and oppress the people only for revenge – in short it is banditry.[61]

This attitude, which the French called *attentisme*, was typical of the Vietnamese peasantry throughout the long struggle. 'Most of the South Vietnamese have a very simple dream', Colonel Nguyen Van Dai, an RVN National Police commandant, remarked. 'They wanted to have peaceful lives and not worry about having food. They didn't want to be afraid of someone capturing them or torturing them or killing them. They supported anyone who could bring peace.'[62] Thus, loyalty was like a flag which changed direction in a capricious wind. 'Communists want to save us from colonialism and underdevelopment, and anti-communists want to save us from communism', a leading monk

---

60 Mark Moyar, 'Villager attitudes during the final decade of the Vietnam War', Texas Tech University Vietnam Center website.

61 Popkin, 'Pacification, politics and the village', pp. 662–3.

62 Moyar, 'Villager attitudes'.

complained at the time of the Tet Offensive. 'The problem is that we are not being saved, we are being destroyed. Now we want to be saved from salvation.'[63] Or, as Kim McQuaid has remarked, 'Everyone was killing the peasants in order to save them from somebody else'.[64]

The RVN, heavily funded by the US, could flood a village with material benefits. Fertilizers, machinery, good seed stocks, schools, and medical care did improve living standards. But these benefits could not entirely erase the bitter taste of corrupt government. Minds were won, but not hearts. Allegiance based upon these benefits waned when the benefits dried up. No emotional link existed between Saigon and the hinterlands, therefore no sense of identity – essential to true nationalism – could develop.

The identity issue is extremely important. Villages in which there was a strong commitment to the Cao Dai or Hoa Hao, or even to Catholicism, were conspicuously successful at resisting infiltration. These sects provided strong leadership, a sense of order, a moral code and a feeling of unity which challenged communist influence. Allegiance to the sect was a matter of faith and faith tended to strengthen under duress. The RVN could never encourage similar allegiance. What is perhaps ironic is that the government was so keen to eradicate the influence of the sects, which seemed to threaten central government authority.

Crude surveys like the HES could not take account of *attentisme*. The Americans frequently misunderstood why peasants supported the NLF. Lieutenant-Colonel William Corson, an exception, concluded that

> The Vietnamese peasant has a strong desire to survive and more often than not hopes the Vietcong will win because he imagines a Vietcong victory will eradicate the conditions he currently faces. Our experience showed that the Vietnamese peasant will help the Vietcong when there is not too much risk in doing so and that in the great majority of cases the peasant considers it unthinkable to betray the Vietcong to the enemy.[65]

To the peasant, aiding the revolution was often merely a matter of survival. But to an American or ARVN soldier it was a treacherous crime, worthy of severe punishment. There was very little understanding

63 McQuaid, *Anxious Years*, p. 101.
64 Ibid., p. 99.
65 Kolko, *Anatomy*, p. 136.

of the dire predicament which so many faced. A tormented peasant desperate simply to survive was often dealt with as severely as a fanatical party member. 'To us there were no friendly civilians, only ones who posed no immediate threat',[66] one soldier commented.

'It got to a point where you just didn't trust none of them', a GI recalled. 'So we'd just try to scare the shit out of them.'[67] Soldiers who went to Vietnam with the best intentions about helping to free the native population from their communist oppressors quickly learned that since it was impossible to tell who was a friend, it was best to assume that everyone was an enemy.

> The Vietnamese did not like us and I remember I was shocked. I still naively thought of myself as a hero, as a liberator. And to see the Vietnamese look upon us with fear or hatred visible in their eyes was a shock. . . . all of a sudden my black-and-white image of the world became real gray and confused.[68]

Those who could understand the predicament of the South Vietnamese peasants could still not feel compassion toward them:

> I think one of the biggest disappointments . . . was the attitude of the Vietnamese peasants. None of them seemed to give a shit about us. The feeling was mutual: We didn't even think they were people. Never once did they say, 'Don't go over there – that trail is booby trapped; don't go that way – there's a sniper.' There was never a warning of any kind. Never one ounce of friendliness. On the other hand, I can understand why: If they'd have tipped us off, Charlie would have come that night and slit their throats. But it would have been nice to have seen them take a small risk for us once.

'You don't see your enemy, so the people you do see become your enemy', one GI reflected. 'You become hardened. You could tell some of the old-timers because, instead of tossing their candy or C-rations *to* the kids, they would throw it *at* them.'[69] The fear, frustration and bewilderment which every American soldier experienced bred hatred and contempt. 'I began to hate them because I couldn't stand the idea that we were coming into these people's lives and totally disrupting them', one soldier remarked.[70]

66 Bergerud, *Red Thunder*, p. 223.
67 Mark Baker, *Nam* (New York, NY, 1981), p. 156.
68 Santoli, *Everything*, p. 111.
69 Bergerud, *Red Thunder*, pp. 221, 224.
70 Baker, *Nam*, p. 164.

Effective nation-building required a degree of understanding which most American policy-makers, military planners and ordinary soldiers did not possess. They answered their bewilderment with firepower, reasoning that, if they could not defeat the communist ideology, they could at least kill the ideologues. But the process of separating the revolutionaries from the peasants created 2.4 million refugees by the end of 1966.[71] In the Song Ve valley in June 1967, 8,465 people and 1,149 animals were forcibly removed, in order to 'protect' them and to deny the PLAF the area. Hamlets were destroyed and crops burned in order 'to discourage the return of the villagers'. The officer in charge described it 'an overwhelming success and a model for future operations'.[72] Colonel Eblen was probably sincere about the altruism of the American mission, but the Vietnamese peasant had difficulty understanding altruism delivered through the barrel of a gun.

71 Kolko, *Anatomy*, p. 137.
72 Cecil Currey, 'Vietnam: lessons learned', in Phil Melling and Jon Roper, eds, *America, France and Vietnam: Cultural History and Ideas of Conflict* (Swansea, 1991), p. 80.

4 THE VIETNAMESE ENEMY

'In the military field', Giap argued, 'apart from the great invention of the atomic weapon, there is a greater invention, the people's war.'[1] The unique strength of the revolution lay in the fortitude of those devoted to it. Their achievement should be measured by the force applied against them; no revolutionaries have ever faced such massive power as the United States mobilized. 'This enormous and imposing force of the people' made the PLAF commander Nguyen Thi Dinh feel 'very small, but I was full of self-confidence, like a small tree standing in a vast and ancient forest'.[2] The revolution succeeded because it harmonized perfectly with a people who were 'habituated to suffering . . . tough in the face of hardship' and, toward their enemies, 'pitiless to the point of cruelty'.[3]

HO CHI MINH AND REVOLUTION

Ho Chi Minh's admirers in the West have, for propaganda reasons, presented him as first and foremost a nationalist, even going so far as to suggest that communism was merely a means to an end. But that is merely an indication of how effective was his propaganda. Ho was a devout, if idiosyncratic, Marxist who relished his nation's role as the vanguard of revolution in the developing world. The fact that he occasionally had differences with Moscow or Peking on mainly tactical issues did not negate his inherent loyalty to the Marxist line. Cadres obediently chanted the mantra about a 'New Vietnam' – a vision which implied a great deal more than mere independence. They threw sand in the eyes of the Americans and their own people by stressing the anti-foreign theme and muting the revolutionary one. But what

1 James P. Harrison, *The Endless War* (New York, NY, 1989), p. 161.

2 Kristin Pelzer, 'Love, war and revolution: reflections on the memoirs of Nguyen Thi Dinh', in Jayne S. Werner and Luu Doan Huynh, eds, *The Vietnam War: Vietnamese and American Perspectives* (Armonk, NY, 1993), p. 97.

3 Harrison, *Endless War*, p. 135. The quotation is from the French writer Paul Isoart.

they had in mind was a Vietnam independent not only of foreign influence but also of its own past. The benevolent uncle image which Ho and his propagandists liked to cultivate should not be allowed to obscure the true character of the man. He was tough, ruthless and iconoclastic. 'All those who do not follow the line which I have laid will be broken', he once warned.[4]

Ho originally planned a Maoist three-stage revolution. In the first phase, cadres would mobilize the masses politically, preparing them for protracted struggle. Violence would be restricted to the minimum necessary to secure safe areas which would become logistical bases and model revolutionary centres. The local people, once exposed to practical benefits of the revolution, would join the movement. During the second phase, mobile military operations would force the enemy to disperse. Political indoctrination would be applied in newly secured areas. In the third phase, the main forces of the revolution, now suitably prepared, would leave safe areas and launch a general offensive. This would spark a popular uprising – the people would rise up and crush their oppressors.

The path toward liberation, according to Ho, came through *dau tranh*, a powerful, highly emotive ethic. Like struggle in Marxist canon, *dau tranh* was both an endeavour and an inspiration – a revolutionary gospel. It stressed teamwork, order, discipline and programmed goals. There were two strands to *dau tranh*. Political struggle, or *dau tranh chinh tri*, encompassed three spheres of activity. *Dich van*, action directed at the enemy population, involved non-military exploits designed to lower enemy morale and erode support for the war. For example, when Jane Fonda visited Hanoi and posed atop a PAVN tank, she unwittingly took part in *dich van*. *Binh van*, the second sphere of activity, entailed non-military action amongst enemy troops. Examples included efforts to persuade RVN soldiers to switch sides and selling drugs to American troops. Finally, *dan van* implied action among the people in the liberated areas. This included land reform, re-education, recruitment, taxation, propaganda and assassination.[5]

Military struggle, or *dau tranh vu trang*, had to be adapted to enemy strengths and to the capabilities of the revolutionary force. In the context of fighting the Americans, it was necessary to abandon the Maoist three-stage strategy, though it still proved useful for propaganda purposes in rallying the people. The third stage of the Maoist

4 David Halberstam, *Ho* (New York, NY, 1983), p. 71.
5 Douglas Pike, *PAVN: People's Army of Vietnam* (Novato, CA, 1986), pp. 216, 233–52.

strategy, which implied big unit war, was simply too dangerous against an enemy as mobile and powerful as the Americans. The Americans could not be given the sort of war they most wanted. The object instead was to create a strategic stalemate which would eventually exhaust the resources and morale of the US. As Henry Kissinger argued in a seminal essay in *Foreign Affairs* in 1969, 'the guerrilla wins if he does not lose. The conventional army loses if it does not win.'[6]

Two sub-strategies were pursued simultaneously to achieve the goal of stalemate during the American war. In the 'village war', PLAF regional troops and village militia waged classic guerrilla war. Action was more important than objectives – action *was* the objective. Guerrilla warfare succeeds by appearing ubiquitous and incessant. 'There is no fixed line of demarcation, the front being wherever the enemy is found', wrote Giap.[7] While no single action is fatal, eventually enemy morale erodes because the war seems endless and inescapable. Time defeats the enemy and patience is a weapon. As Truong Chinh explained in 1947, 'the war must be prolonged . . . Time works for us – time will be our best strategist, if we are determined to pursue the resistance war to the end.'[8]

A regular force strategy was simultaneously pursued by PAVN and PLAF main force units. Giap devised two tactical variants which would permit confrontations with American military might in a protracted war context. The first, *cach dang doc lap*, or the 'gnat-swarm' technique, involved dozens of small attacks, launched incessantly, which were designed to attrite his physical and moral strength. Their frequency and location were unpredictable, forcing American or ARVN forces to disperse and depriving them of the initiative. The second, or *cach dang hop dang*, involved medium-sized attacks against relatively important targets, designed for maximum impact. These had to be perfectly planned and flawlessly executed, so as to provide revolutionary forces with a brief tactical advantage which could be exploited.

According to Maoist precepts, the struggle was supposed to climax in a general offensive, in the style of Dien Bien Phu. The general offensive was supposed to spark *khoi nghia*, or the general uprising:

> the revolutionary consciousness of the people has been
> gradually raised through the use of *dau tranh* strategy to

6 Henry Kissinger, 'The Viet Nam negotiations', *Foreign Affairs* 47 (January 1969), p. 214.

7 Vo Nguyen Giap, *The Military Art of People's War*, ed. Russell Stetler (New York, NY, 1970), p. 105.

8 Truong Chinh, *Primer for Revolt* (New York, NY, 1963), p. 112.

the point where it explodes in a great human spontaneous combustion which, like a forest fire, consumes all before it. The people rise up energized. The enemy's army shatters. The old society crumbles. The people seize power.[9]

In 1954, 1968, 1972 and 1975 general offensives failed to spark *khoi nghia*. But what the people believe is more important than what is true. Like all good myths, *khoi nghia* served as a focus for action. It united the people behind a common revolutionary goal. The 1967–68 Campaign, in which the Tet Offensive played a prominent part, was not really the classic stage three action, though propagandists suggested otherwise. It was instead an attempt by Hanoi to force the pace of American disintegration by underlining the vulnerability of the RVN and by sowing defeatism among the American people. As will be discussed in Chapter 6, it was not the turning point which the communists hoped to engineer.

After Tet, revolutionary forces were left in disarray. In order to regroup, the Politburo adopted a modernized variant of protracted war. Traditional guerrilla methods were amalgamated with new weaponry. Highly professional, well-disciplined sapper teams carried out sudden, violent actions against sensitive American installations. For instance, a few American aircraft might be destroyed with some well-aimed missiles, whereupon the guerrillas would disappear before the Americans could respond. This was not a strategy for victory, since no action could be decisive, nor could sufficient attritional damage be caused. It was, however, an effective way of playing for time while political *dau tranh* eroded enemy strength.

In 1972 came a new variant of armed *dau tranh*. Over the previous three years PAVN had been transformed into a conventional army, capable of big unit mobile war. The Easter Offensive was the culmination of this development. In fact, the metamorphosis was incomplete, which explains the defeat. The necessary logistical matrix had not been fully developed; attacks stalled for lack of supplies. Nor was PAVN able to master American airpower, which remained formidable. Three years later, however, logistical improvements were complete, and the Americans were absent. Success was finally achieved.[10]

Ho was once asked by a journalist how he thought he could defeat the French. 'We will be like the elephant and the tiger', he replied. 'When the elephant is strong and rested and near his base we will retreat. And if the tiger ever pauses, the elephant will impale him

---

9 Pike, *PAVN*, p. 218.
10 See ibid., pp. 212–30.

on his mighty tusks. But the tiger will not pause and the elephant will die of exhaustion and loss of blood.'[11] Giap's instructions to his troops played on a similar theme:

- If the enemy advances, we retreat.
- If he halts, we harass.
- If he avoids battle, we attack.
- If he retreats, we follow.[12]

Communist strategy did not seek a military defeat of the adversary, but sought instead to exhaust his 'aggressive will' (*y chi xam luoc*).[13] The elusiveness of revolutionary forces frustrated both the French and the Americans. Neither solved the dilemma of how to defeat an enemy who would not stand and fight. Central to revolutionary strategy was the concept of *thoi co* – the opportune moment. Giap explained: 'At the right time, a pawn can bring victory: at the wrong time a bad move can lose two knights'.[14] The communist sense of timing was usually adept, but the revolution's worst defeats came when troops were ordered to attack in unfavourable circumstances or when goals were unrealistic.

Like intertwining strands of a single cable, military and political *dau tranh* were separate but inseparable. 'Every military clash, every demonstation, every propaganda appeal was seen as part of an integrated whole', Truong Nhu Tang confessed. 'Each had consequences far beyond its immediately apparent results.'[15] Early in the revolution, the political strand was strongest. As the revolution proceeded, the military struggle gathered importance, but never completely superseded the political. In 1959–63, 90 per cent of cadres were engaged in political *dau tranh*, the rest in military. By 1971–74, the ratio was 55/45.[16] But proportions were by no means rigid; the nature of *dau tranh* varied according to the challenges encountered.

Dau tranh was supposed to involve the people – all people – at all levels. Everyone was mobilized, physically *and* mentally. '*Dau tranh* is all important to a revolutionary', a soldier confessed. 'It shapes his thinking, fixes his attitudes, dictates his behavior. His life, his revolutionary work, his whole world is *dau tranh*.'[17] Or, as Pike has commented:

---

11 Halberstam, *Ho*, p. 89.

12 Peter MacDonald, *Giap* (London, 1993), p. 82.

13 David W.P. Elliott, 'Hanoi's strategy in the Second Indochina War', in Werner and Huynh, eds, The Vietnam War, p. 70.

14 MacDonald, *Giap*, p. 32.

15 Truong Nhu Tang, *A Vietcong Memoir* (San Diego, CA, 1985), p. 87.

16 Pike, *PAVN*, p. 234.

17 Ibid., p. 217.

The struggle movement became the great social fantasy of the Vietnam War. Against a backdrop of high drama it offered the Vietnamese a hero role. The young could embark on a quest to look the dragon, or authority, in the face. The timid villager, all his life a persevering tortoise, found his moment of destiny. The struggle movement meant that there was still magic in the mature world, one needed only to march and mumble the secret incantation – solidarity, union, concord – and the meek would inherit the earth.[18]

Because the struggle was not exclusively military, it could not be defeated by military force alone. Communist doctrine held that one guerrilla could hold a village if the people were sympathetic to his cause and that an entire battalion of government forces could not hold a hostile village. 'We maintain that the *morale factor is the decisive factor in war, more than weapons, tactics and technique*', a party document proclaimed. 'Politics forms the actual strength of the Revolution: Politics is the root and *War is the continuation of Politics*.'[19] Neither the Americans nor the RVN developed a viable counter-strategy. Defeat was therefore inevitable. Once the NLF established a political hold over a liberated zone, that hold could only be broken if the RVN offered the people a better alternative, which it was unable or unwilling to do. Applying force to break the hold was contradictory, since force alienated the local population and enhanced the revolution's appeal.

THE REVOLUTION AND THE PEOPLE

'Our Party', Ho once said, 'is great because it covers the whole country and is at the same time close to the heart of every compatriot.'[20] 'The people are the eyes and ears of the army, they feed and keep our soldiers', Truong Chinh added. 'The people are the water and our army the fish.'[21] In order for the revolution to succeed, the people had to be radicalized and organized. Peasants, the revolutionary raw material, were (according to Ho and Chinh) 'unlucky and simple-minded' people who 'accept their wretched state because they do not understand the cause of their misery'. The revolution would enlighten them and re-mould them. Once aroused, they 'leap into battle, determined

---

18 Ibid., p. 238.
19 Gabriel Kolko, *Anatomy of a War* (New York, NY, 1994), pp. 139–40.
20 Frances Fitzgerald, *Fire in the Lake* (New York, NY, 1972), p. 302.
21 Truong Chinh, *Primer*, pp. 116–17.

to wage a decisive struggle against their exploiters . . . they fight as though they would rather die than continue to endure such suffering'.[22]

For most of the war, military operations were not intended to produce great victories, but rather to provide the screen behind which political indoctrination could proceed. Nevertheless, military and political *dau tranh* acted in symbiosis. Successfully indoctrinated peasants provided manpower, transport, food, cover and intelligence which soldiers needed. Likewise, military success meant that the revolution was better able to protect the people and improve their lives, making them more supportive of it. The revolution did often bring improvements. But, as one defector admitted, there was no point in rescuing peasants prematurely, since Saigon's cruelties were an asset:

> according to a saying of Mao Tse-tung: 'A firefly can set a field ablaze.' Yet for a firefly to set a whole field ablaze the field must be extremely dry. 'To make the field dry' in this situation meant that we had to make the people suffer until they could no longer endure it. Only then would they carry out the Party's armed policy. That is why the party waited until it did.[23]

Patience was paramount. *Thoi co* would come when the people were sufficiently alienated, the government sufficiently weak and the revolution sufficiently strong.

Under Maoist doctrine, controlling the countryside is paramount, since it supplies the urban areas with human and material resources. As the revolution extends its control of the countryside, cities wither on the vine. 'The rule of revolutionary warfare is to progress from small units to large commands of coordinated combat branches and to destroy the enemy's force on a large scale, and finally to attack the cities, attack the nerve centers and smash the enemy's administration.'[24] The NLF's control of the countryside was based on the Maoist concept of the liberated zone. These varied in size from several hundred square kilometres to much smaller areas consisting of a few hamlets. Within these areas, the NLF was the government, collecting taxes, administering services and maintaining order. By 1967, there were zones within 30 miles of Saigon which had not seen a RVN official for over three years.

The key to NLF success was organization. 'On the road to the seizure of power, the only weapon available to the revolutionary masses is organization', Le Duan argued. 'All activities [seek] to bring the

22 Harrison, *Endless War*, p. 145.
23 Jeffrey Race, *War Comes to Long An* (Berkeley, CA, 1972), p. 112.
24 Van Tien Dung, *Our Great Spring Victory* (New York, NY, 1977), pp. 13–14.

masses to the point when they will rise up and overthrow the ruling classes . . . organize, organize, organize.'[25] The NLF had to transform village life, not just so that living standards could be improved, but also that peasant behaviour could be controlled. This meant establishing a new social code, and new institutions to regulate lives. Part of this transformation followed automatically from land redistribution which fundamentally altered economic life. Educational and other intellectual activities gradually altered the peasant's world-view, as did new myths, songs and a folklore suited to the revolutionary ethic. A former activist described how indoctrination affected him:

> We had no private lives to speak of. Although we were teenagers, we didn't have any girlfriends. I told myself that I should live as a real Communist lives, the pure life of the revolutionary. We tried not to think about girls. We would feel guilty if we caught ourselves singing some romantic song. At that time the Party had a slogan called 'Ba Khoan' – 'The Three Delays': 'If you don't have a child, delay having one. If you aren't married, delay getting married. If you aren't in love, delay love.' So we delayed love. Instead we built up our feelings about the mountains and the rivers and the flowers in the places we lived. We loved these things and we felt strongly that we were ready to die for them.[26]

It was not easy to join the NLF. Members were recruited over a long period; anyone eager to join was automatically suspect. Commitment had to be demonstrated through various tests of loyalty. Thus the party was constantly served by eager aspirants intent upon proving their worthiness. The candidate had first to be recommended by two party members, then screened by two inspectors, and then had to pass an oral examination. Talented and especially committed individuals, discovered at the 'rice roots' level, worked their way up the party hierarchy. The revolution was a great deal more unsentimental, authoritarian and coldly clinical than the myths woven into Western youth culture at the time implied, or than stubborn romantics still believe. Students in the 1960s who taped posters of Uncle Ho on to dormitory walls had no idea that they were worshipping a communist control freak.

The Central Office for South Vietnam (COSVN) determined grand strategy. The next tier, the Interprovincial Party Committee (IPC),

25 Harrison, *Endless War*, p. 164.
26 David Chanoff and Doan Van Toai, *'Vietnam' – A Portrait of its People at War* (London, 1996), p. 61.

had separate branches dealing with military affairs, proselytizing, security, economics and miscellaneous functions. Below it were the Provincial Party Committees, the District Party Chapters, and the Village Party Chapters, with each organized into similar branches as the IPC. Mass organizations were established along gender, age, ethnic, religious or occupational lines, with chapters in each village. These included the Liberation Youths' Association, Liberation Women's Association and the largest of all, the Liberation Farmers' Association, which numbered 1.3 million members by 1963.[27]

At the core of the revolution were the party cadres, or *can bo*, who embodied the cherished qualities of the movement – morality, optimism, heroism. 'A revolutionary must be patient, loyal, sociable and brave to the point of sacrifice', the journal of the Youth League declared. 'He must obey the general will and die if need be for the community.'[28] *Can bo* constituted 10–20 per cent of total membership.[29] They were drawn mainly from poor peasant stock in the South and therefore understood peasant life. Party doctrine stressed the 'three withs': cadres had to live, eat and work with the people they sought to indoctrinate.[30] By sharing the experiences of the people, they were better able to earn trust. Secrecy was, however, paramount. *Can bo* in a single area might not know each other by sight; they would often mask their faces at party meetings.

Indoctrination had elements of cult-like mind control. Members were placed in cells of three to ten individuals and subjected to frequent (sometimes daily) self-criticism sessions, conducted by *can bo*. They were repeatedly required to demonstrate their understanding of the ideals of the movement and their loyalty to its goals. But while mind control certainly hardened devotion, it could not create loyalty. The revolution fed on, but did not create, the political culture in Vietnam which craved independence, hated foreigners and desperately desired land. As Konrad Kellem, who studied prisoner attitudes for the Rand Corporation, concluded: 'you do not have to indoctrinate the indoctrinated'.[31] Most were motivated by patriotism – the NLF seemed the only viable nationalist road. Their intense loyalty is especially extraordinary given the hardships they had to endure.

27 Michael Lanning and Dan Cragg, *Inside the VC and the NVA* (New York, NY, 1992), p. 337; William J. Duiker, *Sacred War* (New York, NY, 1995), pp. 43–4.

28 Harrison, *Endless War*, p. 138.

29 Kolko, *Anatomy*, p. 52.

30 Harrison, *Endless War*, p. 166.

31 Stanley Karnow, 'Commentary: the two Vietnams', in Peter Braestrup, ed, *Vietnam as History: Ten Years After the Paris Peace Accords* (Washington, DC, 1984), p. 78.

'We ... expect to be killed, if we decide to fight for the revolution', a cadre in My Tho confessed. 'Our death will serve our children's interests.'[32]

For dynamic young men and women the party embodied their personal ambitions and their desire to share in the moulding of a new nation. In contrast, the RVN seemed staid, prescriptive and elitist – a conglomeration of all the worst elements of old, colonial Vietnam. The RVN was not a meritocracy; advancement within it was based on arcane and arbitrary criteria. In contrast, in the NLF 'a poor peasant could hope to become the village secretary, the district secretary, or even higher – his lack of education and his inability to speak flawless French would not weigh against him. In fact, they would be in his favor.'[33] While it is dangerous to make sweeping generalizations about the characteristics of the two competing movements, it is fair to say that intelligent, highly motivated idealists joined the NLF, while the RVN attracted a fair share of cynics for whom power meant the power to exploit. It is also important to remember that for activists who opposed the Diem regime, there was no legal avenue of political expression, since opposition parties were outlawed. Much of the appeal of the NLF was therefore Diem's creation.[34]

It is important to differentiate between members of the NLF and those who merely supported it. At the height of the war, Pike estimated that only 10 per cent of the population of the South were 'true believers'.[35] Most peasants were opportunistic, their allegiance shifting with the fortunes of the war. While they preferred to sit on the fence, neutrality was difficult to maintain. Those who could not prove they were friends of the revolution risked being judged enemies of it. Wartime studies indicate that the bulk of supporters were poor peasants who sought a better life. Very few believed in socialism, but many saw the NLF as the only way to secure a parcel of land. Others had been alienated by the Saigon government and its capricious system of justice, its corrupt officials and its crippling taxes. In many cases the peasant's loyalty to the NLF was inversely proportional to the cruelty he had experienced from RVN officials.

The party discovered early that land was the single most important factor affecting peasant loyalty. In 1950 an escalation of the

---

32 Harrison, *Endless War*, p. 182.

33 Race, *Long An*, p. 170.

34 See Carlyle Thayer, *War by Other Means* (Sydney, 1989), pp. 188–9; and Douglas Pike, *Viet Cong: The Organization and Techniques of the National Liberation Front of South Vietnam* (Cambridge, MA, 1966), p. 83.

35 Harrison, *Endless War*, p. 173.

war against the French coincided with an accelerated redistribution programme. Land was promised in exchange for joining the military struggle. A defector from Long An province explained how the party manoeuvred peasants into a position of dependency advantageous to the revolution: 'Only by sending their sons into the army and paying taxes could the war be won, and only by winning the war could they keep their land'.[36] Assurances were made that, if a soldier died, the land would go to his relatives. On the eve of the final assault at Dien Bien Phu, Giap told his armies that victory would 'help to ensure that the land reform achieves success'.[37] But, as the struggle continued, the ever-increasing need for soldiers left the party in a serious bind: thousands of small landowners were created who had no ideological commitment to socialism.

The party worked the land issue very well, but in doing so encountered some thorny problems which were never quite resolved. Those peasants who owned their land and farmed it (numerically quite a few) and those who owned some and rented part (an even greater number) might not have liked the French or later the Americans, but they feared the party. These fears were justified, since the party had every intention eventually to take their land. The tension between landed and landless peasantry was very real and caused the party no end of worry. The best cadres came from what might be called the 'lower middle class': people who had some education and an awareness of life outside their hamlet. But this group found talk of collectivism very frightening. The party's cannon fodder came from the landless masses. It was not easy, and ultimately not possible, to please both groups.

Ho understood how support could evaporate if his troops treated the peasantry badly. Soldiers were instructed to respect local customs and to refrain from petty cruelties or wanton destruction. Acts of extortion or bribery were severely punished. There were three main rules of discipline:

1. Obey orders in all your actions.
2. Do not take a single needle or piece of thread from the masses.
3. Turn in everything captured.

'Eight Points of Attention' governed behaviour:

1. Speak politely.
2. Pay fairly for what you buy.

36 Race, *Long An*, p. 129.
37 Kolko, *Anatomy*, p. 60.

3. Return everything you borrow.
4. Pay for everything you damage.
5. Do not hit or swear at people.
6. Do not damage crops.
7. Do not take liberties with women.
8. Do not ill-treat captives.[38]

A strict party morality governed how members related to each other, how much they worked and studied, even how much they should eat (revolutionaries should never be fat!). Thrift, modesty, unselfishness and asceticism were the outward and visible signs of inner dedication. Mutual sacrifice demonstrated commitment and bound the committed together. Here, Ho and his disciples led by example. With few exceptions, they were modest men who subordinated egos to the revolution. Their quest for unity transcended internal disagreements. Many revelled in their anonymity, and few exploited power for material gain.[39]

'The NLF and the people it influenced', writes Douglas Pike, 'lived in a muzzy, myth-filled world of blacks and whites, good and evil, a simplistic world quite out of character with the one to which the Vietnamese was accustomed.'[40] It was also out of character with reality. Only the naive or ideologically blinkered would claim that the moral codes were followed religiously by every soldier and party member. When manpower was in short supply, moral purity became a luxury. One soldier admitted that, by 1967, 'the authorities were taking everyone they could . . . It didn't matter if you were a good element or a bad.'[41] Given the obvious iniquities of the Saigon regime, it is safe to assume that a revolution as morally pure and respectful of the peasantry as Ho envisaged would have succeeded much earlier. Yet at no time were these supposedly righteous revolutionaries able to inspire *khoi nghia*. Though most peasants insisted that they were treated better by NLF soldiers than by ARVN, the struggle was not painted in black and white. Thugs existed on both sides.

The distinguishing feature of the revolution was not its righteousness but rather its naked strength. Vietnamese revolutionary strategy, in contrast to that of Mao, assigned considerable importance to terror.[42]

38 Lanning and Cragg, *Inside*, p. 331.

39 But some apparently used their power to enable their sons to escape military service, by sending them abroad to study. See Chanoff and Toai, *Portrait*, p. 44.

40 Robert J. McMahon, *Major Problems in the History of the Vietnam War* (Lexington, MA, 1990), p. 323.

41 Chanoff and Toai, *Portrait*, p. 48.

42 See Anthony Clayton, *The Wars of French Decolonization* (London, 1994), pp. 40–1.

Members were advised to 'Fragment the opposition's . . . leadership, if necessary using assassination and torture'.[43] The process of 'liberating' a village often involved killing individuals of influence: village chiefs, landowners, district officials and school teachers. According to Lewy, 36,725 assassinations and 58,499 abductions were carried out between 1957 and 1972.[44] Terror, argued Giap, raised the morale of insurgents, frightened opponents, and kept the masses in line. Honest officials were most at risk, since they posed the greatest threat to NLF influence. This also persuaded otherwise virtuous officials to take a dishonest path, giving credence to NLF claims that all RVN officials were corrupt.

The NLF's terror seems to contradict its institutionalized morality. Apologists might argue that every terrorist act had a specific purpose: if violations of the 'Eight Points' occurred only with respect to 'enemies of the revolution', they were not violations at all. Generally speaking, the communists won this propaganda point: their terror seemed to be controlled and purposeful, that of the RVN and the US appeared indiscriminate and vindictive. But the propaganda is bunk. The term 'enemy of the revolution' was widely defined – often only 20 per cent of the victims were government officials or police.[45] The 1968 massacre of innocent civilians in Hué was, by any definition, an unrestrained atrocity.

There are two explanations for these apparent violations of party code. First, as the revolution became more successful it inevitably became less ideologically pure, attracting a greater number of sadists. Maintaining discipline in a party of 5,000 was relatively easy, but less so in one ten times that size. Occasional attempts to purge undesirables (in 1951 one-third of the members were expelled, with a similar proportion in 1960) could not entirely eradicate malfeasance. In theory, all assassinations were supposed to be approved by provincial committees, but in practice perhaps 75 per cent were the work of freelance village activists keen to settle scores.[46]

Secondly, the codes should not be taken too seriously. Thuggery was often official policy. The rules were themselves part of *dich van*; they were as much a piece of propaganda as a code of conduct. *Dich van*, according to Pike, 'shaped perceptions that dissolve if subjected to even casual inspection, yet inspection seldom happened. It created myths that defy elementary logic, yet they endure and threaten to

43 MacDonald, *Giap*, p. 82.
44 Guenter Lewy, *America in Vietnam* (Oxford, 1978), p. 272.
45 Ibid., p. 273.
46 Kolko, *Anatomy*, p. 127.

become the orthodoxy of history. It . . . blinded honourable men to immorality.'[47] The greatest success of the revolution was its ability to create a virtuous façade which obscured a deep and widespread cruelty. Even when clear cases of sin became apparent, revolutionaries (and their apologists) could always claim that the American devil made them do it.

Tran Van Don, a bitter enemy of the NLF, felt that the communists demanded 'a fearful price in terms of human dignity and Vietnamese customs and tradition. They sought to generate a struggle between classes in a backward country where class differences were never known.'[48] His claim to speak for the masses seems hollow, as does his rejection of class conflict. But, that said, the communist record in Vietnam reveals that there is some truth to his argument. Peasant support for the revolution was founded on the twin principles of nationalism and land reform, not socialism. The peasant wanted enough land to feed his family and to make some profit in a capitalist market. But for the communist, land reform was merely a halfway house on the road to collectivization. Peasants generally found the class war distasteful. Murdering a cruel landlord had a certain rough justice, but killing a respected teacher was wanton terror. Persecutions and assassinations did not inspire loyalty, only fear. This fear and a smattering of material benefits inspired a pragmatic devotion to the movement, but not an ideological conversion. The aphorism 'grab 'em by the balls and their hearts and minds will follow', a favourite of the Americans, could be applied equally to the revolution.

WOMEN OF THE REVOLUTION

In October 1931 the Communist Party unanimously agreed that 'the Vietnamese woman is the most persecuted element in society'.[49] In principle, Ho supported sexual equality: 'Without the complete emancipation of women, the building of socialism is not completed'.[50] The importance given to women is demonstrated by the prominence within the NLF of the Women's Liberation Association, which numbered one million members by 1965.[51] The party promised to abolish

---

47 Pike, *PAVN*, p. 243.

48 Tran Van Don, *Our Endless War* (Novato, CA, 1978), p. 25.

49 Mai Thi Tu, 'The Vietnamese woman yesterday and today', in Michael Klein, ed., *The Vienam Era* (London, 1990), p. 192.

50 Tu, 'Vietnamese woman', p. 195.

51 It should be pointed out that the members' primary goal was to 'liberate' South Vietnam, not themselves.

polygamy, give every woman the right to choose her profession, equalize pay, allow common ownership of property within marriage, and allocate land without consideration of gender.

'Women are not only equal to men in society, they are also equal to their husbands', an NLF document proclaimed.[52] But two obstacles impeded real equality: the stubborn vestiges of Confucianism and the masculine nature of war. The Confucian Book of Rites held that 'Morals forbid [a woman] to step out of her room. Her only business is in the kitchen.'[53] Confucian tradition not only hindered the acceptance by men of women's equality, it also made women less likely to perceive for themselves a new status and to abandon habits of obeisance to husbands or fathers. Since most peasants were attracted to revolution for reasons of nationalism or land reform, rather than to its feminist ideals, the liberation of women, no matter how sincerely pursued by the party, faced a rough road.

War opened doors for Vietnamese women, but also closed them. Party manifestoes stressed three responsibilities: (1) women would replace men at work, (2) they would care for their families, and (3) they would serve in militia units.[54] With men away fighting, women were forced into previously masculine roles in manufacturing, agriculture and transport. In many agricultural cooperatives, 80–90 per cent of the workers were women.[55] But this shift in work patterns did not significantly improve female status because it was widely assumed to be temporary and because the work women performed freed men for soldiering, still the most important wartime task.

Giap was fond of quoting the Vietnamese proverb: 'When pirates come into the house, even women must take up arms'.[56] Propagandists distributed widely a poem scratched on a prison wall by a woman revolutionary martyred during the French war:

> A rosy-cheeked woman, here I am fighting side by side with
>   you, men!
> On my shoulders weighs that hatred which is common to us.
> The prison is my school, its mates my friends,
> The sword is my child, the gun my husband.[57]

52 Duiker, *Sacred War*, p. 145.
53 Tu, 'Vietnamese woman', p. 187.
54 Duiker, *Sacred War*, pp. 202–3.
55 Tu, 'Vietnamese woman', p. 195.
56 Harrison, *Endless War*, p. 135.
57 Tu, 'Vietnamese woman', p. 192.

But, in truth, though many women were trained to fight, actual combat was rare. They were more often guards, porters and scouts, or the customary nurses and cooks. Wartime roles were the logical extension of peacetime domesticity.

War reinforces traditional gender divisions: men, with few exceptions, do the fighting, while women assume feminine, caring roles. 'Go and achieve brilliant exploits', a woman wrote on the wall of a cooperative club in Hatay province; 'I'll take care of the house and the village fields.'[58] The need to replenish the population placed an enhanced value on motherhood. 'The woman should not wait for a government or party decree to free her', Ho once declared, 'she must struggle for her own freedom.'[59] This seems to have been a clue to the revolution's actual commitment to emancipation and also an indicator of the limitations of institutional reform in a traditional society.

THE SOLDIERS OF THE REVOLUTION

The model Vietnamese citizen was the farmer ready to drop his hoe and take up his rifle in defence of his homeland. Military service was not, therefore, unfamiliar. The martial heritage of the Vietnamese people was focused and enhanced by the communist revolution, creating what Pike calls 'probably the most outstanding military phenomenon of our lifetime'. Victory was the result of 'a peculiar alchemy: a messianic leadership of extraordinary insight acting as a catalyst on a singular, centuries-old martial spirit'.[60]

The forces of the revolution were divided into four groups. PLAF village militia were part-time soldiers who engaged only rarely in combat, but provided logistical support for larger units. They received little training and few weapons and were concerned primarily with village defence. What they lacked in experience they made up for in motivation, given their strong ties to the area they defended. PLAF regional troops, much better armed than the militia, were full-time soldiers who supported bases and villages and carried out guerrilla operations. There was usually one battalion per province and one company per district. PLAF main force units – uniformed soldiers organized into battalions under the direct command of COSVN – were responsible for large actions throughout the country. The system

---

58 Ibid., p. 194.
59 Ibid., p. 197.
60 Pike, *PAVN*, p. 1.

rewarded soldierly skill through promotion to higher grades of service. Militia became guerrillas if they proved their worth; guerrillas likewise rose to main force units. In theory, manpower was utilized so that no one was assigned a task he or she could not handle and no talent was wasted.

Finally, the North Vietnamese Army, or PAVN, was a highly-trained, professional force, organized into divisions, independent regiments and battalions. In contrast to American forces, the vast majority of soldiers were combat personnel. Hanoi preferred highly motivated volunteers, but as the demands in the South rose, the regime began to recruit virtually all able-bodied men between 18 and 25. Conscription evoked a reaction not unlike that which occurred in the United States:

> All the students had deferments the whole time I was at the university, up until 1967 ... Many parents tried to keep their sons out of the army. They would hide them when they were called up by the recruiting center. ... they would try to scrape up enough to bribe a recruiting official ... Other draftees mutilated themselves or managed to find other ways to fail the physical. People with money were able to pay doctors to disqualify their children. ... it was ... easier to hide in the cities and there was more information about how to stay out. The result was that the big majority of the Northern army was made up of young people from the countryside. They were just more naive. ... In my family none of the four brothers went. My youngest brother dropped iodine in his eyes before he went to take the army physical. We bribed the examining officer to fail another. The third one tried to hide from the draft but he was put in jail.[61]

Nearly 200,000 males reached adulthood annually, producing a pool of 120,000 eligible men. By 1967, eligibility was extended to all those aged 16 to 45. During the French war, the goal was for 40 per cent of troops and 90 per cent of officers to be members of the Communist Party,[62] but, by necessity, these standards were relaxed during the 1960s and 1970s.

In the South, soldiers were given first priority to redistributed land, a powerful recruiting tool. But many fought for ideological reasons, among them Nguyen Tan Thanh, a captain in a VC main force unit:

---

61 Chanoff and Toai, *Portrait*, pp. 62–5. The individual in question avoided the draft because he was politically suspect.
62 Harrison, *Endless War*, p. 161.

I was poor. I had lost my land and I didn't have enough money to take care of my children. In 1961, propaganda cadres of the Front . . . told us that if the poor people don't stand up to the rich people, we would be dominated by them forever. The only way to ensure freedom and a sufficient life was to overthrow them. . . . So I joined the Liberation Front. I followed the VC to fight for freedom and prosperity for the country.[63]

An artist who joined the PAVN, against his better instincts, described another motivation:

I volunteered . . . because of a personal tragedy. During one of the airstrikes in Haiphong my fiancee was killed by an American bomb. Immediately afterwards I decided that I had to go South to fight. At the time – this was in the summer of 1967 – I thought the Liberation Army was riding the crest of a wave. If I didn't join up right away I'd miss my chance to take revenge. . . . But I'll tell you, had I realized that everything we were hearing about victory was nothing more than a big bluff, I would never have left.[64]

Families of PAVN soldiers were compensated financially for the absence of a son or husband, or if he was killed. His children might, for instance, receive a small allowance or special access to education or jobs. For obvious reasons, a less institutionalized system existed in the PLAF, but some compensation was usually paid.

The Rand Corporation found that 'The VC army seems strikingly undisciplined, with persuasion rather than order, forebearance rather than punishment, the generally applied rule'. Spit and polish regimentation characteristic of Western militaries was missing, giving the appearance of chaos. But this was misleading. In fact, great effort was devoted to preparation and training for battle. Even the smallest guerrilla attack was carefully planned. Decisions were supposed to be collective. Indoctrination sessions were frequent, with the role of the political cadre within any unit supremely important. One soldier recalled:

right from the start, we had to learn the basic political drill. Fight the Americans and save the country. The political cadres stressed that soldiers are part of the proletariat, that our job was even more important and more honorable than what the

63 Chanoff and Toai, *Portrait*, p. 43.
64 Ibid., pp. 45, 47.

people were doing. It was our duty to liberate the Southern population that was in misery under the domination of the American imperialists. After a continuous week of this my morale was a lot higher than it was when I left my village.[65]

In contrast to most armies, ordinary soldiers were encouraged to keep diaries, in order to record their feelings about the war and to chart their political indoctrination. These diaries were then used in self-criticism sessions. Both the PAVN and the PLAF were remarkably successful at creating a sense of brotherhood and *esprit de corps*. Soldiers were supremely confident of their abilities and of the right-eousness of their cause:

We had such hatred for the enemy and such devotion to the noble cause of liberating our suppressed people that we felt we could overcome any difficulty and make any sacrifice. . . . We were defending our country and our people and punishing the aggressors. . . . we had faith in the cause we were fighting for, and this faith was reinforced by effective propaganda.[66]

Cadres could resort to discipline to control a unit, but were con-sidered failures if they did so, since persuasion was the standard method of control.[67]

Morale remained high in part because soldiers were not constantly in combat. Most fought only two or three days out of a month, spend-ing the rest of their time growing their food or engaging in political activities. Yet despite all the care which went into maintaining morale, the seemingly interminable war dampened the spirits of even the most hearty:

Our hard lives are deprived of happiness. Everything is despair. What will our lives be like tomorrow? It will be hard and unfair if our lives tomorrow are the same as they are today! . . . We hold no hope of life. No words can express the hardship of our lives. I feel pessimistic and down hearted! Can anyone understand my inner feelings?[68]

Desertions were high, often as high as in the ARVN. During the bloodi-est year of the war, 1969, they peaked at 28,405, and did not drop below 10,000 per year during the American involvement.[69] The problem

65 Ibid., p. 49.
66 Ibid., p. 155.
67 Kolko, *Anatomy*, p. 254.
68 Lanning and Cragg, *Inside*, p. 3.
69 Lewy, *America in Vietnam*, p. 174.

was exacerbated by the fact that communist soldiers were offered significant incentives to desert. The *Chieu Hoi* (Open Arms) programme, heavily funded by American money, offered the defector a pardon, training and sometimes a job. It is possible that some desertions were officially sanctioned. Tired, hungry soldiers would sometimes defect, collect incentives, recuperate, and then return to their old units, gathering valuable intelligence along the way.

LOGISTICS

Since air transport was non-existent and trucks were in short supply, attacks required long preparation. Men and munitions were moved into the surrounding area well before the attack was launched. Supplies were carefully hidden in predesignated caches, often underground. Soldiers were deployed in small groups, travelling to the battlefield on night manoeuvres and arriving according to a precise schedule. The system had to work perfectly if it worked at all, for any compromise of the plans allowed the Americans to exploit their mobility and massive firepower.

Each regular division of 10,000 soldiers needed 50,000 porters, or *dan cong*. Loads were carefully calculated: a man could carry 55 pounds of rice or 40 pounds of other stores over 15 miles if travelling by day, or 12 miles in the dark. A buffalo cart could carry 770 pounds for 7½ miles per day, a horse drawn cart 470 pounds over 12 miles.[70] Weaponry, men and supplies were funnelled south along the Ho Chi Minh Trail. Early in the war, soldiers travelled on foot, with supplies carried on specially adapted bicycles. Soldiers and porters would walk as much as eighteen hours per day, six days per week, resting during the night at specially constructed rest camps. The whole trip might take six months, depending upon the final destination. Troops carried their own provisions, which included a food ration of one or two pounds of rice per day, with bits of meat and vegetable when available. A soldier wrote how he would never forget

> the image of the columns of combatants moving along the track, some of them carrying stretchers, climbing mountain passes roughly cut into thousands of steps, then across bridges dangling high above torrents, and finally stopping over at some liaison station where they would take their frugal meals, sometimes consisting of nothing but salt and bamboo shoots.[71]

70 MacDonald, *Giap*, p. 93.
71 Harrison, *Endless War*, p. 201.

The hazards of the trail, mainly malaria and bombing, but also tigers, bears, snakes and treacherous rivers, claimed between 10 and 20 per cent of any column. Some simply lost their way or died of exhaustion or starvation. It is no wonder that every staging post, sited at intervals of around 25 kilometres, included a cemetery.[72]

The propaganda machine venerated Nguyen Viet Sinh, who, it was claimed, carried 55 tons over 41,000 kilometres during a four-year period. He was designated a Hero of the Liberation Armed Forces.[73] But after 1965, the myth of the trail lost much significance since the vast majority of supplies were carried by truck. In 1966 and 1967 the number of soldiers infiltrating southward may have been as high as 90,000 per year. The trail was upgraded into a major highway, under the supervision of Colonel Dong Si Nguyen. Soviet and Chinese machinery was used to build bridges, tunnels, underground barracks, storage facilities, fuel depots and even hospitals. A vast array of personnel, including drivers, mechanics, construction workers, radio operators, traffic engineers, doctors and nurses permanently staffed outposts dotted along the trail. A sophisticated system of air defences and a ready supply of engineer battalions ensured that the artery was never cut. Engineers laboured round the clock to repair bombed bridges in time for the arrival of the next convoy.

There were always at least two routes to a single destination. Information was supplied to troops on a strictly need-to-know basis. Therefore, names of landmarks passed *en route*, or of turning off points, were not disclosed. A Control of Infiltration Routes Section coordinated route documentation, rest areas, medical care, liaison stations and rations. Liaison agents, frequently women, operated from ordinary shops or houses, their location a tightly guarded secret. They would receive letters of introduction from couriers, authenticate documents and arrange for guides along the next section of the route. The soldiers themselves were led blindly through the jungle. Since spies were everywhere, secrecy was paramount, and anyone asking questions was automatically suspect. Every last detail was carefully monitored; camouflage, for instance, fully occupied thousands of workers. Soldiers were taught that simple errors like throwing away a cigarette butt or defecating in the open might endanger an entire unit.

At the end of the journey, men, munitions and supplies went to base areas usually located along the Cambodian border in sites protected by mountains, swamps, rivers and dense vegetation. Base areas

72 Duiker, *Sacred War*, pp. 196–7.
73 MacDonald, *Giap*, p. 249.

housed supply dumps, hospitals, headquarters, motor pools, training centres, and sometimes primitive arms manufacturing plants. Troops were assembled, trained and equipped for future operations. The most sophisticated base areas were constructed largely underground. The US developed no effective response to these tunnel complexes. American commanders in general lacked the patience to remain in an area long enough to destroy an entire complex.

POSTSCRIPT

Americans encountered an enemy in Vietnam whose fortitude and dedication was beyond their comprehension. Certain 'truths' – the righteousness of democracy, the power of money and the insurmountability of modern weaponry – were refuted by this war. Most soldiers developed a grudging admiration for their perplexing enemy:

> To give you an idea of how steadfast the people were that we were fighting: I found a dead VC medic who had tied himself to a bamboo clump, with a morphine syringe stuck in his arm. He had a large wound in his leg and a large wound in his arm and had bled to death. He had an RPG [rocket-propelled grenade] at the ready, with the safety off. . . . We had him blown up because he was like a booby trap himself. . . . That impressed me. When a person is willing to do that, he must have a pretty strong will.[74]

Because these soldiers seemed so formidable, it was natural to assume that they had been turned into maniacal automatons by a repressive system. For some Americans defeat seemed understandable because the enemy was not really human.

But the soldiers of the revolution felt pain, sorrow and fear like any other. One conscript described his departure from his family:

> My oldest sister . . . got very upset when she heard that I had been drafted. . . . She told me that she wished I could stay home, even though she knew there was nothing we could do about it. When I picked up my knapsack and was about to leave the house, she broke into tears. We were hugging each other and crying. Both of us were crying.[75]

74 Eric Bergerud, *Red Thunder, Tropic Lightning* (New York, NY, 1994), p. 177.
75 Chanoff and Toai, *Portrait*, p. 44.

Even cadres, who epitomized a selfless devotion to the struggle, could not always exorcize their concern for a loved one:

> One of my uncles was Hoang Tan Linh, the deputy chief of the Central Cadres Organizing Office in Hanoi. When he heard that I had volunteered he said, 'Why are you joining? Don't you know that the war in the South is a colossal sacrifice of troops? They're sending soldiers to the South to be killed at a merciless rate. They've taken most of the young men from Hanoi and from all over already, and they'll keep taking them. In war there has to be death. But this war isn't like when I fought against the French. Now the losses are in the thousands and tens of thousands. If you go now there's only one fate – unbearable hardship and possibly death – a meaningless death.'[76]

It is easy to admire the bravery, sacrifice and will of the these soldiers. But admiration for the revolutionaries should not lead to admiration of the revolution. There was, in truth, little romance to the communist struggle. It was formidable, but in a cruel, cold-hearted, despotic and often cynical way.

76 Ibid., p. 46.

5 LIMITED WAR

By the time Lyndon Johnson became President, Vietnam had assumed a symbolic importance which outweighed its actual strategic importance. At stake was America's reputation as a defender of small nations and her status as anti-communist crusader. In early 1965 John McNaughton, Assistant Secretary of Defense, summarized American aims:

70% – To avoid a humiliating US defeat (to our reputation as a guarantor).

20% – To keep SVN (and the adjacent) territory from Chinese hands.

10% – To permit people of SVN to enjoy a better, freer way of life.

ALSO – To emerge from crisis without unacceptable taint from methods used.[1]

Failure in Vietnam, Secretary of State Dean Rusk argued in 1965, would cause 'the communist world . . . [to] draw conclusions that would lead to our ruin and almost certainly to a catastrophic war'.[2] Americans responded to the challenge, but still found themselves in a catastrophic war which ruined their self-belief.

In the defence of her principles, the US committed great acts of destruction. 'We had to destroy Ben Tre to save it', an American major once confessed.[3] That could be a parable for the entire war. Saving Vietnam meant laying waste the countryside and destroying an ancient culture. Saving America's reputation meant destroying her people's confidence in themselves. 'If you let a bully come into your

1 George Herring, ed., *The Pentagon Papers*, abridged edn (New York, NY, 1993), p. 115.

2 David Steigerwald, *The Sixties and the End of Modern America* (New York, NY, 1995), pp. 74–5.

3 Cecil B. Currey, *Victory at Any Cost* (Washington, DC, 1997), p. 268.

front yard one day', Johnson once remarked, 'the next day he'll be up on your porch and the day after that he'll rape your wife in your own bed.'[4] Johnson's solution was to burn down the house. The great irony of this destructive conflict is that both sides pursued a strategy of *limited* war.

THE US GOES TO WAR

At the Ninth Plenum of the Communist Party in 1963, argument raged over the future course of the revolution. An aggressive faction wanted quick deployment of the PAVN, in order to topple the crumbling Saigon regime. The other side was satisfied with the pace of the revolution and warned that intervention by the PAVN would annoy Moscow, worry Beijing, and alarm Washington. After heated debate, a compromise was reached. A new phase would begin; armed struggle would henceforth be 'direct and decisive'.[5] The PLAF would focus upon destroying ARVN units in large-scale actions, setting the stage for a general uprising (*khoi nghia*). But PAVN units would not be deployed. Instead, the PLAF would be strengthened by extra supplies from the North. The illusion of internal insurrection would be maintained.

The strategy nearly worked. The ARVN came perilously close to defeat. American intelligence estimated in March 1964 that the NLF controlled about 40 per cent of the South's total land area.[6] By autumn, analysts were predicting that, without American intervention, the Saigon regime would not survive another six months.[7] General Duong Van 'Big' Minh, who had succeeded Diem, was powerless to arrest the ARVN's decline. Nor did his successor, General Nguyen Khanh, brought to power by a coup in January 1964, offer greater hope. The regime of Khanh, Bui Diem reflected, 'put an end to the idea of bringing alive in South Vietnam a democracy vital enough to ward off the political and military challenges of the Vietnamese Communist Party'.[8] In March 1964 McNamara warned that 'The greatest

4 Stanley Karnow, *Vietnam: A History* (Harmondsworth, 1993), p. 337.

5 William J. Duiker, *Sacred War* (New York, NY, 1995), p. 162.

6 Herring, ed., *Pentagon Papers*, p. 88.

7 William Duiker, 'Waging revolutionary war: the evolution of Hanoi's strategy in the South, 1959–1965', in Jayne S. Werner and Luu Doan Huynh, eds, *The Vietnam War: Vietnamese and American Perspectives* (Armonk, NY, 1993), p. 32.

8 Eric Bergerud, *The Dynamics of Defeat* (Boulder, CO, 1991), p. 68. Bui Diem was ambassador to the US from 1966 to 1972.

weakness in the present situation is the uncertain viability of the Khanh government'.[9]

The PLAF launched guerrilla raids against US bases, designed to alarm the Americans and impress the local population. Johnson, faced with an election in November 1964, was reluctant to deploy combat troops to counter this aggression. 'We are not about to send American boys nine or ten thousand miles away from home to do what Asian boys ought to be doing for themselves', he stressed repeatedly during the campaign.[10] For the same reason, he rejected JCS demands for immediate air strikes upon the North. He did, however, approve OPLAN 34-A, officially described as 'an elaborate plan of covert military operations', which would form part of a programme of 'progressively escalating pressure' against North Vietnam. The covert nature allowed 'plausible deniability', an important requirement in an election year.[11] The Pentagon nevertheless recognized that American responsibility 'for the launching and conduct of these operations was unequivocal and carried with it an implicit symbolic and psychological intensification of the United States commitment' – a 'firebreak had been crossed'.[12]

If the US were to go to war, Johnson needed an incident of sufficient magnitude to fire the wrath of the American people. This came on 2 August 1964, when North Vietnamese patrol boats attacked the destroyer *Maddox* in the Tonkin Gulf. Two days later, the *Turner Joy* was also supposedly attacked. Johnson subsequently claimed that since these incidents were totally unprovoked, significant retaliation was justified. On 4 August he reminded the American people of 'our determination . . . to carry out our full commitment to the people and to the Government of South Vietnam'. For the moment, however, the American response would be 'limited and fitting'. 'We Americans know – although others appear to forget – the risk of spreading conflict. We still seek no wider war.'[13]

Johnson used the incident to gain Congressional authorization to deploy military force as needed in Vietnam. The Tonkin Gulf Resolution held that 'the United States regards as vital to its national interest and to world peace the maintenance of international peace and security

9 Herring, ed., *Pentagon Papers*, p. 88.

10 Karnow, *Vietnam*, p. 411.

11 James P. Harrison, *The Endless War* (New York, NY, 1989), pp. 246–7; Larry Berman, *Planning a Tragedy* (New York, NY, 1982), p. 32; H.R. McMaster, *Dereliction of Duty* (New York, NY, 1997), pp. 59, 60, 86, 95, 119–22.

12 James Clay Thompson, *Rolling Thunder: Understanding Policy and Program Failure* (Chapel Hill, NC, 1980), p. 17.

13 *New York Times*, 5 August 1964.

in southeast Asia'. The President was given the power 'to take all necessary measures to repel any armed attack against the forces of the United States and to prevent further aggression'. The resolution was open-ended and without restriction. It would remain in force until 'the president shall determine that the peace and security of the area is reasonably assured'.[14]

With little debate and less dissent, Congress passed the Tonkin Gulf Resolution on 7 August. The House approved it unanimously (416–0), after a 40-minute debate. In the Senate, the vote went 88–2, with only Wayne Morse of Oregon and Ernest Greuning of Alaska disapproving. Their warnings seemed at the time crankish, though in retrospect perspicacious. Greuning was 'opposed to sacrificing a single American boy' in a 'war in which we have no business . . . into which we have been misguidedly drawn, which is steadily being escalated'. Morse warned that 'a "snow-job" is being done on us by the Pentagon and the State Department'.[15] He feared that a fundamental check upon presidential power, namely the right of Congress to declare war, had been squandered. 'Within the next century, future generations will look with dismay and great disappointment upon a Congress which is now about to make such a historic mistake.'[16] Yet most Americans found Morse and Greuning annoying whingers. The public had been offered a righteous war against an evil aggressor, and had bought it enthusiastically. A Harris survey found that 85 per cent supported administration policy in Vietnam. Presidential approval rose from 42 to 72 per cent overnight.[17]

It is tempting to speculate that the Tonkin Gulf incidents were cleverly engineered to produce the blanket authorization Johnson desired. In his memoirs, McNamara argues that a resolution would in any case have been submitted to Congress within a matter of weeks had the incident not occurred and that 'very likely it would have passed'. But he admits that events in the Gulf made passage easier; without them 'the resolution would have faced far more extensive debate, and there would have been attempts to limit the president's authority'.[18] A bad odour lingers for those inclined to smell a rat. There is little doubt that the *Maddox* was attacked. Photographs of

14 William Appleman Williams *et al.*, eds, *America in Vietnam: A Documentary History* (New York, NY, 1975), pp. 236–7.
15 Walter Capps, *Unfinished War* (Boston, MA, 1990), p. 49.
16 Williams *et al.*, eds, *America in Vietnam*, pp. 236–9.
17 Loren Baritz, *Backfire* (New York, NY, 1985), p. 130, George C. Herring, *America's Longest War* (New York, NY, 1986), p. 123.
18 Robert S. McNamara, *In Retrospect* (New York, NY, 1995), p. 128.

the attacking ships are available and the damage was indisputable. But the mission of the *Maddox* remains cloudy, as does the actual fate of the *Turner Joy*.[19]

The *Maddox* was part of the DESOTO Patrol programme, an operation, begun in 1962, designed 'to collect intelligence concerning Chicom electronic and naval activity . . . [and] serve as a minor cold war irritant to Chicoms'. Morse alleged that the *Maddox* was in North Vietnamese waters on a mission to provoke, and that it was furthermore assisting in clandestine 34-A operations. McNamara, with ingenuousness worthy of an Oscar, rejected these 'monstrous insinuations'. The *Maddox*, he claimed, 'was operating in international waters, and was carrying out a routine patrol of the type we carry out over the world at all times'.[20] He further maintained that DESOTO patrol ships were not involved in 34-A operations. Recently declassified documents suggest otherwise. McNamara has since admitted that his reply to Morse was 'totally incorrect'. He claims that he was misinformed and that his statement was therefore 'honest but wrong'.[21]

There was no photographic evidence for the attack upon the *Turner Joy*, and no reported physical damage. According to action reports, enemy vessels were supposed to have passed between the *Maddox* and the *Turner Joy*, yet radar operators on the *Maddox* reported strong contact with no other vessel than the *Turner Joy*. No enemy vessels were visually sighted by crew on either ship. Furthermore, the *Turner Joy* was in an area which, due to fuel, radar and navigation limits, was inaccessible to North Vietnamese navy squadrons.[22] In other words, the second attack was either an outright fabrication or an innocent misassumption.[23] When Johnson spoke to Ball a few days after the incident, he seemed to favour the latter explanation: 'Hell, those dumb, stupid sailors were just shooting at flying fish'.[24]

On 5 August 1964, in direct retaliation for the alleged attacks, US aircraft pounded the port and oil storage facilities at Vinh, just north

---

19 McNamara still held to the idea that the attack on the *Turner Joy* was 'probable but not certain' when he published his memoirs in 1995 (*In Retrospect*, p. 128). He backed away from this assertion in the subsequent paperback edition.

20 Anthony Short, *The Origins of the Vietnam War* (London, 1989), p. 298. 'Chicom' was official jargon for Chinese Communist.

21 McNamara, *In Retrospect*, p. 137.

22 K. Weitzman, 'The relevance of the Tonkin Gulf incidents: U.S. military action in Vietnam, August 1964', 1996 Vietnam Symposium, Texas Tech University Vietnam Center website.

23 Edwin Moïse, *Tonkin Gulf and the Escalation of the Vietnam War* (Chapel Hill, NC, 1996) favours error over subterfuge. Moïse's book is the most responsible analysis of the controversy.

24 George Ball, *The Past Has Another Pattern* (New York, NY, 1982), p. 379.

of the 17th parallel. This was a carefully calculated act of aggression by Johnson, designed to impress American voters as much as to frighten the North Vietnamese. 'I'll tell you what I want', Johnson told McNamara, 'I not only want those patrol boats that attacked the *Maddox* destroyed, I want everything at that harbor destroyed; I want the whole works destroyed. I want to give them a real dose.'[25] To a reporter Johnson privately boasted 'I didn't just screw Ho Chi Minh, I cut his pecker off'.[26] The raids seemed to presage a new phase in which the President would wield a big stick to punish the North for communist sins in the South. But subsequent days brought no repetition. For the moment, Johnson was inclined to hold fire. The Tonkin Gulf Resolution was like a shiny silver dollar which he was pleased to possess, but not yet ready to spend.

The Tonkin Gulf affair initially had a more profound impact upon DRV strategy than on American. Hanoi concluded that Johnson was waiting for the right moment to send in combat troops. An aggressive offensive suddenly seemed sensible in order to hasten the RVN collapse, before the Americans could come to the rescue. The Politburo's new strategy coincided with General Nguyen Chi Thanh's promotion to the rank of senior general, a status heretofore reserved for Giap. Thanh, who wanted to 'attack unremittingly', took over strategic direction in the South.[27] Giap's caution was suddenly out of fashion.

Given the situation in 1964, Thanh's boldness seemed logical. In his view, the Saigon regime was at death's door and the faction-torn ARVN was incapable of defending itself. But much depended on the American reaction. Thanh assumed that the US would not be able to mobilize sufficiently quickly to prevent the ARVN's collapse and would not remain in Vietnam after that collapse occurred. But Giap, more politically astute, realized that military defeats seem reversible in a way that political disintegration does not. He concluded that, while the US might come to the rescue of an embattled ARVN, she was less likely to intervene to save a government which had lost the mandate to rule. The Americans, Giap stressed, 'will never retreat of their own accord unless . . . [we] use all forms of revolutionary struggle to combat them'.[28] Political disintegration should be allowed to run its course, admittedly a long process.

25 McMaster, *Dereliction*, p. 126.

26 Lloyd C. Gardner, *Pay Any Price* (Chicago, IL, 1995), p. 139.

27 Duiker, *Sacred War*, p. 188.

28 Cecil Currey, 'Giap and Tet Mau Than 1968: the year of the monkey', in Marc Jason Gilbert and William Head, eds, *The Tet Offensive* (Westport, CT, 1996), p. 80.

Thanh's rise was not unrelated to Ho's decline; the latter's poor health limited his influence over strategy. Le Duan, whose star brightened as Ho's faded, was, like Thanh, aggressive and impatient. Politburo rivalries also mirrored tensions in the wider communist world. Le Duan resented Khrushchev's strategy of accommodation and felt that Giap, infected by the Russian leader's pragmatism, had lost touch with the true spirit of the revolution. The disagreement was merely a symptom of long-running antagonism between the two men. Le Duan once described Giap as 'fearful like a rabbit' and incapable of real leadership.[29] The fall of Khrushchev in October 1964 brought a new Kremlin line more in accord with Le Duan's aggression and more inclined to allow the Vietnamese to determine their own course. By February 1965, the Politburo had settled upon a strategy which sought 'a decisive victory within a relatively short period of time'.[30]

Thanh immediately ordered the construction of a base area in the Central Highlands, similar to the Viet Bac base used during the French war. This alarmed General Maxwell Taylor, who had replaced Lodge as ambassador. In September he warned that drastic action would be necessary to counter the infiltration of troops and supplies from the North. Equally disturbing was the increasingly frequent guerrilla attacks upon American targets. In August Saigon's Caravelle Hotel, a favourite haunt of foreign journalists, was bombed, destroying the city's illusion of impregnability. On 1 November a mortar attack on the Bien Hoa airbase killed three Americans and destroyed five aircraft. Meanwhile, the destruction of the ARVN continued apace. Early in December the 9th PLAF Division seized the village of Binh Gia, 40 miles from Saigon, annihilating two of the best ARVN battalions.

While Hanoi still hoped that the war would be won by the PLAF, preparations had to be made in case the US intervened in force or, worse, invaded. In April 1965 Ho announced a new military and civilian service law. Some 300,000 new soldiers were enlisted. Though most were under 25, some who had fought the French were recalled. Two million labourers (*dan cong*) were conscripted to provide logistical support. The Air Force was increased from one regiment to three, and a new transport ministry was formed to handle the increasing flow of Chinese and Soviet arms. The Soviets also provided significant technical support and training for sophisticated weaponry.[31]

29 Ibid., p. 74.
30 Duiker, 'Waging revolutionary war', p. 32.
31 Peter MacDonald, *Giap* (London, 1993), p. 198.

By early 1965, the revolution was on the verge of victory. A majority of the population was now under NLF control, the Saigon regime was steadily weakening, and the ARVN was virtually moribund. Though free to respond to the worsening situation, Johnson remained reluctant. He instructed Taylor that US forces could react to provocation, but proactive attacks were not permitted, nor were reprisal strikes in response to guerrilla attacks on American bases. Johnson's reluctance convinced the Politburo that the US would not send ground troops to rescue the ARVN from complete destruction. It therefore seemed advisable to allow PAVN units to complete the job. Le Duan and Thanh confidently predicted that 'the work of twenty years might be achieved in a day'.[32]

A new plan called for three PAVN regiments to sweep through the Central Highlands in October 1965 and lay siege to the Special Forces Camp at Plei Me. This, it was hoped, would lure an ARVN armoured column out of Pleiku, which would be ambushed and destroyed. The PAVN would then take Pleiku, before advancing on Qui Nhon, gaining control of the Central Highlands and cutting South Vietnam in two. At the same time, PLAF attacks around Saigon would entice ARVN units out of the capital, leaving it weakly defended and ripe for *khoi nghia*.

But there were limits to Johnson's patience. On 7 February the PLAF attacked the American camp at Pleiku, killing nine. The National Security Adviser, McGeorge Bundy, who was in South Vietnam at the time, angrily reacted: 'We cannot stand by'.[33] Johnson agreed: 'We have kept our gun over the mantel and our shells in the cupboard for a long time now . . . And what was the result? They are killing our boys while they sleep in the night.'[34] On Bundy's advice, he approved Operation Flaming Dart, a series of bombing strikes against targets in the North. The official White House statement explained that American attacks were 'in response to provocations ordered and directed by the Hanoi regime'. Then came the customary assurance: 'we seek no wider war'.[35] The beauty of reprisal strikes of this type, the administration believed, was that they 'kept responsibility for escalation on the other side'.[36]

32 Duiker, *Sacred War*, pp. 170–1.
33 McMaster, *Dereliction*, pp. 215–16.
34 Lyndon Baines Johnson, *The Vantage Point* (London, 1971), p. 125.
35 McMaster, *Dereliction*, pp. 215–16.
36 Lawrence Freedman, 'Vietnam and the disillusioned strategist', *International Affairs* 72 (1996), p. 140.

Bundy had long wanted a sustained bombing programme, and advised as much in his memo to Johnson on the day of the Plieku attack. Under the circumstances, he did not feel it necessary to 'connect each specific act against North Vietnam to a particular outrage in the South'. He was not certain that bombing would 'succeed in changing the course of the contest ... It may fail.'[37] But, even if it did, it would be a valuable demonstration of American resolve, and would hearten the RVN. Bundy also stressed the need to 'ma[k]e clear to our own people' that 'at its very best the struggle in Vietnam will be long'.[38] Johnson would do nothing of the sort. For him, the appeal of bombing lay in the fact that it did not imply a huge troop commitment; it offered a way to hurt the DRV 'without escalating the war'.[39]

The Bundy memorandum reveals a preoccupation with the importance of America's reputation as the defender of the 'free world'. In a similar way, the McNaughton memo quoted at the beginning of this chapter clearly indicates just how important matters of honour were. In other words, the struggle was not just about defeating the communist threat in South Vietnam. It was, in a wider sense, about demonstrating that communist aggression – anywhere in the world – would not go unchallenged. As Bundy suggested, it was not essential that the US be successful in Vietnam, as long as the American resolve appeared credible. But this linked the prestige of the US to a very weak regime. How much force would the United States need to apply in order to demonstrate its point? Clearly, the US had to be seen to reinforce the RVN regime, thereby upping the stakes in the struggle for South Vietnam. But, as Lawrence Freedman has pointed out, this led to a nasty Catch-22: 'The South could not be stabilized without pressure on the North; the North could not be pressurized without a more stable South'. If, as Bundy suggested, success was not essential, was there a point at which the US might extricate itself from the crisis with prestige intact? McNaughton, for one, did not know the answer to this question. He warned that 'if we haven't stopped it today, then the reasons for not stopping it will still exist tomorrow, and we'll be in even deeper'. Tom Schelling, a friend and adviser to McNaughton, later confessed that 'nobody could think of a graceful way of getting out'.[40]

On 10 February PLAF units struck the US Army base at Qhi Nhon, killing 23 Americans. Johnson responded with a programme of 'measured and limited air action ... against selected targets in the

---

37 Herring, ed., *Pentagon Papers*, pp. 109–112.
38 Johnson, *Vantage Point*, p. 127.
39 Brian VanDeMark, *Into the Quagmire* (New York, NY, 1981), pp. 67–8.
40 Freedman, 'Disillusioned strategist', pp. 136, 139, 149.

DRV . . . south of the 19th parallel until further notice'.[41] This would become known as Operation Rolling Thunder, launched on 24 February.[42] Instead of a tit-for-tat reprisal, it was a sustained bombing campaign like Bundy had demanded, designed to persuade Hanoi to restrain the PLAF.

Despite the appearance of decisive action, Johnson was like Canute, trying to hold back a Red tide. He responded as presidents often respond, by sending in the Marines. On 8 March elements of the 9th Marine Expeditionary Brigade hit the beaches northwest of Da Nang. Events moved so quickly that Taylor, who opposed the deployment, had little time to obtain the obligatory formal request for assistance from Pham Huy Quat, the new RVN premier. Quat, who feared that the troops would underline the puppet status of his regime, had to have his arm twisted.[43] The Marines' arrival was ill-befitting those who had stormed the halls of Montezuma and the shores of Tripoli. A surreal scene awaited: a group of South Vietnamese dignitaries staged an official welcome and local schoolgirls presented Brigadier General Frederick Karch with a garland of flowers. He was not pleased: 'When you have a son in Vietnam and he gets killed, you don't want a smiling general with flowers around his neck'.[44]

The Marines had been mobilized to protect the Da Nang airbase from terrorist strikes and thus free ARVN troops for operations against the PLAF. Orders specifically stated: 'The US Marine force will not, repeat will not, engage in day to day actions against the Viet Cong'.[45] In other words, the deployment was not supposed to be a major change of policy, since Johnson still hoped that bombing would bring quick victory. But, as the Marines arrived, the ARVN's disintegration continued. Hanoi responded to the Marine deployment by sending additional PAVN units. A new war had begun.

THE DECISION TO ESCALATE

Johnson's political apprenticeship in the 1930s provided two significant lessons. First, his commitment to the New Deal made him keen to extend its beneficence through his own Great Society. Second, he

41 Herring, ed., *Pentagon Papers*, p. 114.

42 The bombing campaign is discussed in greater detail in Chapter 7.

43 Gardner, *Pay Any Price*, p. 184.

44 Jack Shulimson and Charles Johnson, *US Marines in Vietnam, 1965: The Landing and the Buildup* (Washington, DC, 1978), p. 12.

45 Jack Shulimson, 'The Marine war: III MAF in Vietnam, 1965–1971', 1996 Vietnam Symposium, Texas Tech University Vietnam Center website.

learned that totalitarian dictators could not be appeased. 'The central lesson of our time is that the appetite of the aggressor is never satisfied', he declared on 7 April 1965.[46] But, in the context of the 1960s, these two lessons were contradictory. That contradiction plagued the President:

> I knew from the start . . . that I was bound to be crucified either way I moved. If I left the woman I really loved – the Great Society – in order to get involved with that bitch of a war on the other side of the world, then I would lose everything at home. All my programs. All my hopes to feed the hungry and shelter the homeless. All my dreams to provide education and medical care to the browns and the blacks and the lame and the poor. But if I left that war and let the Communists take over South Vietnam, then I would be seen as a coward and my nation would be seen as an appeaser, and we would both find it impossible to accomplish anything for anybody anywhere on the entire globe.[47]

Warnings about the dangers of appeasement were not mere talk, designed for a naive public. In April 1965 McNamara told a *New York Times* journalist off the record that if the US withdrew from Vietnam, 'there would be a complete shift of world power. Asia goes Red, our prestige and integrity damaged, allies everywhere shaken.'[48] During the Tonkin Gulf crisis, Johnson remarked: 'The world remembers – the world must never forget – that aggression unchallenged is aggression unleashed'.[49]

Clearly, the communists in Vietnam had to be challenged. But that did not mean they had to be beaten. Johnson did not want simply to turn the problem over to the generals, who, he felt, were 'always so narrow in their appraisal of everything. They see everything in military terms.' The military, he feared, would respond in a blinkered, brutal, hell-for-leather way, quickly transforming a molehill into a mountain. Johnson felt that generals always chose war because they needed 'battles and bombs and bullets to be heroic'.[50] Like others in his administration, he was deeply proud of the way the Cuban missile crisis had been handled. While the military had pushed immediately for tough action, the politicians had used all the tools at their disposal

---

46 Williams *et al.*, eds, *America in Vietnam*, p. 243.

47 Doris Kearns, *Lyndon Johnson and the American Dream* (London, 1976), pp. 251–2.

48 Williams *et al.*, eds, *America in Vietnam*, p. 247.

49 Jeffrey P. Kimball, ed., *To Reason Why* (New York, NY, 1990), p. 62.

50 Freedman, 'Disillusioned strategist', p. 137.

(including military threats) to find a peaceful, diplomatic solution. The same approach would be applied to Vietnam.

Johnson, the quintessential bargainer, believed he could persuade Ho to accept a settlement which would allow South Vietnam to survive as an independent non-communist state. 'If only I could sit down with Ho Chi Minh', he once confessed, 'if we could just talk together, we could settle this terrible business and get our ass out of that country and that miserable war.'[51] As a sweetener, he offered massive funding for a Mekong River economic development project. 'The vast Mekong River can provide food and water and power on a scale to dwarf even our own TVA', argued Johnson on 7 April 1965, betraying his New Deal roots. 'The task is nothing less than to enrich the hopes and existence of more than a hundred million people.'[52] 'Old Ho can't turn me down', he boasted privately.[53] Ho could, and did. 'They are devastating our land and massacring our people', came the stinging reply, 'yet they hypocritically boast that they will grant one billion dollars to the people of Vietnam . . . "to develop their economies and improve their livelihood".'[54]

While Johnson was trying to pull together a deal, the military was preparing for a real war. The JCS feared that South Vietnam might be lost if the US did not act quickly. They wanted an immediate commitment of three divisions, an end to the defensive posture assumed by American troops, and a sustained bombing campaign against the North. McNamara agreed with the JCS about the extent of the crisis, but did not feel that he could sell their bold plan to the President. He nevertheless warned that Hanoi was 'moving into the third phase of revolutionary warfare, committing regiments and subsequently divisions to seize and retain territory and to destroy the government's troops and eliminate all vestiges of government control'.[55]

Both McNamara and William Westmoreland, the MACV commander, assumed that a shift to the third phase would be advantageous for the United States, since it would allow American forces to fight their type of war. They failed to understand that the traditional three-phase strategy had long been abandoned in favour of protracted war designed to erode American commitment. The aggressive strategy pursued by Thanh and Le Duan over the previous few months was an

51 Jack Valenti, 'The night LBJ surrendered', *George* (March 1998).
52 Williams *et al.*, eds, *America in Vietnam*, pp. 243–4.
53 Karnow, *Vietnam*, pp. 336–7.
54 Capps, *Unfinished War*, p. 64.
55 Berman, *Planning a Tragedy*, p. 135. The 'third phase' is explained in Chapter 1, p. 32 and Chapter 4, pp. 103–5.

attempt to raise the stakes in the conflict and warn the Americans that if they intervened they would find themselves propping up a mortally wounded ally.[56] Ball correctly surmised that there was 'no basis for assuming that the Viet Cong will fight a war on our terms when they can continue to fight the kind of war they fought so well against both the French and the GVN [Government of Vietnam]'.[57] His opinion was backed up by the State Department Office of Intelligence and Research, which doubted 'that the criteria established by Giap for the third stage . . . have been or are about to be met'.[58]

McNamara underestimated the dangers of a protracted war. He could not accept that a minor power like North Vietnam might be able to force Americans into the type of war they did not want to fight. Nor did he understand that in a long war, communist morale was likely to be more durable than American. 'Every quantitative measure we have shows that we are winning' he announced in 1962, and every year thereafter. Ball felt that McNamara

> was a superb Secretary of Defense – brilliantly skilled in planning, budgeting, devising and administering efficient procurement policies, and controlling all aspects of a great sprawling . . . department. But the very quantitative discipline he used with such effect as Secretary of Defense did not always serve him well as Secretary of War. . . . He could not help thinking that because the resources commanded by the United States were greater than those of North Vietnam by a factor of X, we could inevitably prevail if we only applied those resources effectively.

McNamara failed to take into account how the indomitable communist commitment enabled Hanoi to fight a long war. Obsessed with statistics, he tended to ignore that which could not be measured, namely the communists' exceptional spirit. 'With the unquantifiable omitted from the McNamara equation', Ball concluded, 'the answer never came out right.'[59] Suitably chastened, McNamara later admitted that 'The problem lay not in any attempt to deceive but rather in a signal

---

56 David W.P. Elliott, 'Hanoi's strategy in the Second Indochina War', in Werner and Huynh, eds, *Vietnam War*, p. 81. See also William J. Duiker, *The Communist Road to Power in Vietnam* (Boulder, CO, 1981), pp. 223–7; William Turley, *The Second Indochina War* (New York, NY, 1986), pp. 69–72.

57 Ball, *The Past*, p. 399.

58 Berman, 'Waiting for smoking guns: presidential decision-making and the Vietnam War', in Peter Braestrup, ed., *Vietnam as History: Ten Years After the Paris Peace Accords* (Washington, DC, 1984), p. 19.

59 Ball, *The Past*, pp. 369–70.

and costly failure to foresee the implications of our actions. Had we done so, we might have acted differently.'[60]

At a conference in Honolulu in late April, the JCS presented their case for further escalation. Taylor, who had opposed the original deployment of Marines on the grounds that the American soldier 'is not a suitable guerrilla fighter for Asian forests and jungles', was averse to further escalation. It would, he feared, 'lead to ever increasing commitments until, like the French, we would be occupying an essentially hostile country'.[61] But he could not resist the tide of military opinion. The conference recommended increasing troop strength to thirteen battalions (82,000 men). The bombing campaign would continue at its present level for another six months, but since it was agreed that 'bombing would not do the job alone', targets in South Vietnam would henceforth have first call on air assets – an overt commitment to the ground war. It was confidently assumed that the escalation would 'break the will of the DRV/VC by denying them victory'.[62] Back in Washington, Johnson approved the recommendations, despite strident opposition from Ball. But, significantly, Johnson decided 'not . . . to announce the whole program now but rather to announce individual deployments at appropriate times'.[63] In other words, the reality of mobilization would be cleverly disguised in order to fool the American people for as long as possible.

Three months later, disagreements within the administration again surfaced. McNamara visited Vietnam in mid-July and left with a sense of foreboding. During a meeting on 21 July, he backed Westmoreland's requests (backed by the Pentagon) for an extra 200,000 troops by early 1966. Such an escalation, he argued, stood a 'good chance of achieving an acceptable outcome within a reasonable time'. He did not relay to Johnson his misgivings about 'the loose assumptions, unasked questions, and thin analyses underlying our military strategy' which he later claimed to have felt.[64] Alarmed by McNamara's proposals, Ball reiterated that the PLAF would 'stay away from confrontation and not accommodate us', to which Wheeler replied that 'by constantly harassing them, they will have to fight somewhere'. Ball then warned of the 'perilous voyage' which beckoned and voiced his

60 McNamara, *In Retrospect*, p. 175.

61 VanDeMark, *Quagmire*, pp. 51, 93; Maxwell Taylor, *Swords and Plowshares* (New York, NY, 1972), pp. 340–2.

62 Herbert Y. Schandler, *The Unmaking of a President* (Princeton, NJ, 1977), p. 24; Herring, *America's Longest War*, p. 132.

63 McNamara, *In Retrospect*, p. 183.

64 Ibid., pp. 203–4.

'great and grave apprehensions' of the disasters which lay ahead. When Johnson suggested that a relentless escalation might mean that casualties would rise exponentially, Wheeler argued: 'The more men we have . . . the greater likelihood of smaller losses'. If the DRV sent more troops, the US would enjoy a greater opportunity 'to cream them'. Frightened by Wheeler's naiveté, Ball again warned: 'We cannot win, Mr. President. The war will be long and protracted. The best we can hope for is a messy conclusion.'

The discussion continued the next day, along similar lines. Johnson expressed doubts that 'westerners can ever win a war in Asia'. He confessed:

> I don't know how we are going to get the job done. There are millions of Chinese. I think they are going to put their stack in. Is this the best place to do it? We don't have the allies we had in Korea . . . Are we starting something that in two or three years we simply can't finish?[65]

McNamara had no illusions about the difficulties ahead, but, in retrospect, even his pessimism seems optimistic. 'The tide almost certainly cannot begin to turn in less than a few months', he advised, 'and may not for a year or more; the war is one of attrition and will be a long one.'[66] His definition of 'long' was decidedly different from that of Ball, who was not sure

> that we can beat the Viet Cong or even force them to the conference table on our terms, no matter how many *white, foreign* (US) troops we deploy. No one has demonstrated that a white ground force of whatever size can win a guerrilla war . . . in jungle terrain in the midst of a population that refuses cooperation.[67]

Failure would be catastrophic: 'The worst blow would be that the mightiest power on earth is unable to defeat a handful of guerrillas'.[68]

Johnson sided with McNamara, out of fear more than conviction. 'This is what I could foresee', he explained in 1971, 'from all the evidence available to me it seemed likely that all of Southeast Asia would pass under Communist control, slowly or quickly, but inevitably, at least down to Singapore but almost certainly to Djakarta.'[69]

65 Williams *et al.*, eds, *America in Vietnam*, pp. 248–53.
66 Robert J. McMahon, *Major Problems in the History of the Vietnam War* (Lexington, MA, 1990), p. 233.
67 Herring, ed., *Pentagon Papers*, p. 123.
68 Williams *et al.*, eds, *America in Vietnam*, p. 251.
69 Johnson, *Vantage Point*, p. 151.

He was also worried about domestic political consequences, specifically a 'mean and destructive debate' over who was responsible for 'losing' Vietnam. It would 'shatter my presidency'; Truman's difficulties after the 'loss of China . . . were chickenshit compared to what might happen if we lost Vietnam'.[70] He feared that

> If I don't go in now and they show later I should have gone, then they'll be all over me in Congress. They won't be talking about my civil rights bill, or education, or beautification. No sir, they'll push Vietnam up my ass every time. Vietnam. Vietnam. Vietnam. Right up my ass.[71]

Finally, he feared that 'our allies not just in Asia but throughout the world would conclude that our word was worth little or nothing'.[72]

Taking all these considerations into account, Johnson decided that 'we should do what was necessary to resist aggression but we should not be provoked into a major war. We would get the required appropriation in the new budget, and we would not boast about what we were doing.'[73] This meant, in reality, that neither the American people nor even Congress would be told about the financial ramifications of the deepening military commitment. When McNamara recommended, out of fiscal prudence, an immediate tax rise, his advice was roundly rejected.[74] Johnson agreed to send 50,000 troops immediately and privately sanctioned the deployment of an additional 50,000 before the end of the year. But, against the advice of almost all of his advisers, he refused to mobilize the reserves.[75] The US would not go on a war footing. Despite these limitations, Johnson had accepted the logic of escalation, which rendered American commitment open-ended.

The July discussions have become a battleground for historians who argue over the legacy and reputation of Johnson. Larry Berman, in *Planning a Tragedy*, characterizes the events as an elaborate charade engineered by Johnson to create the illusion of advice and consensus. Others, such as Brian VanDeMark, Arthur Schlesinger and David Barrett, are more charitable, suggesting that a reluctant Johnson was sucked into the quagmire of war. In *The Irony of Vietnam*, Leslie Gelb and Richard Betts have suggested that Johnson understood the

70 Kearns, *Lyndon Johnson*, pp. 252–3.
71 David Halberstam, *The Best and the Brightest* (New York, NY, 1972), p. 643.
72 Johnson, *Vantage Point*, p. 152.
73 Ibid., p. 149.
74 See McNamara, *In Retrospect*, pp. 204–6.
75 Gardner, *Pay Any Price*, pp. 249–51.

war to be a quagmire, but that, within this context, he still exercised control by finding a middle way between advocates of escalation and of disengagement. Much depends on whether Johnson seems a cynical manipulator or a sincere man who struggled valiantly against an inevitable tide of events. All the arguments have their merits, but a resolution of them is beyond the scope of this book, even assuming it would be possible.[76]

More fascinating than the argument itself is the vehemence with which it has been conducted. A nation bewildered by its involvement in a frustrating and ultimately futile war is desperate to find the cast iron explanation for its involvement – the moment at which it fell over the brink, and the person responsible for the 'accident'. In truth, no such point exists. That is where the quagmire metaphor is useful. As is clearly revealed in the Pentagon Papers, the aims of the United States did not change, though the means of achieving them became increasingly aggressive. The chief aim was not to save South Vietnam, but to preserve America's reputation as the defender of the free world. Each escalation was sanctioned not because the administration thought it would succeed, but in order to avoid the humiliation of failure. Even David Halberstam, who invented the quagmire analogy, believed in 1964 that withdrawal would mean 'that the United States' prestige will be lowered throughout the world . . . we would dishonor ourselves and our allies by pulling out'.[77] Kennedy, one of the chief escalators in this war, nevertheless realized that each escalation was 'like a drink . . . the effect wears off and you have to take another'.[78]

Johnson escalated sufficiently to suit his objectives, but not sufficiently to defeat communism in Vietnam. A full-scale war was out of the question because he was obsessed with the fear that he might set off the provisions of an imaginary secret treaty between Hanoi and Beijing.[79] The CIA opined that China would intervene only 'if US ground forces invaded North Vietnam in such strength as to control the country' or if the Chinese frontier was threatened, but Johnson did not trust this advice.[80] He decided to do 'enough but not too much'. 'I'm going up her leg an inch at a time', he told Senator George

---

[76] See Berman, *Planning a Tragedy*, especially pp. 79–129; VanDeMark, *Quagmire*; David M. Barrett, *Uncertain Warriors* (Lawrence, KS, 1993); Arthur Schlesinger, *The Bitter Heritage: Vietnam and American Democracy*; and Leslie Gelb and Richard Betts, *The Irony of Vietnam: The System Worked* (Washington, DC, 1979).

[77] David Halberstam, *The Making of a Quagmire* (New York, NY, 1964), pp. 332–4.

[78] Michael Sherry, *In the Shadow of War* (New Haven, CT, 1995), p. 251.

[79] Kearns, *Lyndon Johnson*, p. 270.

[80] Berman, 'Smoking guns', p. 18.

McGovern. 'I'll get to the snatch before they know what's happening.'[81] The extra troops, he hoped, would be like a magic wand which, when waved over the Vietnam problem, would make it disappear. At the very least, they would allow him to buy time to push through his legislative programme, particularly the civil rights and Medicare bills, which had entered a crucial stage.

The US went to war pretending that it was not doing so. The nation would not be mobilized; there would be no declaration of war and no emergency tax rise. The reserves would not be called up, nor would the people be given any indication of the military commitment which lay ahead. Johnson did not want a war fever, which might shift attentions away from more important domestic goals. When he asked McNamara in July 1965 how much the war would cost, the latter replied 'twelve billion dollars in 1966'. Both agreed that it 'would not require wage and price controls'.[82] In other words, Americans could have guns and butter: victory in Vietnam would not destroy the Great Society. Johnson was confident that the economy could handle the strain of domestic reform and foreign war: 'We are a nation with the highest GNP, the highest wages, and the most people at work. We can do both. As long as I am president we will do both.'[83]

For the moment, the sleight of hand worked. Johnson's support stayed solid, and, aside from some rumbling on college campuses, the people supported this strange war. But the demon which Johnson failed to slay in the summer of 1965 grew into a monster within six months. By clinging to the Great Society, he made the war unwinnable. By going to war he made the Great Society unaffordable. A clever politician had responded to a problem which required a statesman.[84] 'A determined President', Ball has argued, 'might at any point have overruled those advisers, accepted the costs of withdrawal, and broken the momentum, but only a leader supremely sure of himself could make that decision, and Lyndon Johnson, out of his element in the Vietnam War, felt no such certainty.'[85] Had a different decision been taken in July, the worst that would have happened is that Johnson would have been blamed for losing a small war. By escalating, he ensured that America eventually lost a big one.

[81] Gloria Emerson, *Winners and Losers* (New York, NY, 1992), p. 377.

[82] Williams *et al.*, eds, *America in Vietnam*, p. 253.

[83] Gardner, *Pay Any Price*, p. 258.

[84] For interesting speculation on the way Johnson's personality might have affected his direction of the war, see Blema Steinberg, *Shame and Humiliation* (Pittsburgh, PA, 1996), chaps 2 and 3.

[85] Berman, *Planning a Tragedy*, pp. 149–50.

WESTMORELAND'S WAR

Johnson's limited war strategy seemed to solve the conflict between the need to prevent the communist conquest of South Vietnam and the equally important need to avoid a major war in Asia. Limited war presumed that at a certain point the conflict would become intolerable for Hanoi. A steady but slow escalation would eventually persuade Ho to negotiate. Victory meant proving to the communists that they could not win. The limited nature of American aims is evident in the objectives drawn up by the JCS in August 1965. These included: (1) to stop the DRV from supporting insurgents in the South, (2) to defeat the PLAF, thus allowing the Saigon regime to assert control over all of South Vietnam, and (3) to keep China from intervening.[86] These points illustrate clearly the accepted view that the real enemy was North Vietnam. A government white paper dated 27 February 1965 asserted that 'the hard core of the Communist forces attacking South Vietnam [are] trained in the North and ordered into the South by Hanoi'.[87]

The arrival of US combat troops did not radically alter Hanoi's strategy. Thanh still assumed that the US would not remain in the war if the ARVN were defeated. Deploying PAVN units seemed the best way to hasten that outcome. As Le Duan advised in November 1965,

> At present *fighting the Americans and fighting the puppets are both important*. . . . But we would like to reassert the point that in deploying on the battlefield, we must aim at annihilating the puppet army first, because of the enemy forces they are the weaker.
>
> In fighting the American troops we must try to select their weak points and situations where they are weak in order to annihilate them. With regard to the strong points or the situation in which they are strong we should temporarily avoid them.[88]

The strategy combined guerrilla insurgency with big unit confrontations. Thanh's troops would 'stick close to the Americans and hit them where it hurts', but contact would be limited to flank attacks rather than frontal assaults.[89] Meanwhile, the political struggle would

---

86 Duiker, *Sacred War*, p. 185.

87 'Aggression from the North': State Department White Paper on Vietnam, 27 February 1965, Internet source.

88 Elliott, 'Hanoi's strategy', p. 82.

89 Duiker, *Sacred War*, p. 182.

dominate; the US would not be allowed to turn the war into an exclusively military contest. Hanoi calculated that if it managed to dictate politics in South Vietnam, while maintaining a stalemate on the battlefield, the revolution would eventually succeed. In other words, Hanoi pursued its own version of limited war. Its aim was to 'limit the conflict with the enemy and defeat the enemy within those limits, inflicting many serious losses, and pushing him into a posture of becoming progressively more and more bogged down and seriously defeated'.[90]

'The first, the grandest, the most decisive act of judgment which the Statesman and General exercises', Clausewitz advised, 'is rightly to understand . . . the war in which he engages, not to take it for something, or to wish to make of it something, which by the nature . . . it is impossible for it to be.'[91] The US ignored this fundamental precept. American troops were sent to Vietnam with definite aims, but no recognizable strategy. 'It was startling to me that we had no military plan to win the war',[92] wrote Clark Clifford, who succeeded McNamara as Defense Secretary in 1968. American action was in truth reaction; Hanoi assumed the strategic offensive throughout, controlling the pace and nature of the war. This lack of purpose, evident even to lower echelon troops, eroded morale. 'I'm not sure that anyone in the higher up levels knew what we were supposed to be doing', one officer recalled. 'Like my troops, I just wondered, . . . if we do all this, what's going to happen, what are we doing, what's the goal of the whole thing?'[93]

When the Americans escalated they established a number of fortified enclaves along the coastline, designed to provide security even if the ARVN collapsed. Action was to be restricted to a 50 mile radius of the bases. The enclaves reflected the unease of Johnson and Taylor, who doubted that American soldiers could win a counter-insurgency contest. As Taylor explained, the enclaves

> would have the advantage of placing our forces in areas of easy
> access and egress with minimum logistic problems associated
> with supply and maintenance. The presence of our troops
> would assure the defense of . . . important key areas and would
> relieve some GVN forces for employment elsewhere. The troops
> would not be called upon to engage in counter-insurgency

90 Elliott, 'Hanoi's strategy', pp. 83–4.
91 Karl Clausewitz, *On War*, ed. Anatol Rapaport (Harmondsworth, 1980), p. 121.
92 MacDonald, *Giap*, p. 219.
93 Ronald Spector, " 'How do you know if you're winning?'': perception and reality in America's military performance in Vietnam, 1965–1970', in Werner and Huynh, eds, *Vietnam War*, p. 159.

operations except in their own local defense and hence would be exposed to minimum losses.[94]

Enclaves limited US commitment, while at the same time demonstrating loyalty to South Vietnam. They were designed to slow the progress of the PLAF, while the bombing forced the North to negotiate.

But the enclave concept was not sufficiently aggressive for Westmoreland, who judged it an 'inglorious, static use of US forces'.[95] He was 'convinced that US troops with their energy, mobility and firepower can successfully take the fight to the VC'.[96] The failure of the bombers to erode Hanoi's resolve acted in his favour – by June 1965 the enclave strategy was dead. Westmoreland then tried to create a type of war more familiar to Americans. He wanted his army to manoeuvre PAVN/PLAF main force units into colossal encounters which would allow his firepower to prevail. He had no doubts about American ability to defeat an Asian guerrilla enemy, confidence typical of the military he had served with such distinction. A standard American formula would be applied in Vietnam: the best men would wield the biggest quantity of the best weaponry to achieve a quick victory. Communism would be crushed by American wealth.

For Westmoreland, defeating the communists involved three tasks. First, the country had to be pacified by neutralizing PLAF guerrillas. Second, PAVN/PLAF main force units had to be defeated. Third, the South Vietnamese people had to be offered a viable political alternative. Westmoreland saw the second problem as the key. He assumed that, if main force units were eliminated, PLAF regional and guerrilla forces would be fatally weakened. Pacifying the guerrillas was a sufficiently minor task to be left to the ARVN. American forces would confront main force units in the hinterlands, thus neutralizing the threat they posed to major population centres, and keeping Americans away from the cities, minimizing their potentially abrasive effect. Westmoreland was not actually against pacification, but doubted it could bring quick victory.

Westmoreland envisaged a three-phase strategy. In the first phase, American troops would protect their bases and build logistical facilities. Troops would respond to enemy aggression as it occurred. In the second phase, Americans would push into the hinterlands to eliminate enemy sanctuaries, inflicting heavy casualties. Finally, the US would mount sustained operations against main force units. The overriding

94 Schandler, *Unmaking*, p. 27.
95 Richard A. Hunt, *Pacification* (Boulder, CO, 1995), p. 33.
96 Schandler, *Unmaking*, p. 27.

tactic would be to locate, then pin down, then annihilate enemy units – a method henceforth known as 'search and destroy'. It did not matter where battles took place, since territory was unimportant. Operations were designed to maximize the kill ratio, on the assumption that intolerable casualties would eventually force the North to negotiate. 'Our mission was . . . simply to kill: to kill Communists and to kill as many of them as possible', Philip Caputo recalled. 'Stack 'em like cordwood. Victory was a high body count, defeat a low kill ratio, war a matter of arithmetic. The pressure on unit commanders to produce enemy corpses was intense, and they in turn communicated it to their troops.'[97]

For five months after the first American landings, the PLAF carefully avoided combat. But on 15 August intelligence revealed that the 1st PLAF Regiment was threatening the enclave at Chu Lai, 55 miles southeast of Da Nang. In Operation Starlite, launched on 17 August, Marines surrounded and annihilated the PLAF force. In five days of fighting, 688 enemy were killed, with American casualties numbering 45 killed and 204 wounded.[98] This first major confrontation seemed a resounding success. Helicopters had proved decisive, allowing Americans to trap enemy troops, neutralizing their extraordinary mobility. But Hanoi interpreted things differently. Thanh pointed out that, even though the Americans had chosen the time and place for the confrontation, they had not eradicated the PLAF presence. He was right. Shortly afterward, insurgents returned unmolested.

Starlite provided a hint of this war's tactical dilemmas. Only one weapon was captured for every six bodies discovered, an indication that many unarmed civilians were killed and included in the body count.[99] In February 1966 Representative Clement Zablocki provided the House Foreign Affairs Committee with statistics that, on average, two civilians were killed for each enemy in South Vietnam, and, in some search and destroy missions, the ratio was nearer six to one.[100] This not only reveals the difficulty of measuring the actual rate of attrition, but also the inherent contradiction in the American way of war. Killing peasants was not a very effective way of winning their loyalty. If fighting erupted in a hamlet, soldiers would sometimes destroy it in order to nullify its potential as a guerrilla sanctuary. Yet this inevitably alienated the peasantry and cast doubt upon the

---

97 Philip Caputo, *A Rumor of War* (New York, NY, 1977), p. xix.
98 Guenter Lewy, *America in Vietnam* (Oxford, 1978), p. 54.
99 Ibid., pp. 54–5.
100 George McT. Kahin, *Intervention* (New York, NY, 1986), p. 403. Zablocki, a hawk, was not inclined to exaggerate.

morality of the US mission. Fred Downs, an infantryman, recognized a dangerous fallacy in the American approach: 'On my farm in Indiana, if I had a squad of Vietnamese come through and stomp through my garden the way I did, go through my house the way I went through their houses, and search, and kill all the chickens and cows, you know, this wouldn't do anything to win my heart and mind'.[101]

In early summer, three PAVN regiments crossed into South Vietnam. Commanded by General Chu Huy Man, their original mission was to gain control of the Central Highlands and cut South Vietnam in two. But with the arrival of US combat troops in the area, Man was instructed to carry out only the first phase of the original strategy, an assault upon the Special Forces Camp at Plei Me, designed to flush out the recently arrived American 1st Cavalry Division. 'We did not have any plans to liberate the land; only to destroy troops', Man later explained.[102] In response to this incursion, Brigadier General Harry Kinnard, the 1st Cavalry commander, launched Operation Silver Bayonet, better known as the Ia Drang Valley Campaign.

On 14 November Lieutenant-Colonel Harold Moore's 1st Battalion, 7th Cavalry, dropped into landing zone X-Ray near the Chu Pong massif. Man responded by rushing three battalions to the area. A ferocious battle erupted, continuing virtually uninterrupted for 48 hours. Ia Drang provided a glimpse of the extraordinary firepower the US could deploy in this war. A total of 33,000 rounds of 105 mm artillery were directed upon PAVN positions.[103] Guns and ammunition had to be airlifted over dense jungle, yet American fighters were never short of firepower. Air Force fighter bombers dropped bombs and napalm. B-52 bombers also saturated the area, their first employment in tactical support.

After repeated assaults upon the American position were repulsed, Man withdrew. The 1st Cavalry lost 79 killed and 121 wounded. The PAVN had 634 known dead, with perhaps an equal number dragged away. Moore concluded that 'Brave American soldiers and the M-16 rifle had won a victory'.[104] Since the Americans had achieved their purpose of killing the enemy, they too departed. En route, one battalion was ambushed. The resultant mêlée left 151 American and 403 PAVN dead.[105] After first experiencing a classic search and destroy

---

101 Capps, *Unfinished War*, p. 91.

102 Harold G. Moore, *We Were Soldiers Once . . . and Young* (New York, NY, 1992), p. 57.

103 Phillip B. Davidson, *Vietnam at War* (Oxford, 1988), p. 362.

104 Moore, *We Were Soldiers*, pp. 232–3.

105 Ibid., pp. 366, 374.

operation, which they could control, the Americans had been introduced to a more sinister aspect of combat in Vietnam – the ambush – which they could not. But fate had been kind. Mere luck was all that separated pyrrhic victory from complete annihilation. Luck of this kind should not inspire confidence, but Westmoreland, like many senior commanders, was congenitally optimistic. Ia Drang convinced him that the enemy could be forced to stand and fight. He concluded that 'the ability of the Americans to meet and defeat the best troops the enemy could put in the field of battle was once more demonstrated, as was the validity of the Army's airmobile concept'.[106] With more helicopters and more troops, the battle could be duplicated on a larger scale.

But, in truth, Man had not been forced to fight. He had chosen to do so. He and Thanh had wanted to see how their troops would respond to American tactics and weaponry. Though satisfied with the performance, they concluded that the costs were too high. In future, large battles like this would be avoided. The US would be defeated by the ubiquity of its enemy. 'The Americans didn't understand that we had soldiers almost everywhere', Giap remarked; 'it was very hard to surprise us.' After Ia Drang, he concluded that 'the way to fight the American was to "grab him by his belt" . . . to get so close that your artillery and air power were useless'.[107]

By the end of 1965, progress had been made. The military situation was stabilized. In theory, the revitalization of the RVN government and military could now proceed. In Saigon, Quat's ministry, in power for just three months, was brought down by Nguyen Cao Ky, an Air Force colonel more impressive for his dress sense than his leadership qualities. Washington assumed the new government would soon replicate the fate of the old. But, fortified by the steady American build-up, Ky's ministry proved surprisingly sturdy. By the end of the year the situation was more stable than at any time since Diem's assassination. Johnson and his advisers convinced themselves that a corner had been turned. The war, it seemed, had been transformed into a contest reassuringly familiar and easily controlled.

But success was an illusion. Ball was correct when he predicted: 'We can scarcely expect [Hanoi] to accommodate us by adopting our preferred method of combat'.[108] The Maoist three-stage strategy had long been abandoned, though propagandists still spoke of impending

---

106 Andrew F. Krepinevich, *The Army and Vietnam* (Baltimore, MD, 1986), p. 169.
107 Currey, *Victory*, p. 257.
108 Berman, 'Smoking guns', p. 19.

khoi nghia. Hanoi had settled upon a strategy which aimed not at total military victory but instead combined all aspects of *dau tranh* – political, military and diplomatic – to trap the US in a protracted war which it could not win. The revolution spread like cancer since the communists still dominated the struggle for peasant loyalty. Americans failed to realize that military escalation did not negate that struggle, but merely camouflaged it.

SEARCH AND DESTROY

The American answer to the problem of the guerrilla was air mobility, rooted in the helicopter. 'Superior mobility is essential in counter-guerrilla operations to achieve surprise and so successfully counter the mobility of the enemy force', an Army manual proclaimed. 'The extensive use of airmobile forces, if used with imagination, will ensure the military commander superior mobility.' Starlite and Silver Bayonet seemed to demonstrate this principle. Air mobility allowed Americans to impose their offensive spirit upon this war. The speed, manoeuvrability and firepower of helicopters provided the illusion of offensive mastery. Unfortunately, as Larry Cable has argued, historical experience had shown that the key to successful counter-insurgency lay in 'the strategic defensive . . . expressed in offensive small-unit operations in which the goal was not so much killing as demoralizing the enemy by depriving him of sanctuary'.[109] This experience was ignored because Americans could not contemplate fighting a defensive war.[110]

Helicopters were not, in truth, the answer to guerrilla mobility, since the US never solved the tactical dilemma of how to find the enemy. The vast majority of search and destroy operations did not result in combat. Traditional methods of location were useless. As the war progressed, ever more sophisticated detection devices were developed, but each inspired an equally ingenious response. As one soldier

109 Larry Cable, *Unholy Grail* (London, 1991), p. 34.

110 Historians continue to argue over the best way to have fought this war. Cable and Krepinevich both contend that the US erred by not pursuing a counter-insurgency strategy which concentrated on the 'village war'. Colonel Harry Summers (*On Strategy: A Critical Analysis of the Vietnam War*, Novato, CA, 1982) argues the opposite, namely that the US lost because it devoted too much attention to counter-insurgency, instead of doing what it did best, namely fighting a conventional war against PAVN. Eric Bergerud (*Dynamics of Defeat*) feels that a counter-insurgency strategy would have played into the hands of the PLAF by dispersing American troops into small units which could be easily routed. On balance, he feels that a more aggressive conventional strategy offered the most promise, but still doubts that an alternative strategy actually could have won the war. See also Chapter 10.

recalled: 'With the number of men we had in the field, which was generally less than 50 per cent of our combat troops at any given time, the NVA/VC units, which were often small to begin with, only had to move a half a mile or so and we would miss them.'[111] A memorandum sent to the White House in early 1966 succinctly summarized the American dilemma:

> The Viet Cong are continuing to avoid South Vietnamese and Allied troops participating in large-scale search and destroy missions. They are, however, persisting in their aggressive campaign of terrorism, sabotage and harassment of lightly defended and isolated outposts and villages.[112]

It is doubtful that anyone at the time realized just how dire were the implications of this memo.

The US had difficulty keeping its operations a secret, which partly explains why most located no enemy activity. Helicopters were very noisy. Blasting the landing zone with artillery, bombs and rockets prior to landing troops alerted enemy units that it was time to disperse. In addition, since communist sympathizers had infiltrated every level of South Vietnamese political and military bureaucracy, they found it relatively easy to discover when and where a big operation was planned. The more elaborate the operation, the greater the likelihood of leaks.

Search and destroy was also extremely costly. The 1st Cavalry, during three and a half months of fighting in Binh Dinh province, fired 136,769 artillery shells, not including 5,105 rounds fired from American warships. Fighter bombers flew 2,622 sorties dropping 2.5 million pounds of explosives and 500,000 pounds of napalm. B-52s flew another 171 sorties dropping 3,078 tons of bombs. All of this firepower resulted in just 1,100 PLAF and 657 PAVN dead, and 479 weapons captured. Americans used firepower to vent their frustration with an elusive enemy – noise implied power and progress. But there was no real evidence that all the explosions were winning the war. One uniquely perceptive analyst argued that 'air strikes have rarely been justified in terms of enemy casualties'. Data collected suggested that 'more noncombatants than fighters have been killed and that other noncombatants were driven into insurgency through resentment'.[113]

By mid-1966, the PLAF no longer roamed the countryside with impunity. But the pace of the war was still controlled by Hanoi. Some

---

111 Eric Bergerud, *Red Thunder, Tropic Lightning* (New York, NY, 1994), p. 100.
112 Cable, *Unholy Grail*, p. 43.
113 Lewy, *America in Vietnam*, p. 59, 96.

88 per cent of all fights were initiated by PLAF or PAVN units and half of these began as ambushes.[114] The enemy not only controlled when combat took place, he also usually determined when it was over. These small engagements were eroding American military might. Mines, ambushes, small fire fights and booby traps took a heavy toll. American forces were being nibbled to death. The steady drip of the nation's blood sapped morale.

BIG BATTLES

At the Honolulu conference on 7–9 February 1966, Johnson expressed a desire to 'nail the coonskin to the wall'. Another sharp escalation was approved. Troop levels, which stood at 184,000 at the end of 1965, would rise to 429,000 by the end of 1966.[115] On 1 July 1966, at another meeting in Honolulu, McNamara outlined six major goals for the new troops to achieve by the end of the year. The two most important called for the attrition of enemy forces at a rate exceeding their capacity to recruit new soldiers (the 'cross-over point') and the elimination of 40–50 per cent of all PAVN and PLAF base areas.[116] Search and destroy, so far tested on a small scale, would henceforth be applied to large multi-division operations.

One such operation, codenamed Attleboro, was designed to penetrate War Zone C in Tay Ninh province along the Cambodian border and root out enemy forces sheltering near the Michelin rubber plantation. Because of its proximity to Saigon, the area was strategically important. Neutralizing the threat to the capital was a necessary prelude to extending RVN influence into the hinterland. The American plan called for one battalion to land between Don Dien and Suoi Da, whereupon other battalions would move toward it, flushing out the PLAF.

The area was first deforested with defoliants and bulldozers. Villages were destroyed, with the population forcibly resettled. This created a free fire zone – any remaining Vietnamese were assumed to be insurgents. For the first few days, enemy ambushes frustrated the offensive. The tide turned when elements of the 4th and 25th Infantry Divisions, the 173rd Airborne Brigade and the 11th Armoured Cavalry Regiment began their sweep. Two ARVN battalions provided reinforcement, making a total of 22,000 allied soldiers. Confronted

114 Shelby Stanton, *The Rise and Fall of an American Army* (Novato, CA, 1985), p. 86.

115 Berman, *Lyndon Johnson's War*, p. 10.

116 Stanton, *Rise and Fall*, p. 84.

by such massive firepower, the 9th PLAF Division retreated into Cambodia. Afterwards, a frustrated Major-General William Depuy commented:

> [The PLAF] metered out their casualties, and when the casualties were getting too high . . . they just backed off and waited. I really thought that the kind of pressure they were under would have caused them perhaps to knock off the war for awhile, as a minimum, or even give up and go back north. But I was completely wrong on that. I was surprised a little bit, too . . . We hit more dry holes than I thought we were going to hit. They were more elusive. They controlled the battle better. They were the ones who decided whether there would be a fight.[117]

In contrast, Westmoreland studied the kill ratio and pronounced the operation a success. The PLAF lost perhaps 1,100 men, and significant quantities of supplies. American casualties totaled around 650, with 155 dead.[118] Westmoreland concluded that the communists could not long survive this rate of attrition. Attleboro seemed to provide the answer for winning the war.

In early 1967 Westmoreland and General Cao Van Vien, chief of the South Vietnamese Joint General Staff, formulated a new Combined Campaign Plan which called for a series of large-scale assaults against enemy base areas. For Westmoreland, these seemed to offer a way to force the communists to stand and fight. He presumed that enemy units would have to defend their base areas, providing him with the opportunity to annihilate them. Using Attleboro as a model, he planned to attack base areas located in the 'Iron Triangle' and War Zone C, northwest of Saigon.

Operation Cedar Falls saw 20 American battalions pour into the Iron Triangle in early January 1967. A huge land-clearing effort was launched beforehand, using defoliants, bombing and bulldozers. Over 6,000 civilians were evacuated. In the first attack wave, Lieutenant-Colonel Alexander Haig's 1st Battalion, 25th Infantry, captured and destroyed Ben Suc with light casualties. The 1st Infantry Division and the rest of the 25th then formed a blocking force, toward which the APCs and tanks of the 11th Armoured Cavalry advanced from Ben Cat. The advance uncovered significant logistical installations, but few Viet Cong. On 26 January the operation was terminated.

---

117 Krepinevich, *Army and Vietnam*, p. 190.
118 John Pimlott, *Vietnam: The Decisive Battles* (London, 1990), p. 83.

Westmoreland then launched Operation Junction City, a multidivision assault into War Zone C involving 22 American and four ARVN battalions. Like the Iron Triangle, War Zone C had been communist-controlled since the French war. US intelligence indicated that elements of the 9th PLAF Division and the 101st PAVN Regiment were present. American troops formed a horseshoe on three sides of War Zone C, into which troops of the 25th Infantry Division and 11th Armoured Cavalry swept on 22 February. Aside from two fierce clashes at Prek Lok, the anticipated major battle never materialized. Sweeps over the next three months encountered empty countryside. The operation was terminated on 14 May.

Cedar Falls and Junction City cost the enemy around 3,500 killed. American losses totaled 354 killed and 1,913 wounded.[119] Though the results fell short of American expectations, Thanh and Giap concluded that it was no longer wise to base large concentrations of main force units near populated areas. Henceforth, Hanoi shifted to greater reliance upon border sanctuaries. This weakened guerrillas in the populated areas who depended upon main force support. But the two operations revealed the flaw in the base area theory. Contrary to expectations, the enemy had refused to stand and fight.

IMAGINARY SUCCESS

By the end of 1967, the RVN was more stable than it had been for years. Pressed by the United States, Ky brought in a new constitution and held elections in September 1967. These were cleverly exploited by his close associate General Nguyen Van Thieu, who became President. Ky reluctantly settled for the vice-presidency. Buoyed by this progress and by the apparent success on the battlefield, Johnson, speaking in San Antonio, Texas, on 29 September, boasted that 'There is progress in the war ... steady progress considering the war that we are fighting; ... [and] the situation that actually prevailed when we sent our troops there in 1965'. He insisted that 'the grip of the Vietcong on the people is being broken', and went on to propose what became known as the 'San Antonio formula': if Hanoi agreed to negotiations, bombing of the North would stop.[120] In private he was much more pessimistic, especially after the DRV failed to respond to the San Antonio offer. 'It doesn't seem we can win the war militarily', he

119 Davidson, *Vietnam at War*, p. 428.
120 Williams *et al.*, eds, *America in Vietnam*, p. 266.

confessed to colleagues on 23 October. 'We can't win diplomatically either.'[121]

Incessant American pressure was taking its toll. In order to make up losses, the better PLAF guerrillas were drafted into main force and regional units, thus weakening the NLF's hold upon the villages. According to some estimates, it lost control of between 500,000 and 1 million people in rural areas, shrinking its tax and food base and complicating recruitment. Taxation rates rose, in some areas doubling to 20 per cent of a farmer's gross income. Because of the difficulty in getting volunteers to shore up the ranks, the PLAF relied increasingly upon conscription. Morale declined, with reports of corruption and a lack of enthusiasm for combat. Soldiers often took out their frustration on the local population.[122]

These developments allowed some Americans to convince themselves that they were in control. But, according to Sam Adams, a CIA analyst, US officials habitually exaggerated the PLAF decline, over-emphasizing statistics which were 'peripheral to the real strengths and weaknesses of the Vietcong. The main enemy strength lay not in the number of troops deployed but in other areas that US intelligence had hardly considered.'[123] Conventional intelligence produced conventional order of battle (OOB) figures which suggested that the US was winning the war. Adams felt that American authorities consistently underestimated the revolution's hold upon the villages, which the defeat of a local guerrilla unit did not necessarily break.

Adams initially encountered delusion, not deception. A colleague admitted: 'We've fallen gradually into the same pattern of mistakes as the French. They didn't begin by faking intelligence; they merely assumed success in the absence of clear failure. We've been doing that for some time.' But then, as the war progressed, subterfuge became necessary in order to bridge the gap between wish and reality. Creighton Abrams, Westmoreland's deputy, reminded Adams that, given the 'image of success' which had consistently been presented, if accurate figures for enemy strength were suddenly released, 'all available caveats and explanations will not prevent the press from drawing an erroneous and gloomy conclusion . . . All those who have an incorrect view of the war will be reinforced and the task will become more difficult.'[124] The official solution was to leave militia figures out of

121 David M. Barrett, ed, *Lyndon B. Johnson's Vietnam Papers* (College Station, TX, 1997), p. 509.

122 Duiker, *Sacred War*, pp. 206–7.

123 Sam Adams, *War of Numbers* (South Royalton, VT, 1994), p. xxx.

124 Ibid., pp. 80, 106.

154

OOB calculations. But a clever public relations gambit could not alter the reality on the ground. 'Here's the horror of it', the father of a dead GI concluded: 'We lost our *only child* . . . in 1968. Ambushed in a damn hamlet in Qui Nhon province. Let's assume he was briefed to expect *x* numbers of irregulars – and instead he was ambushed by people *Westmoreland did not think should be carried in the order of battle!*'[125]

The communists still controlled the pace of the war. Less than 1 per cent of the nearly 2 million small unit operations conducted by the Americans or ARVN during 1967 and 1968 resulted in contact with the enemy. 'It was a sheer physical impossibility to keep the enemy from slipping away whenever he wished it if he were in terrain with which he was familiar', an American general remarked in frustration.[126] In 1967 an official at the Department of Defense Systems Analysis Office advised McNamara:

> The VC/NVA started the shooting in over 90% of the company-sized fire fights. Over 80% began with a well-organized enemy attack. Since their losses rise (as in the first quarter of 1967) and fall (as they have done since) with their choice of whether or not to fight, they can probably hold their losses to about 2,000 a week regardless of our force levels. If, as I believe, their strategy is to wait us out, they will control their losses to a level low enough to be sustained indefinitely, but high enough to tempt us to increase our forces to the point of US public rejection of the war.

From January 1965 to December 1967, approximately 344,000 PAVN/ PLAF soldiers were either killed, seriously injured, taken prisoner or defected. This is admittedly a huge number, but during the same period, main force strength actually increased by 80,800 men. Two thousand losses per week was easily manageable, since by late 1967, according to Westmoreland's own figures, the North Vietnamese were infiltrating 8,400 men into the South each month, and the PLAF was recruiting (or conscripting) another 3,500.[127] Clearly, in the short term at least, no meaningful attrition was taking place.

Westmoreland had demonstrated that his forces could win big battles, but on the political front little progress was being made. Major John Wilson, senior US adviser in Long An province, commented on 11 March 1967:

125 Myra MacPherson, *Long Time Passing* (New York, NY, 1984), p. 417.
126 Krepinevich, *Army and Vietnam*, p. 191.
127 Lewy, *America in Vietnam*, pp. 83–4.

> For every hectare we pacify, we have devoted to this province more men, more dollars and other means than any other province in South Vietnam. Yet, the results of these efforts are meager. . . . In reality, we can only control a very small area . . . I would say that we control only four percent in the daytime and one percent during the night.

The strategy of attrition worked against the complex task of achieving a politically viable society in South Vietnam, which enjoyed the support of the local population. Between 1965 and 1969 approximately 3.5 million people in the south, or 20 per cent of the population, were refugees at one time.[128] In Long An guerrilla recruitment *increased* in direct proportion to American pressure. 'At the end of the day the villagers would be turned loose', William Ehrhart, a young Marine officer, commented. 'Their homes had been wrecked, their chickens killed, their rice confiscated – and if they weren't pro-Vietcong before we got there, they sure as hell were by the time we left.'[129]

It is commonly held that the US won every single significant encounter with PAVN or PLAF troops.[130] Americans confused 'significant' with 'big', never realizing that elaborately staged big battles had little bearing on the outcome of the war. Cedar Falls and Junction City resulted in an average of 70 American dead per month over a five-month period. During the same period, in the rest of South Vietnam, the Americans lost on average 730 men per month. This means, ironically, that one of the safest places for an American combat soldier was in one of Westmoreland's big battles since those operations provided the best opportunity to minimize contact with the enemy.

It was the little clashes all over the country, usually initiated by the enemy, which were proving decisive. 'They were superb at masking their true position', Lieutenant-Colonel Thomas Rhame of the 1st Air Cavalry said of the enemy. 'They were absolute masters at choosing the right terrain at the right place at the right time to blow your crap away.'[131] Because this war had no fronts and few set-piece engagements, American forces were unable to exploit their one distinct

---

128 Ngo Vinh Long, 'The Tet Offensive and its aftermath', in Gilbert and Head, *Tet Offensive*, pp. 97, 108

129 Karnow, *Vietnam*, p. 482.

130 See Harry Summers, 'The last years of the war: a personal view', in Elizabeth Jane Errington and B.J.C. McKercher, eds, *The Vietnam War as History* (New York, NY, 1990), p. 163. Summers's statement to a PAVN commander that the Americans had never been defeated on the battlefield is as stupid as it is popular. It is discussed in greater detail in Chapter 10.

131 Spector, 'How do you know', p. 156.

advantage – abundant firepower. They were unable to turn Vietnam into their type of war. They were losing the war of attrition. As PAVN General Nguyen Xuan Hoang later commented, 'Time was on our side. We did not have to defeat [the Americans] militarily; we had only to avoid losing. A victory by [the] brave [American] soldiers did nothing to change the balance of forces or to bring [them] any closer to victory.'[132]

American deaths in the first half of 1967 averaged 816 per month, compared with a monthly average of 477 in 1966.[133] For the American people, this seemed too high a price for a war which was not being won. The war was also hugely expensive. A single firebase on a single day might use up US$300,000 worth of artillery ammunition. In the first quarter of 1967 artillery units connected to the 25th Division fired over 200,000 rounds, a bombardment which resulted in just 231 enemy killed.[134] When Westmoreland assumed command of MACV, the war cost the US taxpayer less than half a billion dollars a year. When he left Vietnam in 1968, that figure had risen to US$26.5 billion.[135]

Johnson's limited war was not sufficiently limited. The problem with the American approach was that it did not take into account the issue of duration. The great strength of the communist approach was that it did. Hanoi knew that Americans would not tolerate a long war, so a long war was what the communists provided. 'The most crucial limitation', Samuel Huntington has observed, 'is not the limitation on weapons, or geographical scope or goals, but rather the limitation on *time*.'[136] By 1968 Vietnam was a war too long.

Hanoi sought gradually to erode American morale. That strategy had certainly succeeded as far as the American Defense Secretary was concerned. In a very pessimistic memo to Johnson dated 19 May 1967, McNamara confessed that he could see 'no attractive course of action'. He rejected Westmoreland's calls for yet more troops, arguing that

> The picture of the world's greatest superpower killing or seriously injuring 1,000 noncombatants a week, while trying to pound a tiny backward nation into submission on an issue whose merits are hotly disputed, is not a pretty one. It could conceivably produce a costly distortion in the American

132 Currey, *Victory*, p. 258.
133 Lewy, *America in Vietnam*, p. 73.
134 Bergerud, *Red Thunder*, p. 77.
135 Harrison, *Endless War*, p. 317.
136 Samuel Huntington, 'Vietnam reappraised', *International Security* 6 (Summer, 1981), p. 7.

national consciousness and in the world image of the United States – especially if the damage to North Vietnam is complete enough to be 'successful'.

McNamara called for a 'political-military strategy' which involved restricted bombing, a less aggressive ground strategy, a shifting of the military burden to the RVN and greater flexibility toward a diplomatic deal with Hanoi. But, in retrospect, even that solution seems to him to have been inappropriate. 'Today', he confessed in his 1995 memoirs,

> it is clear to me that my memorandum pointed directly to the conclusion that, through either negotiation or direct action, we should have begun our withdrawal from South Vietnam. There was a high probability we could have done so on terms no less advantageous than those accepted nearly six years later – without any greater damage to US national security and at much less human, political, and social cost to America and Vietnam.[137]

The publication of McNamara's memoirs caused huge controversy. A nation still divided by the war did not unanimously accept his admission of error. But, though his apology may seem hollow to some, the pertinence of the above statement is beyond dispute.

---

137 McNamara, *In Retrospect*, pp. 266–71.

6   TURNING POINT?
TET AND THE 1968 ELECTION

Many liberals found the Johnson presidency tortuous. LBJ offered the best hope for domestic reform, but for those disenchanted with the war (and their number steadily swelled), the 1968 election inspired a sense of foreboding. Four more years of Johnson seemed a catastrophic prospect. The war would continue and the divisions within society which it engendered would deepen. But the alternative was Richard Nixon, who could not be trusted with the war or with the Great Society.

Into the breach strode Eugene McCarthy, a little known senator from Minnesota, who declared his candidacy on 30 November 1967. That an incumbent President who had won so resoundingly four years earlier should now be challenged by a fellow Democrat reveals how deep were the divisions in party and society. McCarthy offered himself as healer: 'I am hopeful that this challenge . . . may alleviate . . . [the] sense of political helplessness and restore to many people a belief in the processes of American government'.[1] The new candidate appealed because he was gentle, urbane, introspective, innocent – in every way a marked contrast to the President. Anti-war liberals were immediately enthralled. But the war was only one cause of disenchantment. McCarthy symbolized and gave expression to white, middle-class anxieties, but the Democrats were also supposed to be the party of urban workers and poor blacks, whose very different concerns he could not effectively voice. In healing some wounds, he opened others. It is perhaps no wonder that, a year before the election, Johnson did not take seriously his challenge.

But then came Tet.

TET OFFENSIVE – THE PRELUDE

Toward the end of 1967, US forces fought two battles which left Westmoreland in an upbeat mood. On 29 October the PLAF attacked

1 John Morton Blum, *Years of Discord* (New York, NY, 1991), p. 290.

the RVN district headquarters and Special Forces camp at Loc Ninh, 70 miles north of Saigon. After a week of fighting they were driven back, suffering some 850 casualties. Westmoreland called it 'one of the most significant and important operations' of the war. As Loc Ninh ended, the battle of Dak To began. The largest PAVN concentration in the war so far deployed around the Dak To Special Forces camp in the dense jungle north of Pleiku. A savage battle began on 3 November and raged for nineteen days. The Americans lost 287 killed, 985 wounded and 18 missing. But PAVN losses exceeded 1,200 dead. Westmoreland confidently decided that the 'crossover point' had been reached.[2] There was, he promised, 'light at the end of the tunnel' – blissfully unaware of the irony of such a statement.[3]

'I am absolutely certain that, whereas in 1965 the enemy was winning, today he is certainly losing', Westmoreland announced on 21 November 1967. He further pledged that 'within two years or less, it will be possible . . . to phase down our level of commitment and turn more of the burden . . . over to the Vietnamese armed forces'. The Johnson administration sang in harmony. On 26 November Vice-President Hubert Humphrey claimed 'there has been progress on every front in Vietnam; military, substantial progress, politically, very significant progress . . . There is no military stalemate. There is no pacification stalemate.' Johnson echoed: 'We are making progress'.[4] Victories, ersatz or otherwise, were important in an election year.

Behind the scenes, anxiety fermented. According to official HES findings, by August 1967, the NLF controlled 3,978 of 12,537 hamlets, the RVN just 168.[5] McNamara was growing increasingly disillusioned with the war. 'Ho Chi Minh is a tough old S.O.B.', he confessed in private, 'he won't quit no matter how much bombing we do.'[6] The realization of failure eventually drove him to tears. 'He [cries] . . . all the time now', a secretary confessed.[7] On 19 May he advised Johnson:

> We should not bomb for punitive reasons if it serves no other purpose – especially if analysis shows that the actions may be

2 Robert Pisor, *The End of the Line: The Siege of Khe Sanh* (New York, NY, 1982), pp. 69–74.

3 Don Oberdorfer, *Tet!* (New York, NY, 1984), p. 107. The French made the same promise before Dien Bien Phu. See p. 39.

4 Peter Braestrup, *Big Story* (Novato, CA, 1994), pp. 49–52.

5 Ngo Vinh Long, 'The Tet Offensive and its aftermath', in Marc Jason Gilbert and William Head, eds, *The Tet Offensive* (Westport, CT, 1996), p. 97. In the remaining number, control was contested, with the RVN usually exercising power during the day, the NLF at night.

6 Henry Trewhitt, *McNamara* (New York, NY, 1971), p. 235.

7 Deborah Shapley, *Promise and Power* (Boston, MA, 1973), p. 444.

counterproductive. It costs American lives; it creates a backfire of revulsion and opposition by killing civilians; it creates serious risks; it may harden the enemy.[8]

The rest of the administration circled the wagons in an attempt to project a mood of resolve. McGeorge Bundy, responding to McNamara's pessimism, reminded the President that 'our effort in Viet-Nam in the past two years has not only prevented the catastrophe that would otherwise have unfolded but has laid a foundation for a progress that now appears truly possible and of the greatest historical significance'.[9] Johnson rejected McNamara's advice but, deep down, shared his misgivings. 'Bomb, bomb, bomb, that's all you know', he chided the JCS. He would not de-escalate, but neither would he send more troops, since 'When we add divisions . . . the enemy add[s] divisions. Where does it all end?'[10]

There was also unease in Hanoi. Granted, the ARVN was fragile and Americans were losing patience. But the war seemed stuck in stalemate. The collapse of the RVN was less likely in late 1967 than it had been three years earlier. According to the Maoist formula, the revolution would climax with a popular uprising (*khoi nghia*), triggered by a general offensive. Politics and war would converge at a single point when the enemy was fatally weakened and the people absolutely confident in the revolution. In 1967 this fusion seemed distant; the revolution was still a long way from critical mass.

Stalemate on the battlefield was physical and, as Napoleon once said, in war the moral is to the physical as three is to one. The communists were morally better equipped than the Americans to endure a protracted war. Hanoi was winning, but in a way which contradicted Maoist precepts. Guerrilla action was not supposed to win by itself. Yet in hundreds of small battles, the communists were gradually eroding American will. By itself, this erosion would soon have become serious.

Given this situation, it seems bizarre that the Politburo should decide in April 1967 to push for a 'spontaneous uprising in order to win a decisive victory in the shortest possible time'.[11] The decision was hardly unanimous. Nguyen Chi Thanh, arguing that the time for *khoi nghia* was fast approaching, was backed by Le Duan and the

---

8 David M. Barrett, ed., *Lyndon B. Johnson's Vietnam Papers* (College Station, TX, 1997), p. 428. This is the same memo quoted at the end of Chapter 5.

9 George C. Herring, ed., *The Pentagon Papers*, abridged edn (New York, NY, 1993), pp. 205–6.

10 George C. Herring, *America's Longest War* (New York, NY, 1986), p. 178.

11 Cecil Currey, 'Giap and Tet Mau Than 1968', in Gilbert and Head, eds, *Tet Offensive*, p. 82.

firebrands within COSVN. But Giap and Truong Chinh vehemently insisted that protracted war, with its emphasis upon political revolution, should be allowed to run its course. It seemed wiser to exhaust the Americans than to attempt to defeat them on the battlefield. A high-ranking COSVN official later explained the internal dynamics which ensured that the bold course prevailed: 'The one who has the weapon in his hand has the most prestige. So, any policy supported by the military forces will develop and progress vigorously – no one can stop it.'[12]

The PLAF commander Tran Van Tra explained the reasoning behind the decision to launch a general offensive: 'The war had reached its peak but still offered [the US] no way out'.[13] In other words, the offensive would highlight the failure of Johnson's limited war strategy. As the party officially maintained, 'taking advantage of a time that the American imperialists are confronted with a situation in which both advance and retreat are difficult, at a time when the United States is about to elect a president, we need to inflict a decisive blow, to win a great victory, creating a great leap forward in the strategic situation'.[14] The Politburo predicted three possible outcomes for the offensive. First, it might lead to a 'major victory' which would force the US to negotiate 'in accordance with our demands'. Second, it might produce 'important victories' though 'the enemy . . . would continue to fight'. Third, 'the Americans might send in many more troops, and expand the conflict'.[15] The risk seemed worth taking, since the third outcome – the only wholly negative one – seemed highly unlikely. Hanoi decided that, at this stage in the war and with an election looming, Johnson could not possibly escalate.

The offensive was to begin with a massive nation-wide attack, planned to coincide with Tet (the Lunar New Year), traditionally a time of raucous celebration. 'The basic guiding method', Tra explained, 'was to combine attacks by military units with mass urban uprisings, attacks from within the cities with those from outside, and military activities in rural areas with those in urban centers.'[16] The party was careful to stress that the Tet attacks were only the initial phase of the

12 Eric Bergerud, *The Dynamics of Defeat* (Boulder, CO, 1991), p. 203.

13 Tran Van Tra, 'Tet: the 1968 general offensive and general uprising', in Jayne S. Werner and Luu Doan Huynh, eds, *The Vietnam War: Vietnamese and American Perspectives* (Armonk, NY, 1993), p. 39.

14 David Elliott, 'Hanoi's strategy in the Second Indochina War', in Werner and Huynh, eds, *Vietnam War*, p. 85.

15 Ibid., p. 87.

16 Tra, 'General offensive and general uprising', p. 43.

general offensive: '[The] general offensive/general uprising is a process, I repeat, a process. A process of extremely arduous and complicated military combats and protracted political struggles. . . . It is wrong and dangerous . . . to think that the general offensive/general uprising is a one-blow effort.'[17] In two subsequent phases, reserves would be committed leading eventually to decisive victory, perhaps by the end of the year. 'Decisive' did not mean 'complete'. Hanoi did not imagine driving the Americans into the sea, nor even completely annihilating the ARVN. The example of Dien Bien Phu was stressed. At that battle, the French were not completely defeated, but the victory was decisive because French 'aggressive will' was shattered, preventing continuation of the war. Hanoi planned a similar outcome in 1968.

KHE SANH

On 21 January 1968 PAVN troops overwhelmed a number of American firebases in the mountainous region south of the DMZ, with the result that the Marine camp at Khe Sanh came under siege. Thus began the most dramatic battle of the war. In no other action did American soldiers face such extreme adversity for so long. At home, the battle became a symbol of American determination. Brave Marines provided atonement for the dominating disappointments of this war. Khe Sanh was the Alamo transplanted to Indochina.

Khe Sanh straddled Route 9, which linked the Vietnamese coast with Laotian market towns along the Mekong. As such, it was, for the communists, an important link to sanctuaries in Laos. US Special Forces maintained a small camp there to train and recruit local tribesmen and thus harass the supply route. During the summer of 1967 Westmoreland decided to strengthen the base in preparation for a more aggressive interdiction campaign. A marine battalion was despatched, huge arms supplies were stockpiled and the airstrip was upgraded.

Argument still rages over what PAVN troops were actually trying to achieve by attacking the garrison. There are sufficient similarities to Dien Bien Phu to suggest that a sequel was planned. The possibility certainly plagued Johnson, who was driven to a state of near panic. Westmoreland, though more composed, was genuinely concerned that a relatively small defeat of the Marines might have a huge psychological impact at home – as in Paris in 1954. He responded by exploiting an advantage which the French had lacked, namely his virtually unlimited capacity to supply the garrison by air.

17 Ronnie E. Ford, *Tet 1968: Understanding the Surprise* (London, 1995), p. 81.

But in taking this action, Westmoreland may have been walking blindly into a trap. Giap may have wanted him to believe that another Dien Bien Phu threatened, so that he would take appropriate steps to avoid it. In other words, Khe Sanh was possibly a feint, designed to draw American troops away from crucial objectives of the Tet Offensive. The fact that Hué, one of Hanoi's prime objectives, was left weakly defended in order to protect Khe Sanh suggests that the feint worked.

Khe Sanh possibly had dual goals. Dien Bien Phu had mystical importance to the revolution; the idea of recreating it would have been attractive, especially to a leadership attuned to the psychological consequences of its actions. But Hanoi's plans were always flexible; troops were primed to exploit a number of contingencies. Giap's comments, though written in retrospect, bear this out:

> Khe Sanh was not that important to us. Or it was only to the extent that it was to the Americans. It was the focus of attention in the United States because their prestige was at stake, but to us it was part of the greater battle that would begin after Tet. It was only a diversion, but one to be exploited if we could cause many casualties and win a big victory.[18]

Johnson gave Khe Sanh its importance when he said that 'The eyes of the nation and the eyes of the entire world – the eyes of all of history itself – are on that little band of defenders'.[19] In other words, if the Marines had capitulated, the United States would have been dealt a psychologically catastrophic blow. But, if instead the Marines were caught in a long siege from which they eventually extracted themselves, the operation would still divert American men and supplies from more important areas. It was the latter outcome which transpired.

'THE GREATEST BATTLE EVER FOUGHT'

The general offensive was not, strictly speaking, general, since PAVN units did not play a large part. 'We are not so dumb as to use our main force units', Le Duan confessed.[20] But this does not mean that Hanoi saw Tet as a convenient way to destroy the PLAF and consolidate its hegemony over the South, as some have argued. In fact, most NLF leaders were delighted at the opportunity to play a major role in the general offensive: 'The Party's new strategy gave the South what

18 Ibid., p. 108.
19 Peter Brush, 'The battle of Khe Sanh, 1968', in Gilbert and Head, eds, *Tet Offensive*, p. 208.
20 William J. Duiker, *Sacred War* (New York, NY, 1995), p. 212.

we wanted, the right to determine the political future of the South as equal participants'. They hoped that the offensive would lead to a decisive victory which would allow the NLF a major role in subsequent negotiations.[21]

PLAF units were singularly appropriate to the first phase when hundreds of attacks were launched around the country. These units, in theory, possessed the necessary awareness of local conditions. In the weeks prior to Tet, arms were stockpiled and plans formulated. Local committees were given considerable autonomy in determining precise tactics. COSVN inspired more than directed:

> To conduct an uprising, you must have a roster of all the tyrants and spies and be familiar with the way they live and where they live. Then use suicide cells to annihilate them by any means.
> ... make use of the populace immediately in sabotage and support activities, and in raid operations against the spies. The masses should be encouraged to go on strike, dig trenches and make spikes all night long ... All people in each family regardless of their ages should be encouraged to take part.[22]

On the eve of the attacks, COSVN's message to the troops maintained that the offensive 'will be the greatest battle ever fought throughout the history of our country. It will bring forth world-wide change but will also require many sacrifices. It will decide the fate and survival of our Fatherland and will shake the world and cause the most bitter failure to the imperialist ringleaders.'[23] The attacks were originally supposed to begin just after midnight on 30 January, but, at the last moment, it was decided to delay for 24 hours.[24] This decision was not, however, communicated to several units in the northern region. They struck prematurely, thus alerting US and South Vietnamese forces and blunting subsequent attacks. Eventually, some 84,000 communist troops went into action, attacking 36 provincial capitals, 64 district capitals, and a number of military bases.[25]

In only a few places was even a modicum of success achieved. In the most conspicuous attack, 20 suicide terrorists penetrated the

---

21 Robert Brigham, 'The NLF and the Tet offensive', in Gilbert and Head, eds, *Tet Offensive*, p. 68.

22 James P. Harrison, *The Endless War* (New York, NY, 1989), p. 267.

23 Oberdorfer, *Tet!*, p. 75.

24 There is some speculation that COSVN was using a new lunar calendar not used in the North.

25 Harrison, *Endless War*, p. 268.

American Embassy compound and held back a counter-attack for just over six hours, in full view of television cameras. The attack was always doomed, but the suffering and fear of American soldiers around the Embassy caused ripples of distress across the United States. Americans naturally wondered how the most secure building in South Vietnam had been penetrated by a few guerrillas. Given this moral effect, the assault, argues Eric Bergerud, 'must be considered one of the most successful small-unit actions in the history of modern warfare'.[26]

The revolution placed great importance upon capturing Hué, which would create a huge liberated zone in the north and impose a gigantic moral defeat upon the RVN and the US. PLAF detachments, reinforced by PAVN units, swept aside the Americans and held the city for a number of weeks. During this period, the revolution's real brutality was revealed. Hundreds, perhaps thousands, were rounded up and executed, regardless of whether they were in fact 'enemies of the revolution'. A party report on the offensive remarked in clinical fashion: 'Hué was the place where reactionary spirit had existed for over ten years. . . . it took us only a short time to drain it to its root.'[27]

Elsewhere, Tet was little more than a brief disturbance which conveniently flushed out PLAF insurgents. Suddenly conspicuous, they were rounded up or executed on the spot. A movement which had taken years to build was decimated in a moment. According to Tra, the fault lay partially in organization. Key cadres in the South were not informed of plans for the offensive until late October – 'too short a time for such a colossal and complex undertaking . . . [which] required the extraordinary efforts of hundreds of thousands of devoted and self-sacrificing revolutionaries'.[28] He concluded:

> Our shortcomings and weaknesses were that we were not
> able to destroy a significant number of enemy forces and their
> top leaders. The operations were not effective enough to lend
> leverage to the people's uprising. . . . Therefore, although the
> Political Bureau correctly identified the turning point of the
> war and clearly discerned the precious opportunity it offered . . .
> the approach we employed and the concrete strategic goals we
> set . . . were in effect unrealistic . . . They also underestimated
> the US reaction and its capabilities.[29]

26 Bergerud, *Dynamics*, p. 216.
27 Oberdorfer, *Tet!*, p. 231.
28 Tra, 'General offensive and general uprising', p. 42.
29 Ibid., pp. 52–3.

General Tran Do, who played an influential part in the offensive, concurred: 'Had the Politburo given the campaign a less ambitious name ... and had it clearly stated the campaign's limited objectives, then the people in the fields would have been able to come up with better plans for the attacks and would have made better use of the forces available to them'.[30]

Many commentators have smugly pointed out that the offensive failed to spark *khoi nghia*, a judgement as indisputable as it is simplistic. The attacks could not have taken place without the substantial support of the local population to shelter guerrillas, hide weapons and provide sustenance. In some places, such as Tra Vinh in the Mekong Delta, locals did revolt, at considerable cost to themselves.[31] But the Politburo once again misjudged the mood of the average peasant – a *general* uprising did not occur. *Attentisme* still prevailed: civilians realized that the communists would eventually win the war, but until that eventuality occurred, it made sense to lie low.

By any reckoning, the Tet Offensive was a strategic blunder. But some credit is due to American forces for ensuring this outcome. They performed with extraordinary courage, resilience and adaptibility, particularly during the crucial first day. Quick-witted, highly skilled troops prevented strategically important sites like Tan Son Nhut airbase from falling into the hands of the insurgents, thus foiling the offensive. It was also fortunate that so many soldiers were in the right place at the right time. Hanoi's strategy was based on the fact that Westmoreland had deployed his troops in the hinterlands; in other words, cities and towns would be attacked while American defenders were occupied elsewhere. But on 10 January General Frederick Weyand, commander of American ground forces in the provinces surrounding Saigon, presented Westmoreland with intelligence which suggested an imminent threat to the capital. Westmoreland decided to bring half the battalions in the hinterlands closer to base. As a result, when the PLAF struck, it encountered not lightly defended objectives, but the cream of the American force.

'The enemy has been badly beaten', *Quan Doi Nahn Dan,* the communist military paper, announced. But 'he still remains very stubborn' and the 'struggle is still very difficult'.[32] But it would continue. Hanoi's response to failure was familiar. When plans go awry, the customary response is to launch renewed attacks, with greater intensity.

30 Long, 'Aftermath', p. 116.
31 Harrison, *Endless War*, p. 270. See also Long, 'Aftermath', pp. 101–5.
32 Gabriel Kolko, *Anatomy of a War* (New York, NY, 1994), p. 309.

If a door is locked, push harder. The pushing continued for the next 18 months – the bloodiest period of the war. In some places, genuine success was achieved. But the revolution paid a bitter cost. By the end of the offensive, victory was more remote than it had been on the eve of Tet. According to an official history, the Politburo concluded that 'although Tet had been a great victory and a turning point in the war, further military successes might be delayed for years'.[33] It required a healthy optimism not to be bothered by the inherent contradiction in that statement.

PANIC IN WASHINGTON

In the immediate aftermath of the Tet attacks, Westmoreland announced that the enemy had suffered a 'colossal military defeat'. The US had 'never been in a better position in South Vietnam'.[34] As usual, he had statistics at hand to 'prove' his case. The PLAF, according to conservative estimates, suffered 40,000 deaths, compared to 1,100 Americans and 2,300 ARVN.[35] Westmoreland wanted an immediate shift in strategy to exploit this 'great opportunity',[36] namely amphibious operations against bases in North Vietnam, attacks upon sanctuaries in Laos and Cambodia and an intensified bombing offensive. 'I saw the ability to destroy the enemy's ability to continue the war', he later commented.[37] All this required more troops. After discussions with Wheeler in Saigon, Westmoreland asked for approximately 206,000 additional men, a figure high enough to force the mobilization of reserves.

On 27 February Wheeler cabled Johnson that Tet had been 'a very near thing'. The enemy had 'suffered severely', but 'with replacements, his indoctrination system would seem capable of maintaining morale at a generally adequate level. His determination appears to be unshaken.'[38] While Wheeler's assessment might indeed have been sincere, he probably thought that a gloomy picture increased the chances of the troop request being approved. 'Westy's forces are stretched thin in view of the enemy threat and the course of action open to the

33 Duiker, *Sacred War*, p. 216.

34 Robert Buzzanco, 'The myth of Tet: American failure and the politics of war', in Gilbert and Head, eds, *Tet Offensive*, p. 247.

35 Currey, 'Giap and Tet Mau Than 1968', p. 84.

36 Herring, *America's Longest War*, p. 193.

37 William Westmoreland, *A Soldier Reports* (Garden City, NY, 1976), p. 355. See also Charles F. Brower, 'Strategic reassessment in Vietnam: the Westmoreland "Alternate Strategy" of 1967–1968', *Naval War College Review* 44 (1991), pp. 20–51.

38 Herring, *Pentagon Papers*, p. 214.

enemy', he added in another cable to the President. 'I do not have any apprehension that we will be run out of the country by military action, but I do believe that to achieve victory we must expand our effort substantially and promptly.'[39]

In public, Johnson still projected a combative attitude. 'I do not believe we will ever buckle', he told reporters. 'There will be blood, sweat and tears shed. The weak will drop from the lines, their feet sore and their voices loud. Persevere in Vietnam we will and we must.'[40] But Johnson's brave face was merely cosmetic. Lady Bird Johnson admitted that her husband was 'deeply worried' about the war.[41] He was painfully aware that, if he rejected Westmoreland's request, he might lose the war, yet if he approved it, he might lose the election. Tet had destroyed the illusion of his 'middle way': limited war would no longer suffice. In that sense, Hanoi's strategy had succeeded brilliantly. Uncertain what to do, Johnson looked to Clark Clifford, who would shortly succeed McNamara, for a solution. 'I thought that a new pair of eyes and a fresh outlook should guide this study', Johnson later explained. Privately, he told Clifford: 'Give me the lesser of evils'.[42]

Clifford's deliberations occurred against a backdrop of public anxiety. 'The American people', the *Wall Street Journal* commented, 'should be getting ready to accept, if they haven't already, the prospect that the whole Vietnam effort may be doomed, that it may be falling apart beneath our feet.'[43] Apparently, that realization had already dawned. Gallup found that one person in five shifted from hawk to dove between early February and mid-March.[44] Confidence in Johnson's handling of the war was rapidly evaporating. Before Tet, public support stood at 39 per cent, afterwards it plummeted to 26 per cent.[45] On 27 February the CBS anchorman Walter Cronkite struck at the heart of Middle America's unease:

> We have been too often disappointed by the optimism of the American leaders, both in Vietnam and Washington, to have faith any longer in the silver linings they find in the darkest clouds. . . . For it seems now more certain than ever that the bloody experience of Vietnam is to end in stalemate.[46]

39 Larry Berman, 'The Tet offensive', in Gilbert and Head, eds, *Tet Offensive*, p. 40.
40 Ibid., p. 43.
41 Lady Bird Johnson, *White House Diary* (London, 1970), p. 702.
42 Lyndon Baines Johnson, *The Vantage Point* (London, 1971), pp. 392–3.
43 Oberdorfer, *Tet!*, p. 245.
44 Ibid., p. 241.
45 David M. Barrett, *Uncertain Warriors* (Lawrence, KS, 1973), p. 113.
46 Berman, 'The Tet offensive', p. 43.

Frank McGee of NBC, eager to get in on the act, commented:

> Today . . . the President has before him a request for another
> two hundred thousand men . . . This has brought warnings the
> enemy will match any new force we put in the field. All that
> would be changed would be the capacity for destruction. . . .
> Laying aside all other arguments, the time is at hand when we
> must decide whether it is futile to destroy Vietnam in the effort
> to save it.[47]

Many Americans, even those who supported the war, justifiably wondered why, if communist forces had been so decisively beaten during Tet, Westmoreland needed so many more troops.

The Johnson administration could not ignore the national temper. Under the circumstances, it would have been extremely difficult to sell further escalation to the American people. But, when Clifford formulated his advice, he was not guided by the popular mood. As he confessed:

> We can no longer rely just on the field commander. He can
> want troops and want troops and want troops. We must look
> at the overall impact on us, including the situation here in the
> United States. We must look at our economic stability, our
> other problems in the world, our other problems at home; we
> must consider whether or not this thing is tying us down so that
> we cannot do some of the other things we should be doing.

McNamara estimated that Westmoreland's demands would cost US$2.5 billion in 1968, US$10 billion in 1969 and US$15 billion in 1970, leading to rampant inflation, skyrocketing taxes, or both.[48] They were also strategically unsound. 'I do not understand what the strategy is in putting in 205,000 men', McNamara confessed. 'It is neither enough to do the job, nor an indication that our role must change.'[49] In his advice to Johnson, Clifford argued:

> The country we are trying to save is being subjected to
> enormous damage. Perhaps the country we are trying to save is
> relying on the United States too much. When we look ahead,
> we find that we may actually be denigrating their ability to take
> over their own country rather than contributing to their ability
> to do it.[50]

47 Oberdorfer, *Tet!*, p. 273.
48 Lloyd Gardner, *Pay Any Price* (Chicago, IL, 1995), pp. 436, 440.
49 Barrett, ed., *Johnson's Vietnam Papers*, p. 628.
50 Ibid., p. 644.

'I was convinced that the military course we were pursuing was not only endless, but hopeless', Clifford later reflected.[51] He recommended that Westmoreland's request be denied and that henceforth efforts should be made to shift the military burden toward the ARVN. Johnson agreed with the thrust of Clifford's recommendations and approved only a token troop increase of 22,000.

Admiral U.S.G. Sharp, at the time Commander-in-Chief, Pacific (CINCPAC), reflected on Johnson's decision:

> The reality of the 1968 Tet offensive was that Hanoi had taken a big gamble and had lost on the battlefield . . . Our powerful air force and navy air resources were poised and ready. We could have flattened every war-making facility in North Vietnam. But the handwringers had center stage; the anti-war elements were in full cry. The most powerful country in the world did not have the willpower needed to meet the situation.

Sharp blamed 'the rampant sensationalism of the media' which ensured that 'a traumatic aura of defeatism was generated at the seat of government'.[52] Westmoreland made a similar accusation: 'American reporters undoubtedly contributed to the psychological victory the enemy achieved in the United States. . . . In the race to drain every possible sensation . . . reporters made little apparent effort to check facts.'[53] The argument that the media prevented the exploitation of a major victory after Tet, and thus perhaps even squandered victory in the war, remains durably popular to this day. Those who find the American defeat difficult to swallow find in the fourth estate an easy scapegoat.

'Rarely has contemporary crisis-journalism turned out, in retrospect, to have veered so widely from reality', Peter Braestrup argues. 'To have portrayed such a setback for one side as a defeat for the other . . . cannot be counted as a triumph for American journalism.'[54] But journalists *always* misunderstand the battles they witness. Commanders often do so too – that is called the fog of war. To argue that journalists *wilfully* misreported Tet in order to create opposition to the war or sell papers, as some have done, is a bogus accusation unworthy of serious consideration. Those who blame the press for

51 Clark M. Clifford, 'A Vietnam reappraisal: the personal history of one man's view and how it evolved', *Foreign Affairs,* (July 1969), p. 613.

52 U.S.G. Sharp, *Strategy for Defeat* (Novato, CA, 1978), pp. 215, 218.

53 Westmoreland, *Soldier Reports*, p. 325.

54 Braestrup, *Big Story*, p. 508.

171

defeat in the war tend to forget how, up to 1968, most journalists willingly relayed Westmoreland's rosy assessments to a gullible public.[55]

Even Braestrup realizes that it is difficult to make a connection between public opinion and the reporting of the war:

> There is nothing to show that there was a decisive drop in support [for the war] during February–March 1968. Mass public opinion had shown a steady downward decline since 1965. . . . In any case, public opinion didn't go through the floor at Tet. What did drop was the popularity of the president of the United States. . . .
>
> Tet was a disaster for Johnson at the personal level. The reason the press and TV were incoherent at Tet was that the government was incoherent at Tet.[56]

The media reflected, it did not create, the public despondency. Harry McPherson, a presidential aide who had access to top secret military assessments of the war, eventually came to believe 'what I saw on the tube' because, like many other Americans, he 'was fed up with the "light at the end of the tunnel" stuff. I was fed up with the optimism that seemed to flow without stopping from Saigon.'[57]

But the main fallacy in Sharp's argument is the assumption that a greater military effort could have won the war. In judging the outcome of Tet, he draws the same erroneous conclusions from the 'kill ratio' that Westmoreland made during the war. Vietnam demonstrated that American cultural conceptions of 'acceptable loss' could not be applied to the enemy. As Tra explains: 'Certain people must have seen those battles as defeats, and could only see the dark side of death. But in our eyes, those fallen heroes had won.'[58] The war could not be won by killing lots of communists. Ellsworth Bunker, US ambassador to the RVN, at the time concluded that the offensive 'revealed more clearly than ever before the nature and extent of Viet Cong organization, discipline and power. It confirmed what has been said many times, that the solution of the Vietnam problem must be political, not simply military.'[59]

55 For a contrary view of the role of the press in the war, and especially during Tet, see Oberdorfer, *Tet!*, and Daniel C. Hallin, *The Uncensored War* (New York, NY, 1986). Kathleen Turner, in *Lyndon Johnson's Dual War* (Chicago, IL, 1985), takes a balanced view of the media's effect upon the Johnson presidency.

56 Braestrup, 'A look back at Tet 1968', in John Norton Moore, ed., *The Vietnam Debate* (Lanham, MD, 1990), pp. 266–7.

57 Herbert Y. Schandler, *The Unmaking of a President* (Princeton, NJ, 1977), p. 82.

58 Tra, 'General offensive and general uprising', p. 62.

59 Larry Cable, *Unholy Grail* (London, 1991), p. 220

The Tet Offensive is one is one of the battlegrounds on which opposing schools in the Vietnam debate fight. The simplistic 'military victory/psychological defeat' explanation is favoured by those like Sharp and Phillip Davidson who cannot accept that Vietnam was in any sense a defeat of American forces.[60] It provides the enticing opportunity to blame the war's outcome on a collapse of will within American society. On the other side, Marilyn Young, James Harrison and Gabriel Kolko, among others, encourage the assumption that a psychological defeat of the Americans was always part of Hanoi's grand plan.[61] All of the explanations unfortunately have pieces missing which render the nature of the puzzle unclear. To understand the aims and outcome of Tet requires an appreciation of communist strategy, American perceptions *and* the state of affairs on the ground in Vietnam. The collection of essays edited by Marc Jason Gilbert and William Head, by approaching the problem from many different angles, provides the most plausible reconstruction of the tumultuous events.[62]

According to Tra, 'Tet . . . shook the enemy's aggressive will to its foundation and put an end to the US dream of achieving "victory" by escalating the war; it awakened the United States to the fact that might, resources and money have their limits'.[63] That is an accurate assessment. Tet *was* a psychological defeat for the Americans. Those inclined to admire all things emanating from Hanoi conclude that clever communists planned this outcome. After the war, Giap encouraged this interpretation: 'we wanted to project the war into the homes of America's families, because we knew that most of them had nothing against us'.[64] This is tripe, all the more indigestible coming from a man who originally considered the offensive insane. Granted, the communists were expert propagandists; they did monitor the war's effect upon the American people. But no nation is so stupid as to sacrifice thousands of its soldiers for the elusive hope of a psychological victory. Tet was supposed to lead to a decisive *military* victory, not to a massive defeat which could be packaged as a psychological victory. Tran Do admitted: 'In all honesty, we didn't achieve our main objective,

---

60 See Sharp, *Strategy for Defeat*, and Phillip B. Davidson, *Vietnam at War* (Oxford, 1988), passim.

61 See Harrison, *Endless War*, Kolko, *Anatomy*, and Marilyn Young, *The Vietnam Wars, 1945–1990* (New York, NY, 1991).

62 Gilbert and Head, eds, *Tet Offensive*. Eric Bergerud's explanation in *Dynamics of Defeat* also seems very sensible.

63 Tra, 'General offensive and general uprising', p. 60.

64 S. Karnow, 'An interview with General Giap', in W. Capps, ed., *The Vietnam Reader* (New York, NY, 1991), pp. 133–4.

which was to spur uprisings throughout the south. . . . As for making an impact in the United States, it had not been our intention – but it turned out to be a fortunate result.'[65]

ENTER ROBERT KENNEDY

The Tet débâcle was a boon to McCarthy. On 12 March voters went to the polls in the New Hampshire primary, the first test in the presidential race. McCarthy drew 42 per cent in the Democratic primary. Johnson was not on the ballot, but a write-in campaign yielded 49 per cent. It was technically a victory for the President, but technicalities were irrelevant. By any measure, the result was a disaster. Those who wanted a quick end to the war immediately interpreted the result as an endorsement of their position. But, ironically, psephologists later discovered that, among those who voted for McCarthy, hawks outnumbered doves by three to two, an indication that his appeal was more anti-Johnson than anti-war.[66]

Lurking in the background was Robert Kennedy, the senator from New York, who despised Johnson as much as Johnson despised him. Since entering the Senate in 1966, RFK had urged a radical expansion of the Great Society and conciliation toward North Vietnam, policies popular with anti-war liberals. By early 1967, polls taken on university campuses revealed that Kennedy was the students' undisputed hero.[67] In tones reminiscent of his brother, he told Berkeley students that they had 'the opportunity and the responsibility to help make the choices which will determine the greatness of this nation. . . . If you shrink from this struggle . . . you will betray the trust which your own position forces upon you.'[68]

But this left Kennedy open to charges of hypocrisy, since he shrank from that same struggle. He earnestly believed that Johnson was unfit to be President and that 'We've got to get out of Vietnam . . . It's destroying the country.'[69] But pragmatic considerations rendered him reluctant to enter the race. He preferred to wait until 1972. To oppose

---

65 Currey, 'Giap and Tet Mau Than 1968', p. 84.

66 Braestrup, 'A look back', p. 266.

67 RFK Papers: 1968 Presidential Campaign Papers; Press Division, box 14, John F. Kennedy Library (JFKL).

68 Kennedy, speech to students at University of California at Berkeley, 22 October 1966. RFK Senate Papers: Speeches and Press Releases; box 3, JFKL. See also Clare White, 'Two responses to student protest: Ronald Reagan and Robert Kennedy', in Gerard DeGroot, ed., *Student Protest: The Sixties and After* (London, 1998), pp. 117–30.

69 Blum, *Discord*, p. 295.

Johnson now would, Kennedy feared, cause voters to conclude 'that I was splitting the party out of ambition and envy. No one would believe that I was doing it because of how I felt about Vietnam and poor people.'[70] Kennedy was also keenly aware that, before Tet, there was little chance of winning. He was sufficiently prudent not to commit political suicide for the sake of a principle. But McCarthy's performance in New Hampshire demonstrated that Johnson was vulnerable. RFK declared his candidacy on 16 March 1968. 'These are not ordinary times', he said, 'and this is not an ordinary election.'[71] To some he seemed a messiah, to others a cynical opportunist.

EXIT JOHNSON

On the announcement of Kennedy's candidacy, Johnson went ballistic. He would, he promised, destroy 'that grandstanding little runt'.[72] Through bluster, he attempted to reassert his authority over the nation and the war. 'Let's get one thing clear', he informed his aides, 'I am not going to stop the bombing.' 'Make no mistake about it', he told one audience; 'We are going to win.'[73] But whistling, or even shouting, in the dark did not frighten away the demons. On 26 March a much more subdued Johnson summoned a group of senior advisers (the 'Wise Men') to give their thoughts on the war. Included were McGeorge Bundy, George Ball, Matthew Ridgeway, Maxwell Taylor, Cyrus Vance and Dean Acheson. The previous November, the same group had given an overwhelming endorsement of the war effort. Now, shaken by Tet, few could muster confidence. As an indication of how times had changed, Bundy confessed: 'I must tell you what I thought I would never say – that I now agree with George Ball'.[74] Though Taylor still pushed for escalation, the majority favoured disengagement. Acheson summarized the general feeling: 'The issue is can we do what we are trying to do in Vietnam. I do not think we can. . . . The issue is can we by military means keep the North Vietnamese off the South Vietnamese. I do not think we can.'[75] This was

---

70 Jack Newfield, *Robert Kennedy, A Memoir* (New York, NY, 1988), p. 186.

71 Larry Berman, *Lyndon Johnson's War* (New York, NY, 1989), p. 187.

72 Blum, *Discord*, p. 300. See also Jeff Shesol, *Mutual Contempt: Lyndon Johnson, Robert Kennedy, and the Feud that Defined a Decade* (New York, NY, 1997); and Paul R. Henggeller, *In His Steps: Lyndon Johnson and the Kennedy Mystique* (Chicago, IL, 1991).

73 Gardner, *Pay Any Price*, p. 447.

74 George Ball, *The Past Has Another Pattern* (New York, NY, 1982), p. 408.

75 William Appleman Williams *et al.*, eds, *America in Vietnam: A Documentary History* (New York, NY, 1975), p. 272.

not the conclusion Johnson had sought, but neither was it one he could ignore. The 'establishment bastards' had deserted him.[76]

In a televised speech on 31 March, Johnson, shocked by Tet and worn down by public acrimony, announced a halt to the bombing offensive above the 20th parallel and invited Hanoi to the conference table. Then came perhaps the most dramatic and shocking ending to any presidential speech in American history: 'I shall not seek, and I will not accept, the nomination of my party for another term as your President'.[77]

Jack Valenti, the President's friend and assistant, spoke to Johnson two days later. 'He was calm, almost serene, as if whatever plague had been visited upon him was now exiled from his mind and heart.' Valenti asked: 'Why would you do this? You can beat Nixon.' The President nodded.

> Yes, I think I would beat him. But [the race] would be too close for me to be able to govern. The nation would be polarized. Besides, the presidency isn't fun anymore. Everything has turned mean. No matter what I accomplish, the damn war infects everything.

After a short pause, Johnson elaborated:

> I hope my speech will prove to the Vietnamese that I have no political agenda, that I am no longer going to be president next year. Maybe they will understand that all I want is to negotiate something that is fair and honorable, so we can get out – and now. That ought to appeal to them, I think. This is the best way to do it. I'm free now to end this goddamned war.[78]

Johnson was no coward. A veteran of many bruising political campaigns, he was not the sort to shirk the contest which lay ahead. Though he was not always an honest man, one is inclined to believe his reasons for dropping out. It is a measure of the man that he recognized that the welfare of the nation and the cause of peace were better served if he did not run. 'I never was surer of any decision I ever made in my life', he confessed at the time. 'I have 525,000 men whose very lives depend on what I do, and I must not be worried about primaries.'[79]

---

76 Roger Morris, *An Uncertain Greatness: Henry Kissinger and American Foreign Policy* (New York, NY, 1977), p. 44.

77 Williams *et al.*, eds, *America in Vietnam*, p. 275.

78 Jack Valenti, 'The night LBJ surrendered', *George*, (March 1998).

79 Johnson, *Vantage Point*, p. 436.

Momentous events in Washington did not profoundly alter the character of the war. Both sides attempted to exploit a perceived military advantage after Tet. As a result, 1968 became the bloodiest year of the war. Westmoreland, mortally wounded by the Tet embarrassment, was kicked upstairs, becoming Army Chief of Staff. He was replaced by Creighton Abrams. Johnson still hoped that a noncommunist South Vietnam could be firmly established, but did not come up with any distinctively different strategies to achieve this purpose, other than more of the same. The effort to shift the military burden to the Vietnamese was given added urgency; American taxpayers liberally financed the ARVN's expansion. In the South, the air war was intensified; bombers dropped huge payloads on sometimes flimsy intelligence of insurgent activity. The Accelerated Pacification Program sought to extend control of the hinterlands in anticipation of a peace deal, and the Phoenix Program eliminated insurgents by whatever sinister means.[80] Johnson was racing against time to shape the war in a way that would allow his eventual absolution by historians. But the limiting factor was American patience: 'the collapse of the home front', Johnson realized, 'was just what Hanoi was counting on'.[81]

TWO TRAGEDIES: LOS ANGELES AND CHICAGO

Johnson had pulled out of the race, but was still determined to win through his surrogate, Humphrey, who declared his candidacy in late April. Humphrey was Johnson neutered and lobotomized, a decent but spineless man who lacked the leadership attributes which the portentous times demanded. Homilies about restoring the 'politics of happiness, the politics of purpose and the politics of joy' had as much relevance to the crises the nation faced as an aspirin to a terminal cancer patient.[82] But Humphrey could rely on those who would have supported Johnson, still a large constituency. He could also depend upon the Democratic city machines, particularly that of Mayor Richard Daley of Chicago, where the convention would be held. Without doing, or being, anything, he became the frontrunner.

Unlike McCarthy, RFK realized that the election could not be won exclusively on the anti-war vote. But the more he tried to widen his constituency, the more contradictions he encountered. If he pushed for the expansion of the Great Society, he risked losing working-class

---

80 Phoenix is explained in greater depth in Chapter 8.
81 Johnson, *Vantage Point*, p. 422.
82 Kim McQuaid, *The Anxious Years* (New York, NY, 1989), p. 34.

Democrats fearful of higher taxes. If he spoke out against the war, he alienated those who still supported it. During one interview, he made a clear concession to the anti-war lobby: 'I don't think that we're automatically correct or automatically right and morality is on our side . . . because we're involved in a war'. But then, moments later, he suggested that there was still a virtuous task to be accomplished in Vietnam: 'it's important that the United States associate itself with – with those forces within a country who are in favor not just of change for change's sake, but – but for a better life for the people of these nations'.[83]

Victories in the Indiana, Nebraska and District of Columbia primaries demonstrated that Kennedy was the only candidate who could poll well among those who represented the future of the party and those of its past. Then came the California primary on 3 June, which Kennedy won with 46 per cent to McCarthy's 42. At his victory address, Kennedy called upon McCarthy supporters to cast aside their differences and join his campaign. He felt that the momentum was his, and that it was strong enough even to overwhelm Humphrey. 'On to Chicago and let's win there', he told the admiring throng in Los Angeles. A few moments later he was dead.

Kennedy was the only man in America who could embrace radical students, blacks *and* working-class whites worried by the deepening divisions in their society. His ties to old politics won him the support of traditional Democrats, and the 'Kennedy Mystique' – so strong since his brother's assassination – widened his appeal further. But the political commentator Tom Wicker felt that this alliance was not really 'feasible': Kennedy wanted 'to have Mayor Daley's support and the support of the college students. The two are incompatible in the long run.'[84] The student activist Tom Hayden concurred:

> In one corner of his [RFK's] very complicated mind, he believed he could use the structure and then destroy it. Use Mayor Daley to become President and, at the same time, encourage the ghetto to rise up against Mayor Daley. . . . It doesn't work. It leads back to embracing the Mayor Daleys and right wingers because they ultimately become the people you must depend on to remain the leader of their power structure.[85]

83 Transcript, 'Town Meeting of the World', 15 May 1967. RFK Senate Papers, Speeches and Press Releases, Subject File Box 3, JFKL.

84 Jean Stein and George Plimpton, eds, *American Journey. The Life and Times of Robert Kennedy* (New York, NY, 1970), p. 266.

85 Ibid., p. 266.

It is quite possible that Kennedy would have failed in his attempt to unite his party and the nation. It is also quite evident that, after his assassination, there was no one left who could even remotely hope to do so.

Democratic disunity was painfully exposed at the Chicago convention. Though McCarthy made a brief surge after Kennedy's death, there was really no stopping Humphrey. But that did not prevent the party from flagellating itself while the whole world watched. Inside the convention hall, delegates hurled abuse at each other. Outside, Daley's police fought a pitched battle with hordes of young rabble-rousers. There was provocation and excess on both sides, but one expects better of the police. The forces of the establishment were also more organized in their brutality (and better armed) than their counter-cultural foes.

Amid the tumult, the convention endorsed Johnson's candidate and Johnson's Vietnam policy. While the party tore itself apart, Humphrey spouted platitudes. 'Put aside recrimination and disunion', he urged. 'Turn away from violence and hatred.'[86] Had he been speaking from an Apollo space capsule orbiting the Earth, he could not have been more detached from the strife which engulfed him. Theodore White, perennial chronicler of presidential campaigns, observing the Chicago spectacle, wrote: 'The Democratic Party is finished.'[87]

THE NEW NIXON

The National Commission on Violence concluded that the Chicago police had been 'unrestrained and indiscriminate' in dealing with the demonstrations. Yet, when polled, only one in five Americans expressed the opinion that too much force had been used.[88] Within this difference of opinion lay a promising political constituency. The country was turning against the war but still despised those who stridently opposed it. Of the candidates who remained in the race, only Nixon could capitalize on this anomaly. He sought to build a candidacy from what he called the 'forgotten Americans, those who did not indulge in violence, those who did not break the law, people who pay their taxes and go to work, people who send their children to school, who go to their churches, people who are not haters, people who love this country'.[89]

86 Blum, *Discord*, p. 309.
87 Ibid., p. 308.
88 Ibid., pp. 310–11.
89 Ibid., pp. 313–14.

The opinion polls suggested that the American people were steadily losing faith in the war. But polls are easily misinterpreted. Throughout the war, the standard question asked of Americans was: 'Do you support continued American action in Vietnam?' – or a variation thereof. Those who answered 'No' were carelessly labelled 'doves', those who said 'yes' were crudely termed 'hawks'. But the 'Nos' spanned a wide variety of opinions. Some were genuine pacifists. Others were troubled by the nature of this war, its morality or lack of purpose. Others had pragmatically decided that the war could not be won at tolerable cost. When people crossed the line from hawk to dove, they took their political principles with them, discarding only their unquestioning support for the war. The new doves, in other words, were still patriotic citizens who believed in the good of their country. While keen for an end to the war, they did not want to sacrifice American honour. This explains why the 1968 election did not produce an avowed peace candidate, despite the loud demands for peace across the country. It also explains why Nixon's platform was so appealing: though he promised to withdraw the troops he would still aggressively defend American values.

In stark contrast to the agonized process by which Humphrey emerged as Democratic candidate, the selection of Nixon was smooth, dignified and peaceful. His campaign was helped enormously by the independent candidacy of George Wallace, whose bigoted conservatism appealed to traditional working-class Democrats disenchanted with Johnsonian liberalism and still determined to win the war. In order to limit Wallace's appeal, Nixon brought on board as his running mate Spiro Agnew, the thuggish Governor of Maryland whose penchant for populist banter made him a folk hero among those who liked their politics raucous, profane and simple.

Nixon's victory at first seemed a certainty. Vague references to a 'secret plan' to end the war satisfied those inclined to wishful thinking. He would bring 'fresh ideas' which eluded the 'tired men around the president'.[90] Since the people had grown disenchanted with Johnson, they were not about to get inspired by a pale imitation. But, late in the campaign, Humphrey rallied, helped in part by an erosion of the Wallace vote. Even hawks felt uncomfortable when Wallace's running mate, General Curtis LeMay, boasted about bombing North Vietnam 'back to the Stone Age'.[91] But Humphrey also did himself a service when he publicly distanced himself from Johnson. In Salt Lake

90 Gardner, *Pay Any Price*, p. 516.
91 Blum, *Discord*, p. 314.

City on 30 September, he promised to stop the bombing of North Vietnam 'as an acceptable risk for peace'. He further proposed to 'take the risk that the South Vietnamese would meet the responsibilities they say they are now ready to assume in their own self-defense'.[92] In truth this was not a far cry from Johnson's own policies at that very moment, but the American people thought it a significant departure. Humphrey's 'conversion' rendered him acceptable among those whose support for Nixon had been heavily laden with fear.

Humphrey was also helped by a sudden breakthrough in the peace negotiations. Talks in Paris had gone nowhere; Hanoi's intransigence was easily matched by Washington's. Then, under pressure from party leaders keen to avert electoral disaster, Johnson indicated to W. Averell Harriman, his Paris negotiator, that he would halt the bombing in exchange for concessions from the North Vietnamese. Hanoi responded positively, and a vague arrangement was tentatively accepted calling for negotiations which would include the RVN government and, crucially, the NLF. The deal had the backing of President Thieu. On 31 October Johnson announced to the nation that he was stopping the bombing. But on the next day Thieu reversed his position. Anna Chan Chennault, co-chairwoman of Republican Women for Nixon, had used her considerable Asian connections to stir up opposition to the peace plan in Saigon, promising Thieu that he would get a better deal from Nixon.

On 5 November Nixon secured 43.4 per cent of the vote, Humphrey 42.7 per cent, and Wallace 13.5 per cent. Given the tiny margin of victory, it is intriguing to conjecture whether Humphrey might have won if not for Chennault's scheming. Such speculation appeals because the sordid affair seems in keeping with the corrupt character of Nixon.[93] But the Democrats lost the election; they did not have it stolen from them. They squandered the constituency which had served them well for so long. Humphrey lost because blue-collar workers deserted the party for Nixon or Wallace, because the Old South had become a no-go area for Democrats, and because many blacks and anti-war liberals decided to stay at home on election day.

Nixon won the victory which might have been Johnson's. According to Valenti, Johnson bowed out because he knew the election would be too close and the nation would be polarized. He was right. Far from uniting the country around a single candidate, the election tore open

92 Theodore H. White, *The Making of the President 1968* (New York, NY, 1969), p. 441.
93 See Jeffrey Kimball, *Nixon's Vietnam War* (Lawrence, KS, 1998), pp. 56–62.

wounds and poured salt on them. Nixon did not have the temperament or grace to act as healer.

POSTSCRIPT

The Tet Offensive was a turning point in the war, but, for Hanoi, a turn in the wrong direction. The communists were winning the war before the offensive; they were a shattered force after it. The PLAF was virtually destroyed; the PAVN had henceforth to shoulder a much greater burden of combat. As for the US, it fought for two and a half years before Tet, and five years after it. Nearly as many Americans died after the battle as before. Johnson was a mediocre Commander-in-Chief whose direction of the war was deeply flawed. By 1968, McNamara was a broken man and his replacement, Clifford, could not muster enthusiasm for an aggressive war. In their place came Richard Nixon, Henry Kissinger and an assorted group of very hard men who, though intent on disengagement, were nevertheless determined to make North Vietnam pay dearly. In this light, the Tet Offensive hardly seems a clever psychological victory. It was in fact a colossal blunder which prolonged the war, causing unnecessary suffering on both sides.[94] The true nature of the calamity might be gauged from the reaction of Ho Chi Minh. According to the historian Thai Van Kiem, Ho 'silently regretted not having listened to Vo Nguyen Giap ... Following this burning debacle, Ho's health declined day by day. He never got over this defeat. Unable even to sleep, he died the next year, in 1969.'[95]

94 I am grateful to Eric Bergerud, whose argument I have summarized here. See *Dynamics of Defeat*, chaps 6, 7 and 8.
95 Currey, 'Giap and Tet Mau Than 1968', p. 84.

7   ROLLING THUNDER

Vietnam was a bomber's war. The US and its allies dropped almost 8 million tons of bombs in all theatres, over double the tonnage dropped by Allied powers during the Second World War. During the peak years of the Rolling Thunder campaign, an average of 800 tons of bombs per day were targeted on North Vietnam, or roughly 300 pounds per resident per year.[1] Yet this massive campaign had no significant effect upon the outcome of the war.

'The aeroplane is the offensive weapon *par excellence*', wrote General Giulio Douhet before the Second World War. The marriage of manned flight and high explosives brought new meaning to the concept of total war. 'No longer can areas exist in which life can be lived in safety and tranquillity', Douhet argued, 'nor can the battlefield any longer be limited to actual combatants.' Enthusiasts assumed that since the bomber would always get through, the nature of war had permanently changed. 'To have command of the air means to be in a position to wield offensive power so great that it defies human imagination', wrote Douhet. '*To be defeated* in the air . . . is . . . to be at the mercy of the enemy . . . compelled to accept whatever terms he sees fit to dictate.'[2]

Douhet's thesis was tested in the Second World War, with mixed results. German bombers were unable to destroy the will of the British people, nor were they able to cripple Britain's industries. Allied bombers, in a campaign of unprecedented intensity, could not bring Germany to its knees. Studies suggest that British and German morale actually rose during bombing campaigns. But, despite this evidence, advocates of strategic bombing emerged from the war with faith intact.[3]

1 Earl H. Tilford, 'Why and how the US Air Force lost in Vietnam', *Armed Forces and Society* 17 (Spring, 1991), p. 327.

2 Giulio Douhet, *The Command of the Air*, trans. Dino Ferrari (New York, NY, 1942), pp. 12–16.

3 This is, admittedly, my judgement on the effectiveness of the Second World War campaigns, though it is widely shared. Others, of course, disagree. For a summary of the opposing view, see Melden E. Smith Jr, 'The strategic bombing debate: the Second World War and Vietnam', *Journal of Contemporary History* 12 (1977), pp. 175–91.

Modern nations love to bomb. The two world wars placed a high premium on human lives, contributing to a widespread determination to avoid repetition of the carnage. Bombers offered apparent salvation from high casualty ground battles. They seemed a cheap way of waging war – cheap in lives lost, if expensive in weaponry. The dramatic impact of bombs allowed aircrews to wage symbolic war disproportionate to their actual contribution. The loss of a crew, while tragic, seemed miniscule in comparison to its offensive contribution. But as British Air Marshal John Slessor argued in 1954, the bomber's perceived value was grossly inflated. Citing evidence from Korea, he warned that there was no 'short cut to victory . . . The idea that superior air power can in some way be a substitute for hard slogging and professional skill on the ground . . . is beguiling but illusory.'[4] Enthusiasm nevertheless remained buoyant. 'The Korean War was a special case', Air Force Secretary Thomas Finletter insisted. 'Air power can learn little from there about its future role.'[5]

Bombs are notoriously inaccurate, as Second World War statistics revealed. Bombers of the Vietnam generation were, admittedly, more accurate, but targets were harder to hit. The more primitive the war effort the more difficult it is to destroy from the air. Small makeshift arms factories were hard to find and the largely truck-based transport system was less vulnerable than a rail system would have been. But air commanders stubbornly ignored these indications of their arm's impotence: 'To moan the lack of strategic targets . . . and therefore conclude that air power is limited is to overlook the inherent flexibility of the air vehicle', a 1962 report concluded. 'There is no such thing as limitations or impossible conditions, only incorrect tactics or poor employment.'[6]

Early bombing raids had a mainly psychological purpose. The Flaming Dart missions against targets in the DRV were direct reprisals for specific PLAF raids in the South. As McGeorge Bundy explained to Johnson on 7 February 1965, the day after the raid on Pleiku: 'our primary target in advocating a reprisal policy is the improvement of the situation in *South* Vietnam'.[7] 'Sustained reprisals'

---

4 M.J. Armitage and R.A. Mason, *Air Power in the Nuclear Age* (Chicago, IL, 1983), p. 45.

5 Ibid., p. 18.

6 Dennis Drew, 'Wars of the third kind and Air Force doctrine', 1996 Vietnam Symposium, Texas Tech University Vietnam Center website.

7 George C. Herring, ed., *The Pentagon Papers*, abridged edn (New York, NY, 1993), p. 111.

would enable the US 'to speak in Vietnam on many topics and in many ways, with growing force and effectiveness'.[8] They would hearten the Saigon regime, frighten the NLF, demonstrate American resolve, and eventually erode the will of the North. Maxwell Taylor argued that it was not even necessary for targets of 'intrinsic military value' to be hit. The 'really important target is the will of the leaders of Hanoi . . . virtually any target north of the 19th parallel' would 'convey the necessary message'.[9] 'As practical men, they cannot wish to see the fruits of ten years labor destroyed by slowly escalating air attacks.'[10] Bundy admitted:

> We cannot assert that a policy of sustained reprisal will succeed in changing the course of the contest in Vietnam. It may fail, and we cannot estimate the odds of success with any accuracy – they may be somewhere between 25% and 75%. What we can say is that even if it fails, the policy will be worth it. At a minimum it will drop down the charge that we did not do all that we could have done, and this charge will be important in many countries, including our own.[11]

To George Ball, the logic of bombing the North to save the South seemed distorted. As a director of the Strategic Bombing Survey after the Second World War, he was well-acquainted with the bomber's limitations. There was, he argued, 'little evidence to suggest that the South Vietnamese would have their hearts lifted by watching the North suffer a sustained aerial bombardment'.[12] He later argued that those who argued otherwise were guilty of 'classical bureaucratic casuistry . . . Dropping bombs was a pain-killing exercise that saved my colleagues from having to face the hard decision of having to withdraw.'[13] Johnson was nevertheless swayed by those, like Bundy and Taylor, who argued that bombing would allow the US to avoid the commitment of large ground forces. It seemed a cheap way to make a point in Vietnam. On 13 February he approved Operation Rolling Thunder, a programme of 'measured and limited air action' which would remain in force 'until further notice'.[14]

8 Lloyd C. Gardner, *Pay any Price* (Chicago, IL, 1995), p. 170.
9 H.R. McMaster, *Dereliction of Duty* (New York, NY, 1997), p. 238.
10 Gardner, *Pay any Price*, p. 162.
11 Herring, ed., *Pentagon Papers*, p. 112.
12 Gardner, *Pay any Price*, p. 147.
13 Larry Berman, *Planning a Tragedy* (New York, NY, 1982), p. 45.
14 Herring, ed., *Pentagon Papers*, p. 114.

THE CAMPAIGN

Rolling Thunder began on 2 March 1965. Confidence in American air power and a lack of respect for North Vietnamese resilience encouraged a belief that bombers would achieve their objectives quickly. The JCS envisaged a campaign lasting no more than twelve weeks. Taylor, a bit more pessimistic, argued that it might take six months.[15]

The original Air Force plan listed 94 specific targets whose obliteration would 'destroy North Vietnam's capacity to continue as an industrially viable state'.[16] The JCS endorsed the list and urged Johnson to authorize strikes against all 94 targets. He instead chose to escalate slowly, in the hope that the North's breaking point would be reached at a point short of blanket annihilation. On 17 February McNamara explained that 'we should try to destroy the will of the DRV to continue their political interference and their guerrilla activity. We should try to induce them to get out of the war without having their country destroyed and to realize that if they do not get out, their country will be destroyed.'[17]

The 'slow squeeze', according to McNaughton, would allow the US 'the option at any point to proceed or not, to escalate or not, and to quicken the pace or not'.[18] A memo on 6 April proposed that strikes could be added 'in response to a higher rate of VC activity'.[19] Since guerrilla activity did not abate, what quickly evolved was a steadily escalating sustained bombing campaign. In 1965, 25,000 sorties dropped 63,000 tons of bombs. This increased to 79,000 sorties and 136,000 tons in 1966, 108,000 sorties and 226,000 tons in 1967, and 82,000 sorties and 180,000 tons in 1968.[20]

Central to the strategy was the bombing pause. During the campaign, eight complete halts and seven partial cessations occurred; the former lasting from 24 hours to 36 days.[21] Pauses were designed to give the North time to reflect upon the wisdom of negotiation, or, as Bundy advised, 'We want to keep before Hanoi the carrot of our desisting as well as the stick of continued pressure'.[22] In reality, the pauses backfired. They did not persuade the DRV to negotiate and

15 David Barrett, ed., *Lyndon B. Johnson's Vietnam Papers* (College Station, TX, 1997), p. 153.

16 Drew, 'Wars of the third kind'.

17 Barrett, ed., *Johnson's Vietnam Papers*, p. 122.

18 David Richard Palmer, *Summons of the Trumpet*, 75–6.

19 Barrett, ed., *Johnson's Vietnam Papers*, p. 142.

20 John T. Smith, *Rolling Thunder* (Walton on Thames, 1994), p. 212.

21 Lyndon B. Johnson, *The Vantage Point* (London, 1971), p. 578.

22 Herring, ed., *Pentagon Papers*, p. 112.

forced the US to take up again the mantle of aggressor each time bombing was resumed. 'We received little credit for stopping the bombing and heavy criticism for renewing it', Johnson admitted.[23]

Air Force and Navy targeteers made weekly proposals for bomber strikes, and relayed these up the chain of command, via CINCPAC and the JCS, to McNamara, who presented them at regular Tuesday meetings with Johnson and a few other advisers, all civilians.[24] Approved targets were then relayed back to Vietnam, by the same route. Political considerations remained paramount; targets were chosen with the aim of keeping 'collateral damage' (civilian casualties) to a minimum. The areas around Hanoi and Haiphong, and along the Chinese border, were initially off limits, partly because Johnson was concerned about the consequences of hitting the foreign diplomatic corps which resided in Hanoi, or of striking a Soviet or Chinese vessel in Haiphong harbour. Less than 5 per cent of sorties were directed against strategic targets on the JCS list, an indicator that there was in truth little of significance to bomb.[25] The vast majority were armed reconnaissance missions directed against the transport system, with pilots authorized to strike targets of opportunity within a specified area. In other words, Rolling Thunder became a sustained interdiction campaign of unprecedented intensity. Though figures for sorties flown and bombs dropped seem huge, most bombs were wasted blowing up bits of jungle. The snakes, pigs and tigers on the ground did not have a good war.

ZEALOTS AND DOUBTERS

Just two weeks into the campaign, doubts began to surface. Bundy confessed that it seemed 'questionable' that the DRV could be forced to mend its ways 'under the pressure of our air operations alone'. Taylor admitted that 'no amount of bombardment . . . is going to convince Hanoi to call off its action'.[26] On 29 June a State Department memo concluded that the effect of bombing was

> rather limited . . . convincing evidence indicates that US strikes against North Vietnam have had no significantly harmful effect

---

23 Johnson, *Vantage Point*, p. 235.

24 It was not until late 1967 that General Wheeler, Chairman of the JCS, joined the meetings.

25 Smith, *Rolling Thunder*, p. 212. See also Douglas Pike, 'North Vietnamese air defenses during the Vietnam War', in William Head and Lawrence Grinter, eds., *Looking Back on the Vietnam War* (Westport, CT, 1993), pp. 161–2.

26 Brian VanDeMark, *Into the Quagmire* (New York, NY, 1991), pp. 97–8, 126, 151.

on popular morale. *In fact*, the regime has apparently been able to increase its control on the populace and perhaps even to break through the popular apathy and indifference which have characterized the outlook of the average North Vietnamese in recent years.[27]

At the end of the year, a Pentagon report expressed grudging admiration for how the DRV, despite encountering 'many difficulties', had survived. 'Its economy had continued to function. The regime had not collapsed and it had not given in. And it still sent men and supplies into SVN.'[28]

Limited results convinced bombing enthusiasts that the only logical response was escalation. On 2 April CIA Director John McCone advised

we must . . . change the ground rules of the strikes against North Vietnam. We must hit them harder, more frequently, and inflict greater damage. Instead of avoiding the MIG's, we must go in and take them out. A bridge here and there will not do the job. We must strike their air fields, their petroleum resources, power stations and their military compounds . . . promptly and with minimum restraint.[29]

'We shall continue to achieve only limited success in air operations', the JCS advised, 'if required to operate within the constraints presently imposed.' They wanted 'an immediate and sharply accelerated program which will leave no doubt that the US intends to win and achieve a level of destruction which they will not be able to overcome'.[30]

Doubters and zealots argued for the rest of the year. Both sides used the same evidence to prove a different point. A total bombing pause beginning on 17 December brought the debate to a head. Ball repeatedly stressed that 'We are not breaking the will of North Vietnam. They are digging in', while adding that 'Bombing never wins a war'.[31] Taylor countered: 'If we give up bombing, we will seriously hurt the war effort. We should punish Hanoi, [or] else we will be there 20 years.'[32] Johnson appears to have been most impressed by the fact that the pause had not brought a response from Hanoi. He

27 Berman, *Planning a Tragedy*, p. 51

28 James Clay Thompson, *Rolling Thunder: Understanding Policy and Program Failure* (Chapel Hill, NC, 1980), pp. 46–7.

29 Berman, *Planning a Tragedy*, p. 59.

30 Thompson, *Rolling Thunder*, p. 48.

31 Barrett, ed., *Johnson's Vietnam Papers*, p. 288.

32 Ibid., p. 313.

did not think he could 'sell the American people on the merits of stopping the bombing'.[33] On 31 January 1966, therefore, bombing resumed with greater intensity.

But still Hanoi did not budge. On 6 May Walt Rostow, who had replaced Bundy, argued that a 'sustained' attack on the DRV's oil storage facilities would 'seriously affect the infiltration rate'. He cited American success in bombing German oil facilities during the Second World War, apparently oblivious to the fact that the DRV's war effort was not heavily dependent upon the internal combustion engine. A CIA report of February 1966 estimated that 'an average of about 12 tons daily has been required by the VC/PAVN from external sources over the past year'.[34] Twelve tons meant that only six Molotova trucks had to sneak over the border each day. Johnson nevertheless went along with Rostow, permitting strikes on seven POL (petroleum, oil and lubricants) facilities in the Hanoi/Haiphong vicinity between 29 June 1966 and the end of July. The CIA surmised that storage capacity in the North was reduced by 85 per cent, though others put destruction at around 70 per cent.[35] This was a tactical success but a strategic failure since morale in the North, and its ability to continue the war, were not seriously affected. POL storage was henceforth dispersed throughout the country, with sites often consisting of nothing more than a collection of suitably camouflaged 55 gallon drums. Tanks were deliberately sited close to dikes, on the assumption that the Americans, fearful of atrocity charges, would not want to cause widespread flooding.[36]

On 29 August 1966 the Institute of Defence Analysis (IDA), an independent think-tank, advised the government that 'the US bombing of North Vietnam (NVN) has had no measurable effect on Hanoi's ability to mount and support military operations in the South at the current level'.[37] Duly convinced, McNamara warned Johnson on 14 October that 'to bomb the North sufficiently to make a radical impact upon Hanoi's political, economic and social structure, would require an effort which we could make, but which would not be stomached either by our own people or by world opinion, and it

---

33 Ibid., p. 288.

34 Larry Cable, *Unholy Grail* (London, 1991), pp. 111–12.

35 Robert J. McMahon, *Major Problems in the History of the Vietnam War* (Lexington, MA, 1990), p. 267; Raphael Littauer and Norman Uphoff, eds, *The Air War in Indochina* (Boston, MA, 1972), p. 39.

36 Mark Clodfelter, *The Limits of Air Power: The American Bombing of North Vietnam* (New York, NY, 1989), p. 132. AA batteries were often also placed near the dikes.

37 Smith, *Rolling Thunder*, p. 223.

would involve a serious risk of drawing us into open war with China'.[38] The CIA chipped in, arguing that 'during the course of the Rolling Thunder program the North Vietnamese capability to support the war effort has improved. . . . We see no signs that the air attack has shaken the confidence of the regime.'[39]

A pessimist might have concluded that bombing was futile, but pessimists do not make it far in the military. At stake was the credibility of air doctrine. Once the decision to bomb had been made, the only choice was to escalate until success was achieved, for to do otherwise would be to admit that the doctrine was fallacious. Alarmed by McNamara's gloomy assessment, Wheeler argued: 'The Joint Chiefs of Staff . . . believe our air campaign against NVN to be an integral and indispensable part of our overall war effort. To be effective the air campaign should be conducted with only those minimum constraints necessary to avoid indiscriminate killing of population.'[40] The case for escalation was strengthened when a noticeable increase in resupply activity occurred during the five-day bombing pause in February 1967. Johnson yielded to the hawks, approving new targets, including a cement plant, the steel mill at Thai Nguyen, and electrical power plants. Rivers and estuaries along the southern coast were mined and targets along the Chinese border were removed from the prohibited list.

The futility of the 1967 campaign can be illustrated by the attacks on the Paul Doumer bridge, which carried rail and road traffic over the Red River into Hanoi. From August through December 1967, American bombers managed to blast gaps in the bridge and disrupt traffic on it, but were not able to destroy it completely. Damage was repaired with astonishing speed. In December, when damage grew too great, repairs were halted and rail traffic immediately shifted to a pontoon bridge which lay in readiness for just such an eventuality. An even more stubborn target was the Thanh Hoa bridge over the Ma River, approximately 80 miles south of Hanoi. It defied destruction during the entire campaign, despite some 700 sorties being directed against it, at the cost of eight American aircraft.[41]

The administration was now deeply divided on Rolling Thunder. At one extreme McNamara wanted immediate de-escalation, at the other the JCS demanded more intensive bombing of Hanoi and Haiphong.

38 Herring, ed., *Pentagon Papers*, p. 162.
39 Barrett, ed., *Johnson's Vietnam Papers*, p. 372.
40 Ibid., p. 368.
41 Bernard Nalty, ed., *The Vietnam War* (London, 1996), p. 92. It was not until 1972 that the US Air Force was able to destroy the bridge using laser-guided bombs.

On 8 August Rostow suggested that bombing had impeded the DRV's supply efforts by as much as 50 per cent, to which McNamara replied that the figure was closer to 1 per cent and that malaria among coolies was more effective than bombs at cutting the flow.[42] Johnson sought a middle line between the two extremes, but privately expressed a desire to 'pour the steel on'. He felt certain that the bombs were sapping North Vietnamese strength – 'I feel it in my bones' – though evidence suggested otherwise.[43]

The Senate Preparedness Subcommittee, chaired by Senator John Stennis, then entered the fray. It was packed with pro-bombing hawks out to get McNamara.[44] The Stennis hearings began on 9 August when Admiral U.S.G. Sharp, the CINCPAC, testified that bombing had significantly reduced the level of infiltration, thus limiting 'considerably the enemy's ability to conduct major sustained operations in South Vietnam'. Still clinging to Douhet's theories, he wanted restrictions removed so that the US could 'make our air presence felt over the cities of Hanoi and Haiphong'.[45] McNamara delivered a 'masterful performance' on the 25th, warning the subcommittee that 'You cannot win the war on the cheap by bombing'.[46] The subcommittee concluded rather predictably that Rolling Thunder's failure to achieve its objectives 'cannot be attributed to inability or impotence of airpower. It attests, rather, to the fragmentation of our air might by overly restrictive controls, limitations and the doctrine of "gradualism".' In other words, McNamara was blamed for not listening to the advice of the JCS. Keen to deflect criticism, Johnson eventually permitted strikes against 52 of the 57 targets advocated in the Stennis report, including some within the Hanoi circle and near the Chinese border.[47]

At the same time, Johnson gave wide latitude to those within his administration, including McNamara and Rusk, who were pursuing peace initiatives. They urged an extended bombing pause as a gesture to Hanoi. The President demurred, but on 29 September did unveil his 'San Antonio formula' which proposed that 'The United States is willing to stop all aerial and naval bombardment of North Vietnam when this will lead promptly to productive discussions'.[48] The offer was far too

42 Barrett, ed., *Johnson's Vietnam Papers*, p. 458.

43 George C. Herring, *LBJ and Vietnam* (Austin, TX, 1994), p. 117.

44 Thompson, *Rolling Thunder*, p. 56.

45 Guenter Lewy, *America in Vietnam* (Oxford, 1978), p. 383.

46 Herring, *LBJ and Vietnam*, p. 56.

47 Lewy, *America in Vietnam*, p. 385. See also Robert S. McNamara, *In Retrospect* (New York, NY, 1995), pp. 284–95.

48 William Appleman Williams *et al.*, eds, *America in Vietnam: A Documentary History* (New York, NY, 1975), p. 266.

vague for Hanoi, but did at least suggest to those at home that efforts were being made to find a peaceful solution. Johnson still feared that 'a unilateral and unrequited bombing stand-down would be read in both Hanoi and the United States as a sign of weakening will'.[49]

By December 1967, almost every target of military value defined by the JCS had been destroyed or severely damaged. Then came the Tet Offensive, which demonstrated conclusively that, even as an interdiction campaign, Rolling Thunder had failed. In his dramatic speech of 31 March, Johnson announced a restriction of the bombing, 'in the hope that this action will lead to early talks'.[50] But his 'very limited bombing', restricted to targets south of the 19th parallel, still meant that, over the next six months, 77,081 sorties were flown against infiltration routes, nearly 5,000 more than were flown against all of North Vietnam during the same period in 1967.[51] Rolling Thunder officially ended when peace talks began in November 1968. By the end, 'success' was measured by the tonnage of bombs dropped and the number of sorties flown, since the effect upon the DRV was at best obscure. 'We were playing sortie games', one Navy flyer confessed. 'It didn't make a shit what you did over there, as long as the aircraft got off the ship.'[52]

AIR DEFENCES

One of the more powerful myths of the war, which the DRV exploited to great effect, was that American bombers, in the words of one critic, let loose 'sophisticated destruction on a relatively defenseless, essentially peasant people'.[53] Critics of the campaign have carelessly assumed that, since the tonnage of bombs greatly exceeded the totals dropped in the Second World War, Vietnam must have suffered at least as badly as Germany. A sense of moral outrage was encouraged by the highly inaccurate and sensationalist accounts published by Harrison Salisbury, the American journalist who visited North Vietnam in December 1966. Unfortunately, many subsequent historians have accepted Salisbury's judgements at face value, failing to understand the way he was manipulated by North Vietnamese propagandists.[54] In

---

49 Barrett, ed., *Johnson's Vietnam Papers*, pp. 568–9.

50 Williams *et al.*, eds, *America in Vietnam*, p. 274.

51 Ibid., Lewy, *America in Vietnam*, p. 387.

52 Smith, *Rolling Thunder*, p. 226.

53 See Lewy, *America in Vietnam*, p. 412.

54 Salisbury's reports were published in the *New York Times*, and later repeated in *Behind the Lines* (New York, NY, 1968). Some of the most irresponsible accusations regarding the bombing are found in Gloria Emerson, *Winners and Losers* (New York, NY, 1992), passim.

fact, the level of destruction and death in Vietnam was relatively small. This was partly because there were few good targets to bomb, but also because American pilots flew into the most sophisticated and deadly air defence system ever deployed in wartime. One pilot called North Vietnam 'the center of hell with Hanoi as its hub'.[55]

As Rolling Thunder progressed, the Soviets (and, to a lesser extent, the Chinese) provided an ever-increasing supply of complex weaponry. By the end of 1966, the DRV had around 150 surface-to-air missile (SAM) sites, 70 MIG interceptors, over 100 radar sites, and 5,000 AA guns. In the following year, SAMs increased to 250, AA guns to 7,000, and MIGs to 80.[56] Gunners and pilots were trained by Russian and Chinese experts who occasionally exceeded their remit and took part in active combat.

The system was highly coordinated. In order to evade radar detection, American pilots flew into DRV airspace at low altitude. But this brought them within range of small arms fire. Every worker or peasant with access to a weapon (perhaps as many as 150,000 were so armed) was instructed to fire at approaching American aircraft.[57] According to Giap:

> With 'plough in one hand and rifle in the other', young and
> old people, men and women, in the countryside and the towns,
> actively participated in shooting down enemy planes, forming
> a low altitude anti-aircraft fire network that covered the whole
> country. . . . Using infantry weapons, militias and guerillas shot
> down many modern American jet planes and captured a large
> number of pilots.[58]

Actual losses from small arms fire were minor, but the image of an ordinary peasant downing a modern jet with a primitive rifle had obvious propaganda value to a country engaged in a people's war. It fostered the idea that every civilian had a role to play.

Small arms fire did force attackers to altitudes above 1,500 feet where they could be detected by radar, and were susceptible to AA fire, the most deadly element of the DRV's defence. If American pilots

---

55 Clodfelter, *The Limits of Air Power*, p. 131.

56 Ibid., Micheal Clodfelter, *Vietnam in Military Statistics* (Jefferson, NC, 1995), pp. 229–31.

57 Earl Tilford, 'Crosswinds: cultural imperatives of the air war', in Phil Melling and Jon Roper, eds, *America, France and Vietnam: Cultural History and Ideas of Conflict* (Swansea, 1991), p. 113.

58 Peter MacDonald, *Giap* (London, 1993), p. 316. See also Cecil B. Currey, *Victory at Any Cost* (Washington, DC, 1997), p. 252.

tried to avoid the flak by flying even higher, they came within range of SAMs. Though SAMs were responsible for relatively few 'kills', they did distract bombers from primary targets. Measures taken to reduce an aircraft's vulnerability to SAMs increased its vulnerability to MIG attack. Though the US lost relatively few aircraft to enemy fighters, the MIGs did force the Americans to expend a huge amount of energy and expense on fighter escorts for its bomber force.

Air defence was made easier by the hubris and tactical rigidity of the Americans, who assumed that they possessed an invincible weapon which did not therefore need to be wielded with great subtlety. American planes often attacked at 10.00 a.m., 2.00 p.m. and 4.00 p.m. because maintenance engineers preferred to work to a prescribed schedule. It did not take long for the North Vietnamese to figure out when bombs were likely to arrive.[59] The desire of many American pilots to earn the title of 'ace' by downing enemy fighters caused them to dump bombs and give chase when MIGs appeared. This was exactly what DRV pilots wanted them to do.[60]

CIVIL DEFENCE

The task of defending the civilian population against air attack revealed the ingenuity and resolution of the Vietnamese people. Surviving the bombers became a sublime patriotic act. 'Call the Shelter Your Second Home' was the official slogan, reiterated from hoardings and loudspeakers. People were expected to protect themselves from air attack and participate in the massive programme of shelter construction. The goal was at least three shelters per person – one at home, another at work, and a third on the way to work. Some shelters accommodated several people but most were 'spider holes', 5 feet deep and 2½ feet in diameter, which provided a single individual with protection from almost anything short of a direct hit. Hanoi claimed to have constructed 20 million shelters and 30,000 miles of reinforced trenches.[61] Tran Van Truong, a Haiphong resident, recalled that by 1967

> everyone was prepared for [the bombing]. We had a bunker dug into the floor of the house underneath the heavy divan. It was an excavation about four feet deep in the dirt floor, with the opening next to the divan, which served as a roof. That was a

59 Tilford, 'Crosswinds', pp. 112–13.
60 Ibid., p. 122.
61 William J. Duiker, *Sacred War* (New York, NY, 1995), p. 200.

common kind of arrangement. . . . All of the students had also gotten training in school about how to treat wounds. Every house had a supply of bandages, alcohol and cotton for first aid.[62]

In 1966 Salisbury visited a school near Hanoi in which the playground was honeycombed with trenches and each child had access to a foxhole directly under his or her desk.[63]

Non-essential members of the population were moved out of urban areas susceptible to bombing. Beginning in February 1965, refugee camps and collective farms were set up in the countryside to accommodate this surplus population. Though this policy was less successful than other measures, mainly due to people's deep reluctance to move from their homes, it is nevertheless estimated that one-third of the population of Hanoi had departed by late 1966.[64] Government offices, schools and small factories were also moved out of the cities. Production processes were broken up with components manufactured at scattered small units and assembled at another site, thus presenting the Americans with few large targets.

Much of the civil defence programme served little concrete purpose, but did encourage a communal spirit of resistance. Children walking to school occasionally attached leafy vegetation to their shoulders to aid concealment. They wore hats and coats of heavily matted straw to defend themselves against bomb pellets and shrapnel. The Vietnamese delighted in devising primitive responses to American technological wizardry. Hot surfaces on trucks were insulated with banana leaves so as to avoid detection by infrared devices. Aluminium foil wrapped around electrical components of engines prevented detection by electromagnetic sensors. Trails and roads were disguised with ash, sand, leaves and potted plants. Civil defence was based on the premise that the Americans could not destroy that which they could not detect. On the Ho Chi Minh Trail, the slogan went '*di khong dau, nau khong koi, noi khong tieng*' – 'walk without footprints, cook without smoke, speak without sound'.[65]

62 David Chanoff and Doan Van Toai, '*Vietnam*' – *Portrait of its People at War* (London, 1996), p. 127.

63 Salisbury, *Behind the Lines*, p. 70. Though Salisbury witnessed the effectiveness of North Vietnamese civil defence, he remained convinced that civilian casualties were very high.

64 Duiker, *Sacred War*, p. 203.

65 Barton Meyers, 'Vietnamese defense against aerial attack', 1996 Vietnam Symposium, Texas Tech University Vietnam Center website.

ASSESSMENT

Up to 22 October 1968, bombers destroyed or put out of commission 77 per cent of all ammunition depots, 65 per cent of POL storage, 59 per cent of power plants, 55 per cent of major bridges, and 39 per cent of railroad shops. Iron and steel, cement, and explosives plants (the North had one of each) were all put out of action. Armed reconnaissance flights destroyed 12,521 vessels, 9,821 vehicles and 1,966 railroad cars. And, because of the bombing, perhaps 600,000 people in the North were diverted from other tasks to repair the damage, and another 145,000 were occupied in air defence.[66] But, as with the 'kill ratio' on the ground, these figures are open to doubt. Pilots supplied evidence of extraordinary destruction, but the proof of the pudding was lacking. The DRV did not falter and the PLAF was not starved of supplies.

'Perhaps the most important measure of the effects of the bombing', Sharp argued, is 'the consideration of the situation if there had been no bombing at all'. He felt that an 'uninhibited flow of men, weapons and supplies through North Vietnam to confront our forces in South Vietnam' would have meant 'considerably heavier casualties at a smaller cost to the enemy'.[67] But this is strange justification, based as it is on what might have happened without the bombing rather than what did happen with it. In any case, it is spurious to justify the campaign on the basis of its limited interdiction success, since it was never intended to be primarily an interdiction effort. The bombers were supposed to convince the DRV that it was senseless to continue fighting. They failed. The most massive bombing campaign the world has ever seen did not stop the DRV from carrying on to victory.

An interdiction campaign could serve the war effort, but could never be a war winner. The PLAF sought to minimize its dependence upon the DRV, partly to decrease its vulnerability to the air campaign, but mostly to retain a sense of autonomy. The CIA estimated that, during the heavy fighting in 1967, the revolution required just 25 per cent of its supplies to come from outside, or around 55 tons per day.[68] That equates to just 20 or 30 truckloads, which demonstrates that no interdiction campaign could hope to succeed – the

---

66 Lewy, *America in Vietnam*, p. 390. The Pentagon admitted in 1967 that these diversions did not have a significant effect on the DRV's ability to wage war, since they did not significantly decrease the pool of potential soldiers. See Kolko, *Anatomy*, p. 191.

67 Lewy, *America in Vietnam*, p. 390.

68 Cable, *Unholy Grail*, p. 209. Lewy gives a slightly higher figure of 100 tons per day, but the point remains. See Lewy, *America in Vietnam*, pp. 390–1.

volume of traffic was simply too small. Interdiction was also inextricably dependent upon the progress of the ground war. In other words, if the bombers were to have any effect, American infantry had to maintain the tactical initiative in order to force the adversary to use up his supplies. This never occurred. By controlling the pace of the war, the PLAF negated its susceptibility to interdiction.

Sir Robert Thompson concluded in 1969 that since 'the bombing had a minimal effect on infiltration and on the capacity of North Vietnam to wage . . . war, which were the only two advantages the Americans may have got from it, then all the benefits have been derived by Hanoi'. Chief among these was that it 'enabled the North to organize the whole country on a war footing with the full support of the people'.[69] The IDA report concluded that the 'bombing clearly strengthened popular support of the regime by engendering patriotic and nationalistic enthusiasm to resist the attacks'.[70] Anecdotal evidence supports these findings. Nguyen Van Mo, a PAVN master sergeant, felt that 'during the early attacks [the Americans] hit proper military targets and . . . their flying techniques were pretty good'. But escalation meant that 'A large number of civilians were unexpectedly killed. After that people began to hate the Americans.'[71] Tran Van Truong came from a 'bourgeois' Haiphong family deeply suspicious of the Hanoi government. 'None of us would have minded at all if the Saigon army had invaded the North and liberated us from them.' But, when the bombers came, 'I began to hate the Americans, really hate them'.[72]

If all else failed, the proponents of bombing tended to fall back on the justification that it heartened supporters of the Saigon regime. At the beginning of the campaign, Bundy argued that 'the immediate and critical targets are in the South – in the minds of the south Vietnamese and in the minds of the Vietnamese cadres'.[73] But, as McNamara discovered, diminishing returns were apparent as early as July 1965:

> Morale in South Vietnam was raised by the initiation of the
> bombing program . . . Now – with the bombing programs
> having become commonplace and with the failure of the
> situation to improve – morale in South Vietnam is not

69 Robert Thompson, *No Exit from Vietnam* (New York, NY, 1969), p. 139.

70 Herring, ed., *Pentagon Papers*, p. 151.

71 Chanoff and Toai, *Portrait*, p. 126.

72 Ibid., p. 127.

73 Lawrence Freedman, 'Vietnam and the disillusioned strategist', *International Affairs* 72 (1996), p. 146.

discernibly better than it was before the program began. In a sense, South Vietnam is now 'addicted' to the program ...'[74]

'There had been an appreciable improvement in South Vietnamese morale immediately after the bombing began and subsequent buoyancy always accompanied major new escalations', the IDA reported. But 'the effect was always transient ... fading as a particular pattern of attack became a part of the war. There was no indication that bombing could ever form a permanent support for South Vietnamese morale if the situation in the South itself was adverse.'[75]

Those who supported the bombing always believed that the campaign would succeed tomorrow if only a bit more force were applied. 'The effect of the air campaign is a cumulative one and no one can predict which blow will be the crucial blow', General Harold Johnson, the Army Chief of Staff, reassured the President in September 1967. 'Every blow makes him stretch his resources and at some point his resources will not be able to be stretched anymore.'[76] Diehard proponents still held to this argument after the war. 'Rolling Thunder was working by the end of the summer of 1967', Colonel Jacksel Broughton, a US Air Force pilot, has argued. 'Only the lack of perspective by the President and the Secretary [of Defense] and their dedication to doom allowed our nation to stumble past yet another opportunity to close our Indochinese involvement with honor.'[77] Needless to say, there are those who maintain that Rolling Thunder demonstrates the folly of placing military direction in the hands of 'unskilled amateurs'.[78]

'The severe restrictions under which our Air Force operated', argued Sharp, 'resulted in markedly decreased effectiveness of the tremendous power we had available and resulted in wide misunderstanding of the effectiveness of airpower when properly used.'[79] Westmoreland decried the way 'interference from Washington seriously hampered the campaign.... This or that target was not to be hit for this or that nebulous non-military reason.'[80] The former chairman of the JCS,

74 Thompson, *Rolling Thunder*, pp. 44–5.

75 Smith, *Rolling Thunder*, p. 214.

76 Gardner, *Pay any Price*, p. 384.

77 Jacksel M. Broughton, 'Rolling Thunder from the cockpit', in John Norton Moore, ed., *The Vietnam Debate* (Lanham, MD, 1990), p. 158.

78 See J. Terry Emerson, 'Making war without will: Vietnam rules of engagement', in Moore, ed., *Vietnam Debate*, p. 168.

79 U.S.G. Sharp, 'Airpower could have won in Vietnam', *Air Force Magazine* 54 (1971), pp. 82–3.

80 William Westmoreland, *A Soldier Reports* (Garden City, NY, 1976), p. 119.

Admiral Thomas H. Moorer, felt that gradual escalation 'granted the enemy time to shore up his air defenses, disperse his military targets, and mobilize his labour force for logistical repair and movement. From a military point of view, gradualism violated the principle of mass and surprise which airpower has employed historically to attain maximum effectiveness.'[81] Moorer contends that a sudden air attack of maximum intensity in 1965, perhaps directed against the 94 original JCS targets, would have yielded greater success. Air defences, at that time quite primitive, would not have been able to cope with an attack of such intensity, making targets easier to hit and keeping losses to a minimum. There is some merit to this argument. Former PAVN Colonel Bui Tin admitted that 'If all the bombing had been concentrated at one time, it would have hurt our efforts'.[82] But a bombing campaign which crippled the DRV still would not have meant the complete emasculation of the PLAF.

Johnson's 'nebulous non-military reasons' for limiting targets made political sense in a political war. He once commented that, if all restrictions on the bombing of Hanoi and Haiphong were removed, 500,000 anti-war protesters would climb the fences of the White House and lynch him.[83] Hyperbole aside, he had a point. He also had to worry about Chinese and Soviet reaction. 'In the dark at night', he later confessed, 'I would lay awake picturing my boys flying around North Vietnam, asking myself an endless series of questions. What if one of those targets you picked today triggers off Russia or China? What happens then?'[84] The Korean War demonstrates that the risk of Chinese intervention was no chimera, as Westmoreland believed. Ball understood that the great problem with the Chinese was that it was impossible to know what level of American aggression in Vietnam would provoke an adverse response. 'We will not find out until after the catastrophe', he warned.[85]

'I thought the North Vietnamese would reach a point, like the Chinese and North Koreans in Korea, and Stalin during the Berlin airlift, when they would finally give in', Rusk confessed.[86] But by

81 Lewy, *America in Vietnam*, p. 393.

82 Joseph P. Martino, 'Vietnam and Desert Storm: learning the right lessons from Vietnam for the post-Cold War era', 1996 Vietnam Symposium, Texas Tech University Vietnam Center website.

83 Meyers, 'Vietnamese defense'.

84 Doris Kearns, *Lyndon Johnson and the American Dream* (London, 1976), p. 270.

85 Lewy, *America in Vietnam*, p. 393.

86 Mark Clodfelter, 'Of demons, storms, and thunder: a preliminary look at Vietnam's impact on the Persian Gulf air campaign', in Head and Gritner, eds, *Looking Back*, p. 146.

1967, American bombs had destroyed almost everything possible or worthy of destruction, and the DRV continued to fight. Hanoi's resilience survived long past the point where American logic said it should crumble. The cost of this failed effort was prodigious. The US lost 938 airplanes and 818 airmen.[87] In early 1967 the CIA estimated that each dollar of damage caused to North Vietnam by the air campaign cost the United States US$9.60.[88] The bombing also spurred the campus peace protesters and, according to Bill Moyers, 'escalated the war to the front page of every newspaper'.[89] The image of sophisticated, highly armed American bombers destroying primitive villages damaged America's reputation and eroded homefront morale.

On 19 February 1968 White House aides met the crew of the *Constellation* to obtain their view of the bombing. Senior officers provided the usual rosy assessment, but one lieutenant was a great deal more candid:

> We are going through the worst fucking flak in the history of man, and for what – to knock out some twelve foot wooden bridge they can build back a couple of hours later. We can't hit the [Haiphong] docks where they unload the war matériel because we might hit the ships, and we can't hit the ships because some of them might be Russian. . . . We've got a great big country with sophisticated equipment, trained pilots, expensive aircraft and it's not worth a damn . . .[90]

Rolling Thunder was a disaster because bombing was not appropriate to this type of war.

87 MacDonald, *Giap*, p. 234; Tilford, 'Crosswinds', p. 119.
88 Clodfelter, 'Demons', p. 146.
89 Gardner, *Pay any Price*, p. 177.
90 Don Oberdorfer, *Tet!* (New York, NY, 1984), p. 195.

8   PEACE WITH HONOUR?

To assess Richard Nixon's handling of the Vietnam War requires negotiating a minefield of contradictions. He ended the war, but took rather long to do so. Detente with the USSR and China was a triumph, but the Cambodian corpse still festers. To some, Nixon's Christmas bombing of 1972 was a clever ploy, to others machismo gone mad. If one ignores Nixon's character flaws, his Vietnam policy seems adept and occasionally brilliant. If one considers those flaws, that policy seems foolhardy and frequently irrational.[1]

Nixon's Cabinet was probably more turbulent than most, partly owing to the times, but mostly to the idiosyncrasies of the President and his National Security Adviser, Henry Kissinger. They developed a bunker mentality, marginalizing those with contrasting opinions, such as Defense Secretary Melvin Laird and Secretary of State William Rogers. The situation differed markedly from the Johnson presidency, when McNamara, Rusk, Rostow, Bundy and others had significant input. In the Nixon White House, mutual distrust reigned. Kissinger thought Nixon a 'dark and dangerous . . . madman'; Rogers a vain, uninformed 'fag'; and Laird a scheming megalomaniac. Rogers despised Kissinger's Machiavellian arrogance. Nixon bugged Kissinger's phones, and Kissinger listened in on Nixon.[2] The two men forged a partnership not out of mutual esteem but because Kissinger's diplomatic skills and Nixon's brutishness proved formidable when fused. Both men imposed their flawed personalities on the peace process. Withdrawal was prolonged because their goals went beyond merely extricating America from the war.

1 Nixon's war in Vietnam has received surprisingly little attention from historians. Aspects of 'his' war – the Phoenix Program, the Easter Offensive, the bombing campaigns, etc. – have been the focus of quite a few studies, but very few books have examined the broad topic of Nixon's conduct of the war. Jeffrey Kimball's *Nixon's Vietnam War* (Lawrence, KS, 1998), is a notable exception.

2 Loren Baritz, *Backfire* (New York, NY, 1985), pp. 196–7; Kimball, *Nixon's Vietnam War*, p. 64.

DISENGAGEMENT

The Tet Offensive was disastrous for the revolution. One PLAF sapper of ten years service who defected in 1970 felt that 'Communism was not winning' because 'the ARVN was growing too strong'. In his unit, 'the morale . . . was low because the men were tired of fighting, afraid of death, and felt they were losing the war'.[3] A local party official felt that many members had

> lost confidence in the higher echelon leadership and in the revolutionary capability of the people. They think that our assessment of enemy capabilities is inaccurate, our strategic determination is erroneous . . . They become doubtful of victory, pessimistic and display a shirking attitude.[4]

The rank and file were warned that victory would come 'not suddenly but in a complicated and tortuous way'.[5] But rehabilitation would be difficult. 'We . . . lost many cadre during the 1968 offensive and its aftermath', a defector revealed. 'The result was that many cadre were making it to the top who in former times would never have been considered.'[6]

The improvident offensive was paid for in large part by the peasantry, whose taxes soared in NLF-controlled villages, and whose sons were wantonly sacrificed. A district-level NLF defector confessed:

> Before the Tet events, the VC said that they needed only seven days to achieve the revolution. They needed the support of the population; they collected very heavy contributions arguing that they needed the contributions to bring about peace and prosperity; but after the anticipated seven days they said that this was only a first stage, the first wave. When the second stage came on 7th of May [1968] they said there was then an almost complete destruction of the enemy, to step up to the third stage which would be in August, 1968, and which was also to be the final stage; but, as a matter of fact, there has been no final stage at all . . . These facts have accounted for the cadres' and the

---

3 John M. Del Vecchio, 'The importance of story: individual and cultural effects of skewing the realities of American involvement in Southeast Asia for social, political and/or economic ends', 1996 Vietnam Symposium, Texas Tech University Vietnam Center Website.

4 William J. Duiker, *Sacred War* (New York, NY, 1995), p. 219.

5 Ibid., p. 225.

6 Eric Bergerud, *The Dynamics of Defeat* (Boulder, CO, 1991), p. 218.

general population's losing confidence in the success of the revolution by the Front.[7]

A former NLF finance director recalled: 'the people were disenchanted with us. We had promised to topple the puppet government . . . and had collected extremely heavy taxes on the basis of this pledge. In 1969, when I attempted to tax again, the people were angry about this.'[8] But the situation was not entirely gloomy. Removing cadres did not always remove the revolution's hold over an area. 'Despite the military setbacks the Communists have suffered, they are not losing politically in Vietnam today', the journalist Robert Shaplen commented in late June 1968. 'There is scant reason to doubt that the options at the moment belong to Hanoi.'[9]

The new administration seems to have agreed. The NSC advised Nixon on 21 January 1969 that 'The North Vietnamese and the Viet Cong have access to sufficient manpower to meet their replenishment needs . . . for at least the next several years'. The North would still be able to 'launch major offensives, although not at Tet levels'. Especially crucial was the fact that 'the enemy basically controls both sides' casualty rates'.[10] This meant that, if nothing changed, years of stalemate beckoned. Before his appointment Kissinger argued that 'our military operations . . . have little relationship to our declared political objectives'. An attrition strategy was pointless since it did not extend political authority – 'the only meaningful definition of "victory" in guerrilla warfare'.[11] None of this surprised Nixon. 'There's no way to win the war', he admitted privately nearly a year before becoming President. 'But we can't say that, of course. In fact, we have to seem to say the opposite, just to keep some degree of bargaining leverage.'[12]

By 1968, Nixon's strident anti-communism had given way to a more accommodating attitude. Victory in Vietnam was not as important as it had seemed in the early 1960s. But he could not simply pull out of Vietnam on the day after his inauguration. As he saw it, he

---

7 Mark Moyar, 'Villager attitudes during the final decade of the Vietnam War', 1996 Vietnam Symposium, Texas Tech University Vietnam Center website.

8 Bergerud, *Dynamics*, p. 218.

9 Robert Shaplen, *The Road from War* (New York, NY, 1970), p. 234.

10 Robert J. McMahon, *Major Problems in the History of the Vietnam War* (Lexington, MA, 1990), pp. 443–5.

11 Henry Kissinger, 'The Viet Nam negotiations', *Foreign Affairs* 47 (January, 1969), pp. 214, 216.

12 Arnold R. Isaacs, *Without Honor: Defeat in Vietnam and Cambodia* (Baltimore, MD, 1983), p. 489.

faced three essential tasks. 'First, I would have to prepare public opinion for the fact that total military victory was no longer possible.' This was not difficult, since most Americans agreed that the war could not be won at tolerable cost. 'Second, I would have to act on what my conscience, my experience, and my analysis told me was true about the need to keep our commitment.' This was probably more important to Nixon than to most Americans. Pride prevented him from accepting a peace which might be interpreted as an abandonment of South Vietnam. The war had always had more to do with America's future than with Vietnam's and never more so than now. 'Third, I would have to end the war as quickly as was honorably possible.'[13] Here lay a thorny dilemma: honour and speed contradicted each other. But Nixon did not entirely understand this; he assumed he could master problems which had defeated his predecessor. 'I'm not going to end up like LBJ, holed up in the White House afraid to show my face in the street', he boasted immediately after his election. 'I'm going to stop that war. Fast.'[14] 'I played a little poker when I was in the Navy', he told delegates to the Republican convention in August 1968, 'When a guy didn't have the cards, he talked awfully big. But when he had the cards, he just sat there – had that cold look in his eyes. Now we've got the cards.'[15]

The Paris talks had degenerated into a forum for each side to air inflexible demands and abuse the other, what Shaplen called a 'dialogue of the deaf'.[16] Recognizing their futility, US representatives proposed secret high-level talks. Hanoi agreed, and in late March 1969 direct negotiations between Kissinger and Le Duc Tho began at a flat in an undistinguished Paris neighbourhood. While these talks were proceeding, Nixon went public with his own peace plan. On 14 May he offered to set a precise timetable for the mutual withdrawal of all foreign troops in South Vietnam as a preliminary to free elections under international supervision. 'Foreign' was defined to include North Vietnamese.

'Measures of great consequence and force' would, Nixon promised, be taken if no progress toward peace was made by 1 November 1969.[17] Nixon thought that his past reputation could be used to good effect in frightening the North Vietnamese:

13 Richard M. Nixon, *RN: The Memoirs of Richard Nixon* (New York, NY, 1978), p. 349.

14 H.R. Haldeman, *The Ends of Power* (New York, NY, 1989), p. 81.

15 Kimball, *Nixon's Vietnam War*, p. 83.

16 Shaplen, *Road from War*, p. 300.

17 Nixon, *RN*, pp. 393–4.

I call it the Madman Theory . . . I want the North Vietnamese
to believe I've reached the point where I might do *anything* to
stop the war. We'll just slip the word to them that 'for god's
sake, you know Nixon is obsessed about Communism. We
can't restrain him when he's angry – and he has his hand on
the nuclear button' – and Ho Chi Minh himself will be in Paris
in two days begging for peace.[18]

According to Nixon, the Korean War had been brought to an end
when Eisenhower threatened massive retaliation if North Korea refused to negotiate. He would take a similar approach in Vietnam. The
key was to make the Politburo believe that if negotiations stalled, the
US might still push for complete victory. A frightened Hanoi would
be like putty in Nixon's hands. Kissinger agreed that Nixon's 'brutal
unpredictability' could be put to good effect.[19] 'What the potential
aggressor believes', he once argued, 'is more crucial than what is
objectively true.'[20]

The NSC's Operation Duck Hook was designed in part to sow
fear and uncertainty. The proposal included bombing Hanoi and other
cities, destruction of dikes, mining of rivers and harbours, a land
invasion of the North, and the possible use of nuclear weapons. It was
more a propaganda exercise than a serious strategic plan. 'We wouldn't
go out of our way to allay their fears about [nuclear weapons]',
Winston Lord, a Kissinger aide, confessed. 'Let them worry about
that, even though we know it's not true.'[21] Careful 'leaks' were designed to frighten Hanoi. 'Once the enemy recognizes that it is not
going to win its objectives by waiting us out', Nixon told a press
conference in September 1969, 'then the enemy will negotiate and we
will end this war before the end of 1970.'[22]

Hanoi refused to play its assigned role. Nixon's proposals were
rejected as 'absurd' and a 'farce'. Mutual withdrawal was irrelevant
since, DRV negotiators claimed, the North had no troops in the
South.[23] Hanoi preferred to negotiate from a position of strength and,
at this moment, did not feel strong. The old tactic of *danh va dam,
dam va danh* ('fighting while talking, talking while fighting') was

18 Haldeman, *Ends of Power*, pp. 82–3.

19 Kimball, *Nixon's Vietnam War*, p. 66.

20 Henry Kissinger, 'Domestic structure and foreign policy', *Daedalus* (Spring 1966),
p. 506.

21 Kimball, *Nixon's Vietnam War*, p. 163.

22 Richard M. Nixon, *The Nixon Presidential Press Conferences*, ed. George W.
Johnson (London, 1978), p. 65.

23 Shaplen, *Road from War*, p. 300.

instead pursued. This 'aimed at stimulating and developing the enemy's internal contradictions and thereby making him more isolated, in order to deprive him of his propaganda weapons'.[24] Unremitting pressure on the battlefield would make the Americans more desperate for peace, while, at the same time, the fact that peace was being discussed would erode the morale of American troops. A communist spokesman promised to stay in Paris 'until the chairs rot'.[25]

Nixon's bluff had been called. He railed against 'the other side's absolute refusal to show the least willingness to join us in seeking a just peace. . . . it is convinced that all it has to do is to wait for our next concession, and our next concession after that one, until it gets everything it wants.'[26] This was indeed Hanoi's strategy, and one which had a high chance of success. Bluster aside, it was difficult for Nixon to deliver on his threat to escalate the war since he had promised Americans that troops would come home. On 8 June 1969 he informed Thieu that the US was committed to a programme of disengagement, beginning with 25,000 troops by 31 August. On 16 September another cut of 35,000 was announced, followed by 50,000 on 15 December.[27] More than 100,000 troops were expected to leave during 1970.

The driving force behind the withdrawal was Laird, the former hawk who had become disillusioned with the war. For him, America's global role, which had originally inspired intervention in Vietnam, now dictated departure. By 1969, the war was consuming 37 per cent of the total military budget, thus delaying much-needed modernization of American forces.[28] Laird decided that the best course was to get out before the war prevented the United States from realizing more important foreign policy objectives in, for instance, Western Europe.

On 24 November 1969 Nixon warned the American people that 'A nation cannot remain great if it betrays its allies and lets down its friends'. A precipitate withdrawal from Vietnam would

> result in a collapse of confidence in American leadership not only in Asia but throughout the world. . . . Far more dangerous, we would lose confidence in ourselves. Oh, the immediate reaction would be a sense of relief that our men were coming home. But as we saw the consequences of what

24 Truong Nhu Tang, *A Vietcong Memoir* (San Diego, CA, 1985), p. 210.
25 Shaplen, *Road from War*, p. 301.
26 McMahon, *Major Problems*, p. 449.
27 Bernard C. Nalty, ed., *The Vietnam War* (London, 1996), p. 172.
28 Gabriel Kolko, *Anatomy of a War* (New York, NY, 1994), p. 347.

we had done, inevitable remorse and divisive recrimination would scar our spirit as a people.

Nixon, like Eisenhower, Kennedy and Johnson before him, was keen that a non-communist, independent South Vietnam should survive. But there had to be limits to America's sacrifice. 'The great question', he argued, was 'How can we win America's peace?'[29] His choice of words was significant: it would be America's peace, not South Vietnam's. The main goal was to preserve American credibility. As Kissinger wrote, 'He took credibility and honor seriously because they defined America's capacity to shape a peaceful international order'.[30]

His solution was the 'Nixon Doctrine'. As its main points revealed, this was in truth Eisenhower's 'New Look' recycled:[31]

- First, the United States will keep all of its treaty commitments.
- Second, we shall provide a shield if a nuclear power threatens the freedom of a nation allied with us or of a nation whose survival we consider vital to our security.
- Third, in cases involving other types of aggression, we shall furnish military and economic assistance when requested in accordance with our treaty commitments. But we shall look to the nation directly threatened to assume the primary responsibility of providing the manpower for its defence.

Applied to Vietnam, the doctrine meant that henceforth 'the primary mission of our troops is to enable the South Vietnamese forces to assume the full responsibility for the security of South Vietnam'. If the ARVN could be sufficiently strengthened, while Hanoi's capacity to wage war was weakened, a stalemate and Korea-style settlement might result. 'In the previous administration we Americanized the war in Vietnam', Nixon explained. 'In this administration we are Vietnamizing the search for peace.'[32] At the very least there would be a 'decent interval' between American departure and RVN defeat, as Kissinger admitted in his more candid moments.

In presenting his 'strategy', Nixon appealed directly to those Americans who, though tired of the war, still wanted 'peace with honour'. He dubbed them the 'silent majority'. Those who agitated for 'an immediate precipitate withdrawal' were savagely attacked. 'The policy

29 Richard Nixon, transcript of 24 November 1969 ('Silent Majority') speech.
30 Henry Kissinger, *Diplomacy* (New York, NY, 1994), p. 675.
31 'There was less to the Nixon Doctrine than met the eye', Kissinger later admitted. 'That we would no longer involve ourselves in civil wars was – in 1969 – conventional wisdom.' *White House Years* (Boston, MA, 1979), p. 225.
32 'Silent Majority' speech.

of this nation', Nixon insisted, would not be dictated by 'the minority who hold that point of view and who try to impose it on the nation by mounting demonstrations in the streets'. Nixon, perhaps the most aloof President of the postwar period, was playing the populist card, drawing a line between the 'folks' and the 'elitists'.[33] His Vice-President Spiro Agnew weighed in with colourful diatribes against the 'effete corps of impudent snobs' and 'nattering nabobs of negativism' who advocated precipitate withdrawal.[34] This vast public relations campaign included inviting Merle Haggard to the White House. Haggard's songs, especially 'Okie from Muskogee' and 'Fighting Side of Me', were the 'silent majority' speech with Country Western phrasing.

According to Nixon, American withdrawal would be paced according to the enemy's behaviour on the battlefield and at the negotiating table. 'Hanoi could make no greater mistake than to assume that an increase in violence will be to its advantage', he warned. 'If I conclude that increased enemy action jeopardizes our remaining forces in Vietnam, I shall not hesitate to take strong and effective measures to deal with that situation.'[35] If the DRV settled into a protracted war, US troops would supposedly remain indefinitely, and the ARVN would in theory grow stronger. But this was in truth another bluff, as Hanoi well understood. So far, American withdrawal had been unilateral, and there was every indication that it would continue to be so. 'Nixon on the one hand was threatening bombing and on the other withdrawing troops', Nguyen Co Thach, one of the Paris negotiators, later reflected. The signal he gave was consequently 'very vague. The question for us was not bombing or any other kind of force. We should have been able to survive, to stay on. But for the Americans, in any case, they must leave. That was their problem.'[36]

The 'silent majority' speech gave Nixon a window of opportunity to pursue Vietnamization. For the moment, the American people were on his side. His approval rating soared to its highest since he took office. But Nixon realized that time was not on his side. 'I was under no illusions that this wave of . . . support could be maintained for very long. I knew that under constant pounding from the media and our critics in Congress, people would soon be demanding that new actions be taken to . . . end the war.'[37]

---

33 Ibid.

34 Richard Melanson, *Reconstructing Consensus: American Foreign Policy Since the Vietnam War* (New York, NY, 1991), p. 225.

35 'Silent Majority' speech.

36 Kimball, *Nixon's Vietnam War*, p. 113.

37 Nixon, *RN*, p. 411.

VIETNAMIZATION IN PRACTICE

Vietnamization was not, in truth, Nixon's idea. In early November 1967 Creighton Abrams, then Westmoreland's deputy, was assigned a specific remit to improve the armed forces of South Vietnam. American factories went into high gear to provide modern weaponry. Numbers in uniform steadily increased, especially after 19 June 1968 when Thieu, frightened by the Tet attacks, issued a general mobilization order applying to all males aged between 16 and 50. Almost 100,000 new conscripts were processed by the end of the year, while another 215,000 volunteered to avoid being drafted. The total in uniform by the end of the year reached 819,200, increasing to 1.1 million, or half of the male population between 18 and 35, by 1973.[38] All ARVN units were supplied with the M-16 by April 1969, and 95 per cent of the Regional and Popular Forces were so equipped a year later. At the beginning of 1972, South Vietnam had 120 infantry battalions, 58 artillery battalions, 19 battalion-sized armoured units, 1,680 naval craft, over 1,000 airplanes, and 500 helicopters. Its Air Force was the fourth largest in the world. The National Police Force expanded to 116,000 and Regional and Popular Forces reached 550,000.[39]

RVN forces were bigger, but not proportionately better. There was 'a reluctance to go out and fight . . . There are many [soldiers] . . . who are not sure which way the war is going to end, including military officers. They don't want to be the first to die if it ends the wrong way, so they practice a "Live and let live" philosophy.' Desertions steadily increased, reaching 140,000 in 1971, up 24,000 from three years earlier.[40] The government was too weak and disorganized to apprehend and punish culprits. The problem was most pronounced in combat units, which fought far from soldiers' homes. This meant that, as the ARVN took over the American mobile role, desertion worsened.

Expansion placed an enormous strain on the officer corps, traditionally the weakest link in RVN forces. Wealthy, intelligent or powerful young men easily avoided service, or took commissions which guaranteed soft assignments or plenty of graft. Unsatisfactory commanders were hardly ever dismissed since replacements were scarce. 'It is generally acknowledged that a rise in rank or a change in

38 Guenter Lewy, *America in Vietnam* (Oxford, 1978), p. 166; Kolko, *Anatomy*, p. 378.

39 Kolko, *Anatomy*, p. 378; Lewy, *America in Vietnam*, pp. 166–7; Nalty, ed., *Vietnam War*, p. 172.

40 Lewy, *America in Vietnam*, pp. 172, 195.

assignment signifies a change in political fortune rather than a recognition of service on the battlefield', an American analyst commented on the ARVN in 1970. Thieu's 1971 election campaign was heavily funded by General Dang Van Quang, a hopelessly ineffectual commander who made a fortune in the narcotics trade. In mid-1969, the Censorate, the anti-corruption bureau set up by Thieu to please the Americans, rather bravely went after General Nguyen Van Toan, one of the most blatant racketeers, who also had an unsavory affection for very young girls. Thieu promptly promoted Toan,[41] thus ensuring his loyalty.

By May 1971, 35 per cent of infantry battalions were commanded by captains, many of whom had less than six months command experience. A senior American adviser complained:

> When we mention a deficiency and ask what's been done about it we get the indignant answer, 'I give order'. And so he has, but no one ever follows up to see if the order was carried out. Few Vietnamese leaders ever get out to the company and platoon to see what's going on; they are content to listen to bullshit briefings . . . and consume leisurely lunches . . . The commander who is aggressive and effective doesn't last long, because he makes too many enemies on both sides.

American advisers were bothered by the low regard for civilian life displayed by ARVN commanders. In 1971 the Rand Corporation warned about their 'addiction to the opium of heavy weapons':

> When soldiers have helicopters they seem to worry less about the disposition of the population along the roads they would otherwise have to travel. When they have armor, the attitudes of the villagers seem less important. The indifference is reciprocated. Some people in South Vietnam have come to regard their own army as a foreign army . . . Its destructive style of fighting coupled with the bad behavior of many of its soldiers cause the people to fear that the army that is supposed to be defending them is a bigger threat to their own security than the enemy.[42]

The US put great effort into training ARVN officers, but to little effect. Some 12,000 were sent to the US, and special schools were established in South Vietnam. Training was, however, hindered by

---

41 William Appleman Williams *et al.*, eds, *America in Vietnam: A Documentary History* (New York, NY, 1975), p. 307; Kolko, *Anatomy*, p. 382.
42 Lewy, *America in Vietnam*, pp. 171, 182.

language difficulties; instead of instructors learning Vietnamese, the students were taught English, which swallowed up training time.[43] But the most serious problems could not, in any case, be solved with better training. 'These people don't need advisers; or, if they do, then we have already failed', one American officer complained. 'Charlie doesn't need advisers when he conducts a sapper attack. He doesn't need Tac air, or gunships or artillery. He's hungry and he's got a cause and he's motivated. Therein lies the difference. On our side nobody is hungry and few are motivated.'[44]

A survey of American field commanders in February 1969 voiced a common opinion that the ARVN would be able to deal with an indigenous PLAF threat, but would not stand up to PAVN regulars. Most felt that real reform required a complete social and political transformation in South Vietnam, which was inconceivable. The senior American adviser in Phu Yen remarked in September 1970:

> The real question . . . is whether the Vietnamese have the *will* to bring the war to a successful conclusion. The problems presently facing the GVN and its armed forces are not significantly different than they were in 1963; corruption is rampant; public officials are indifferent to the problems at hand; the logistics system is bogged down in bureaucracy; the troops are undisciplined . . . the list could go on and on.[45]

A 1969 Senate report summarized perfectly the American dilemma: 'The present government will probably remain in power as long as the United States continues to support it . . . [but] If the present government remains in power . . . Vietnamization will fail'.[46] Three years later the Senate Foreign Relations Committee found 'no indications that Thieu intends to make the sweeping changes which . . . are needed to transform the ARVN into a well led army and to enhance the effectiveness of the government's control over the countryside'.[47]

But Vietnamization did not actually need to work, as long as it *appeared* that progress was made. Laird realized that if evidence leaked out that the ARVN remained weak, this might slow troop withdrawals. Senior commanders were therefore encouraged to make positive comments about ARVN progress, which were then distributed widely via the propaganda network. The charade worked too well;

43 Kolko, *Anatomy*, pp. 378–9.
44 Lewy, *America in Vietnam*, p. 172.
45 Ibid., p. 169.
46 Kolko, *Anatomy*, p. 381.
47 Williams *et al.*, eds, *America in Vietnam*, p. 307.

many Americans began to believe that Nixon had found the magic formula to get the US out of the war *and* defeat the communists.

MILITARY OPERATIONS

According to Kissinger, Nixon 'did not believe that negotiations would amount to anything until the military situation changed fundamentally. He thought Hanoi would accept a compromise only if it had no other choice.'[48] Thus, it suited the Americans to maintain the intensity on the battlefield. Huge operations like Junction City were a thing of the past, but Americans still died in large numbers.

Hanoi also decided to keep the kettle on the boil. But this was a high-risk strategy. At the end of 1968, the forces of the revolution were devastated but not dead. 'The greatest danger to the Front, even greater than US and GVN exertions, was that the leaders of COSVN and the politburo in Hanoi would ask too much', writes Bergerud. That is what happened during 1969 and, as a result, the NLF came close to destruction. A PAVN lieutenant captured near Cu Chi confessed that it was 'very difficult for the Viet Cong to mount an offensive due to the demoralization of their troops and lack of support of the people'.[49] Samuel Popkin noted how, before Tet, '18-year-old villagers would lie and say they were 13 to get out of the [RVN] draft'. But, after Tet, '13- and 14-year-olds would lie and say they were 18 to get into the draft before the Communists got to them'.[50]

During 1969, incessant American and ARVN pressure was devastating for the revolution, with casualty rates often exceeding those of the Tet Offensive. In December 1969 American officials in the III Corps area reported success on all fronts:

> the progress made in pacification ... during 1969 has been remarkable. If one recalls the situation a year ago, one cannot help but be impressed with the changes wrought. Only a miniscule percentage of the population remains 'under VC control'. Roads which were either closed or extremely dangerous are now teeming with civilian traffic. Curfew hours have been eased. Areas which lay fallow are back under cultivation. The harvest has been bountiful.[51]

48 Kissinger, *White House Years*, p. 263.

49 Bergerud, *Dynamics*, pp. 239, 252.

50 Samuel Popkin, 'Commentary: the village war', in Peter Braestrup, ed., *Vietnam as History: Ten Years After the Paris Peace Accords* (Washington, DC, 1984), p. 102.

51 Bergerud, *Dynamics*, p. 254.

The revolution might not have been able to survive this sort of pressure for much longer. But the US could not sustain it. As in the past, time proved the most important factor. The patience of the American public was wearing thin. The war was supposed to be ending.

The operation at Ap Bia Mountain, or 'Hamburger Hill', in May 1969 left the people at home bewildered. American tactics would have impressed the Grand Old Duke of York. Troops marched up the hill because the enemy was at the top, and killing the enemy was what the war was about. After six days, nine assaults, and heavy casualties, they took the hill, then marched back down again, abandoning it. Hamburger Hill, one of the few large actions of 1969, received more attention than it perhaps deserved. To the American people it was important because it was unimportant; good men died in a futile pursuit.

After 1970, Hanoi pursued a modifed version of protracted war, designed to compensate for the severe losses of the previous two years. The number of small unit actions, which stood at 1,374 in 1968, increased to over 2,400 in 1972, while battalion-sized attacks decreased correspondingly.[52] Communist forces aimed primarily to disperse enemy forces while preserving their own strength. Sappers caused immense damage to American installations and morale. PAVN and PLAF soldiers became even more elusive, refusing, except under the most favourable circumstances, to stand and fight. Hanoi did not want to disturb the American withdrawal by launching major operations, but neither did it want American casualties to be so reduced that the anti-war momentum subsided. A path between these two extremes was successfully negotiated.

This period of relative quiescence also allowed long-delayed economic rejuvenation of North Vietnam, a prerequisite to a future major offensive, to take place. Thus, a strange dichotomy characterized the forces of the revolution. On the battlefield, elementary guerrilla tactics placed great emphasis upon primitive booby traps, mines, and small unit ambushes. Meanwhile, behind the scenes, the PAVN was turning itself into a modern army capable of division-strength mobile operations and armed with sophisticated Soviet weaponry.

American troop withdrawals did not initially reduce combat strength. First to leave were logistical personnel, whose duties were either consolidated more efficiently or transferred to the Vietnamese. It was not until 1971 that combat strength began to drop significantly. But, by that stage, the intensity of combat operations had already declined, as

---

52 Richard A. Hunt, *Pacification* (Boulder, CO, 1995), p. 253.

American units refrained from aggressive search and destroy operations, preferring instead to consolidate control over secure areas. US forces also concentrated more heavily on artillery and air power. More than half the tonnage in shells and bombs used during the entire war was expended during Nixon's first term. Hanoi cooperated by decelerating offensive activity, concentrating instead on mines and ambushes, in the secure knowledge that Nixon's troop withdrawals had their own momentum.

HEARTS AND MINDS AGAIN

Vietnamization coincided with increased efforts to reassert control over rural areas long under NLF domination. Earlier attempts had snagged on the RVN's reluctance to introduce meaningful land reform. On 26 March 1970 a concession was made: the Land to the Tiller Law stipulated that those who cultivated land should own it. The law would have been revolutionary in 1945, but by the time Thieu took action, land was no longer the problem it once was, partly because NLF redistribution was so advanced, but more importantly because the transformation of the RVN economy had rendered South Vietnam a net importer of food. Land prices consequently fell, farms were abandoned, and landlords found that money could be made more easily in the cities. By May 1972, the government had, in theory, created an additional 800,000 landowners, but most were peasants who were formally granted land earlier given by the NLF. It also bears noting that NLF redistribution had strings attached: the peasant was expected to pay taxes, provide intelligence and loan his sons to the military. Thieu's reform had no such conditions, which meant that the government derived little benefit in return. The peasant could accept the RVN's offer, but still support the NLF.[53]

Thieu concentrated reform in the Mekong Delta where, because NLF redistribution was well-advanced, landlords were keen to be compensated for land lost.[54] They could not have been happier. Money earned for worthless land was invested in new methods of exploitation. The American-inspired agricultural revolution provided plenty of opportunities. By 1973, nearly half of Vietnam's agricultural land was mechanically ploughed. Former landlords supplied seeds, fertilizers or machinery, at punishing rates of interest. Usury, which had been dying out, was miraculously rejuvenated by Thieu's 'progressive' reforms.

---

53 See Jeffrey Race, *War Comes to Long An* (Berheley, CA, 1972), pp. 271–6.
54 Kolko, *Anatomy*, pp. 389–91.

A new system of local government was simultaneously implemented, supposedly to reduce the arbitrary power of landlords. Eventually, over 90 per cent of all hamlets had councils and chiefs elected by the local population.[55] But this, too, was more impressive on paper than in reality. Frequently, the only name on the ballot was the individual selected by the Thieu regime. The reform was a cynical attempt to extend central government authority more deeply into the hinterland. 'Thieu's purpose has not been to enact major reforms giving peasants a role in government', an American analyst commented, 'but rather to develop a power base outside ARVN command.'[56] The new bureaucrats brought with them Saigon's talent for extortion.

Pacification got an enormous boost from the Tet Offensive, which decimated the PLAF. HES statistics suggested that the NLF controlled over 4,000 villages in March 1968, less than 1,000 four years later.[57] Though the HES was a crude measurement, the trend it indicated is accurate. In Long An, guerrillas surrendered at an average of 200 per month during 1969, and about 80 per month during 1970. By the end of 1970 perhaps only 420 assorted activists remained in the province.[58] The 320th main force regiment had to be broken up and sent into the region to replace village militia units and political cadres who had been exterminated.[59] After interviewing peasants in eighteen villages in 1970, Samuel Popkin concluded that

> Under the pressures of war the Vietcong were no longer able to deliver social benefits to the population, while the GVN living on American resources was able to begin flooding the countryside with schools, fertilizers, Hondas, infirmaries and hundreds of thousands of non-agricultural jobs. The peasants, although they often realized the superior quality of Viet Cong government, were nonetheless attracted by the better and safer living conditions in GVN controlled areas.[60]

Pacification made great strides, but that does not mean that the population was won over to the RVN. 'People follow the GVN now because it is strong and it offers a chance to make a living', an American

55 Lewy, *America in Vietnam*, p. 188.

56 Samuel Popkin, 'Pacification: politics and the village', *Asian Survey* 10 (August 1970), p. 670.

57 Lewy, *America in Vietnam*, p. 198.

58 Race, *Long An*, p. 269.

59 David W.P. Elliott, 'Hanoi's strategy in the Second Indochina War', in Jayne S. Werner and Luu Doan Huynh, eds, *The Vietnam War: Vietnamese and American Perspectives* (Armonk, NY, 1993), p. 89.

60 Popkin, 'Pacification', p. 663.

215

adviser reflected. 'Should it be unable to maintain both security and a reasonable livelihood for individuals, it will be deserted as was Macbeth by his thanes.'[61] In many places the old dichotomy still existed: hamlets were controlled during the day when government officials felt safe, but the night belonged to the guerrillas. By the end of 1972, despite its severe depletion, the NLF still had *access* to two-thirds of the population.[62]

As in the past, pacification might root out guerrillas, but in the process alienate local peasants, rendering them more susceptible to communist infiltration. There was a great deal of 'coerced population resettlement' in which peasants were herded out of troublesome hamlets. One American observer felt that these were merely 'a gimmick' to remove a black mark from the HES book. 'Putting the people behind barbed wire against their will is not the first step towards earning their loyalty and support',[63] commented another evaluator, who would surely have won first prize for stating the obvious.

The importance of covert operations rose as the American withdrawal gained pace. The most notorious was the Phoenix Program, begun in 1967 under the general direction of Ambassador Robert Komer. It sought to centralize intelligence-gathering and counter-insurgency by way of a network of carefully trained agents inserted into villages and hamlets. Eventually over 300 villages were infiltrated. Funding to the tune of US$4 million was provided by the embassy, and the programme itself was administered by MACV, in cooperation with the CIA.[64] But the agents answered to the RVN Ministry of Rural Development, which meant that the US incurred the criticism, but had little control.

Phoenix became yet another manifestation of Saigon venality and corruption. There were those within the RVN security infrastructure who saw the programme as an opportunity to fight the war in the way the communists had long done so. Their motives were sincere, even if their methods rather brutal. But, in addition to them, the programme also attracted a motley collection of sadists, tricksters and embezzlers interested more in self-aggrandizement than in real counter-insurgency. Opportunities for corruption were immense, and monitoring minimal. Since rewards of up to US$11,000 were offered for a live communist, half that for a dead one, temptations were immense.[65] Individuals were often imprisoned merely for the bribes which could

61 Lewy, *America in Vietnam*, p. 193.
62 Kolko, *Anatomy*, p. 397.
63 Race, *Long An*, p. 219; Lewy, *America in Vietnam*, pp. 181, 184.
64 Douglas Kinnard, *The War Managers* (Wayne, NJ, 1985), p. 102.
65 James P. Harrison, *The Endless War* (New York, NY, 1989), p. 203.

be extracted to obtain their release or to satisfy arbitrary quotas set by overzealous regional administrators. Some NLF members were unmasked, but, in the process, the innocent suffered terribly. Much of the programme's 'success', demonstrated by the number of cadres supposedly neutralized, was in fact bogus. NLF infiltration was high. Communist double agents would inform on political enemies, who would then be 'removed', making life easier for the local NLF cell, not to mention confusing villagers. This infiltration ensured that most big fish escaped the net, a fact which caused the CIA enormous frustration. According to Richard Hunt, in 1970–71 only 3 per cent of those eliminated were full or probationary party members above district level.[66]

The Phoenix Program has received a tremendous amount of bad publicity, much of it inspired by sensationalist rumour. The reputation of the United States, through its sponsorship of the programme, has suffered proportionately. The *New York Times* called it 'one of the most degrading enterprises carried out by Americans in Vietnam'.[67] Because Phoenix was a covert operation, getting to the truth has been difficult: much of what actually happened is still shrouded in secrecy, while at the same time the operation attracted its share of fantasists keen to boast about what they witnessed. Yoshia Chee, who allegedly served as an adviser to a South Vietnamese People's Reconnaissance Unit (PRU), claimed that one of the favourite forms of torture was 'popping . . . eyeballs out with a spoon'.[68] PRU operatives allegedly exercised a 'no holds barred' approach to interrogation. Kenneth Barton Osborn, an enlisted man with the 149th and 525th Military Intelligence Groups, told a Congressional committee in 1971 that

> I never knew an individual to be detained as a VC suspect who ever lived through an interrogation in a year and a half, and that included quite a number of individuals . . . There was never any reasonable establishment of the fact that any of those individuals was, in fact, cooperating with the Vietcong, but they all died and the majority were either tortured to death or things like thrown from helicopters.

The more virulent condemnations of the American role in the Phoenix Program have relied heavily on Osborn's evidence. It is, however, very suspect. Another adviser to a PRU, Richard Welcome, claimed:

66 Hunt, *Pacification*, p. 249.
67 *New York Times*, 22 August 1975.
68 Mark Moyar, *Phoenix and the Birds of Prey* (Annapolis, MD, 1997), pp. 91–2. Since Moyar has found no evidence to show that Chee actually served as a PRU adviser, it is safe to assume that his claims are bogus.

Prisoners were abused. Were they tortured? It depends on what you call torture. Electricity was used by the Vietnamese, water was used, occasionally some of the prisoners got beat up. Were any of them put on the rack, eyes gouged out, bones broken? No, I never saw any evidence of that at all.

It is entirely possible that Welcome's testimony is as unreliable as that of Osborn. But the weight of evidence favours the former. It seems that the Phoenix Program was not quite as brutal and sadistic as many would like to believe.[69] Cruelty makes good copy.

Phoenix was in truth an escalation of a battle between underground representatives on both sides of the conflict, which had been going on since the French era. The secret war was suddenly less secret, more open and a great deal more violent. In some respects, Phoenix was merely Saigon's variant of Hanoi's 'extermination of traitors' campaign. For elite members of the RVN National Police, many of whom had lost family members to communist assassination, the programme presented a welcome opportunity for retribution. Pay-back was possible for one very simple reason: for the first time since the early 1960s the countryside was sufficiently secure for RVN officials to go into the villages and kill cadres.

Figures for Phoenix 'neutralizations' vary widely, with estimates as high as 100,000 and as low as 25,000.[70] Whatever the correct figure, it is generally agreed that Phoenix must have weakened the revolution. Since the movement was by this stage spread very thinly, the elimination of a few cadres in a particular area could cripple local organization. One PLAF defector told the CIA analyst Frank Snepp in January 1973 that 'politically the VC were defunct'. But, at best, Phoenix probably hastened a development which was inevitable in any case, namely the transfer of power in the South from the PLAF to PAVN. It obviously did not affect the outcome of the war, though some armchair strategists are intrigued by the theoretical possibilities of such a programme had it been attempted earlier and with greater energy. But at what cost? The operation undoubtedly spread alienation among the peasants. America's moral mission was sullied by the association with torture and wholesale assassination. 'I sometimes think we would have gotten better publicity for molesting children', an

---

69 Ibid., pp. 99–107.

70 Moyar, who has provided what appears to be the most carefully counted figure, claims some 26,369 killed from 1968 to 1972. See p. 236. Higher estimates are often derived from reports emanating from Hanoi. The communists often tended to lump almost all executions of cadre occurring after 1967 under the Phoenix umbrella.

American official confessed in 1972.[71] Komer concluded that Phoenix was 'a small, poorly managed and largely ineffective effort'.[72]

An American study concluded in 1972 that fewer than one in five peasants wanted American troops to stay, even though it was widely understood that when they left the communists would triumph. The NLF had been significantly weakened, but, according to Komer, 'we never were able to translate this into positive and active rural support for the Government of Vietnam. . . . we were never able, ourselves, to generate a counterattraction in Saigon that ever had the charisma, the capability, the administrative effectiveness'.[73] Aggressive pacification at best created a vacuum; the NLF was removed, but no new focus of power replaced it. Minds were won, but not hearts.

Guy Pauker, a Rand pacification analyst, claimed in 1971 that 'a feat of political alchemy' had occurred: the South Vietnamese government now seemed viable, given a continuation of American aid and the acceptance of 'low-level Communist violence'. Assuming that Pauker was an honest man, one has to conclude that he had been sucked into a swamp of self-delusion. At every level from the White House to the ordinary platoon, artifice was endemic. Some lied wilfully, some tacitly, others quite innocently. Even the wary were duped. In December 1969 the respected journalist Stewart Alsop praised pacification in an issue of *Newsweek*. The article was inspired by a supposedly unescorted trip Alsop took with Ambassador William Colby in the Mekong Delta. In fact,

> armed teams proceeded and followed the car, close enough
> to provide protection but distant enough not to be seen by
> occupants. A number of armed helicopters, out of sight, also
> accompanied the 'unescorted' tour, and outposts along the way
> were constantly informed of their progress. Unfortunately, this
> kind of deception was not uncommon.[74]

Clearly, the Americans still had much to learn about winning hearts and minds. A Senate Foreign Relations study of 1972 quoted one adviser who blithely remarked, 'All I know is that there has been progress, and progress as I see it is tractors and Hondas'.[75]

71 Hunt, *Pacification*, p. 236.
72 Andrew F. Krepinevich, *The Army and Vietnam* (Baltimore, MD, 1986), pp. 228–9.
73 Kolko, *Anatomy*, pp. 396–7.
74 Kinnard, *War Managers*, pp. 108, 146.
75 Williams *et al.*, eds, *America in Vietnam*, p. 305.

CAMBODIA AND LAOS

The ease with which Hanoi had violated the neutrality of Laos and Cambodia had been a source of deep frustration for the US. The sanctuaries in and infiltration routes through the two countries rendered it impossible to control insurgent activity in South Vietnam. Enemy units would slip across the border whenever the tide of battle shifted unfavourably. COSVN was located just inside the Cambodian border, 50 miles from Saigon, yet was impervious to American interference. Likewise, the port of Sihanoukville became an increasingly important conduit for supplies destined for the PLAF. Souvanna Phouma and Norodom Sihanouk, the leaders of Laos and Cambodia, respectively, did not resist Hanoi's incursions, since they did not want to anger communists in their own countries, nor spark a wider war. Meanwhile, the US, while it had resisted temptations to invade both countries with ground troops, did pound the Ho Chi Minh Trail, so much so that more American bombs fell on Laos during the war than on North or South Vietnam. In other words, both sides in the war cruelly exploited Laos and Cambodia, to such a degree that by 1969 their fragile neutrality had become very precarious.

The Cambodian situation was complicated by the rise of Pol Pot, one of the founders of the Kampuchean Communist Party (KCP), or Khmer Rouge. He wanted Cambodian communists to distance themselves from Hanoi, an idea which delighted the Chinese, who preferred Indochinese communists to be divided, the better to limit the DRV's influence. Pol Pot justifiably felt that Hanoi was exploiting the Cambodian people. The KCP's increasingly successful guerrilla campaign in the northwestern provinces disturbed Sihanouk's carefully cultivated neutrality. He assumed that Pol Pot was Hanoi's puppet, and therefore moved closer to the United States. Nixon was happy to exploit Sihanouk's predicament. Before his inauguration, he advised Kissinger that 'a very definite change of policy toward Cambodia should be one of the first orders of business when we get in'.[76] The President hoped that eliminating enemy installations in Cambodia would benefit Vietnamization.

On 18 March 1969 the US began bombing Cambodia, with the aim of cutting the Ho Chi Minh Trail, destroying supplies destined for southern insurgents, and eliminating COSVN. Under Operation Menu, 3,630 B-52 sorties dropped over 100,000 tons of bombs during

---

76 Caroline Page, *US Official Propaganda During the Vietnam War, 1965–1973* (London, 1996), p. 252.

a fourteen-month period.[77] The operation was kept secret – except from those underneath the bombs. As late as 11 May 1970, in a nation-wide address, Nixon insisted that 'American policy . . . has been to scrupulously respect the neutrality of the Cambodian people'.[78] According to Kissinger, had the bombing been made public, Sihanouk would have been forced to condemn it, or reveal his complicity. Secrecy also averted an outcry within the United States, where most people assumed that the war was being brought to an end, not widened.

The bombing failed on all counts. COSVN was not destroyed, nor is there any evidence to suggest that PLAF/PAVN soldiers in South Vietnam were starved of supplies. By this stage in the war, they were sufficiently adept at camouflage, tunnelling and fortification to provide sanctuaries from American bombers. In any case, since American intelligence had failed to provide a precise location for COSVN, hitting it with bombs was rather difficult.

The B-52s did, however, succeed in further destabilizing Cambodian politics. A year after the bombing began, Sihanouk was ousted by his own ministers. The new government under General Lon Nol immediately demanded that all Vietnamese troops leave Cambodia, much to Nixon's delight. Sihanouk subsequently claimed that the US had engineered the coup, an allegation perhaps just short of the truth. Washington knew it was coming and supported it once launched. Lon Nol's brother, Lon Non, confessed that 'We would not have done what we did, had we not been absolutely sure President Nixon would support us'.[79] But, though Nixon was pleased by the rise of Lon Nol, few expected the latter to hold his country together. The ultimate benefactor was Pol Pot, whose insurrection fed on government weakness. By May 1970 Khmer Rouge troops had forced Lon Nol's forces back into the major towns and cities. Phnom Penh was surrounded.

Nixon then decided to invade. Fifteen thousand American and ARVN troops crossed the border on 1 May 1970. 'Cambodia . . . has sent out a call to the United States . . . for assistance', Nixon subsequently claimed. In truth, Lon Nol had not been fully informed of the operation, which was designed to bolster American efforts in Vietnam, not to aid the struggle against the Khmer Rouge. Nixon admitted as much when he promised that the campaign would 'protect our men

77 Earl H. Tilford, 'Bombing our way back home: the commando hunt and menu campaigns of 1969–1973', in William Head and Lawrence Grintner, eds, *Looking Back on the Vietnam War* (Westport, CT, 1993), p. 130.

78 McMahon, *Major Problems*, p. 453.

79 Ben Kiernan, 'The impact on Cambodia of the US intervention in Vietnam', in Werner and Huynh, eds, *Vietnam War*, p. 221.

who are in Vietnam and ... guarantee the continued success of our withdrawal and Vietnamization programmes'.[80] When critics questioned the legality of the operation, Nixon angrily replied that 'the legal justification ... is the right of the President of the United States under the Constitution to protect the lives of American men'.[81]

The Cambodian operation gave justification to Nixon's madman image. Frustrated by the limits imposed on his use of power in Vietnam, he could not resist lashing out elsewhere. Despite his acceptance of the need to de-escalate, he seems to have been uncomfortable in the cloak of a peace president, and perhaps convinced himself that he could further peace by waging his own little war in Cambodia. His explanation was appropriately aggressive:

> If, when the chips are down, the world's most powerful nation, the United States of America, acts like a pitiful, helpless giant, the forces of totalitarianism and anarchy will threaten free nations and free institutions throughout the world. ... I have rejected all political considerations in making this decision. ... I would rather be a one-term President and do what I believe is right than to be a two-term President at the cost of seeing America become a second-rate power and to see this nation accept the first defeat in its proud 190-year history.[82]

The nation was not convinced. Most people had trusted the President to find an honourable exit from the war. He was attacked from all angles. For perhaps the first time, ordinary Americans questioned the morality of their mission in Southeast Asia. College campuses, relatively quiet since the election, again erupted in violence.[83] Four administration aides resigned in protest. The Senate Foreign Relations Committee angrily repealed the Tonkin Gulf Resolution and placed a time limit on the deployment of troops in Cambodia. The country was conforming to the President's paranoid delusions, rendering him even more stubborn. 'Don't worry about divisiveness', he told his staff. 'Having drawn the sword, don't take it out – stick it in hard. ... Hit 'em in the gut.'[84] 'A siege mentality was setting in', presidential aide Charles Colson recalled. 'It was now "us" against "them". Gradually,

---

80 McMahon, *Major Problems*, pp. 452–3.
81 Richard M. Nixon, *A New Road for America: Major Policy Statements, March 1970 to October 1971* (New York, NY, 1972), pp. 675, 683.
82 McMahon, *Major Problems*, pp. 454–5.
83 See Chapter 12, pp. 309–10.
84 William Safire, *Before the Fall* (New York, NY, 1975), p. 190.

as we drew the circle closer around us, the ranks of "them" began to swell.'[85]

Nixon convinced himself that the raids had knocked the 'living bejeesus' out of COSVN. 'Anything that walked is gone', he boasted in private.[86] He was more temperate in public: 'We have ended the concept of Cambodian sanctuaries, immune from attack'.[87] On 8 May he claimed:

> we have bought at least 6 months and probably 8 months of time for the training of the ARVN ... We have also saved hundreds, if not thousands, of Americans ... by buying time, it means that if the enemy does come back into those sanctuaries next time, the South Vietnamese will be strong enough to handle it alone.[88]

MACV boasted that 2,000 PAVN soldiers were killed, 8,000 bunkers destroyed and 1,600 acres of jungle cleared, while large caches of food and ammunition were captured.[89] But numbers had never been an adequate measure of success in this war and were not now. In fact, COSVN was never found, and PAVN moved back into its sanctuaries within weeks of the American withdrawal. There is no conclusive evidence that the invasion upset a planned PAVN offensive in the South, as presidential sources subsequently claimed.[90] Nor did it interrupt the relentless march of the Khmer Rouge to Phnom Penh. In Paris, negotiations between Kissinger and Tho were suspended by an angry Hanoi, thus undermining Nixon's assumption that aggression would force the communists to negotiate.

Pol Pot could not have asked for a better recruiter than Nixon. Refugees (the Pentagon estimated a total of 130,000) were particularly susceptible to Khmer Rouge indoctrination. 'The bombers may kill some Communists, but they kill everyone else, too', a disgruntled villager remarked. Chhiht Do, a former KCP leader, described how Pol Pot used American raids for propaganda purposes:

> they would take the people to see the craters, to see how the earth had been gouged out and scorched. . . . The ordinary

85 Charles W. Colson, *Born Again* (Old Tappan, NJ, 1976), p. 41.
86 William Shawcross, *Sideshow* (London, 1979), pp. 152–3.
87 Baritz, *Backfire*, p. 198.
88 Nixon, *Presidential Press Conferences*, p. 103.
89 George C. Herring, *America's Longest War* (New York, NY, 1986), p. 236.
90 See Phillip B. Davidson, *Vietnam at War* (Oxford, 1988), p. 628, and Bruce Palmer, *The 25 Year War* (New York, NY, 1984), p. 102 for a more positive assessment of the achievements of the campaign.

people . . . sometimes literally shit in their pants when the big bombs and shells came. . . . Their minds just froze up and they would wander around mute for three or four days. Terrified and half-crazy, the people were ready to believe what they were told. . . . That was what made it so easy for the Khmer Rouge to win the people over.[91]

Nixon achieved what had hitherto seemed impossible, namely harmony between Pol Pot and Sihanouk. A new alliance called the National United Front for Kampuchea (FUNK) was formed, in which Sihanouk was the figurehead and Pol Pot the brute strength. Some 200,000 new followers joined the KCP by 1972.[92]

Next on the invasion list was Laos. In Operation Lam Son 719, launched on 30 January 1971, ARVN troops, supported by US air cover, were supposed to cut the Ho Chi Minh Trail, destroy sanctuaries, and decimate PAVN troops. In a conventional war such a bold move might have been strategically sound, but this was not a conventional war. In any case, PAVN troops were too numerous, too well-entrenched and too experienced to be dislodged by 16,000 ARVN conscripts operating in a hostile environment.[93] 'We were asking the South Vietnamese to conduct an operation that we had refused to take when we had 500,000 troops in Vietnam', Kissinger later admitted.[94] Six weeks after invading, ARVN troops were in headlong retreat. As they fled, they trampled over the reputation of Vietnamization.

Thieu had instructed his commanders to terminate operations once casualties reached an unacceptable level.[95] This annoyed the Americans, but was probably quite a sensible decision since Thieu did not want to sacrifice troops needed for his own protection in an operation designed to aid American withdrawal. Hanoi concluded that Lam Son 719 had resulted in a 'profound transformation' of the struggle. 'As we begin 1972, we are facing a great opportunity and can develop it quite beautifully.'[96] This was a fair assessment. The Laotian operation, designed to pre-empt a future PAVN offensive by cutting supply lines, in fact made such an offensive more likely by exposing ARVN weaknesses. There had been conspicuous cases of panic, cowardice, desertion and faking of wounds. Yet not long after the last bedraggled

91 Kiernan, 'The impact on Cambodia', pp. 222–5.
92 Duiker, *Sacred War*, p. 231.
93 Norman Hannah, *The Key to Failure: Laos and the Vietnam War* (Lanham, MD, 1987), p. 284.
94 Kissinger, *White House Years*, p. 999.
95 Palmer, *25 Year War*, p. 112.
96 Kolko, *Anatomy*, p. 376.

ARVN soldier stumbled out of Laos, Nixon announced, in a nation-wide broadcast, 'I can report tonight that Vietnamization has succeeded'. Privately, both he and Kissinger admitted that the operation 'was clearly not a success'.[97]

THE TURN OF DIPLOMACY

Nixon entered the White House confident that he was 'the one man in this country' who could end the war within a year.[98] But as the 1972 election approached, his 'plan' lay in tatters: negotiations had stalled and Vietnamization seemed a sham. American troop levels, which stood at 542,000 when Nixon took office, shrunk to around 200,000 by the end of 1971, and to less than 50,000 by June 1972. An irresistable momentum governed the withdrawal; American voters would not tolerate any deviation from it. The North Vietnamese, realizing that troops once departed would not return, saw advantage in being patiently uncooperative at the peace talks. The Nixon approach had clearly failed, since Vietnamization was supposed to convince the Politburo that it was wiser to negotiate a compromise than to delay and face a much-strengthened ARVN. On 26 January 1972 Kissinger accused Hanoi of holding out for a peace settlement 'in which the probability of their taking over is close to certainty'.[99] Truer words were seldom spoken.

While negotiations in Paris stagnated, Nixon turned to great power diplomacy. He and Kissinger hoped that, by winding down the war, they could improve relations with the USSR and China, and that such a development would in turn facilitate an acceptable settlement in Vietnam. The conflict in Indochina would become an insignificant local difficulty instead of a potent symbol of Cold War tension. An easing of the diplomatic situation with respect to both countries would, it was hoped, allow partition to become acceptable to all parties. But, whatever happened, Vietnam would not be allowed to hinder detente with the USSR and China, which was the overriding goal. Where Kissinger erred was in believing that he could mould the world as he pleased. He encouraged Nixon to think that trade and diplomatic concessions would persuade both countries to loosen ties with Vietnam. But this strategy, formulated before Nixon became President, was far more complicated than he anticipated. Neither China, nor the

97 Kimball, *Nixon's Vietnam War*, pp. 246–7.
98 Haldeman, *Ends of Power*, p. 82.
99 McMahon, *Major Problems*, p. 456.

USSR, nor indeed the DRV, were willing to play to the script Kissinger wrote. Eventually, obstreperous actors manipulated the director.

Nixon and Kissinger failed to appreciate that Chinese attitudes toward Vietnam had more to do with age-old conceptions of Southeast Asian dominance than with new Marxist imperialism. In any case, the idea of a 'Chinese view' was mistaken; her policy was notoriously inconsistent. Despite these obstacles and misconceptions, some progress was made. In March 1971 Chou En lai informed the DRV leaders that, in his opinion, the war was proceeding toward an acceptable conclusion (given the American withdrawal) and that the Vietnamese struggle would not be allowed to impede improvement of Sino-American relations. In July Kissinger made his first secret visit to Beijing. Shortly afterwards the Chinese pressured Hanoi to accept a compromise settlement. In the following November, an alarmed Pham Van Dong, Prime Minister of the DRV, went to Beijing to urge Mao Zedong to cancel Nixon's planned visit to China. Mao flatly refused, and further suggested that Hanoi should prepare for a long-term American presence in South Vietnam and a protracted political struggle.

Diplomacy with the Soviets was more straightforward, but not necessarily more promising. Sheer arrogance perhaps prevented Nixon and Kissinger from realizing that, since the United States was more desperate for a deal than the USSR, the power to exploit rested with the latter. Detente with the Soviet Union gave Moscow a more secure European frontier and important trade concessions. The Americans, in contrast, never got what they really wanted, namely Soviet pressure upon Hanoi to negotiate.

Vietnam was as much an expression of Sino-Soviet rivalry as a source of tension between 'free' and communist worlds. Nixon and Kissinger hoped to exploit this rivalry and thus alter the context within which Vietnam lay. But this part of the plan backfired badly. They did not appreciate that, by playing upon the split, they exacerbated Sino-Soviet differences, and made Vietnam a test of virility for each power. Despite the President's success in achieving detente with both countries, Chinese aid to the DRV doubled between 1971 and 1972 while Soviet aid more than doubled.[100] Diplomatic overtures ultimately benefited the DRV more than the US, especially since 'success' rendered Nixon more confident about troop withdrawals, thus easing the burden facing the DRV. Kissinger and Nixon failed to understand the DRV's role within the complex equation. They thought that superpowers could mould the destinies of small states, that strength alone

100 Kolko, *Anatomy*, p. 429.

determined influence. Instead, Hanoi found itself in the eminently advantageous position of a spoiled child whose parents are in the process of divorce, when each spouse seeks to please the child in order to wound the other.

THE EASTER OFFENSIVE

Diplomatic developments reminded Hanoi once again that the Chinese were motivated more by hard pragmatism than brotherly love. Suitably chastened, the Politburo decided to pursue its own goals by its own means, namely by embarking upon a major military offensive. The idea of a complete victory while US troops were still on Vietnamese soil had intoxicating allure, as did the prospect of defying the Chinese. It is perhaps no coincidence that the offensive, like Tet before it, occurred during an American election year. Hanoi hoped that a worsening military situation would persuade Nixon to make concessions in Paris, in order to placate voters.

In the Nguyen Hue (or 'Easter') Offensive, launched on 30 March 1972, three divisions attacked across the DMZ with the aim of liberating Quang Tri province and threatening Da Nang. A second attack around Kontum, Plieku and Binh Dinh sought to cut South Vietnam in two. A third hit Loc Ninh and An Loc, preparatory to an assault upon Saigon. In all, some 125,000 troops were deployed, supported by hundreds of tanks.[101]

The attack sent Nixon into an incandescent rage. Home-bound air squadrons and Navy carriers were immediately ordered back to Vietnam. 'We should go for broke', he told Kissinger. 'I intend to stop at nothing to bring the enemy to his knees. . . . He has gone over the brink *and so have we*. The only question is whether we have the *will* to use that power. What distinguishes me from Johnson is that I have the *will* in spades.'[102] In Operation Linebacker, bombing of the North was resumed with an intensity and ferocity not seen during the heaviest months of Rolling Thunder. The B-52 force, which had shrunk to 83 by the end of March, swelled to 171 six weeks later.[103] 'The bastards have never been bombed like they're going to be bombed this time', Nixon promised.[104] Hanoi and Haiphong were spared, but elsewhere destruction was widespread. Within America, few shared

---

101 G.H. Turley, *The Easter Offensive* (Annapolis, MD, 1985), pp. 29ff.; Davidson, *Vietnam at War*, pp. 673–7.
102 Nixon, *RN*, pp. 606–7.
103 Peter MacDonald, *Giap* (London, 1993), p. 310.
104 Herring, *America's Longest War*, p. 247.

Nixon's anger and few, therefore, supported the bombing. 'After three years of Richard Nixon, is LBJ back in the White House?', Senator Alan Cranston asked. Fellow Senator John Tunney warned: 'there is despair in this country and it's increasing and it's deepening and it's real and it's legitimate'.[105]

Linebacker was, ironically, more successful than any previous bombing campaign. 'Smart' bombs allowed much greater accuracy. And since Hanoi was now pursuing a strategy of conventional war, the North's war machine was much more dependent upon petroleum and spare parts, and therefore much more vulnerable to bombing. Improved technique also allowed greater damage to be caused with fewer bombs and fewer sorties than during Rolling Thunder. The loss rate consequently fell.[106]

On the ground, the ARVN, fighting virtually without American ground support, was everywhere forced to retreat. By 13 April Loc Ninh was captured and An Loc surrounded. Kontum was only barely held after the ARVN 23rd Division provided timely reinforcement. Most of Quang Tri was overrun by 4 May, placing Hué under enormous pressure. But then the advance slowed. General Ngo Quang Truong, given command of ARVN troops in the north, skilfully relieved the pressure on Hué. ARVN units gradually regrouped, then launched a methodical counter-attack. PAVN was pushed back everywhere, even at the scene of its greatest success in Quang Tri, which was recaptured on 15 September. North Vietnamese losses were heavy, with perhaps 75,000 killed and 700 tanks destroyed.[107]

By attacking along three separate fronts simultaneously, Giap had diffused his strength and failed to deliver a knockout blow anywhere. Supply problems forced him to pause after each tactical success, allowing the ARVN to re-group. In other words, PAVN was ill-prepared logistically for such an ambitious campaign. These deficiencies were further compounded by division commanders who had little experience of conventional warfare. Brave soldiers were wasted by incompetent command and unrealistic strategies.

During the counter-offensive, Abrams remarked: 'By God, the South Vietnamese can hack it!'[108] The fighting was dramatic proof that Saigon, for all its inadequacies, was still able to put together a huge force of men willing to fight and die to stop the communists.

105 Bruce Oudes, ed., *From: The President – Richard Nixon's Secret Files* (New York, NY, 1989), p. 423.
106 Lewy, *America in Vietnam*, pp. 410–11.
107 Kinnard, *War Managers*, p. 150.
108 Palmer, *25 Year War*, p. 122.

American advisers believed they would crack in the first few weeks; that they did not do so came as a huge surprise. In other words, the offensive lends powerful evidence to those South Vietnamese who, to this day, claim that they were building a country and that people were still willing to die for the anti-communist cause. But, though individual soldiers fought well when properly led, good command was unfortunately rare. According to Colonel G.H. Turley, chief adviser with the 3rd ARVN Division, the offensive revealed

> the full array of leadership traits. Heroic, traitorous, skilled and nearly incompetent leaders all passed in review. Unresponsive leadership from the highest levels of command within the South Vietnamese government accounted for much of the tragedy which resulted from the early encounters.[109]

The most significant reason for the PAVN defeat was American airpower, in particular the tactical use of B-52s. Some 50 per cent of PAVN tanks put out of action were destroyed from the air; 74 per cent of all sorties were flown by American pilots.[110] The North Vietnamese tendency to rely on age-old tactics of massed infantry attacks rendered bombing even more lethal. After the battle, Sir Robert Thompson concluded that, while 'it is untrue to say that the battles were won solely by American air power, it would be true to say that they could not have been won without it'.[111]

Though ARVN technically won, the omens were dire. Nixon's diplomatic successes with the Chinese and Soviets had not prevented Hanoi from mounting a major offensive. Pacification was seriously impeded, with the number of hamlets under communist control rising significantly. ARVN never recovered what the Vietnamese dubbed 'Third Vietnam', the area within the II Corps Tactical Zone in the Central Highlands which Hanoi's generals had long concluded would be the ultimate theatre of decision. With PAVN in position around all the cities in the region, there was little Saigon could do but wait for the blow to fall. American analysts concluded that 'the overall enemy position . . . [has] been greatly strengthened in terms of freedom of movement, access to population and food supplies, and a weakening of the faith of the rural population in the ability of the government to protect them'.[112] Furthermore, the destruction of villages by trigger-happy RVN bombers and artillery units spread disaffection. Some

109 Turley, *Easter Offensive*, p. 302.
110 Lewy, *America in Vietnam*, p. 200.
111 Robert Thompson, *Peace is Not at Hand* (London, 1974), p. 110.
112 Kolko, *Anatomy*, p. 428.

970,000 new refugees resulted, of whom 600,000 were confined in miserable camps. An American adviser, Lieutenant-Colonel Robert Wagner, concluded that, up until the Easter Offensive, the people were growing 'more and more committed to the GVN. Now, many are measuring . . . their commitments, waiting for the winner.'[113] But the most worrying omen was the way the offensive exposed the limits of Vietnamization. There was, however, no turning back. On the eve of the 1972 Republican convention, the last American combat soldier left Vietnam.

TALKING, BOMBING AND TALKING

The Easter Offensive gave impetus to the peace process, as Hanoi had hoped, but not in the way anticipated. When secret talks resumed in July, Le Duc Tho was at first confidently intransigent, but turned more accommodating when it became clear that Nixon was certain to be re-elected. The DRV proposed the establishment of a coalition government which would include representatives from both the People's Revolutionary Government (essentially the NLF) and the Thieu government, in addition to neutral elements. But, aware that Hanoi was seriously weakened by its costly offensive, the US refused to countenance a coalition. In early October Le Duc Tho abandoned his insistence upon power-sharing, accepting instead the idea of a cease-fire, followed by the complete withdrawal of US forces. A tripartite Council of National Concord would administer the post-treaty transition.

Kissinger, convinced that 'peace is at hand', was euphoric. But he reckoned without Thieu's determination to wreck the plan. The RVN leader had adopted a 'Four No's' policy: no negotiating with the enemy, no communist activity in South Vietnam, no coalition government, no surrender of territory.[114] Needless to say, this left little room for negotiation with the DRV. When Kissinger met Thieu in Saigon between 18 and 23 October he found that the latter would not budge. Letting loose his anger, Kissinger (according to one account) hissed: '[Thieu] has chosen to act the martyr, but he hasn't got what it takes! If we have to, the United States can sign a separate treaty with Hanoi. As for me, I'll never set foot in Saigon again. Not after this. This is the worst failure of my diplomatic career!'[115] After cooling down, he tried to mollify Thieu by arguing that the bedraggled PAVN

113 Lewy, *America in Vietnam*, pp. 198, 201.
114 Kolko, *Anatomy*, p. 434.
115 Tran Van Don, *Our Endless War* (Novato, CA, 1978), p. 208.

was no match for the mighty ARVN and by promising that Nixon would send American forces to the rescue in the event of a new DRV offensive.

'It is hard to exaggerate the toughness of Thieu's position', an exasperated Kissinger told Nixon. 'His demands verge on insanity.' Nixon realized that Thieu, like a scorned lover, could cause a great deal of embarrassment on the eve of the election. He therefore decided that the time was not ripe to abandon South Vietnam. 'You have got to get Henry to slow down', Nixon told an aide.[116] On Nixon's insistence, Kissinger relayed Thieu's demands to Hanoi, most of which were flatly rejected. Hanoi then tabled a number of new demands, and the talks stalled. Though he had failed to deliver peace, Nixon won the election by one of the largest landslides in American history, defeating the hapless George McGovern. Having secured a huge mandate, he could now act more freely in Vietnam.

Kissinger was becoming increasingly frustrated with the way 'a little fourth rate power like Vietnam' was treating him with disdain. 'They're just a bunch of shits. Tawdry, filthy shits', he remarked.[117] In what he called his 'most difficult decision of the war', Nixon ordered airstrikes on 19 December.[118] The notorious Christmas bombing, or Linebacker II, was a 'brief . . . massive use of force' designed to get the 'message through to Hanoi'.[119] 'I don't want any more of this crap about the fact that we couldn't hit this target or that one', Nixon told Admiral Thomas Moorer. 'This is your chance to use military power to win the war, and if you don't, I'll consider you responsible.'[120] Kissinger took delight in being 'in control of things again' instead of being like a rabbit 'trapped between two [Vietnamese] snakes'.[121]

North Vietnam was attacked around the clock: by night with B-52s and F-111s, during the day with tactical strike aircraft. In a campaign lasting twelve days, 729 B-52 and 640 fighter-bomber sorties dropped around 20,000 tons of bombs on oil storage facilities, railroad yards, supply dumps, and repair depots in the Hanoi–Haiphong area.[122] The operation caused, according to the DRV, between 1,300 and 1,600

---

116 Walter Isaacson, *Kissinger* (New York, NY, 1992), p. 441, 457.

117 Nixon, *RN*, p. 733; Jeffrey P. Kimball, 'Nixon and the diplomacy of threat and symbolism', in David L. Anderson, ed., *Shadow on the White House* (Lawrence, KS, 1993), pp. 159–60.

118 Nixon, *RN*, p. 734.

119 Harrison, *Endless War*, p. 287.

120 Nixon, *RN*, p. 734.

121 Kimball, *Nixon's Vietnam War*, p. 364.

122 Davidson, *Vietnam at War*, pp. 727–8; Kolko, *Anatomy*, p. 441; Nalty, ed., *Vietnam War*, p. 208.

fatalities.[123] This explosion of anger carried a high cost for the US. American pilots paid dearly for complacent assumptions that, because of the success of Linebacker I, raids upon the North could be conducted in relative safety. The DRV's air defence system had grown significantly more sophisticated since Rolling Thunder. The US lost 26 aircraft, including 15 B-52s. Twenty-nine crewmen were killed, 33 captured, and 26 rescued after crashes.[124] The losses were doubly painful for the American people coming, as they did, just before Christmas. The war was supposed to be nearly over and B-52s were supposed to be virtually invulnerable. Hanoi called the battle an 'aerial Dien Bien Phu'. That is perhaps an exaggeration, but what is clear is that the United States could not have continued the attacks much longer given Moscow's willingness to keep Hanoi supplied with SAMs and other AA weaponry.

It is probably safe to say that Hanoi did not anticipate the attacks. One feels instinctively that the DRV fell into a trap which the devious Nixon and Kissinger had set. While the bombing was going on, the US rushed huge amounts of supplies to South Vietnam and a huge effort was devoted to shaping the domestic balance of forces in the South. A multitude of low-level skirmishes called the 'battle of the flags' had been going on for some time in anticipation of an agreement at Paris. The ARVN used the bombing interlude to intervene in this struggle in a big way, in the process mauling scattered PLAF units and assuming control over large tracts of territory. It is also safe to say that the B-52s were designed to impress Saigon as much as Hanoi. Nixon wanted Thieu to believe that the power of the US Air Force would be used if Hanoi did not behave. This, he thought, would persuade Thieu to accept the agreement and perhaps even encourage all friendly elements in the South to believe that there was still logic in continuing the struggle.

The *New York Times* called the action 'war by tantrum'. The *Washington Post* thought that the American people would 'cringe in shame and . . . wonder at their President's very sanity'.[125] But Nixon insisted that there was method to his madness. 'The Russians and the Chinese might think they were dealing with a madman', he explained to a columnist. They would then 'force North Vietnam into a settlement before the world was consumed by a larger war'.[126]

---

123 Lewy, *America in Vietnam*, p. 413.
124 Nalty, ed., *Vietnam War*, p. 208.
125 Nixon, *RN*, p. 738.
126 Baritz, *Backfire*, p. 213.

Talks in Paris did resume. Those who had always believed in bombing drew predictable conclusions: bombs had forced the DRV back to the negotiating table. Westmoreland even surmised that 'Had the United States employed the massive power of the B-52s in 1968 as they did in 1972, Hanoi would have come to the negotiating table then; the war would have been shortened and thousands of American – and Vietnamese – lives would have been saved.'[127] But the fallacy in this argument is bigger than the payload of a B-52. The North Vietnamese returned to the conference table because they knew that at the very least they could get the terms offered in October, which had been acceptable. Those terms were not available in 1968, which explains why they refused to negotiate seriously. Linebacker II caused a change of mind among leaders in Hanoi, but not a change of direction. They were still intent upon the complete conquest of the South, by whatever means. No bombing campaign could change that.

On 9 January 1973 agreement was finally reached. On the crucial question of the future of South Vietnam, Article 15 was studiously vague:

> The re-unification of Vietnam shall be carried out step by step through peaceful means on the basis of discussions and agreements between North and South Vietnam, without coercion or annexation by either party, and without foreign interference. The time for re-unification will be agreed upon by North and South Vietnam.[128]

Thieu would remain in power until elections were held by a trilateral National Council. Crucially, PAVN units would be allowed to remain in the South, in positions occupied prior to the cease-fire. Since these were basically the same conditions on the table in October, it is unclear what the bombing actually achieved.

Thieu felt cruelly betrayed. For him, the most important, and iniquitous, aspect of the settlement was the fact that PAVN troops would remain on southern soil. As Tran Van Don reflected:

> What occurred was a cease-fire in place, rather like a policeman interrupting a robber holding up a candy store. Under the principle agreed to by the United States, the law enforcement officer would leave the robber pointing his weapon at the

127 MacDonald, *Giap*, p. 343.
128 McMahon, *Major Problems*, p. 562.

frightened store owner instead of hauling him off to jail in handcuffs.[129]

By a combination of threats and promises, Thieu was persuaded to accept the agreement. Nixon insisted that the 'problem of North Vietnamese troops is manageable under the agreement', and promised that, if the DRV violated the settlement, America would 'respond with full force'.[130] But, if Thieu remained obstinate, the US would 'proceed . . . if necessary alone'.[131]

Hanoi was patient enough to realize that the best course was to agree a settlement which allowed the Americans to leave with dignity intact. The Politburo was confident that, once they left, victory was certain. The peace deal, COSVN concluded, would bring 'a great opportunity for revolutionary violence, for gaining power in South Vietnam, for troop and enemy proselytizing, and for making great leaps in the balance of forces'.[132]

Washington made much of the fact that the mechanisms for a peaceful settlement had been established, but no one, not even Kissinger, really believed that Vietnam's fate would be resolved by a ballot, instead of by bullets and bombs. During the course of the Nixon administration, the US had abandoned most of its demands. The original reason for the war, namely to determine who should govern South Vietnam, had not been resolved. Rogers admitted that the agreements were 'ambiguous, but deliberately ambiguous. We never pretended that it was definite and if we had attempted to work it out we would still be fighting.'[133] Nixon and Kissinger had achieved the precise conditions necessary to an American departure. The settlement allowed the American people to come to terms with a war which had not been won. Those who had opposed the war were satisfied that it was over, those who had supported it drew solace from the fact that Thieu remained in power. The total victory of the North was sufficiently distant and, to optimists, uncertain. At the very least, there would be a 'decent interval' between American departure and the RVN's complete collapse. Few really believed the administration's claims that the US had won the war; but Americans were not plagued by a sense of defeat. It is in the transformation of Vietnam into a country of no real importance that the magnitude of Nixon's achievement lies.

129 Don, *Endless War*, p. 195.
130 McMahon, *Major Problems*, pp. 557–8.
131 Nixon, *RN*, p. 737.
132 Tang, *Vietcong Memoir*, p. 215.
133 McMahon, *Major Problems*, p. 473.

POSTSCRIPT

In mid-1969 Kissinger admitted that the only option open to the United States was to 'pursue a middle course between capitulation and the seemingly endless stalemate that we had inherited'.[134] The US spent four years pursuing that course, sacrificing over 20,000 American lives in the process. The fact that the settlement was signed in January 1973 and not a year or two earlier seems suspicious. It is tempting to argue that Nixon intentionally delayed so that he would not have to run for re-election as the first President to lose a war. Haldeman gave credence to these assertions when he admitted that troops withdrawals were scheduled with the election in mind:

> Henry . . . feels that if we pull them out by the end of '71, trouble can start mounting in '72 that we won't be able to deal with and which we'll have to answer for at the elections. He prefers, instead, a commitment to have them all out by the end of '72 so that we won't have to deliver finally until after the elections and therefore can keep our flanks protected. . . . If any bad results follow they will be too late to affect the election.[135]

But it is rather too easy to make simplistic judgements about the timing of the peace. With Nixon, diplomatic goals and domestic campaigns worked in a complicated symbiosis. He was never just interested in finding a way out of Vietnam. His other goals – strengthening the ARVN, detente with China and the USSR, punishing the DRV, redefining victory – were designed to make withdrawal palatable, to preserve American self-belief, and to buttress America's global reputation. Those goals took time to achieve, much more time than Nixon anticipated. Given the crisis of confidence with which the US was afflicted after Vietnam, it is not certain that the delay was worthwhile, nor that Nixon achieved his purpose. The extra years of war, and the added sacrifice, did not establish a country at peace with itself.

Nixon found that which had eluded Eisenhower, Kennedy and Johnson, namely a way to withdraw. Yet their failures made his success possible. Many had to die in Vietnam before the American people could accept the idea of a war not won and a nation unable to right every wrong. There are elements of Nixon's performance which were brilliant. His combination of negotiation and aggression thwarted the Hanoi regime, hitherto the masters of *danh va dam, dam va danh*. His

---

134 Ibid., p. 467.
135 Kimball, *Nixon's Vietnam War*, p. 239.

overtures to the Soviet Union and China transformed Vietnam into what it should always have been: a small country of small importance. But along with these achievements came brutal cynicism, Nixon's trademark. Brilliance was tinged with venality. There was, in his handling of the war, elements of a personal vendetta; aggression did not always have strategic justification.[136] He would have argued that there is no room for virtue and honesty in great power politics. His sidekick Kissinger wanted to purge the characteristic sentimentality from American foreign policy.[137] In this they succeeded brilliantly, but the limits of their achievements are defined by their excesses. As Jeffrey Kimball has written:

> Ironically, in prosecuting the war as long as he did, Nixon contributed to the erosion of that domestic consensus which had previously supported military intervention abroad. . . . Blaming others for America's failure in Vietnam, he contributed to the bitterness that haunted American politics and the confusion of purpose and meaning that plagued American foreign policy in the years ahead.[138]

Nixon hoped to preserve American dignity, yet that dignity was seriously eroded by the lies and deceit which were the tools of his trade. He brought American troops home, but he did not bring peace to the region. While he deserves praise for ending the war, he should not escape blame for the killing fields of Cambodia. The Vietnam Memorial in Washington DC lists the names of many men who died needlessly in pursuit of Nixon's peace.

---

136 See Blema Steinberg, *Shame and Humiliation* (Pittsburgh, PA, 1996), p. 203.
137 See Isaacson, *Kissinger*, pp. 654–7.
138 Kimball, *Nixon's Vietnam War*, p. 371.

9 THE FALL OF SAIGON

The Paris Agreements of January 1973 were supposed to end the war in Vietnam, with the future of the South to be decided politically. In truth, the peace was a sham. 'Both the Communists and the government', the CIA analyst Frank Snepp recorded on 13 July, 'are interpreting the new cease-fire agreement selectively, emphasizing . . . those parts of it which favor their respective interests and ignoring those that do not'.[1] While Hanoi and Saigon jockeyed for favourable military advantage, each accused the other of violating the Accords. Neither side had any faith in a peaceful solution. Both expected a final decisive battle.

NO SURRENDER

On 5 January 1973 Nixon promised Thieu that the US would provide 'continued assistance in the post-settlement period and that we will respond with full force should the settlement be violated by North Vietnam'.[2] Thieu trusted Nixon, so much so that he felt safe to use his own troops to extend control over the countryside, rather than to counter a PAVN build-up. He presumed that Hanoi, fearful of American intervention, would try to overthrow the Saigon regime slowly, through political infiltration and protracted war. This assumption inspired his 'no surrender' strategy: communist insurgency would be resisted with maximum force everywhere.

In Long An province, NLF-controlled hamlets were hit by four or five airstrikes and an average of 1,000 artillery rounds per day. Unbridled aggression reaped results. A year after the Agreements, American sources estimated that Saigon had reasserted authority in

1 Frank Snepp, *Decent Interval* (New York, NY, 1977), p. 65.
2 William Appleman Williams *et al.*, eds, *America in Vietnam: A Documentary History* (New York, NY, 1975), p. 309.

770 hamlets.[3] Tran Van Tra, PLAF commander in the South, admitted that the ARVN offensive 'caused considerable difficulties'.[4] Americans were surprised at the resilience of South Vietnamese forces, which they had expected would crumble immediately after the US departure. One intelligence analyst in Saigon described the ARVN as 'an efficient, aggressive military force that [is] capable of defending its territory'.[5] But 'success' had high cost: some 6,000 ARVN soldiers were killed in the first three months after the Paris Accords, a rate of loss higher than during the Tet Offensive.[6] Losses for the first year of the 'cease-fire' totalled 26,500 ARVN, perhaps 39,000 PLAF/PAVN and 15,000 civilians.[7]

No longer impeded by American scruples, Thieu unleashed a vicious vendetta against opponents and neutralists. RVN soldiers were ordered to 'use clubs to beat up' neutralist members of the National Assembly.[8] A worse fate awaited those communists who failed to produce a valid identity card; police were ordered to 'blow [their] brains out on the spot'.[9] Perhaps as many as 80,000 communist suspects were imprisoned.[10] At the same time, an economic blockade of NLF-controlled villages sought to starve out insurgents. Famine spread through the central provinces, where peasants were reduced to eating bark, cacti and banana roots.[11]

Thieu's aggressive strategy left the ARVN in a serious predicament. Communist insurgents were still attacking when and where they chose. Since RVN forces had no idea where blows might fall, troops were dispersed throughout the country. Half of ARVN strength was deployed in static defensive positions, while only 10 per cent of communist strength was.[12] This disadvantage was compounded by the no surrender strategy, which placed an impossible burden on the ARVN. The frenzied land-grabbing which had followed the Paris Accords left the ARVN over-stretched. There were not enough troops to defend every outpost *and* interdict enemy lines of communication.

3 Ngo Vinh Long, 'Post-Paris Agreement struggles and the fall of Saigon', in Jayne S. Werner and Luu Doan Huynh, eds, *The Vietnam War: Vietnamese and American Perspectives* (Armonk, NY, 1993), p. 208.

4 William J. Duiker, *Sacred War* (New York, NY, 1995), p. 240.

5 Gabriel Kolko, *Anatomy of a War* (New York, NY, 1994), p. 462.

6 George C. Herring, *America's Longest War* (New York, NY, 1986), p. 258.

7 Marilyn Young, *The Vietnam Wars, 1945–1990* (New York, NY, 1991), p. 290.

8 Long, 'Post-Paris Agreement struggles', pp. 206–7.

9 James P. Harrison, *The Endless War* (New York, NY, 1989), p. 291.

10 Ibid., p. 293.

11 Long, 'Post-Paris Agreement struggles', p. 209.

12 Robert McMahon, ed., *Major Problems in the History of the Vietnam War* (Lexington, MA, 1990), p. 579.

The former was given priority, which meant that the DRV's logistical preparations were not seriously impeded. Since Thieu would not allow territory to be surrendered in order to consolidate strength, a major offensive to push PAVN forces back into North Vietnam was not possible. Nor were any plans prepared for a strategic withdrawal in the event of a large PAVN attack.

By 1974, the RVN possessed one of the largest ground forces in the world. There were 450,000 ARVN regulars, another 550,000 troops in the RF/PF, 51,000 personnel in the Air Force and a slightly smaller number in the Navy. But these figures must be treated with caution. Only about 200,000 ARVN regulars were in combat units. Logistical and administrative components were huge, a legacy of American influence. Desertion rates of around 20,000 per month were common. About 100,000 'flower soldiers' bribed commanders in order to remain in civilian employment. 'Gold soldiers' paid others to fight for them, and 'phantom soldiers' were in truth dead, though their pay was still collected by corrupt officers.[13] Thus, actual strength was significantly lower than paper strength.

According to Article 6 of the Paris Agreements, American bases in South Vietnam were to be dismantled. But installations such as the Cam Ranh Bay naval facility and the Tan Son Nhut airbase were cleverly transferred to the RVN for 'civilian use'.[14] Around 10,000 American 'civilians' – many of them recently de-activated military personnel – remained in South Vietnam to assist the RVN.[15] In addition, Operation Enhance and Enhance Plus poured around US$1 billion in military equipment into South Vietnam before the January settlement.

Thieu's forces nevertheless suffered badly when the American flow of arms was curtailed. By late 1974, ARVN artillery ammunition stockpiles stood at 20 per cent of 1972 levels. Eleven out of 66 Air Force squadrons had to be disbanded because of lack of fuel, while others had operations severely restricted.[16] The real problem was not the availability of weaponry, but its use. The ARVN fought like its American mentor, with massive, unrestrained firepower. Unfortunately, supplies were now finite. Troops, overly dependent upon tactical air-power, were reluctant to attack without a preliminary airstrike. 'ARVN battalions appear to be completely dependent upon outside fire

---

13 Guenter Lewy, *America in Vietnam* (Oxford, 1978), p. 209–10.

14 Harrison, *Endless War*, p. 291.

15 Kolko, *Anatomy*, p. 449.

16 Lewy, *America in Vietnam*, p. 208; McMahon, p. 582; John Pimlott, *Vietnam: The Decisive Battles* (London, 1990), p. 182; Bernard C. Nalty, ed., *The Vietnam War* (London, 1996), p. 228.

support', an American adviser commented in 1972. He added, rather prophetically, that this was 'a tragic situation because much of this outside fire support will eventually be gone'.[17]

ARVN troops were not universally bad. Though performance had been inconsistent, some units were first-class. Administrative reforms carried out under Thieu had improved quality. The promotion system was overhauled, with greater emphasis upon merit. Pay scales were increased and veteran's benefits expanded. But corruption remained high and morale stubbornly low. Snepp related how

> corruption has gotten so bad, wounded government soldiers have to pay to be medevacked. One chopper hovered for nearly an hour last Monday as the pilot bickered with a hamlet chief by radio over the price of lifting out a bleeding militiaman. They finally settled on six ducks from the hamlet pond.[18]

Pay rises were negated by the fact that actual pay often failed to appear. Due to inflation and the removal of the rice ration, the actual income of soldiers declined by about two-thirds between January 1973 and May 1974. Many deserted to support families. Dwindling supplies further eroded morale. Artillery and mortar fire was severely curtailed, and grenades rationed. Boots were replaced every nine months instead of every six and socks were in short supply. Evacuation of the injured was hampered by the shortage of ambulances and fuel. It was not uncommon to see four or five ambulances, out of fuel, pulled in train by a truck or tractor. 'The morale of the ARVN soldier was adversely affected by so many factors that it is remarkable that he was able to fight at all', a Rand analyst reflected.[19] That many continued to do so with great determination is testimony to the strength of anti-communism within South Vietnam.

ARVN units were usually identified with a particular region, an outgrowth of their static, pacification role. Troops resented moving to new areas, as mobile warfare implied, and were slow to adjust. Desertion rates were lower if troops served close to home, which explains why nearly 40 per cent of ARVN soldiers in 1974 were stationed in the Delta, the one place in the South where a PAVN attack was least likely. More importantly, when fighting in their own locale, their first concern was often for nearby families. As Tran Van Don recalled, if a withdrawal from an area was ordered, 'soldiers were naturally motivated to protect their families and individual possessions, so they might

---

17 Lewy, *America in Vietnam*, p. 182.
18 Snepp, *Decent Interval*, p. 44
19 Kolko, *Anatomy*, pp. 468, 525.

very well [leave] their posts to see to them'. Exit routes inevitably became clogged with camp followers. 'This would, of course, weaken the defensive position, the enemy would exploit the situation further, and eventually what had started as an orderly retreat for good purposes would turn into an utter rout.'[20]

The survival of a non-communist South Vietnam was dependent upon Thieu's ability to ensure economic stability. But by 1973 the RVN economy was a delicate hothouse flower which could not exist outside the controlled environment which the United States had created, nor without the steady fertilization of American aid. An estimated 250,000 South Vietnamese had been employed servicing the American war machine. Most of these jobs disappeared when the Americans departed. Inflation reached 65 per cent.[21] South Vietnam, an agrarian country, did not produce the food to feed itself because so many peasants had fled to the city to escape the war. Further grants could delay, but not avert, economic disaster.

In the past, the United States had propped up the RVN by pouring in money and troops. But Americans no longer wanted to play the role of rescuer. On 31 July 1973 Congress voted (over Nixon's veto) to cut off funds for military action by American forces anywhere in Indochina. The main effect of this was to halt the bombing of sanctuaries in Cambodia, which had continued unabated since the Paris Accords. American B-52s flew their last mission two weeks later, much to Nixon's chagrin. The following November, the War Powers Resolution, restricting presidential authority to wage war, was passed. Just prior to his resignation in August 1974, Nixon approved an aid package for 1975 worth US$1 billion, but Congress subsequently cut the figure to US$700 million. Against this figure US$400 million was charged in shipping costs, leaving just US$300 million in actual hardware, an amount reduced in real terms by high inflation. When Gerald Ford took over the presidency he assured Thieu that 'existing commitments this nation has made in the past are still valid and will be fully honored by my administration'.[22] He warned Congress and the American people that cuts in aid would 'seriously weaken South Vietnamese forces during a critical period when Communist forces . . . are growing stronger and more aggressive'.[23] But rallying Americans for a renewed effort to save the RVN was beyond Ford's power.

20 Tran Van Don, *Our Endless War* (Novato, CA, 1978), p. 231.

21 Harrison, *Endless War*, p. 294; Snepp, *Decent Interval*, p. 100.

22 David L. Anderson, 'Gerald R. Ford and the Presidents' war in Vietnam', in Anderson, ed., *Shadow on the White House* (Lawrence, KS, 1993), p. 188.

23 Ibid., p. 189.

When it became clear that Thieu's line to Washington was broken, what passed for political stability in Saigon began to disintegrate. Huge demonstrations of the hungry and jobless choked major cities. On 27 September 1974 *Dong Phuong*, a newspaper which had reliably supported the Thieu regime, called upon 'the entire people' to 'struggle hard for the eradication of corruption, the elimination of injustices, the implementation of democratic freedoms, the establishment of peace, and the decapitation of those who have created so many tragic situations for our people'.[24] The chaos of the early 1960s had returned.

DELIBERATIONS AND PREPARATIONS IN THE NORTH

The Easter Offensive had demonstrated that a full-scale invasion of the South required a strong economic base and logistical network. The state of the North Vietnamese economy, severely damaged by the December 1972 bombing, militated against such a massive operation. The alternative was to overthrow the Thieu regime mainly by political means. This would entail a return to basics – a comprehensive effort to advance the revolution in every village and hamlet. But the NLF infrastructure upon which such a plan depended had suffered badly since 1968 and could not easily be rebuilt.

At the 21st Plenum of the Vietnamese Communist Party in October 1973, long-standing strategic disagreements resurfaced. There was considerable dispute over the actual strength of the ARVN, which, in purely numerical terms, was five times stronger than revolutionary forces in the South. The future American role was another matter for concern; no one knew how Nixon would react to a PAVN invasion. On the other hand, it was clear that the Watergate scandal had seriously weakened Nixon, leading to a decline in aid to the South. Weighing all these factors, Hanoi settled upon a cautious strategy designed to bring complete victory in 1976. Victory would come through a military offensive, not political subversion.

The three-year strategy involved a gradual escalation of violence. Infiltration of villages would proceed simultaneously with logistical preparations for a big offensive. Le Duan emphasized that 'the national people's democratic revolution in the south and the socialist revolution in the North are inextricably linked, but *the greatest and most decisive force is in the North, in the rear area*. As the war reaches the concluding stage the decisive role of the rear area becomes even more

---

24 Long, 'Post-Paris Agreement struggles', pp. 210–11.

obvious.'[25] At the opportune moment, the general offensive would be launched in three strategic areas. In the far north, attacks would isolate Hué and Da Nang. In the central section, the offensive would pursue the long-held aim of cutting South Vietnam in two by seizing Pleiku, Qui Nhon, Tuy Hoa and Ban Me Thuot. Finally, an assault upon Saigon would follow success further north. The strategy was similar to the Easter Offensive, but the crucial difference was that assaults would not be launched simultaneously. Flexibility was paramount; there would be no attempt to force the pace. Progress would depend on the state of the ARVN and the reaction of the United States.

General Van Tien Dung, formerly Giap's second-in-command, took charge of planning the offensive. Naturally cautious, he sought to avoid the errors of the Easter Offensive through methodical preparation. A huge construction programme provided essential transportation and communication facilities. The Ho Chi Minh Trail was widened and, in most areas, paved. Altogether, 12,000 miles of roads were built. A new pipeline took fuel from North Vietnam deep into the South, and a modern radio network was established. Thirteen new airfields were built in South Vietnam, each supplied with a sophisticated AA system. The RVN air force, lacking the high performance aircraft to attack SAM missile sites, could not counteract this development.

PAVN was reorganized into four major groups: I Corps near Hanoi, II Corps near the DMZ, III Corps in the Central Highlands and IV Corps in the highlands of Cambodia. By January 1975 PAVN strength in the South stood at around 220,000 soldiers, of whom 148,000 were combat troops. A Strategic Reserve of seven divisions was held in the North, and support was still available from perhaps as many as 50,000 PLAF troops. The North had around 700 tanks, of varying make, and some 230 aircraft. Ammunition reserves were sufficient to sustain an operation of the intensity of the Easter Offensive for one year.[26] The most important change in PAVN strength since 1972 was a significant increase in mobile artillery, thanks to Soviet generosity in 1973 and 1974. ARVN troops had always fought with artillery superiority and most had never been subjected to concentrated gunfire. These men would receive a nasty shock when battle began. For a soldier there are few things more demoralizing than being outgunned.

---

25 David W.P. Elliott, 'Hanoi's strategy in the Second Indochina War', in Werner and Huynh, eds, *Vietnam War*, p. 91.
26 Lewy, *America in Vietnam*, p. 206; Harrison, *Endless War*, p. 292.

In spite of these developments, Hanoi had reservations about its military capability. Combat efficiency and morale had been severely dented by the terrible casualties since 1968. 'Our cadres and men were fatigued', wrote Tra, 'we had not had time to make up our losses, all units were in disarray, there was a lack of manpower, and there were shortages of food and ammunition.'[27] Severe losses meant a greater reliance upon young, inexperienced conscripts. Some 40 per cent of replacements had only six months experience, 50 per cent less than three. 'Experience' often meant the time taken to travel down the Ho Chi Minh Trail into the battle zones.[28] The final departure of American troops undoubtedly lifted spirits, but morale was not as resilient as it had once been. Defections had risen markedly since 1967. Younger troops lacked the political indoctrination to prepare them for a long campaign.

BATTLE BEGINS

For most of 1974, PAVN or PLAF units conducted strategic raids upon ARVN outposts, bases and communication centres. ARVN troops everywhere, but especially in the Saigon area, were incessantly harassed. The random nature of these attacks gave the impression that the revolution was everywhere powerful. Hanoi hoped that this would restore communist influence in the hinterlands and damage the morale of those loyal to Saigon.

A propaganda offensive in the United States carefully camouflaged these efforts. The American people were bombarded with evidence of Thieu's cruel repression of alleged communist sympathizers. By suggesting that the DRV was the only one violating the Paris Accords, Hanoi successfully deepened America's alienation from its former ally. Since Nixon's mendacity had been exposed by the Watergate scandal, the public was not inclined to believe his counterclaims. This reinforced the desire to cut aid and lessened the possibility of an eleventh-hour rescue.

Raids around Saigon were designed to isolate the city, in preparation for the final offensive. Tra sought to cut Highway 4, the principal route between the capital and the Mekong Delta, and seize the communications hub at Xuan Loc. In the north, PAVN sought to isolate Hué. The General Staff, recognizing the urgency of these operations,

27 Cecil B. Currey, *Victory at Any Cost* (Washington, DC, 1997), p. 294.
28 Peter McDonald, *Giap* (London, 1993), p. 323.

insisted that assaults should continue through the monsoon season. But, after very heavy fighting, all PAVN advances in the Saigon area were repulsed, though Tra's troops did draw the noose closer. Raids in the north were more successful. By the end of the wet season, PAVN artillery units were in range of every major city – Da Nang, Quang Ngai City and Qui Nhon. But, around Hué, General Ngo Quang Truong fought PAVN troops to a standstill. These mixed results disappointed the General Staff and the Politburo. Hanoi's fears that the ARVN remained a formidable force seemed to be confirmed. Caution seemed justified.

In fact, the opening battles were more successful than Hanoi appreciated. The raids sharpened PAVN effectiveness. Valuable logistic corridors toward strategically important objectives were opened. Most important, ARVN casualties were very heavy and morale was rapidly eroding. Loss of weaponry was doubly significant since supplies were now limited. By autumn 1974, the military balance had shifted. Thieu's strategy of defending aggressively everywhere had seriously weakened his forces. The ARVN was stretched thinly across the country in lines of static defence. There were no spare troops for a strategic reserve nor for attacking enemy lines of communication.

Hung nevertheless argued that the 1974 results demonstrated that strategic raids should continue for at least another year, with final victory delayed until 1976. Tra vehemently disagreed. Certain that a short but determined push would topple Thieu, he advocated an immediate attack upon Saigon. The General Staff, reflecting Hung's caution, vetoed the first stage of Tra's plan, the capture of the key town of Don Luan. Tra then took his case to Le Duan, who partially reversed the General Staff decision. After receiving guarded approval for the Don Luan attack, Tra attacked on 22 December 1974. Though few in Hanoi realized it at the time, the final campaign of the Vietnam War had begun.

THE ARVN DISINTEGRATES

On 26 December Don Luan fell. The next important objective was Phuoc Long province. A rag-tag collection of ARVN units was thrown in the path of Tra's well-armed and highly coordinated force. The ARVN Air Force proved ineffectual, with many pilots refusing to fly into the intense flak. Phuoc Long fell on 6 January 1975, the first liberation of an entire province during the war. Only 900 ARVN troops survived, from an original contingent of 6,000. Two Ranger companies virtually disappeared.[29] The battle heartened the Politburo, since it seemed that the ARVN was indeed a paper tiger. But Phuoc Long was more important for what did not happen than for what did. A heavy communist assault upon a province just 75 miles from Saigon had provoked no reaction from the United States. For Hanoi, the last obstacle to a general offensive had been removed.

Impressed by the Phouc Long result, the Politburo on 8 January gave cautious approval to an offensive in Military Region II, with the aim of bisecting the South. The region had six main strategic sites: Kontum, Pleiku and Ban Me Thuot in the highlands, and Nha Trang, Tuy Hoa and Qui Nhon on the coast. It had always been poorly defended by the ARVN, due in part to the logistical difficulties which steep mountains and inadequate roads presented. In contrast, five PAVN divisions – some 80,000 combat troops – were present, including fifteen tank regiments.

Dung planned to attack Ban Me Thuot first, masking his effort with a feint toward Pleiku. The feint worked brilliantly, leaving ARVN units in no position to defend Ban Me Thuot. Between 4 and 8 March, PAVN units cut the major transport routes, isolating the city. At 2.00 a.m. on 10 March, they attacked. Two days later, the city fell. An ARVN counter-attack verged on the absurd, leading Dung to conclude that enemy morale had 'seriously declined'. He called for 'a spirit of urgency and forcefulness . . . to promptly seize the opportunity to win great victories'.[30]

On 14 March Thieu ordered General Pham Van Phu to withdraw his regular forces from Kontum and Pleiku, move them to the coast, and organize a force to re-take Ban Me Thuot. Phu reluctantly complied, but left the details to junior commanders, while he escaped to safety in Nha Trang. Within Kontum and Pleiku, panic quickly spread among units which had not received the order to evacuate. Soldiers fought among themselves and took retribution on the civilian population. Over US$250 million in equipment and munitions was left for PAVN to collect because no one thought to destroy it.[31] A stream of soldiers and refugees headed south without plan or direction. 'There was no explanation whatsoever of the move to the population', one refugee later complained. 'No organization of any kind was set for the mass evacuation.' As one of the last planes left Pleiku, 'people

29 Phillip B. Davidson, *Vietnam at War* (Oxford, 1988), p. 763.
30 Lewy, *America in Vietnam*, p. 211.
31 Ibid., p. 212.

grabbed for the tail, falling off as the plane taxied. . . . a small baby fell out of the aircraft, killed instantly as it hit the tarmac.'[32]

On 18 March the retreating column stalled at Cheo Reo, when ARVN engineers were unable to build a bridge over the Ea Pa River. Vicious PAVN artillery tore into the chaotic mass of soldiers and civilians. ARVN pilots, mustered to support the column, kept to ineffectively high altitudes to avoid flak. Accuracy suffered so severely that friendly fire destroyed four tanks, raked a Ranger battalion and killed hundreds of civilian refugees. After the column eventually forded the river, it encountered a series of road-blocks and routes littered with mines. Of the 60,000 troops originally evacuated, 20,000 survived, including only 700 of the 7,000 elite Rangers. Perhaps one quarter of the 400,000 refugees made it to safety.[33]

RVN forces, Snepp recorded, 'seemed to be trapped on the sheer face of a glass mountain, and [were] slipping badly'.[34] In Military Region I in the north, Thieu directed Truong to implement what seemed from the outset a foolhardy plan of withdrawal. The aim was to form a defensive line from just north of Tuy Hoa across to the Cambodian border. This meant surrendering most of the highlands, though strategic redoubts would be set up at Hué, Da Nang, Quang Ngai, Qui Nhon and Tuy Hoa, rather like the old American enclave plan. It was hoped that they would, at the very least, provide evacuation points accessible to the sea, though Thieu still dreamed of holding as much of the coast as possible.[35] Truong doubted that his forces were capable of a such an immensely difficult military manoeuvre, and was worried about the clutter of refugees. He decided instead to concentrate his forces in Hué, Da Nang and Chu Lai, eventually transferring the bulk of his force to Da Nang, where it could perhaps be evacuated by sea.

On 19 March PAVN units attacked on a number of fronts. By evening, the whole of Quang Tri province was captured, leaving Hué desperately vulnerable. Within the city, fears of a repeat of the 1968 massacre caused severe panic. On the 20th, Thieu reassured Hué residents that the ARVN would protect them, but then instructed Truong to defend only Da Nang. Two days later, PAVN cut Highway 1 between Hué and Da Nang and attacked Tam Ky, capital of Quang Tin province. It fell two days later.

32 David Butler, *The Fall of Saigon* (New York, NY, 1985), pp. 102, 120.
33 Davidson, *Vietnam at War*, p. 779.
34 Snepp, *Decent Interval*, p. 209.
35 He was apparently keen to retain access to recently discovered offshore oil reserves.

Troung tried on the 24th to evacuate Hué by sea. Thousands drowned or were killed by PAVN artillery. Masses of equipment was left on the beaches. A sea lift from Chu Lai was equally disastrous, with panic ensuing and only 7,000 troops escaping. On 25 March, Hué fell, a disaster of enormous psychological significance. Da Nang was choked with more than 400,000 bedraggled refugees who staggered in from all directions.[36] The tide of exiles was living proof that the revolution had failed to inspire a popular uprising. Though the evacuees were by no means desperate to remain under Saigon rule, they *were* desperate to escape Hanoi's grim authority.

By 29 March Da Nang was surrounded. Evacuation by sea was attempted, but few actually escaped. Truong had to swim for his life. Da Nang fell on the 30th, ten years and three weeks after American Marines had landed. Eight days earlier Ford had tried to rally Thieu by promising that the US would 'stand firmly [behind] the RVN at this critical hour'. He mentioned that he was considering 'actions which the situation may require and the law permit'.[37] In truth, American law no longer permitted meaningful action.

THE HO CHI MINH CAMPAIGN

The Politburo decided that caution was no longer appropriate. The ARVN was weak, Thieu discredited, and the US prepared to let South Vietnam fall. 'Not only has the revolutionary war in the South entered a period of developing by leaps and bounds', a party document proclaimed, 'but the time is ripe for carrying the general offensive and general uprising to the enemy's lair.'[38] On 25 March Dung was ordered to liberate Saigon before the monsoon. The operation would be called the 'Ho Chi Minh Campaign'.

Dung decided on a five-pronged attack, designed to avoid the destruction of Saigon. Each corps at his disposal had a specific axis of advance, from which it would surround opposing forces and then head for five selected strategic targets: Independence Palace, the headquarters of the Joint General Staff, Tan Son Nhut airbase, the National Police headquarters, and the headquarters of the Capitol Zone, whose commander controlled the troops in the Saigon vicinity. Dung calculated that if these five points could be captured quickly, Saigon would fall with comparatively little violence. He wanted to avoid the

---

36 In the chaos, counting was of course difficult. Some estimates place the total refugees at 1,000,000. See Lewy, *America in Vietnam*, p. 213.

37 Anderson, 'Gerald R. Ford and the Presidents' war in Vietnam', p. 194.

38 McMahon, *Major Problems*, p. 586.

devastation which had occurred during the Tet Offensive and did not want to force the ARVN into a desperately brutal last ditch defence.

While Saigon waited for the axe to fall, Ford golfed in Palm Springs. General Frederick Weyand, sent to South Vietnam to report on the RVN's prospects, submitted on 5 April a shopping list of ammunition, fuel and supplies which would allow the ARVN to 'rebuild their capabilities'. The price tag read US$722 million. Ford appended an additional US$250 million in humanitarian aid, then sent the request to Congress. None of his advisers dared suggest that the US$1 billion package would actually buy victory, or even stave off defeat. Kissinger admitted to 'other purposes' which would be 'best served by the granting of this sum' – he was, in other words, still deeply worried about the damage to American credibility if the RVN was simply abandoned. Ford told Congress that the money 'would at least allow the orderly evacuation of Americans and endangered Vietnamese' who numbered in the 'tens of thousands'. But public disapproval, measured in messages to the White House, ran over two to one against the package. Congress took the easy way out by slowly deliberating the request, in the firm knowledge that events in Saigon would soon overtake discussions in Washington.[39]

Before taking Saigon, Dung decided to cut Highway 4, the route to the Mekong Delta, and capture Xuan Loc, which anchored the outer defences along the eastern approach to the capital. Neither attack went well. At Xuan Loc the ARVN ironically performed better than at any time during the entire war. Eventually, however, PAVN numerical strength began to tell. On 20 April ARVN forces were driven back to Long Binh and Bien Hoa airbases, 12 miles east of Saigon. Both sides suffered heavily, but ARVN losses were crippling.

Saigon was now surrounded by around fifteen PAVN divisions, supported by sappers, tanks, artillery and AA units. The logistical problems of 1972 had been solved. Morale was high. In contrast, the ARVN had four divisions hastily regrouped for Saigon's defence, plus tattered remnants of units evacuated from the north. Defensive plans were vague, supplies desperately short, and morale rock bottom. Truong, now Deputy Chief of the Joint General Staff, had the unenviable task of organizing the city's defence. He deployed his forces to cover the five main roads leading into the capital. Blocking positions were sited some 17 to 30 miles out. The resulting area was admittedly too large to defend with the forces at his disposal, yet a tighter circle

39 Anderson, 'Gerald R. Ford and the Presidents' war in Vietnam', pp. 196–9; Snepp, *Decent Interval*, p. 337.

would have implied abandoning the bases at Bien Hoa, Cu Chi, Lai Khe and Long Binh, and would have left the city vulnerable to 130 mm artillery attack.

Within Saigon despair was endemic. As Thieu's grip on power weakened, factional rivalry intensified. Ford's decision to pull all non-essential American personnel out of Vietnam convinced Thieu that the situation was hopeless. Aware that the communists were unlikely to negotiate with him, he resigned on 21 April, complaining that 'The Americans abandoned us. They sold us out. A great ally failed a small ally.'[40] In came General Duong Van Minh, a more benign figure who had entertained talks with the communists during his brief premiership in 1963–64. Those inclined to grasp at straws hoped that Minh would be able to strike a deal with Hanoi.

On 23 April Ford told students at Tulane University that the war 'is finished as far as America is concerned'.[41] His audience erupted in applause. A difficult dilemma nevertheless plagued the President, namely that of evacuating remaining Americans and others deemed worthy of rescue. If they left too early, they would trigger panic and jeopardize the city's defence. Yet if they delayed, it might prove impossible to rescue everyone on approved evacuation lists. Ford decided to wait as long as possible, though influential South Vietnamese businessmen and politicians, and orphans of mixed race, were airlifted from Tan Son Nhut from late March. During one such mercy mission on 4 April, a C-5A Galaxy transport, with 243 orphans on board, crashed shortly after take-off. A witness recalled:

> only after the ambulances began unloading at [the hospital] . . . were we able to sort out the casualties. The nurses would simply pass the children under the shower, saying, 'This one's alive, this one's dead'. . . . None of the babies had name tags, simply wristbands saying 'New York', 'New Jersey', and so on, the addresses of their new foster homes.

Over 200 children and 44 adults were killed in the crash.[42]

On the 26th, Bien Hoa was attacked, along with other outer defences. Three days later, Tan Son Nhut was shelled, closing it to fixed-wing aircraft. Ford then decided to implement Operation Frequent Wind, the final evacuation. Sixty CH-53 helicopters from a Seventh Fleet Task Force in the South China Sea ferried refugees day

40 Pimlott, *Decisive Battles*, p. 180.
41 Anderson, 'Gerald R. Ford and the Presidents' war in Vietnam', p. 199.
42 Snepp, *Decent Interval*, pp. 304–5.

and night from pre-determined points of concentration on roof tops. At the Embassy,

> The hordes of Vietnamese . . . jammed into every corner of the building were a collage of wasted hopes. Many were carrying all they owned in small brown paper bags. Some had dogs and cats underarm. The children stared in bewilderment at the chaos around them, and as the Embassy's air-conditioning system broke down, the stench and heat in the corridors became unbearable. . . . an extraordinarily beautiful woman of mixed Vietnamese-French parentage . . . sat weeping throughout the evening at a desk in a side office with a small child in her arms. In the crush . . . she had become separated from her Vietnamese Army husband and two older children. They had been left in the crowds outside.

Operation Frequent Wind evacuated 1,373 Americans, 5,595 South Vietnamese, and 85 other nationals, in addition to the American ambassador's poodle.[43] The last helicopter, carrying the Marine Guard which had supervised the Embassy evacuation, flew out on the 30th.

With the outer defences now captured, communist forces launched a massive mechanized assault, heading for the five strategic points. Shortly after noon on the 30th, PAVN tanks appeared on the streets of Saigon. ARVN soldiers laid down their arms and quickly changed into civilian clothes. Cheering crowds that lined the streets consisted mainly of opportunists eager to escape retribution and party faithful acting to a pre-arranged dramatic script. The eastern PAVN column, led by Tank 843, made for the symbolically important Independence Palace. Encountering little opposition, it pushed forward along streets littered with the detritus of war before crashing through the Palace gates. Shortly afterwards, Colonel Bui Tin raced inside and demanded the surrender of President Minh. 'I have been waiting since early this morning to transfer power to you', Minh told Tin. 'You cannot give up what you do not have', Tin replied.[44]

The Vietnam War was over. Victory had been achieved by an invading army. The great popular uprising remained elusive.

43 Ibid., pp. 542–3, 563.
44 Pimlott, *Decisive Battles*, p. 187.

10   AN AMERICAN DEFEAT

After the war came the inquest. For a country as unaccustomed to losing as the United States, defeat in Vietnam was bewildering. The despotic nature of Vietnamese communism, revealed after unification, has encouraged revisionist analyses of the conflict. For some, even those who once opposed it, the war now seems a just cause worthy of greater effort. A short leap of reason leads to the conclusion that it might even have been winnable.

STABBED IN THE BACK?

The war produced a rich harvest of scapegoats. Nixon, swayed by his own propaganda, argued that victory was secure by 1973. If not for Watergate, 'we would not have lost the war in Vietnam', he argued in 1988. 'I would have seen to it that we would have forced the North Vietnamese to keep the Paris peace agreement.'[1] Variations of this fantasy have proved popular among those desperate to escape the reality of defeat and those (often the same crowd) keen to focus blame. Colonel Harry Summers, for instance, berates President Ford, who 'did not have the backbone to honor his country's solemn guarantees and . . . chose to golf while Saigon suffered'.[2] Kissinger's culprits resided on Capitol Hill; he had wanted to 'bomb the daylights out of Hanoi' when it violated the Paris Agreements, 'but Congress wouldn't let me'.[3] Ronald Reagan repeated this refrain in 1985:

---

[1] Bruce Oudes, ed., From: The President – Richard Nixon's Secret Files (New York, NY, 1989), p. 621. For an analysis of the Nixon view, see Jeffrey Kimball, Nixon's Vietnam War (Lawrence, KS, 1998), pp. 368–71.

[2] Harry Summers, 'The last years of the war: a personal view', in Elizabeth Jane Errington and B.J.C. McKercher, eds, The Vietnam War as History (New York, NY, 1990), p. 169.

[3] Gabriel Kolko, Anatomy of a War (New York, NY, 1994), p. 472.

the truth of the matter is, we did have victory. . . .

But what happened? We signed the peace accords, . . . and we made a pledge to [Saigon]. And when the North Vietnamese . . . violate[d] the agreement and the blitz started . . . the administration in Washington asked Congress for the appropriations to keep our word, . . . [but] Congress refused. We broke our pledge . . .

And so, we didn't lose the war. When the war was all over and we'd come home – that's when the war was lost.[4]

This is, of course, total nonsense. American aid might have postponed the fall of Saigon, but it could not have bought victory because victory could not be bought. 'The present deteriorating situation', Huynh Trung Chanh, a deputy in the RVN's Lower House, wrote in January 1975, 'is not because of a lack of aid but because of *lack of support of the people*. In previous years, aid was overly abundant and yet what was ever solved?'[5]

The war protesters have also proved popular scapegoats. 'America lost because of its democracy', argues Colonel Joseph P. Martino, a retired US Air Force officer. 'Through dissent and protest it lost the ability to mobilize the will to win.' The war, he feels, provides a useful lesson: 'it must be possible to counter dissent which involves collaboration with the enemy. We must not allow the enemy to intervene in our domestic politics, even under the guise of dissent.'[6] Martino, apparently, belongs to that group for whom politics seems simple and political judgement easy. They find it inconceivable that American power could be defeated by a ragtag group of Third World extremists. The explanation must therefore lie within. Blaming the protesters not only provides a convenient explanation for defeat, it also supplies a handy morality tale: the US must undergo a spiritual regeneration if it is to resume its rightful supremacy in world affairs. Patriotism must become fashionable again. It is no coincidence that the religious right often argues that the Vietnam failure is evidence of a wider moral disintegration.[7]

---

4 Richard Melanson, *Reconstructing Consensus: American Foreign Policy since the Vietnam War* (New York, NY, 1991), p. 154.

5 Ngo Vinh Long, 'Post-Paris agreement struggles and the fall of Saigon', in Jayne S. Werner and Luu Doan Huynh, eds, *The Vietnam War: Vietnamese and American Perspectives* (Armonk, NY, 1993), p. 213.

6 Joseph P. Martino, 'Vietnam and Desert Storm: learning the right lessons from Vietnam for the post-Cold War era', 1996 Vietnam Symposium, Texas Tech University Vietnam Center website.

7 See Walter Capps, *The Unfinished War* (Boston, MA, 1990), pp. 118–36.

Vietnam was not the first unpopular war. Americans were also deeply divided about the First World War and Korea.[8] Vietnam is different because the US lost; therefore the line between defeat and dissension seems straight and clear. But those on the American right who use the Vietnam lesson to justify an assault upon free speech and liberal values ignore an important fact. Dissent did not cause defeat, but defeat did enliven dissent. In 1965 the war was popular and the protesters hugely unpopular. Three years later, support for the war dipped under 50 per cent because victory still seemed elusive. The protesters, for all they might claim otherwise, did not inspire a popular will to end the war.[9] The war itself did that.

The same argument applies to the role of the press. Over 50 per cent of the commanders polled by Douglas Kinnard thought media coverage was at best 'uneven'; another 38 per cent maintained that it was 'disruptive of United States efforts'.[10] Again, Martino confidently condemns the enemy within: 'The failure to report the true nature of the enemy, and the misreporting of US victories, all contributed to the public's sense of the war's futility'.[11] There is no doubt that the media, especially television, presented a one-sided view. Americans were not shown scenes of communist brutality; they could not measure My Lai atrocities against those at Hué. But this one-sidedness exists in every war.[12] And, though the media's criticism of the American effort was subjective, so too was its praise. Early in the war, journalists were willing co-conspirators in efforts to mislead the public about the war's true nature. When the war began to go badly, the media responded accordingly. The press and television did not make the war into a futile stalemate, they simply described it as such when that is what it became.[13]

8 See Angus Johnston, 'Student activism in the United States before 1960: an overview', in Gerard J. DeGroot, ed., *Student Protest: The Sixties and After* (London, 1998), pp. 12–26.

9 A tone of self-congratulation is evident in most of the works published by former protesters. See, for instance, Tom Hayden, *Reunion* (New York, NY, 1988), and Fred Halstead, *Out Now* (New York, NY, 1978). Most of the 'serious' studies of the protest movement merely re-package this heroic tale of successful dissent. The most blatantly reverential homage is, perhaps, *Who Spoke Up?* by Nancy Zaroulis and Gerald Sullivan (New York, NY, 1984).

10 Douglas Kinnard, *The War Managers* (Wayne, NJ, 1985), p. 132.

11 Martino, 'Vietnam and Desert Storm'.

12 The recent Gulf War is perhaps an exception, since cameramen from the allied countries remained in Baghdad throughout the war.

13 This argument is convincingly presented in Daniel C. Hallin, *The Uncensored War* (New York, NY, 1986). See also Kathleen J. Turner, *Lyndon Johnson's Dual War* (Chicago, IL, 1985).

'For the first time in history', argues Robert Elegant, 'the outcome of a war was determined not on the battlefield but on the printed page and, above all, on the television screen.'[14] Such a profoundly stupid statement can only be explained by a deep ignorance of events on the ground in Vietnam, or by a ridiculously inflated view of the media's power. American soldiers had first to taste defeat in Vietnam for the war to become intolerable at home. The inadequacies of the American war effort were real; they have nothing to do with faulty perception or savage betrayal. The US suffered a strategic defeat. This raises a worthy question: would a different strategy have brought victory?

ON STRATEGY

The most popular strategic criticism focuses upon the flaws of limited war, which left soldiers with 'one hand tied behind their backs'. According to the 1980 Myths and Realities survey by the Veterans Administration, 47 per cent of the public and 72 per cent of Vietnam era veterans agree that 'Our troops were asked to fight in a war which our political leaders . . . would not let them win'. Among those who experienced combat duty in Vietnam, 82 per cent agree.[15] This line of argument is popular, as it allows the imagination to conjure up a scenario in which victory was possible. Thus, in the popular *Rambo* films, the hero, upon being ordered back to Vietnam, asks his superior: 'Sir, do we get to win *this* time?'

To Johnson, limited war seemed politically sensible. McNamara, during his confident phase, asserted that 'The greatest contribution Vietnam is making . . . is that it is developing an ability in the United States, to go to war without the necessity of arousing the public ire'.[16] But critics contend that this half-heartedness caused defeat. 'It seems rather obvious that a nation cannot fight a war in cold blood, sending its men and women to distant fields of battle without arousing the emotions of the people', General Bruce Palmer argues. 'I know of no way to accomplish this short of a declaration of war . . . and national mobilization.'[17] Summers feels that a declaration would have made the war 'a shared responsibility of both the government and the American people'. Without it, 'many vocal and influential members of the American public questioned . . . the legality and propriety of [US]

---

14 Robert Elegant, 'How to lose a war', *Encounter* 57 (August, 1981), p. 73.
15 Myra MacPherson, *Long Time Passing* (New York, NY, 1984), p. 59.
16 Loren Baritz, *Backfire* (New York, NY, 1985), pp. 319–20.
17 Bruce Palmer, *The 25 Year War* (New York, NY, 1984), p. 190.

actions'.[18] Westmoreland agrees: 'As a student of the history of war, and remembering the relatively recent Korean War experience, I was aware of the likelihood that a limited war, fought with limited means for limited objectives, would put special strain on the body politic'.[19]

American commitment *was* lacking. 'We never made any effort to create a war psychology in the United States', Dean Rusk admitted. 'We tried to do in cold blood perhaps what can only be done in hot blood.'[20] But the argument that a declaration of war would have inspired greater commitment is deeply flawed. The Korean War, another limited war, was also fought without a formal declaration, yet the US managed to attain its objectives. Disenchantment with the Vietnam War grew because objectives were not obtained, despite the claims of political and military leaders. As the credibility gap widened, support for the war fell. It is difficult to see how a declaration of war would have prevented this development.

Furthermore, for most Americans the war was tolerable up until 1968 because it did not touch their lives. On that score, Johnson was probably right about the need to maintain business as usual. Clausewitz understood that

> War is no act of blind passion, but is dominated by the political object, therefore the value of that object determines the measure of the sacrifices by which it is to be purchased. This will be the case, not only as regards extent, but also as regards duration. As soon, therefore, as the required outlay becomes so great that the political object is no longer equal in value, the object must be given up.[21]

A declaration of war would have implied mobilization of the reserves, a shift to a war economy, cancellation of social programmes, and, one suspects, more stringent control of the media and of civil liberties. It seems unlikely that these measures would have made the war *more* popular. Americans would rightly have asked themselves whether the political object – the fate of South Vietnam – justified such sacrifice.

It is also reckless to assume that Congress or the American people would have approved a declaration of war in 1965. Where was the

18 Harry G. Summers, *On Strategy: A Critical Analysis of the Vietnam War* (Novato, CA, 1982), p. 46.

19 Robert J. McMahon, *Major Problems in the History of the Vietnam War* (Lexington, MA, 1990), p. 272.

20 Robert Divine, 'Historiography: Vietnam reconsidered', in W. Capps, ed., *The Vietnam Reader* (New York, NY, 1991), p. 105.

21 Karl Clausewitz, *On War*, ed. Anatol Rapaport (Harmondsworth, 1980), p. 125.

threat to American security, the vital prerequisite to such a declaration? A lot of dominoes would have had to fall before people in San Francisco felt threatened. The Tonkin Gulf Resolution was popular precisely because it was not a declaration of war. It proposed limited action, which seemed justified in the circumstances. At the time, the resolution did not seem any more monumental than similar measures pertaining to the Middle East and the Formosa Straits that Eisenhower had pushed through Congress in the previous decade.[22]

Summers also argues that the US never formulated a viable strategy designed to win the war. Military planners mistakenly believed that unlimited firepower and modern weaponry could take the place of strategy. American forces were tied to 'the strategic defensive in pursuit of the negative aim of wearing the enemy down',[23] with progress measured solely by the body count, or by the amount of ammunition expended. This line of argument has proved popular. Some 68 per cent of commanders polled by Kinnard thought US objectives lacked clarity. 'The US was committed to a military solution, without a firm military objective', one commander remarked. 'The policy was attrition – killing VC – this offered no solution – it was senseless.'[24]

Summers feels that 'Instead of orienting on North Vietnam – the source of war – we turned our attention to the symptom – the guerrilla war in the south'.[25] The 'tyranny of fashion' meant that counterinsurgency, not conventional warfare, was pursued. In other words, the US abandoned the standard method by which it won wars, in favour of a bad imitation of its enemy's tactics. It should have recognized that, despite appearances to the contrary, the war was not an indigenous insurgency, but an invasion of the South by the North – a conventional war masquerading as a guerrilla conflict. This being the case, 'the Army should have taken the tactical offensive along the DMZ across Laos to the Thai border in order to isolate the battle and then *deliberately* assume the strategic and tactical defensive'.[26]

Palmer advances a similar argument, even going as far as to argue that victory could have been won with four fewer American divisions than were actually mobilized. A five-division force (two American, two Korean, one ARVN) along the DMZ, with a further two American

---

22 Gary R. Hess, 'The military perspective on strategy in Vietnam: Harry G. Summers's *On Strategy* and Bruce Palmer's *The 25 Year War*', *Diplomatic History* 10 (1986), pp. 98–9.

23 Summers, *On Strategy*, p. 165.

24 Kinnard, *War Managers*, pp. 24–5.

25 Summers, *On Strategy*, p. 127.

26 Summers, 'The last years of the war', p. 170.

divisions to extend the line to the Laos–Thai border, would effectively have 'isolated the battlefield', cutting the South off from communist infiltration.[27] According to Palmer, this would have created 'a military shield behind which South Vietnam could work out its own political, economic and social problems. Cut off from substantial out-of-country support, the Viet Cong was bound to wither on the vine and gradually become easier for the South Vietnamese to defeat.'[28]

The United States certainly had the capacity to fight this sort of war. With sufficient force and a willingness to extend the ground war into Laos and Cambodia, it might have isolated the battlefield. But what would the consequences have been? The US fought a *limited* war against a communist threat at the height of the Cold War. Yet none of her major allies actively supported her mission. It is not hard to imagine what the world reaction would have been had the US fought more aggressively. Leaving aside the potentially very dangerous reaction of the USSR and China, one has to bear in mind the effect such a strategy would have had upon the stability of the Western alliance.

Isolating the battlefield could not have been achieved as cheaply or as easily as Summers and Palmer suggest. The logistical complications of trying to create a Maginot Line along the DMZ and through Laos were immense. Vietnam was not Korea, where different terrain and the defence of a peninsula made a barrier feasible. Nor was it the wide open spaces of Eastern Europe, the battleground which American conventional tactics presupposed. Much of the area in question was dense, hilly jungle which favoured the infiltrator. 'Some have considered it practicable to seal the land frontiers against North Vietnamese infiltration', Westmoreland once commented, 'yet small though [South Vietnam] is, its land frontiers extend for more than 900 miles.'[29] If Laos had been sealed off, might the DRV have extended the Ho Chi Minh Trail through Thailand? No barrier can ever be impenetrable, and the frustrating fact of northern incursions was that they did not need to be big to be successful. The revolution could survive on a trickle. Small convoys of trucks could make a huge difference to the PLAF, but if trucks failed to get through, bicycles might. If bicycles proved too obtrusive, supplies could be hauled on the backs of coolies.

The highest level of American casualties during the war was suffered by Marines who guarded the DMZ.[30] Communist guerrillas had

27 Palmer, *25 Year War*, pp. 182–8.
28 Summers, 'The last years of the war', pp. 171–2.
29 William Westmoreland, *A Soldier Reports* (Garden City, NY, 1976), p. 147.
30 Eric Bergerud, *The Dynamics of Defeat* (Boulder, CO, 1991), p. 331.

their greatest success with lightning raids against static targets. As a barrier force, the Americans would have been sitting ducks for incessant sapper attacks and artillery bombardments. But, even assuming that the US could have prevented incursions by northern troops and supplies, victory was still contingent upon neutralizing the NLF (which controlled vast areas of South Vietnam in 1965) *and* building a viable government in the South.

Good government could not be learned overnight, nor could hearts and minds be won quickly. American troops would have had to remain on station during a slow process of nation-building, an open-ended commitment which the American public would have found progressively intolerable. Though the communists claimed otherwise, the US had no imperialistic interest in Vietnam. Unlike the French, they derived no direct advantage from occupying the country. They did not want to stay.

The great problem with the Palmer/Summers thesis is the miniscule role it assigns to the PLAF. There is no evidence to suggest that removing the DRV from the equation would have persuaded the PLAF to lay down its arms. In the vast majority of engagements, Americans fought the PLAF, not PAVN. The PLAF would undoubtedly have been worse off if supply lines from the North had been cut, but it would still have been able to wage war. In 1967 the CIA estimated that the vast majority of supplies used by the revolution originated in the South.[31] Self-sufficiency and adaptation were the NLF's strongest assets. It geared its effort to supply levels, shifting between periods of dormancy and great activity. Time was on its side. It did not need to win the war, it had only to avoid outright defeat. Its strategy was based on the certainty that eventually Americans would tire of the war.

In the 1980s the Summers thesis became the accepted interpretation of the war within the American military establishment. Copies of *On Strategy* were issued to students at the Army War College and the Command and General Staff College.[32] The thesis has great appeal because it postulates a scenario in which the US could have won the war by doing what came naturally. But it is based on a blinkered view of the war. Summers is fond of relating an incident which occurred when he met PAVN Colonel Nguyen Dôn Tu in 1975. 'You know you never defeated us on the battlefield', Summers rather stupidly

31 George R. Vickers, 'US military strategy and the Vietnam War', in Werner and Huynh, eds, *Vietnam War*, p. 124.

32 Bob Buzzanco, 'The American military's rationale against the Vietnam War', *Political Science Quarterly* 101 (1986), p. 560.

remarked. Tu pondered the statement a moment, then replied: 'that may be so, but it is also irrelevant'.[33] He was probably astounded that, after such a long war, Summers should still be so ignorant of its true nature.

THE OTHER WAR

Those who recognize the importance of the NLF to the communist war effort, among them Andrew Krepinevich, advance a decidedly different thesis from that of Summers and Palmer. Krepinevich argues that the US paid insufficient attention to the 'village war', and thus failed to adopt an effective counter-insurgency strategy. Failure resulted because the US tried to mould the war to suit conventional strategy, rather than adapting strategy to suit the war. Instead of fighting big unit engagements, which had little bearing on the eventual outcome, the US should have concentrated upon bringing security to the peasantry, thus allowing the RVN eventually to win hearts and minds. Krepinevich denounces the 'Army Concept':

> the Army's perception of how wars *ought* to be waged . . .
> reflected in the way the Army organizes and trains its troops for
> battle. The characteristics of the Army Concept are two: a focus
> on mid-intensity, or conventional, war and a reliance on high
> volumes of firepower to minimize casualties – in effect, the
> substitution of material costs at every available opportunity
> to avoid payment in blood.[34]

This argument has a great deal of merit. Westmoreland did underestimate the importance of village war and considered PLAF guerrillas mere 'termites' who could be safely left to the ARVN. But the ARVN proved unequal to this task, and the failure to break the NLF's hold upon the peasantry contributed to the American defeat.

To fight a guerrilla insurgency required subtlety, stealth and patience. Americans instead applied raw power. They had some success, but it was success similar to that of the man who burns down his house in order to rid it of termites. The reluctance to sacrifice lives – summed up in the ubiquitous sentiment: 'expend shells not men' – in practice meant that many innocent Vietnamese civilians were killed so that a few Americans could live. John Paul Vann observed in 1972 that

---

33 Summers, 'The last years of the war', p. 163.
34 Andrew Krepinevich, *The Army and Vietnam* (Baltimore, MD, 1986), p. 5.

I have walked through hundreds of hamlets that have been destroyed in the course of a battle, the majority as the result of the heavier friendly fires. The overwhelming majority of hamlets thus destroyed failed to yield sufficient evidence of damage to the enemy to justify destruction . . . Indeed, it has not been unusual to have a hamlet destroyed and find absolutely no evidence of damage to the enemy. . . . The destruction of a hamlet by friendly firepower is an event that will always be remembered and practically never forgiven by those members of the population who lost their homes.[35]

The defence specialist Herman Kahn argued in 1968 that 'The United States must adopt as its working position that the lives of Vietnamese civilians are just as valuable as American lives'. But for the American military such an idea was preposterous. In their efforts to protect themselves, they made more enemies.

But counter-insurgency was not the sure-fire solution which Krepinevich suggests. It required a massive level of commitment. Westmoreland admitted that with 'virtually unlimited manpower, I could have stationed troops permanently in every district or province and thus . . . enabled the troops to get to know the people intimately, facilitating the task of identifying the subversives and protecting the others against intimidation'.[36] To be effective, counter-insurgency had to go hand-in-hand with aid programmes; standards of living had to rise at the same time that security was strengthened. But, as Richard Hunt concludes, this sort of pacification strategy 'would most likely have taken too long and would in any case have exhausted the patience of the American people'.[37] In a conversation with Robert Shaplen in 1970, a demoralized American economic-development worker summarized the immense difficulty of pacification: 'two Vietcong in a hamlet can still undo most of what we've accomplished'.[38]

In *Dynamics of Defeat*, Eric Bergerud argues, rather convincingly, that the chances of winning the war by fighting the 'other war' were less than by pursuing a more aggressive conventional strategy. The problem was one of time and manpower. The US had a very small number of combat troops. Dispersing them to cover a greater area, as Westmoreland recognized, would have been playing into the hands of the PLAF. The guerrillas would have loved to be able to slug

35 Guenter Lewy, *America in Vietnam* (Oxford, 1978), p. 104.
36 Westmoreland, *Soldier Reports*, p. 147.
37 Richard A. Hunt, *Pacification* (Boulder, CO, 1995), p. 279.
38 Robert Shaplen, *The Road from War* (New York, NY, 1970), p. 338.

it out in the hinterlands with lightly armed Americans. The US Army, Bergerud feels, was organized as it was because that was the best way for a modern democracy to fight a war. The Army's motto of 'bullets not bodies' suited a citizenry who accepted the principle of fighting communism, but did not want to lose men. Spreading out and fighting a real counter-insurgency war, while deploying firepower sparingly, would simply have meant more Americans sent home in body bags.[39]

The task of training men for counter-insurgency was in any case hugely complicated, especially since GIs were limited to a one-year tour of duty. It was arguably also a diversion from the American military's intended purpose, which was to fight a conventional war against the Soviet Union. Did it make sense to undergo a massive military transformation in order to win a small war in Asia? 'We're watchdogs you unchain to eat up the burglar', one battalion commander argued. 'Don't ask us to be mayors or sociologists worrying about hearts and minds.'[40] 'I'll be damned if I permit the United States Army, its institutions, its doctrines, and its traditions to be destroyed just to win this lousy war', an American officer once exclaimed. Lewy cites this as evidence of the Army's stubborn refusal to adapt.[41] It seems instead an impressive ability to take the long view.

WAS VICTORY POSSIBLE?

Loren Baritz rejects the Krepinevich thesis on the grounds that cultural conditioning impeded adaptation to the challenges Vietnam posed. 'War is a product of culture . . . Our managerial sophistication and technological superiority resulted in our trained incompetence in guerrilla warfare.' There is plenty of evidence to support this argument. Sophisticated weapons were used because they were available, not necessarily because they were appropriate.[42] Baritz argues that there was no escape from the tyranny of technological war: 'The military's continuing claim that we could have won the war if it had been allowed to fight the war differently is pointless. We could not have

---

39 This argument is also derived from Bergerud's correspondence with the author over the course of this book's preparation.

40 Thomas G. Paterson, 'Historical memory and illusive victories: Vietnam and Central America', *Diplomatic History*, 12 (1988), p. 5.

41 Lewy, *America in Vietnam*, p. 138.

42 For instance, studies have revealed that slower propeller-driven aircraft were more efficient at destroying targets in this type of war than jet aircraft and resulted in fewer civilian casualties and crew losses. Yet over 90 per cent of sorties were flown by jets. Lewy, *America in Vietnam*, p. 98.

fought it differently. . . . The American way of life and war meant that we could not succeed as counterinsurgents.'[43]

This seems excessively deterministic. It is also peripheral to the real issue. Defeat was inevitable not because of strategic failures, but because America backed an ally which had no future in Vietnam. Both Summers and Krepinevich, from different directions, argue that the conditions could have been created in which the RVN could have transformed itself into a benevolent, responsible and representative government. Yet during nearly 30 years of American involvement the Saigon regime provided no evidence that it was capable of such a transformation. The RVN did not become corrupt and cruel because it was, by 1965, losing the war. It was corrupt and cruel by nature. Improving the military situation in South Vietnam would not have eradicated its venality. The RVN could not easily overcome the fact that it was an urban, Westernized and largely Catholic elite which ruled over a rural, eastern, poor peasantry. Those with power were reluctant to change because exploitation was profitable in the short term. Strategic tinkering would not have transformed the social conflict at the heart of the Vietnam War.

Anti-communism had great popular appeal, but the RVN government had little. It was difficult to motivate soldiers to defend a regime which had no real identity, and a state which was an invention of diplomats. These weaknesses forced the regime to look outward for support, namely to the United States. While American assistance undoubtedly made South Vietnam stronger militarily, it weakened the regime politically by exacerbating its worst faults. 'The American dollars have really changed our way of thinking', the ultraconservative Father Nguyen Quang Lam wrote in 1975. 'People compete with each other to become prostitutes, that is to say, to get rich in the quickest and most exploitative manner.'[44] The American presence was living proof that the Saigon government could not control its own fate. The American way of war also fundamentally altered the character of South Vietnam, creating a society and an economy which were not sustainable in the long term.

Some have argued that the US should have forced the RVN to reform. It was a great mistake, Robert Komer contends, that the US did not use 'more vigorously the power over the [RVN] that our contributions gave us. We became their prisoners, rather than they ours.' But forcing the RVN to change (assuming this was possible)

43 Baritz, *Backfire*, pp. 317–21.
44 Long, 'Post-Paris agreement struggles and the fall of Saigon', p. 213.

would merely have underlined its puppet status, leaving the Americans vulnerable to charges of neocolonialism. Some time ago, in a different theatre of war, T.E. Lawrence recognized the difficulties of creating an effective alliance between unequal partners. It is 'better they do it imperfectly than you do it perfectly', he argued, 'for it is their country, their war, and your time is limited'.[45] It is also difficult to force an ally to improve whilst at the same time making it clear that you will not let them fail. For the US, the RVN's survival was always more important than its morality.[46] Powerful cynics in Saigon exploited that situation.

The US was not only saddled with a weak ally, it also faced a formidable enemy. 'They were in fact the best enemy we have faced in our history', one general confessed to Kinnard.[47] In 1945, after the Japanese surrender, General Douglas MacArthur warned General Jacques LeClerc, the new Commander-in-Chief of French forces in Indochina, about the difficulties of fighting Vietnamese nationalism: 'if you expect to succeed in overcoming the resistance of your enemy . . . bring soldiers, and then more soldiers, and after that still more soldiers. But, even after all the soldiers you can spare are there, you probably still will not succeed.'[48] Three-quarters of the commanders polled by Kinnard felt that the US did not sufficiently understand the enemy. One general complained of a 'gross misconception of North Vietnamese capabilities, values and determination'.[49]

David Chanoff, who interviewed many veterans of the revolution, 'came away . . . with an appreciation for why their side triumphed and our side didn't'. He explained:

> Utter ruthlessness and massive social manipulation on the part of the Northern-led party played a large role, of that there's no doubt. . . . But even more important . . . was a quixotic disregard for the impossible, a quality I came to think of as 'ordinary heroism'. So many apparently normal human beings had demonstrated in one way or another a damn the consequences approach to life that it began to seem like a national trait.[50]

45 Lewy, *America in Vietnam*, pp. 439–40.

46 See Richard Hunt, 'Strategies at war: pacification and attrition in Vietnam', in Richard A. Hunt and Richard Shultz, eds, *Lessons from an Unconventional War* (New York, NY, 1982), pp. 43–5.

47 Kinnard, *War Managers*, p. 67.

48 Tran Van Don, *Our Endless War* (Novato, CA, 1978), p. 143.

49 Kinnard, *War Managers*, p. 28.

50 David Chanoff and Doan Van Toai, *'Vietnam' – A Portrait of its People at War* (London, 1996), p. 209.

It is perhaps difficult for Americans raised on stories of the Alamo, San Juan Hill and Iwo Jima to accept that they were defeated by a spirit more powerful than their own. Don Luce, who toured the US with the Indochina Mobile Education Project, encountered 'a tremendous frustration that, with all our bombs, all of our technology, we have not been able to destroy the human spirit. That really bothered people.'[51]

The revolution's potent mix of military and political struggle gave it a profound advantage over its adversaries. It was able, because of its contact with the peasantry, to fight and rule with economy of force, thus making the most of meagre resources and limited personnel. And, no matter how much it might have resorted to cruelty, terrorism and occasionally cynical acts, it retained a moral superiority over the Saigon regime which allowed it to maintain political legitimacy. It represented, in other words, the best causes: economic and social justice and national independence, even if those causes often became distorted in their pursuit.

This political supremacy meant that the revolution could never be defeated purely by military means alone. Sir Robert Thompson feels that the Americans, and by extension their RVN allies, 'fought a separate war which ignored its political and other aspects, and were not on a collision course with the Vietcong and North Vietnamese, who therefore had a free run in the real war'. Or, as Larry Cable states even more succinctly: 'The American war in Vietnam [was] irrelevent to the Vietnamese wars'.[52] Granted, the stubbornness which some Americans displayed in attempting to mould the war into a familiar form was prodigious. 'It is fashionable in some quarters to say that the problems in Southeast Asia are primarily political and economic rather than military', General Earle Wheeler claimed in November 1962. 'I do not agree. The essence of the problem in Vietnam is military.'[53] But, while it is tempting to believe that the war could have been won by an army of sociologists and political scientists spreading a benevolent culture among an ignorant peasant population, such fantasies do not accord with the reality in Vietnam. The PLAF were not a bunch of barefoot guerrillas but a highly trained, fiercely determined and well-armed fighting force which was at its best in small unit actions. A small force of American counter-insurgency specialists, as envisaged by Thompson, might have worked in Malaya, but Malaya was not

51 Gloria Emerson, *Winners and Losers* (New York, NY, 1992), p. 353.
52 Larry Cable, *Unholy Grail* (London, 1991), p. 234.
53 Lewy, *America in Vietnam*, pp. 85–6.

Vietnam. No matter how much money and effort was devoted to pacification, it could not work unless the PLAF main force units were neutralized. This explains why the greatest progress in pacification was made after Tet, when the PLAF effectively removed itself from the contest.

As Wheeler's assertion demonstrates, American decision-makers did not really understand the threat with which they were faced. Edward Lansdale, who had an intimate understanding of revolutionary politics in Southeast Asia, wrote a scathing attack upon American policy in a 1964 article entitled 'Vietnam: Do We Understand Revolution?'. The short answer was 'no'. 'There must be a heartfelt *cause* to which the legitimate government is pledged', Lansdale argued, 'a cause which makes a stronger appeal to the people than the Communist cause, a cause which is used in a dedicated way by the legitimate government to polarize and guide all other actions – psychological, military, social and economic – with participation by the people themselves, in order to bring victory.'[54] Without such a cause, the 'legitimate' government had no real claim to legitimacy. Or, as another expert observed in 1967, 'It is not possible to fight something with nothing'.[55] There *was* a spirit among the non-communists of South Vietnam, and a determination to resist the imposition of an alien ideology. They *were* a massive force. But the government never discovered how to harness their energy and embody their dreams.

Thus, the American effort was never more than a delaying force. When American ground troops began arriving in 1965, the defeat of the Saigon regime was imminent. The Americans delayed that inevitable consequence by around ten years. Both the French and the Americans, not to mention the Saigon regime itself, resorted to force because of the unassailable supremacy of the communists in the political arena. All three learned (or should have learned) that force by itself was inappropriate, because the application of force made the political appeal of the insurgency all the greater. The harder they tried to win the war, the more disruption they caused, and the more remote victory became. As John Del Vecchio writes, good intentions caused great misery:

> We came not to conquer. We came to help. We came to insure security and independence. We came to end conflict. We said and we showed that we would selflessly lay down our lives to

54 Edward Lansdale, 'Vietnam: do we understand revolution?', *Foreign Affairs* 43 (1964), p. 77.
55 Lewy, *America in Vietnam*, p. 94.

end this conflict. And yet our altruism has corrupted itself until we can only be satisfied with annihilation. We define everything about us in terms of conflict. As long as there are two sides there will be conflict and we have said we will not tolerate conflict. We will stamp it out. It is the same as sentencing Vietnam to total destruction and annihilation.[56]

Alternative military strategies such as those proposed by Summers and Krepinevich might have produced a more effective military conduct of the war, but they do not address the political question. It was within the power of the US to effect a stalemate on the battlefield and perhaps even to impose a temporary military defeat upon revolutionary forces, but military dominance could only be sustained if the US commitment was open-ended. Once Americans departed, communist political strength would prevail. The communist strategy was based on the absolute certainty that the US could not stay in Vietnam forever.

LESSONS LEARNED

Was this the wrong war, or a war fought wrongly? The 1980 Myths and Realities survey found that 37 per cent of Vietnam veterans (including non-combat) and 38 per cent of the general public expressed the opinion that the war could never have been won under any circumstances.[57] It is a significant development when over one-third of the citizens of the most powerful nation on earth admit that there are wars they cannot win. It is perhaps no wonder that the Vietnam experience led to a resurgence of isolationism. Just before the fall of Saigon, just 36 per cent of Americans polled agreed that it was important for the US to honour foreign policy commitments. Only 34 per cent expressed a willingness to send troops to defend West Berlin in the event of a Soviet invasion. A majority in favour of intervention could only be found when the hypothetical victim was Canada.[58] This isolationist spirit seems to have endured. In 1989 nearly one half of respondents to a poll argued that the Vietnam failure demonstrated that the US should only go to war to repel an invasion of her own country.[59]

---

56 John M. Del Vecchio, 'The combative structure of the English language', in Jeffrey P. Kimball, ed., *To Reason Why* (New York, NY, 1990), p. 353.

57 MacPherson, *Long Time Passing*, p. 59.

58 George C. Herring, *America's Longest War* (New York, NY, 1986), p. 274.

59 Melanson, *Reconstructing Consensus*, p. 190.

After Vietnam, the American government became noticeably less confident in its exercise of power. Cyrus Vance, Secretary of State in the Carter administration, argued: 'the use of military force is not, and should not be, a desirable American policy response to the internal politics of other nations'.[60] Reagan seemed a great deal more bellicose, but we must not confuse rhetoric with reality. He and Bush struck aggressive postures, but chose their conflicts carefully. Grenada and Panama were safe bets, but Nicaragua looked too much like Vietnam in Central America. But Vietnam also forced American power underground, where it would not arouse the disdain of those who disapproved. Covert forces were active in Central America, Africa and Southeast Asia. The 1980s was a busy time for the CIA.[61]

Carter's National Security Adviser, Zbigniew Brzezinski, felt that 'the tragedy of Vietnam' is that 'we are afraid to use power'. He wanted Americans to accept 'the selective use of that power'.[62] Alarmed by the isolationist trend, Nixon argued that 'it is vital that we learn the right lessons from that defeat. In Vietnam, we tried and failed in a just cause. "No More Vietnams" can mean that we will not *try* again. It *should* mean that we will not *fail* again.'

James Thomson, historian and one time policy-maker, feels that it would be 'no great misfortune if the [Vietnam] war led to a reduction of grandiosity on our part'.[63] That perhaps is the most important lesson: that there are limits to American power and limits on where power should be used. Senator Frank Church recognized the flaws in American thinking in February 1965 when active involvement was still a matter for debate:

> We have come to treat 'Communism', regardless of what form
> it may take in any given country, as the enemy. We fancy
> ourselves the guardians of the 'free' world, though most of it is
> not free, and never has been. We seek to immunize the world
> against further Communist infection through massive injections
> of American aid, and, wherever necessary, through direct
> American intervention. Such a vast undertaking has at least two
> defects: first, it exceeds our national capability; second, among
> the newly emerging nations, where the specter of Western

60 Ibid., p. 106.
61 See Gregory F. Treverton, *Covert Action: The Limits of Intervention in a Postwar World* (London, 1987).
62 Ibid., p. 108.
63 Richard N. Pfeffer, ed., *No More Vietnams?: The War and the Future of American Foreign Policy* (New York, NY, 1968), pp. 258, 288.

imperialism is dreaded more than Communism, such a policy can be self-defeating.[64]

Because Johnson's war seemed affordable and tolerable, few asked whether it was necessary. Military operations were based on the assumption that Vietnam was vital to the security of the United States, when in fact it was (or should have been) a purely local argument.

There are some wars which military power alone cannot solve, and some places where the US does not belong. But power begets responsibility; American isolationism has been as disastrous as overzealous intervention. One is tempted to argue that countries like Vietnam should be allowed to sort out their own internal problems; but recent events in the former Yugoslavia demonstrate that when they are left to do so the results can be terribly tragic. Vietnam does nevertheless provide some sobering lessons about the arrogance of power and the need to consider consequences when power is exercised. The war was about stopping communist expansion, not about the fate of Vietnam. No one stopped to consider what might happen to the poor people in Vietnam when 500,000 American soldiers arrived to fight the Cold War. The US successfully delayed the inevitable for ten years, but thousands of innocent Vietnamese died in the futile pursuit of American state interest.

RENEWAL AND REDEMPTION?

After the Gulf War, President George Bush boasted 'By God, we've kicked the Vietnam syndrome once and for all'.[65] The statement had resonance because it seemed true on a number of levels. The United States had apparently put aside the uncertainty which failure in Vietnam had engendered; Americans were now confident and assertive in the exercise of power. They had also gone to war and fought differently. Bush had carefully constructed the sort of coalition impossible during the Vietnam War; Americans did not go to war alone, and therefore did not feel the eyes of the world upon them in quite the same way. The apparent ease with which the Gulf War was 'won' also seemed to confirm that the lessons of Vietnam had been learned well, particularly with respect to the need for meticulous planning and rapid deployment.

But it would not be overly cynical to see this as a carefully constructed myth. The greatest difference between Vietnam and the Gulf

---

64 Capps, *Unfinished War*, p. 57.
65 Michael Sherry, *In the Shadow of War* (New Haven, CT, 1995), p. 463.

War was that spin-doctors now attended meetings of Cabinet and the JCS. Bush's war may have seemed more open and above board than Johnson's had, but in truth news of it was much more carefully manipulated to encourage a positive public view. (In fact, journalists had much greater access to the battlefield in Vietnam than in Iraq.) The war was also fought in a way calculated to please the public, most notably in the way that the fighting stopped at a point when a dramatic, low-cost victory could be claimed, but still at a point far short of actually defeating the enemy. Unlimited power was used to pursue a limited aim. Had Bush ordered his armies on to Baghdad, they would have encountered the cream of Saddam Hussein's forces in a very determined mood. The war would have been far uglier.

The ruse worked. Bush discovered that a war could be made acceptable if the public could be convinced that military action had somehow changed. The old myth of American military omnipotence was cleverly revived but given a new spin: the US, it seemed, could win wars without killing lots of people. Television reports showed smart bombs guided with ultimate precision into chimneys and ventilations shafts of strategic buildings, leaving civilian housing nearby unscathed. News broadcasts neglected to mention that only a small percentage of the bombs were 'smart', the rest being of the more conventional, less accurate variety. Reporters gladly joined the bandwagon of self-delusion. 'High technology sets this war apart from Vietnam', one reporter argued, apparently unaware that smart weapons were also used in Southeast Asia. Others celebrated the fact that airpower had become the 'determinant of victory in war', unknowingly echoing a sentiment first expressed by Giulio Douhet in the 1930s, and repeated by air enthusiasts ever since. War had become fashionable again. There was even talk of 'postmodern war' which would 'minimize the shedding of American blood while maximizing the destruction on the other side'. War 'now consists of short, quick actions that take days to complete, not months or years'.[66] Tell that to the people of the former Yugoslavia.

Americans learned to love the military again. Books like *Prodigal Soldiers*, by James Kitfield, praised the progress the armed forces had made since Vietnam, and presented a picture which would inspire public pride. Senior commanders in the Gulf War became heroes in the way those of the Vietnam era never did. Properly packaged, Norman Schwarzkopf and Colin Powell seemed intelligent, able and above all humane commanders – more like Eisenhower than Westmoreland.

66 Ibid., pp. 470–71.

The military was presented as a career, not a job of last resort. A new soldierly icon was created, characterized by the recruitment slogan 'The Marines need a few good men'. In future, wars would be won by small bands of courageous, dedicated professionals armed with the most technologically advanced weaponry.

Granted, some progress was made. Reforms to the command structure and bureaucracy addressed the problems which Vietnam had so vividly exposed, chief among them the tendency to allow strategic preconceptions to influence the interpretation of battlefield progress. The American military did become leaner, fitter and more efficient. A bit of adversity seemed good medicine. The indiscipline, drug abuse and racial animosity which had characterized the military in the later years of the war were proactively addressed. It could even be argued that the military became an engine of social change, integrating racially and sexually much more quickly than many private institutions. Perhaps most healthy was the apparent awareness of limitations. In the early 1980s Summers's *On Strategy* fed Army fantasies about a different ending to the Vietnam War. In contrast, in the 1990s some lecturers at the Command and General Staff College suggested that the war was one which an American military could not win.[67]

But it is easy to exaggerate the change which has occurred, easy to wallow in post-Gulf War euphoria. The Gulf War performance seems impressive in part because many groups, for various political reasons, have over-stated the problems of the Vietnam-era military. That soldiers like the brutal Colonel Kurtz of *Apocalypse Now* were supposedly absent from the fighting in Iraq says more about the enduring myths of the Vietnam War than about the actual character of the American military today. Many of the reforms which have occurred since 1975 would have happened anyway, the result of advances in weapons technology or the manifestation of progress in wider society. The problems which beset the military during the Vietnam era resulted mainly from a long and ultimately futile war. End the war, and the problems solve themselves. The American military appears more healthy because it has been able to address its problems during a period of relative peace. The unlikelihood of war has made a military career more attractive and thus improved the overall calibre of the recruit.[68] Nor is it entirely clear that Westmoreland's army was functionally better than Schwarzkopf's. The Gulf War was, after all, a

---

67 My thanks to my sister, Lieutenant Colonel Janet A. Borch, US Army, a graduate of the College, for this information.

68 Many American soldiers complained about being sent to the Gulf, claiming that they had never expected actually to go to war when they joined the military.

very close approximation to the sort of conventional conflict which has figured large in the military's preparations since 1945. In a modern sense, it is not a typical war. Wars of the future, writes Martin van Creveld, will be 'low-intensity conflicts' waged by insurgents, terrorists and outlaw regimes. 'It will be protracted, bloody and horrible'[69] – or, in other words, rather like Vietnam. The frustrations of Somalia will probably be more typical of the future than the triumphs in Iraq. As happened in Vietnam, in such contests the impotence of power will lead to a rapid erosion of American confidence. Schwarzkopf's aplomb will give way to an acerbity reminiscent of Westmoreland. The only way for the military to maintain the myth of 'renewal and redemption'[70] is for the United States to choose its future wars with care.

69 Martin van Creveld, *The Transformation of War* (New York, NY, 1991), pp. 205, 207, 212.

70 A phrase favoured by James Kitfield, as evidenced by the jacket of his book, *Prodigal Soldiers* (New York, NY, 1995).

11   A GRUNT'S LIFE

On the 18th anniversary of D-Day, 2 June 1962, John Kennedy warned the West Point graduating class that American security was threatened by a war

> new in its intensity, ancient in its origin – war by guerrillas, subversives, insurgents, assassins, war by ambush instead of by combat, by infiltration instead of by aggression, seeking victory by eroding and exhausting the enemy instead of engaging him . . . These are the kinds of challenges that will be before us in the next decade if freedom is to be saved . . .[1]

The American military did not prove equal to this challenge. Forces trained to fight a massive conventional war were thrown into a small, claustrophic, bewildering conflict. The war was lost. So, too, was the legendary invincibility of the American soldier.

VOLUNTEERS AND DRAFTEES

Much is made of the statistic that three-quarters of Vietnam veterans were volunteers. Though technically accurate, it is misleading, since many volunteered only when they fully expected to be drafted. They enlisted on the assumption that by doing so they might avoid being sent to Vietnam or might land a rear echelon assignment. 'Volunteers' did have a slightly better chance in Vietnam; they made up 75 per cent of the total force, but suffered 69.6 per cent of the deaths.[2]

Nevertheless, many soldiers did volunteer, often for reasons which seem old-fashioned today. Lieutenant Tom Carhart 'held a few truths to be self-evident. Communism was bad; America, freedom, and West Point were good. That was the extent of [my] political philosophy.'[3]

1 Rick Atkinson, *The Long Gray Line* (London, 1989), p. 22.
2 'Vietnam warriors: a statistical profile', compiled by the Vietnam Veterans Memorial fund.
3 Atkinson, *Long Gray Line*, p. 267.

'The war I thought was like they taught us in high school', one soldier commented. 'You know, you're fighting communism . . . the good guys against the bad guys.'[4] Some went in search of heroic war, like their fathers who had fought good wars in Europe or the Pacific. They grew up watching John Wayne films on Friday nights and re-enacted episodes of *Combat!* on backyard battlefields with plastic guns. War seemed exciting, noble, romantic. Philip Caputo confessed that he

> wanted . . . to find in a commonplace world a chance to live heroically. Having known nothing but security, comfort and peace, I hungered for danger, challenges and violence. . . . the heroic experience I sought was war; war, the ultimate adventure; war, the ordinary man's most convenient means of escaping from the ordinary.[5]

Another soldier experienced a pull common to many men in all wars: 'I was a little gung-ho and I was scared, too. I wanted to prove myself, I wanted to test my manhood.'[6] For those who wavered, society or family provided a gentle nudge:

> My old man, when the war came, he says 'Oh go. You'll learn something. You'll grow up to be a man. Go.'
>
> Shit, if my folks had to send their little poodle, they would have cried more over that than over me. But I'm supposed to go, because I'm a man.[7]

'I told my father I was thinking of going to Canada', one veteran recalled. 'I turned to walk out of the room. I saw my father, his head in his hands, sobbing at the kitchen table. I had never seen him cry before. I knew then that I had to go.'[8]

Most African-Americans would not have felt the same instinctive patriotism as Carhart. Yet many agreed that the war had to be fought or 'the commies would take over'.[9] Others volunteered simply because the military has always proved attractive for those with few career options. It provided a way of gaining acceptance and proving one's worth in white-dominated society. Contrary to popular assumptions, however, African-Americans did not suffer disproportionately

4 Paul Starr, *The Discarded Army* (New York, NY, 1973), p. 9.

5 Philip Caputo, *A Rumor of War* (New York, NY, 1977), pp. 5–6.

6 Stanley W. Beesley, ed., *Vietnam: The Heartland Remembers* (Norman, OK, 1987), p. 15.

7 Mark Baker, *Nam* (New York, NY, 1981), pp. 15–16.

8 Myra MacPherson, *Long Time Passing* (New York, NY, 1984), p. 36.

9 Gerald Gill, 'Black soldiers' perspectives on the war', in Walter Capps, ed., *The Vietnam Reader* (New York, NY, 1991), p. 174.

in this war. They constituted 10.6 per cent of active duty military personnel, 13.5 per cent of the total population, and 12.5 per cent of the combat deaths.[10]

Service in Vietnam reflected not racial discrimination, but discrimination against the young, the under-educated, and the poor. One-quarter of the American force had family incomes below the poverty level. The college graduate who enlisted had a 40 per cent chance of being sent to Vietnam, the high school graduate 65 per cent, the dropout 70 per cent.[11] A distinction nevertheless needs to be made between service and combat. It should not be inferred that, because of the high percentage of high school dropouts in Vietnam, the combat force was generally of low intelligence. The field army was in fact a better representation of society than was the army overall, for good reason. The simpleton who could hardly spell his name was quickly recognized as a danger to his comrades and was often sent back to camp to wash dishes. This might explain why, according to recent research, 'per capita death rates ... were only slightly lower in affluent American communities than in others'.[12] On the other hand, West Virginia, one of the poorest states in the Union, experienced the highest Vietnam death rate at 84.1 per 100,000 males, the national average being 58.9.[13]

The average age of the soldier was nineteen, nearly seven years younger than in the Second World War. Older, more experienced men were more likely to avoid the draft. 'What did I need with shaving equipment?', one Marine recalled of his induction, 'I was only seventeen. I didn't have hair under my *arms*, let alone my face.'[14] Vietnam challenged their youthful imagination. 'We thought we were tough and streetwise, but we were really ignorant', one veteran admitted.[15]

---

10 'Vietnam warriors'.

11 Ibid., Lawrence M. Baskir and William A. Strauss, *Chance and Circumstance* (New York, NY, 1978), p. 10.

12 See Arnold Barnett *et al.*, 'America's Vietnam casualties: victims of a class war?', *Operations Research* 40 (1992), p. 865. According to the authors, the richest decile of their population sample suffered 7.8 per cent of the deaths, while the poorest suffered 9.6 per cent. The highest share of deaths (13.1 per cent) was suffered by the second poorest decile. What the authors do not stress, but is clear from their findings, is that 55 per cent of the deaths occurred among the poorest half of the population sample, 45 per cent among the richest half.

13 'Vietnam warriors'. Death rates continue to divide historians because of their political implications. Tempers flare over the notion of a 'class war'. A clear resolution of the argument seems elusive, in part because both sides have used sophisticated demographic analysis to 'prove' their case.

14 MacPherson, *Long Time Passing*, p. 52.

15 Eric Bergerud, *Red Thunder, Tropic Lightning* (New York, NY, 1994), p. 264.

Shad Meshad, born and raised in the southeastern United States, 'knew nothing about the northeast or even about the southwest. And, for sure, I didn't know a thing about Asia.'[16]

As the war dragged on and the demand for recruits increased, standards fell, partly because the 'best' men found it easier to avoid service. Lily Adams, an Army nurse, found that 'Some of these guys, young boys, just couldn't handle it. They just didn't have it. . . . Their IQ [was] so low. They just weren't Army material, but we used them anyway.' One veteran felt that by 1970, 'replacements . . . didn't have enough time to train and become soldiers. They lacked the desire, dedication and obedience, the two or three years that's required to become the best possible soldier before entering battle.'[17] The problem was compounded by a chronic shortage of quality NCOs, whose leadership skills could not be improvised quickly. Ironically, the best NCOs were rewarded with rear echelon jobs.

Active service for the enlisted man was limited to one year. This created a short-term mentality; soldiers focused not on winning, but surviving.

> Each X on my short-timer's calendar represented a massive act of will. All day long I would fight back the compulsion to scratch away another day as if, by the ritual act of crossing it off my calendar, I would have lived it through. . . . I gathered days in-country as a miser does dollars, and clung to them just as fiercely.[18]

As men grew more experienced, they drew closer to the end of their term. Critics complain that the US fought the war with a different army every year. It is easy to criticize the policy, but much harder to find an alternative. Granted, American soldiers in the Second World War fought for the duration, but the comparison is hardly appropriate since the war was so different. In Vietnam, 'duration' could have meant eight years; it is hard to imagine that morale or commitment would have *improved* had soldiers been forced to stay the distance.

After the war, in Hollywood productions and dime store novels, service in Vietnam became a metaphor for degeneracy and madness. This annoyed those veterans who took pride in their normality. 'It really irritates me to see the soldiers portrayed as drug-crazed, psychopathic murderers, losers, idiots and cowards', Lee Reynolds, a

---

16 Walter Capps, *The Unfinished War* (Boston, MA, 1990), p. 93.
17 Bergerud, *Red Thunder*, pp. 96, 214.
18 Norman L. Russell, *Suicide Charlie* (Westport, CT, 1993), p. 160.

medic, has commented. 'From what I saw over there, nothing could be farther from the truth.'[19] Granted, some inappropriate men became soldiers, but failure in Vietnam was not caused by immaturity, ignorance or insanity. While the intelligent and able often shielded themselves from the draft, those who did serve were still the best-educated force America had ever sent to war. Post-1945 education reform meant that 79 per cent had at least a high school education, compared to 63 per cent in the Korean War and 45 per cent in the Second World War.[20] 'They were very skillful, very professional, probably the most knowledgeable soldiers that our military has ever put on a battlefield', Reynolds felt.[21]

OFFICERS

Tim O'Brien described his platoon commander as 'a professional soldier, an ideal leader of men in the field . . . He did not yearn for battle. But neither was he concerned about the prospect.'[22] Unfortunately, O'Brien's experience was not sufficiently typical. Perhaps in no other war have American soldiers been so contemptuous of their officers. 'The very few . . . I came into contact with were totally incompetent', rifleman Dan Vandenberg commented. 'They were more concerned with how you looked, how your uniform was, or how your hair was cut.'[23] Demand for officers outstripped supply. Due to the unpopularity of the war, Reserve Officer Training Corps (ROTC) enrolment dropped from 231,000 in 1965 to 73,000 in 1972. In 1970, 60 per cent of ROTC members expressed a reluctance to serve in Vietnam.[24] Westmoreland admitted that 'the Army had to lower its standards . . . some marginal types were commissioned'.[25]

At the peak of the war, the proportion of officers to men was almost double that of the Second World War. But though 43,000 officers ranked major or higher served, only 201 were killed in action.[26] One captain described his battalion commander as a man who 'had always his mission in mind and he went about performing

---

19 Bergerud, *Red Thunder*, p. 307.

20 'Vietnam warriors'.

21 Bergerud, *Red Thunder*, p. 307.

22 Tim O'Brien, *If I Die in a Combat Zone* (London, 1989), p. 86.

23 Bergerud, *Red Thunder*, p. 303.

24 Gabriel Kolko, *Anatomy of a War* (New York, NY, 1994), p. 360.

25 William Westmoreland, 'Vietnam in perspective', in Capps, ed., *Vietnam Reader*, p. 119.

26 Kolko, *Anatomy*, p. 360.

that mission with the utmost proficiency. His mission was getting promoted.'[27] The 1970 Study on Military Professionalism, conducted by the Army War College, regretted the prevalence of the

> ambitious, transitory commander – marginally skilled in the complexities of his duties – engulfed in producing statistical results, fearful of personal failure, too busy to talk with or listen to his subordinates, and determined to submit acceptably optimistic results which reflect faultless completion of a variety of tasks at the expense of the sweat and frustration of his subordinates.[28]

Many officers, General Douglas Kinnard felt, 'made a career out of their own careers rather than a career out of leading their units'. Some 87 per cent of the commanders he polled thought careerism was a serious problem.[29]

Since the war was expected to be short, officers were limited to a six-month tour, in order to give as many as possible combat experience. The policy – derogatively known as 'ticket-punching' – engendered enormous ill-feeling among ordinary soldiers who 'were there for their whole tours and never had the luxury of rotating out to a safe and secure assignment'. Lieutenant-Colonel Carl Quickmire thought it was an 'extremely dumb policy ... and very bad for morale'.[30] Inexperienced officers also compromised the efficiency and safety of a unit. According to one study, a battalion commander with less than six months experience lost an average of 2.5 men per month, while those with over six months lost 1.6 men.[31] 'All evidence points to the fact that disintegration in the Army relates directly to the character, integrity and competence of the officer corps', argue Paul Savage and Richard Gabriel in a controversial but convincing essay. 'Nothing in the available data shows any connection between disintegration and such external factors as the "permissive society", fragmenting ideologies, or "a nation being torn apart".'[32]

27 Loren Baritz, *Backfire* (New York, NY, 1985), p. 300.
28 John M. Gates, 'If at first you don't succeed, try to rewrite history: revisionism and the Vietnam War', in William Head and Lawrence Grinter, eds, *Looking Back on the Vietnam War* (Westport, CT, 1993), p. 185.
29 Douglas Kinnard, *The War Managers* (Wayne, NJ, 1985), pp. 110, 112.
30 Bergerud, *Red Thunder*, p. 301.
31 Baritz, *Backfire*, p. 303.
32 Paul L. Savage and Richard A. Gabriel, 'Cohesion and disintegration in the American Army: an alternative perspective', in Grace Sevy, ed., *The American Experience in Vietnam* (Norman, OK, 1989), pp. 96–7.

THE LOGISTICS OF DEPLOYMENT

In 1954 a team of analysts made recommendations to Army Chief of Staff General Matthew Ridgway on the type of force to be mobilized in the event of an American intervention in Vietnam. They warned that casualties would be proportionate to those in the Pacific theatre during the Second World War. Since Vietnam was 'practically devoid of those facilities which modern forces such as ours find essential . . . a tremendous engineering and logistical effort' would be required. This would mean that only a small proportion of troops deployed would take part in combat, but all would be vulnerable to guerrilla attack.[33] The report convinced an already reluctant Eisenhower not to intervene.

Eleven years later, when American troops mobilized, they encountered many of the problems outlined in the above report. In the past, upon mobilization, the reserves provided the logistics, communications and service personnel to the standing army. But since Johnson refused to mobilize them, huge problems arose. The situation was exacerbated by the lack of well-developed port facilities in South Vietnam. Material was dumped on Saigon docks, where a huge logjam developed. Vast quantities were lost, to pilferage, sabotage or bad management. A supply crisis quickly developed. The 173rd Airborne, for instance, arrived at its station with only fifteen days' worth of bullets.[34]

By the end of 1967, the crisis was solved, though wastage remained severe. The logistics system supported more than 1.3 million American and allied soldiers. Approximately 850,000 tons of supplies arrived each month. Troops consumed 10 million field rations, 80,000 tons of ammunition, and 80 million gallons of fuel per month. In order to process this mountain of supplies, the US constructed six new ports, 4,000,000 square yards of airfields and heliports, 20 million square feet of storage areas, 500,000 cubic feet of refrigerated storage, 1,700 miles of roads, 15,000 feet of bridges, and 15 large fortified camps.[35]

In most wars, there is a front line which has to be supplied, and a relatively safe rear from which supplies come. But because there was no front, there was also no rear. Every American installation had to be protected militarily. Supplies had to be stored at large base areas which required huge numbers of personnel to administer, support and

33 Melvin Gurtov, *The First Vietnam Crisis* (New York, NY, 1967), p. 126.
34 Shelby Stanton, *The Rise and Fall of an American Army* (Novato, CA, 1985), p. 21.
35 Bernard Nalty, ed., *The Vietnam War* (London, 1996), pp. 120–1.

defend. This in part explains why American forces had such a long 'tail'. By December 1967, when troop strength totalled 473,200, actual combat strength was only 49,500, or 10.46 per cent of the total. Around 12 per cent were artillery and engineers, 2 per cent aviation, and 75 per cent headquarters and logistics personnel.[36]

Staff officers had difficulty prying soldiers out of safe rear echelon assignments. Divisions theoretically above strength had combat companies dangerously short of personnel. In 1966 combat battalions of the 1st Cavalry Division which were supposed to number 920 men often had less than 550.[37] Rifle companies were frequently one-third below strength. Lieutenant-Colonel Carl Nielson described how these problems reduced combat efficiency:

> although [my] rifle company was authorized 188 personnel, it rarely had more than 120 available ... And when we left the base camp, we always had to leave some of the remainder behind for perimeter defense. So when we actually got out in the field with our company, we were lucky to have 100. And I can recall making several air assaults where the guiding factor of determining the number of infantrymen on the ground was the number of transport helicopters available, each of which could take 10 men. We would rarely have more than 8 or 9, so now you're down to 80 to 90 people actually engaged in combat, that out of an authorized strength of 188.[38]

The shortage of skilled personnel was particularly acute. Aviation and logistics units could not be formed according to schedule, reducing effectiveness of ground units. Heavy losses among helicopter crews meant that the availability of pilots rather than strategic objectives often determined whether an operation went ahead. In June 1966 the Army required 14,300 pilots but could muster only 9,700.[39]

COMBAT

A generous Cold War budget produced a highly trained American military, albeit one prepared for war in Eastern Europe. Thomas Giltner's 'training for combat in Vietnam was non-existent'; it was instead 'conventional ... Monte Casino, North Africa, the Battle of

---

36 'Vietnam warriors'.
37 Stanton, *Rise and Fall*, p. 139.
38 Bergerud, *Red Thunder*, p. 115.
39 Stanton, *Rise and Fall*, p. 95.

the Bulge'.[40] Within the military, the lack of counter-insurgency training was not a cause for concern. In 1962 the Army Chief of Staff, General George Decker, told Kennedy that 'any good soldier can handle guerrillas'.[41] A common view among military professionals held that the war would be won with mobile tank warfare on South Vietnam's 'savannah grasslands and open plains, just like in Europe or west Texas'.[42]

The American answer to guerrilla warfare was air mobility. Helicopters encouraged an unwarranted confidence:

> 'Totally different war now.' The lieutenant flipped his cigarette
> out to the dew-covered ground. 'The French couldn't get
> around like we can.' He patted the Huey's deck. 'Machine's like
> this make all the difference. How'd you like to be a guerrilla
> trying to fight an army that can be anywhere, anytime?'[43]

The US put together the most lavish airmobile effort in history, at huge cost. The 1st Aviation Brigade, established in May 1966, eventually became one of the largest commands in Vietnam, with over 24,000 men and 4,230 aircraft.[44] On an average day a utility helicopter consumed 4,000 pounds of fuel. Almost 5,000 helicopters, each with a price tag exceeding US$250,000, were lost. Nearly 6,000 pilots and crew were killed, one-tenth of war fatalities.[45]

The attrition strategy begat the search and destroy operation. If an enemy presence was suspected, a mission would be launched, its size determined by the anticipated enemy concentration. American units usually did not break down lower than company level, since smaller squads were easily ambushed. A landing zone (LZ) would be chosen by overflying the area. Artillery and air support would first 'soften' the sector, whereupon troop helicopters, flying just above the jungle canopy and supported on the flanks by helicopter gunships, would hit the LZ, arriving within seconds of the last artillery round. Since the LZ was seldom more than 30 minutes from the base area, reinforcements could be ferried in quickly, and casualties removed. As additional ground units arrived, the target would be compressed, with air bombardment intensifying. Finally, infantry would sweep the area.

40 Bergerud, *Red Thunder*, p. 95.
41 Richard Hunt, *Pacification*, p. 19.
42 Andrew Krepinevich, *The Army and Vietnam* (Baltimore, MD, 1986), p. 37.
43 Robert Mason, *Chickenhawk* (London, 1983), p. 362.
44 Stanton, *Rise and Fall*, p. 92.
45 Peter MacDonald, *Giap* (London, 1993), p. 220.

South Vietnam was divided into tactical areas of responsibility, usually covering several provinces. The division (or separate brigade) assigned an area would stay there unless pulled away to contribute to a major operation. For example, the 1st Cavalry Division had its headquarters, commanding general, and principal staff at Phuoc Vinh, north of Saigon. The rear headquarters, where most of the logistical and administrative support was located, was at Bien Hoa. The division's three brigades had separate bases 50 to 100 miles from each other. Division and brigade bases were semi-permanent. Battalions were dispersed to a number of strategically situated firebases, which could be activated or de-activated according to need.

The standard infantry weapon was the M-16 assault rifle. With a stock made of plastic, it was considerably lighter than previous rifles. It fired a .223 calibre bullet, the smallest ever used in war, at a prodigious rate of fire. The advantage of the weapon's lighter weight was lost by the necessity to carry huge supplies of ammunition. The standard load was 200 rounds per man, but many carried 600 rounds to keep the hungry weapon fed. The muzzle velocity (3,800 feet per second) and the tendency of the bullet to be easily deflected on impact meant that it could inflict horrific wounds.

The small bullet lacked range and stopping power and was not terribly accurate – small objects like twigs or leaves could deflect its flight. But the most serious problem with the M-16 was its tendency to jam:

> When the M-16 rifle had a stoppage,
> One could feel enemy eyes
> Climbing
> His
> Bones
> Like
> Ivy.[46]

'They say if you kept the thing clean it worked just fine, which is great as long as you're operating on concrete. But out in the jungle, where it's nothing but dirt, it's totally impossible to keep them clean', one GI remarked. Most soldiers envied the enemy's AK-47. 'You could drive a truck over them, and you couldn't hurt those damn things; you could pour sand down their barrels and they would still fire. Ours would jam if you looked at them wrong.'[47]

---

46 MacAvoy Lane, 'Guns', quoted in W.D. Ehrhart, *In the Shadow of Vietnam: Essays, 1977–1991* (Jefferson, NC, 1977), p. 85.

47 Bergerud, *Red Thunder*, pp. 49–51.

Troops were constantly on the move in search of the enemy. 'You'd be surprised how similar killing is to hunting', a grunt wrote to his brother. 'I get all excited when I see a VC, just like when I see a deer.'[48] Most engagements began as some form of ambush. 'Sometimes we found Charlie, sometimes it was the other way.'[49]

> One night we wandered far and long
> To kill young men who, brave and strong
> And precious to their loved, their own,
> Were coming to kill us.
> Aching, filthy, weak, afraid,
> Creeping through the dripping shades,
> Searching forms through jungle haze,
> We stalked those men as prey.[50]

A great deal of damage could be done in a few seconds of chaos. If ambushed troops called for artillery or air support, deadly moments would pass before help arrived. 'Charlie played his game', one veteran remarked with grudging admiration. 'By the time the mortar rounds got there, he was already gone.'[51]

Limitless weaponry and ammunition eroded combat prowess. Soldiers fired indiscriminately the second the enemy was engaged, often running out of ammunition in the middle of a firefight. Commanders called in artillery barrages and air support to silence the lightest opposition. Officers preferred to waste shells rather than men, thus giving the enemy ample warning of American intentions. 'There developed . . . a great respect and affection for the men we commanded and a powerful reluctance to shed their blood. Our overall effectiveness as a fighting force was diminished', one officer felt.[52] Huge logistical problems arose as support troops struggled to transport and protect the massive supplies needed for an operation. Firepower became the solution to every problem – an expression of power and of fear. The destruction was sometimes senseless, but criticism is easy in retrospect. 'I didn't think of our targets as homes where exhausted and frightened people were praying for their lives', Tobias Wolff comments. 'When you are afraid you will kill anything that might kill you. [When] the enemy had the town, the town was the enemy.'[53]

48 Bernard Edelman, ed., *Dear America: Letters Home from Vietnam* (New York, NY, 1985), p. 94.

49 O'Brien, *If I Die in a Combat Zone*, p. 100.

50 James McLeroy, 'Ambush', in Edelman, ed., *Dear America*, p. 65.

51 Bergerud, *Red Thunder*, p. 74.

52 Ibid., pp. 295–6.

53 Tobias Wolff, *In Pharoah's Army* (London, 1994), pp. 133–4.

Often the only evidence of VC presence was the booby traps or mines which, between 1965 and 1970, caused 11 per cent of American combat deaths and 17 per cent of injuries.[54] The simplest and most common was the punji stake trap, in which sharpened bamboo stakes spread with human excrement were planted in a camouflaged pit. The unsuspecting soldier who stepped on one was certain to suffer immense pain, often followed by infection or gangrene. Traps slowed patrols and eroded morale. O'Brien described an all-pervasive fear:

> You hallucinate. You look ahead a few paces and what your legs will resemble if there is more to the earth in that spot than silicates and nitrogen. Will the pain be unbearable? Will you scream or fall silent? Will you be afraid to look at your own body, afraid of the sight of your own red flesh and white bone?[55]

Primitive weapons were often constructed from material inadvertently supplied by Americans. A beer can, primed with explosive from a dud bomb, became a grenade or mine. The ability to recognize traps came with experience, which explains why green GIs were most vulnerable.

'When you are fighting a war like Vietnam, you have no idea if you're doing anything useful militarily or not', one soldier felt. Another admitted being troubled by 'the knowledge that as soon as we left, they would be back, and most likely, so would we'.[56] O'Brien wrote of his fellow soldiers:

> They did not know even the simple things: a sense of victory, or satisfaction, or necessary sacrifice. They did not know the feeling of taking a place and keeping it, securing a village and then raising the flag and calling it a victory. No sense of order or momentum. No front, no rear, no trenches laid out in neat parallels. No Patton rushing for the Rhine, no beachheads to storm and win and hold for the duration. They did not have targets. They did not have a cause. They did not know if it was a war of ideology or economics or hegemony or spite.[57]

The body count was an inadequate measure of progress:

> no contact was made, and the gunships got bored. So they made a gun run on a hootch with mini-guns and rockets. When

54 Nalty, ed., *Vietnam War*, p. 23.
55 O'Brien, *If I Die in a Combat Zone*, p. 126.
56 Bergerud, *Red Thunder*, pp. 134, 267.
57 Tim O'Brien, *Going After Cacciato* (New York, NY, 1980), pp. 320–1.

they left the area we found one dead baby . . . in its mother's arms, and we found a baby girl about three years old, also dead. . . . When it was reported to battalion, the only reprimand was to put the two bodies on the body count board and just add them up with the rest of the dead people.[58]

The best indicator of progress was, sadly, the way men changed from green recruit to tired, desensitized veteran in a matter of months:

> [We] watched the rest of Bravo Company come and go to the field – each time more scroungy and grungy and hangdog-looking than the time before. There were always fewer faces when they came humping those last three hundred meters up the hill . . . always newer faces, pale and astonished, when they left the camp again. . . . a month or six weeks later, when the company came back . . . those fucking new guys would be indistinguishable from the rest, except for the eyes. . . . the eyes took longer.[59]

'His eyes were what I saw first', one veteran recalled. 'What I saw in Lawrence's eyes was the horror, The Horror. What spooked me . . . was that I could tell immediately that he knew that everything was different now.'[60]

CASUALTIES

The vast majority of GIs were relatively safe, since most were not in combat. Even among combat units the risk varied according to the unit's area of operation and the year of the war. Perhaps as many as 1.6 million men either fought, provided close support, or were regularly exposed to danger between 1965 and 1973. Of those, 58,202 died and 303,704 were injured, roughly half requiring hospitalization.[61] Small arms fire caused 51 per cent of the deaths and 16 per cent of the wounds, with artillery and mortars responsible for 36 per cent and 65 per cent, respectively.[62] As in any war, venereal disease was rampant. Large numbers also fell victim to tropical diseases, insect and snake bites, and the bothersome ailments caused by a hostile

58 Richard Boyle, *Flower of the Dragon* (San Francisco, CA, 1972), pp. 140–1.
59 Larry Heinemann, *Paco's Story* (London, 1989), p. 33.
60 Baker, *Nam*, p. 111.
61 'Vietnam Warriors'. Deaths from combat numbered 47, 378. As with any war, the number of deaths varies from source to source, but this war is unique in the efforts devoted to establishing an accurate figure.
62 Richard Holmes, *Firing Line* (London, 1987), p. 210.

climate and poor hygiene. 'I had jungle rot so bad that the only way I could carry my rifle was to cradle it in the bend in my elbows with my hands in front of my face', one soldier recalled. 'I couldn't hold on to it my hands were so sore and burning. My feet were like that too.'[63] The lack of clearly defined front lines meant a higher than normal number of friendly fire casualties. Over 1,000 died in vehicle crashes and an almost equal number drowned or were suffocated.[64] One in five deaths were 'non-hostile'.[65]

American forces were, perhaps to their detriment, deeply concerned about casualties. 'I guess my standard of success was keeping my soldiers alive', one commander admitted.[66] Troops often performed best when rescuing wounded comrades. The injured received the best medical care ever experienced in war. A soldier was usually rescued and under surgical care in less time than a civilian involved in a car accident on one of America's highways. But since care was better and quicker, more men survived who in earlier wars would have died, which in turn meant many more ended up severely disabled. Amputations and crippling wounds were 300 per cent higher proportionately than in the Second World War and 70 per cent higher than in Korea. Multiple amputations were over three times as high as in the Second World War.[67]

> After our war, the dismembered bits
> – all those pierced eyes, ear slivers, jaw splinters,
> gouged lips, odd tibias, skin flaps, and toes –
> came squinting, wobbling, jabbering back.[68]

At base hospitals, nurses and doctors worked under enormous strain. It was hard to watch young, healthy men being destroyed:

> A bullet went through the base of his skull and ricocheted
> inside his helmet until its momentum ran out. . . . He is fully
> alert but 'locked in', paralyzed from the eyes down from a
> severed brain stem. He is able only to blink, move his eyes

---

63 Mark Baker, *Nam* (New York, NY, 1981), p. 78.

64 Holmes, *Firing Line*, p. 191.

65 'Vietnam warriors'.

66 Ronald H. Spector, 'How do you know if you're winning?: perception and reality in America's military performance in Vietnam, 1965–1970', in Jayne S. Werner and Luu Doan Huynh, *The Vietnam War: Vietnamese and American Perspectives* (Armonk, NY, 1993), p. 159.

67 'Vietnam warriors'.

68 Walt MacDonald, 'After our War', quoted in Ehrhart, *Shadow of Vietnam*, p. 92.

down, and cry, and there's no hope of his ever doing more than that.

How long can he live this way? Ten years? Twenty years? Thirty or forty? What God would permit such a fate? None that I want to believe in.

We print the alphabet on a piece of cardboard, so he can communicate more than yes or no. We run a finger along the letters, and he blinks out a message.

Once in the middle of the night he blinks the message 'L-E-T M-E D-I-E'[69]

A stoical detachment was essential. 'I don't want to get close to anybody', one nurse repeatedly reminded herself. 'I don't want to get to know anything about them. Because if I do, I find myself getting drawn and attached to this person. I can't afford to lose more people like this because it will destroy me and I won't function.'[70]

'We didn't see much shell shock', Lily Adams recalled.[71] Psychiatric casualties composed just 5 per cent of medical evacuations in 1965–66, falling to less than 3 per cent in 1967–68. This compares dramatically with 23 per cent during the Second World War. The explanation seems to be the absence of sustained combat, the one-year rotation and a greater awareness of war's psychiatric effects. There were two neuropsychiatric treatment centre teams, and psychiatrists attached to each division. Line officers were instructed to be sensitive to the mental torment of battle. One psychiatrist reasoned that, due to the one-year rotation, there was 'not the sense of hopelessness that prevailed in previous conflicts where death, injury or peace became the only possible ways in which the soldier could find himself extricated from combat'.[72]

War destroys, but it also creates. Deep emotional bonds were formed between fellow soldiers. A West Point graduate remarked how the Army had taught him how to kill, but not how to handle the death of a comrade. 'No one had ever said, "Cadets, you're going to see a great deal of death and gore, and here are some possible ways to accommodate it." That omission [seemed] ... a serious oversight, almost like sending a man into combat without proper training in marksmanship.'[73]

69 Winnie Smith, *Daughter Gone to War* (London, 1992), p. 200.
70 Bergerud, *Red Thunder*, pp. 209–10.
71 Ibid., p. 214.
72 Holmes, *Firing Line*, pp. 258–60, 263.
73 Atkinson, *Long Gray Line*, p. 263.

MORALE

The war has often been presented as a morality tale: the disintegration of the US Army, it is argued, demonstrates what happens when good men are used for corrupt purposes. Or a different version asserts that the war was lost because inadequate soldiers, polluted by Sixties hedonism, were sent to Vietnam. Ironically, both arguments rely upon a similarly distorted image of the American soldier. Drug-crazed sadists were either victims of a cruel government or symptoms of a sick society.

American soldiers went to war in 1965 firmly committed to their country's cause. From a very early age they underwent a comprehensive, if informal, indoctrination. For most, America was a 'city on a hill' – not only wealthy and powerful, but morally righteous. W.D. Ehrhart

> believed sincerely that if we did not stop the communists in
> Vietnam, we would one day have to fight them in San Diego.
> I had no reason up to that point in my life to doubt either my
> government or my high school teachers or the *New York Times*.
> I believed in my country and in its God-given role as the leader
> of the Free World – that it was the finest nation on earth, that
> its political system and its leaders were essentially good, and
> that any nation or people who opposed us must be inherently
> bad. Furthermore, I valued my freedom, and took seriously the
> notion that I owed something to my country.[74]

These men were the perfect raw material for an army preparing for war. But commitment to *this* war required an act of faith. 'I figured that [the war] was more or less right', one soldier confessed, 'because why would I be going if it wasn't right?'[75] Potential soldiers were given very little formal indoctrination. In contrast, communist political cadres worked tirelessly to indoctrinate fellow soldiers about the righteousness of their war. Formalized propagandizing of this type is antithetic to a liberal democracy like the United States. But without it, American soldiers had difficulty understanding their mission. When they discovered the 'real' war, they had few barriers to disillusionment:

> The American people had been told that we were defending a
> free democracy. What I found was a military dictatorship rife
> with corruption and venality and repression. The premier of

74 Ehrhart, *Shadow of Vietnam*, p. 47.
75 Starr, *Discarded Army*, pp. 8–9.

288

South Vietnam openly admired Adolf Hitler. Buddhist priests who petitioned for peace were jailed or shot down in the streets. Officials at every level engaged in blatant black-marketeering . . . at the expense of their own people.[76]

Chanting the Pledge of Allegiance or recalling amber waves of grain were weak defences against the creeping uncertainty which afflicted nearly every soldier.

The soldier's disillusionment mirrored a crisis of confidence within America as a whole, where the naive certainties of the 1950s gave way to 1970s self-doubt. The evaporation of support for the war at home undoubtedly exacerbated the unease experienced by soldiers. They did not need to be told that they were fighting an ignoble war, but telling them made them feel worse.

> A lot of guys would get newspapers from home and . . . we'd read about all the protesting and rioting back home about the war. We just couldn't understand it. Here we was, over there humping ourselves to death and we were worried about what was going to happen next, and here these bunch of long-haired hippies back home protested on the streets and did what they wanted to do.[77]

Innocent men became scapegoats for an unpopular war. Their sense of betrayal ran deep. Shocked by the outcry when four students were killed at Kent State in 1970, one soldier wrote: 'So why don't your hearts cry out and shed a tear for the 40-plus thousand red-blooded Americans and brave, fearless, loyal men who have given their lives so a bunch of bloody bastard radicals can protest, dissent and generally bitch?'[78]

Thus, by the late 1960s, the sense of purpose which the American soldier took to Vietnam had evaporated. A Marine corporal and Purple Heart winner, on his second tour of duty, wrote to his father after the battle of Hué:

> 15 months in the Nam and I'm still charging the lines with as much balls as any other stud I know because the adventure and pride . . . within me demands it. . . . And why? Suddenly I'm sitting in my vacuum wondering WHY? A nasty collision with reality and I damn well wouldn't give my life for any of this.

76 Ehrhart, *Shadow of Vietnam*, p. 48.
77 Otto J. Lehrack, ed., *No Shining Armor* (Lawrence, KS, 1992), p. 328.
78 Edelman, ed., *Dear America*, p. 226.

You're damned straight. Not for any President who got into office by a fluke to begin with, and now continues to brainwash the troops, and the country, with phoney pretenses accounting for our participation in this cesspool. So, not me. No sir. Not this kid's life. Not even a limb and hopefully not even another goddamn drop of blood. Oh, I'll fight. I'll fight for the adventure and the preservation of my ass, when a damn zip tries to level it. But not for that man ... No sir. I hate that man. I [also] hate these mustard, prideless, ambitionless, leeching bastards, whose government is merely an extension of our own government's corruption.[79]

'I never felt I was fighting for any particular cause', David Parks commented. 'I fought to stay alive and I killed to keep from being killed.'[80] Colonel Robert Heinl admitted in 1971 that ' "Search and evade" ... is now virtually a principle of war, vividly expressed by the GI phrase, "CYA (cover your ass) and get home!" '[81] Soldiers took to painting UUUU on their helmets: 'the unwilling, led by the unqualified, doing the unnecessary, for the ungrateful'.

Drugs became a serious problem. The RVN Navy kept the supply flowing, and top politicians (including Ky and Thieu) profited from the trade. NLF sympathizers also kept American soldiers well-stocked with all manner of mind-numbing drugs. According to one study, by 1971 marijuana use stood at 50.9 per cent of military personnel, heroin and other narcotics 28.5 per cent, and hallucinogenics 14 per cent.[82] During one court-martial, the judge asked the accused how he had earned the Silver Star ribbon he was wearing. The latter replied that he could not remember since he was 'strung out on heroin' at the time.[83]

The decline in morale eroded the soldier's respect for authority. Officers became pariahs. Between 1969 and 1971 there were 730 recorded cases of fragging, with 83 officers killed.[84] The figures for actual cases do not accurately convey the gravity of the problem,

79 Correspondent unidentified, copy of letter in Adam Walinsky Papers, 'Campaign 1968' 4/-S/1968, Kennedy Library. My thanks to Clare White.

80 Holmes, *Firing Line*, p. 281.

81 Kolko, *Anatomy*, p. 362.

82 Guenter Lewy, *America in Vietnam* (Oxford, 1978), p. 154. It should be pointed out that these figures are not seriously out of line with the levels of drug usage at home.

83 Frederic Borch, 'Judge advocates in combat', unpublished manuscript, chap. 3, pp. 11–12.

84 Lewy, *America in Vietnam*, p. 156. So termed because the officer was usually attacked with a fragmentation grenade.

since fear of fragging intimidated officers, seriously undermining their ability to lead. Back at home, some 144 underground newspapers encouraged disobedience among personnel at military bases. 'In Vietnam, the Lifers, the Brass are the true Enemy, not the enemy', a paper distributed at Fort Lewis argued. 'Don't desert', another advised; 'Go to Vietnam and kill your commanding officer.'[85] Problems of indiscipline were not confined to ground troops. In 1972 a House inquiry found 'literally hundreds of instances of damage to naval property wherein sabotage is suspected'. During the Chrismas bombing of 1972, some pilots refused to perform their assigned role of attacking AA batteries. One B-52 commander was tried for refusing to fly, and at one point a state of 'near mutiny' existed.[86] The precipitate troop withdrawals during the Nixon administration should be seen in this light – they were partly intended to save the military from itself.

Racial tension also increased. In 1968, 200 African-American prisoners rioted at Long Binh jail. Two years later, one of the worst race riots of the war occurred at Camp Baxter in Da Nang. Though statistics suggest otherwise, African-American soldiers felt they were bearing the brunt of the war.

> When you're on patrol and moving into an area, it's always the negro who's walking point. That means he is the first to get it if a mine explodes. That's the kind of harassment we get from the whites. . . . Look at the guys who go out on sweeps, who protect the hills. Brothers, as many brothers as they can find.

Some wrote on their helmets 'NO GOOK EVER CALLED ME NIGGER'. It is fair to assume that a significant proportion of fragging incidents were racially motivated, especially as the Army has traditionally had a high percentage of white southern officers and urban African-American enlisted men. African-Americans arriving in Vietnam were astonished to see Confederate flags attached to jeeps. 'We are fighting and dying in a war that is not very popular in the first place and we still have some stupid people who are still fighting the Civil War', one commented.[87]

Desertion was high, but not as high as might be expected for such an unpopular war. In 1965 the desertion rate stood at 15.7 per 1,000 soldiers, peaking at 73.5 in 1971. This compares favourably with a peak rate of 63 in 1944. Rates for soldiers going absent without leave

85 Borch, 'Judge advocates', chap. 3, p. 11.
86 Kolko, *Anatomy*, pp. 364–5.
87 Ronald H. Spector, *After Tet* (New York, NY, 1993), pp. 245–6.

(AWOL) were higher in the Korean War than in Vietnam.[88] A significant number deserted *after* they had served a full term and returned to the United States. The problem was kept in check by the fact that desertion in Vietnam was not easy, since there were few places to hide in the hostile countryside. Only a tiny percentage deserted within Vietnam, and an even smaller fraction from combat.

The disintegration of the American military can be measured by the escalating legal burden. In 1965 the US Army had four lawyers in Vietnam. By 1969, 135 attorneys working ten to twelve hours per day, seven days a week, could not keep up with the case load. Around 25,000 courts-martial were tried by the US Army in Vietnam between 1965 and 1969, peaking in the latter year at 9,922. In the same year, 66,702 Article 15s were administered.[89] Roughly 20 per cent of cases involved drug offences.[90] Judges often faced a dilemma, since many combat soldiers preferred a spell in the stockade to a jungle patrol. Many cases involving rear echelon soldiers which ordinarily would have resulted in courts-martial were handled instead with Article 15 proceedings, with punishment taking the form of a combat assignment.

Combat is often a spur to morale. The survival instinct focuses the mind and distracts attention from corrosive anxieties. This explains why most problems of indiscipline occurred in the rear areas. Dissension on a patrol endangers the lives of everyone in the unit. The same holds true for drug abuse. 'Nobody did drugs or alcohol in the field', one soldier claimed. 'That was the wrong time and place. You needed everything you had to stay alive, and doing drugs wasn't one of them. . . . if you were doing drugs, you might get shot out in the field during a firefight. . . . maybe get the whole squad killed.' Harry Bergson of the 25th Infantry confirmed this view: 'I think that all of that crap took place in the base camp. That's where the drug problems and the black power groups and all of the rest of that junk was.'[91]

Battlefield morale survived much longer than political morale. Men who despised the war still fought like heroes. The glue that held them together was the duty felt to each other. O'Brien mourned the loss of Captain Johansen – 'losing him was like the Trojans losing Hector':

---

88 Lewy, *America in Vietnam*, p. 157.

89 Article 15 of the Uniform Code of Military Justice allows a commander to impose 'non-judicial' punishment for minor violations of the UCMJ. The soldier has the option of accepting the Article 15, or demanding trial by court-martial. The punishments under Article 15 are limited to reductions in rank and forfeitures of pay. The advantage is that it means no court-martial, and no federal conviction.

90 Borch, 'Judge advocates', chap. 2, pp. 6, 38; chap. 3, p. 10.

91 Bergerud, *Red Thunder*, pp. 285, 288.

Vietnam was under siege in pursuit of a pretty, tantalizing, promiscuous, particularly American brand of government and style. And most of Alpha Company would have preferred a likeable whore to self-determination. So Captain Johansen helped to mitigate and melt the silliness, showing the grace and poise a man can have under the worst circumstances, a wrong war. We clung to him.[92]

'Your family was your squad, and that's who you looked after', one soldier commented. 'Mom and apple pie and stuff, that was out the window. You were fighting for each other. You were trying to keep each other alive so you could make it home.'[93]

The military tried to boost morale by making available an endless supply of creature comforts. Soldiers returned from a firefight and within a half hour sat down to steaks, beer, french fries and ice cream. Helicopters brought cold beer to soldiers in the throes of battle. An American major commented wryly to Robert Shaplen in 1967, 'One of these days they'll be pumping Muzak down to company level'.[94] When the Americans left, they abandoned 71 swimming pools, 90 service clubs, 159 basketball courts, 30 tennis courts, 55 softball diamonds, 85 volleyball pitches, 337 libraries and 2 bowling alleys.[95] Prostitutes were cheap, readily available and generally tolerated by the military brass.

Davidson Loehr, trained as a forward artillery observer, 'beat the game' when he landed a job as an entertainment officer:

> They gave me a secretary and an air-conditioned office in Saigon, and my job consisted of meeting movie stars and professional entertainers at the airport, taking them out to dinner on an expense account, and keeping their refrigerator stocked with beer and soft drinks. After work, I stopped . . . for steam bath, massage, and sex; or, less often, spent the night with Thom, my favourite barmaid.[96]

The comfortable existence enjoyed by REMFs ('rear echelon mother fuckers') eroded morale among combat soldiers. They complained about the arbitrary and corrupt process by which others were chosen for easy assignments, and concluded (with justification) that combat was a form of punishment. But the REMFs were sometimes tormented

---

92 O'Brien, *If I Die in a Combat Zone*, p. 145.
93 Bergerud, *Red Thunder*, p. 267.
94 Robert Shaplen, *The Road from War* (New York, NY, 1970), p. 140.
95 William Hauser, *America's Army in Crisis* (Baltimore, MD, 1973), p. 103.
96 Davidson Loehr, 'The fresh kill', in L. Freedman, ed., *War* (Oxford, 1994), p. 51.

by a purposeless life. 'I have had a shit existence on a bad army post in a deserted area', one soldier stuck at Long Binh base complained. 'If I had really been in Vietnam, I might have seen some of the country, talked to its farmers, eaten its food, played with its children or killed some of its men.'[97]

Creature comforts, designed to boost morale, may in fact have eroded efficiency. General Hamilton Howze felt that 'Our base camps became too elaborate, soaked up too much manpower, diverted our attention from the basic mission and lessened our operational flexibility'.[98] The war could seem unreal:

> It was weird, really; you'd be out in the bush for two or three weeks or longer and come in for a stand down. You could have a cookout, go to the PX, see movies at night. It was almost like being back in the world. I personally could never get used to that, and to me, it was one of the problems. We were deceiving ourselves. If we were going to fight the war and win it, let's fight the war and win it and go home. But this artificial living . . . was beyond me. It may have kept the troops entertained, but it prevented them from focusing on what we were there for.[99]

Some of war's sharp edges had been smoothed. 'It was difficult for [the Americans] to suffer all the hardships of the Vietnamese battlefront', one PAVN veteran commented. 'When we had no water to drink, they had water for showers! We could suffer the hardships much better than they could. That, probably, was the main reason we won.'[100]

In another misguided attempt to boost morale, more than 1.25 million bravery medals were awarded, compared to just 50,258 during the Korean War. The total exceeds even the most generous estimate of the number who actually faced danger.[101] Rewards were not, however, distributed equally. During his first 26 weeks of command in Vietnam, Colonel John Donaldson received 27 medals.[102] Perhaps not surprisingly, the number of citations increased as the American

---

97 Edelman, ed., *Dear America*, p. 159.
98 Gates, 'If at first you don't succeed', p. 183.
99 Bergerud, *Red Thunder*, p. 278.
100 MacDonald, *Giap*, p. 336.
101 Holmes, *Firing Line*, p. 356.
102 Baritz, *Backfire*, pp. 296–7. He later became the first American general since 1900 to be charged with a war crime, for which he was acquitted. He was accused of 'gook hunting' – shooting Vietnamese indiscriminately from a helicopter.

combat role decreased. There was little awareness that medals, like money, devalue with inflation.

WAR CRIMES

Because the enemy seemed so alien, a brotherhood of arms did not develop between the two sides. Second World War films have encouraged the cliché of the GI who shares a cigarette with a captured enemy and then perhaps passes around photos of his family. As with all clichés, this one has some truth. But Vietnam was different:

> We did not speak their language, so we could not ask their names, their home villages, or even if they were the same age as us. We were ignorant of their history or culture, so we had no idea if they were even Vietnamese, Cambodian, or possibly Chinese . . . [There was] tremendous group pressure not to feel any compassion . . . Many times I saw individual acts of compassion that were immediately counteracted by cruelty and deliberate steps taken to show . . . that to be human had no place in war.[103]

It was a short step from cruelty to atrocity. Lee Childress saw a fellow soldier shoot an old Vietnamese woman who tried to steal his chewing gum. 'He shot her point blank through the chest and killed her.' His crime went unpunished. 'We got in more trouble for killing water buffalo than for killing people', Childress remarked.[104] Norman Ryman collected ears cut from dead enemy soldiers and photographs of mutilated 'gooks'. He loved the war so much that he volunteered for two extra tours of duty. 'I had an excuse to be hostile and aggressive and I also had a license to kill without prosecution which made my actions enjoyable and my insanity bearable.'[105]

On 16 March 1968 members of Company C, Task Force Barker, a battalion-sized unit of the Americal Division commanded by Lieutenant William Calley, murdered some 350 unarmed civilians in the village of My Lai. According to Calley,

> I was ordered to go in there and destroy the enemy. That was my job . . . That was the mission I was given. I did not sit down and think in terms of men, women and children. They were all

103 Bergerud, *Red Thunder*, p. 256.
104 Albert Santoli, *Everything We Had: An Oral History of the Vietnam War by Thirty-Three American Soldiers who Fought It* (New York, NY, 1981), p. 63.
105 MacPherson, *Long Time Passing*, p. 507.

classified the same . . . I felt then and I still do that I acted as I was directed, and I carried out the orders that I was given and I do not feel wrong in doing so. . . .

We weren't in My Lai to kill human beings, really. We were there to kill an ideology that is carried by – I don't know. Pawns. Blobs. Pieces of flesh. And I wasn't in My Lai to destroy intelligent men. I was there to destroy an intangible idea. To destroy communism . . . I looked at communism as a southerner looks at a Negro, supposedly. It's evil. It's bad.[106]

The incident, the worst atrocity by American soldiers during the war, caused a huge outcry at home, though not everyone condemned Calley. Charges were subsequently brought against thirteen men, with Calley accused of 109 acts of murder. He was convicted and received life imprisonment, a sentence eventually reduced to ten years on the intervention of the Secretary of the Army. This made him eligible for parole after six months, which was granted. The other twelve were acquitted. A further twelve officers of the Americal division were accused of covering up the crime, but only two, Captain Ernest Medina and Colonel Oran Henderson, were court-martialled. Both were acquitted.

In 1970 six Rangers at base club boasted how, after ambushing and killing enemy soldiers, they had 'cut open the bodies from throat to groin and stuffed them with rice'. 'Calling cards' of this type were designed to strike fear in enemy soldiers; a PLAF variant was to stuff an American soldier's genitalia into his mouth. The Rangers were reported, and charges brought. A mission was despatched to search for evidence. Air Force jets and helicopter gunships prepped the area, whereupon a Huey carrying a rifle platoon and the defence lawyer arrived. The team found burlap rice sacks, lots of blood, but no bodies. Since there was no actual proof of the crime, the case was dismissed.[107] It reveals the difficulties of investigating war crimes and of punishing the guilty. Prosecutors faced enormous practical difficulties collecting evidence and finding witnesses in a war zone. The dilemma of precisely defining criminal behaviour in this type of war made conviction even more complicated.

Between 1965 and 1973, around 250 cases of alleged war crimes by Americans came before military authorities. Further investigation revealed that 160 of these were unsubstantiated. Eventually, 36 resulted

106 Michael Bilton and Kevin Sim, *Four Hours in My Lai* (London, 1992), pp. 335, 372.

107 Borch, 'Judge advocates', chap. 3, pp. 26–8.

in trials by courts-martial.[108] It is difficult to say whether these were just the tip of the iceberg. One officer felt that 'My Lai represented to the average professional soldier nothing more than being caught in a cover-up of something which he knew had been going on for a long time on a smaller scale'.[109] Many incidents, especially early in the war, probably went unreported. Others fell into the grey area which exists between cruelty, carelessness and atrocity. Wantonly shooting at an individual running across a paddy attracted adverse attention only if it turned out afterwards that the individual was a fourteen-year-old girl. Death could be random, but cold-blooded murder was probably relatively rare. One must bear in mind the fact that Vietnam was a very public war; especially after 1969 reporters roamed the countryside in search of the genuine atrocity which would win them a Pulitzer Prize.

'War by its nature', writes Caputo, 'can arouse a psychopathic violence in men of seemingly normal impulses.'[110] This war, in particular, did so. Many explanations are offered: the tension of guerrilla war, a futile attrition strategy, racist attitudes toward the enemy, poor quality officers, the shame of defeat, and drugs. As former marine W.D. Ehrhart put it:

It's practically impossible
to tell civilians
from the Vietcong.

Nobody wears uniforms.
They all talk
the same language,
(and you couldn't understand them
even if they didn't).

They tape grenades
inside their clothes,
and carry satchel charges
in their market baskets.

Even their women fight,
and young boys,
and girls.

108 Ibid., chap. 2, p. 15.
109 Kinnard, *War Managers*, p. 52.
110 Caputo, *Rumor of War*, pp. xvii–xviii.

It's practically impossible
to tell civilians
from the Vietcong;
after awhile,
you quit trying.[111]

Vietnam, according to Caputo, was 'an ethical as well as a geographical wilderness' where 'lacking restraints, sanctioned to kill, confronted by a hostile country and a relentless enemy, we sank into a brutish state'.[112] So, too, did the enemy, who regularly mutilated corpses and executed prisoners. Hanoi decided early on that the 'laws of war' did not apply to revolutionary struggle in South Vietnam. While some analysts find it possible to apply a different moral code to communist crimes, there is no doubt that there were Norman Rymans on both sides.

POSTSCRIPT

'Most American soldiers in Vietnam', writes Caputo, 'could not be divided into good men and bad. Each possessed roughly equal measures of both qualities. I saw men who behaved with great compassion toward the Vietnamese one day and burned down a village the next.'[113] Norman Ryman, who should never have become a soldier, was not typical. The myth of an ignorant, psychotic, drug-crazed and murderous military has served as a convenient explanation for defeat. As hard as it might be to accept, good American soldiers got beaten in Vietnam. The defeat can not be blamed on bad men. But defeat did make some men bad.

111 W.D. Ehrhart, 'Guerrilla war', reprinted in Alf Louvre and Jeffrey Walsh, eds, *Tell Me Lies About Vietnam* (Milton Keynes, 1988), pp. 165–6.
112 Caputo, *Rumor of War*, p. xx.
113 Ibid.

OPPOSING THE WAR

Sixties sentimentalists want to believe that the Vietnam War was
brought to an end by a popular movement which began on America's
college campuses. A dispassionate examination of the movement reveals more clowns than heroes, more ignominy than virtue.

The postwar baby boom, which peaked in 1947, lasted until 1965,
by which time 76 million children had been born.[1] They grew up in a
wealthy country profoundly sure of itself. Knowing neither world war
nor great depression, they found no cosy satisfaction in peace and
financial security, as their parents did. The older generation's aspirations seemed prosaic; there was, surely, more to life than a station
wagon, shag carpets and a garbage disposal. Parents seemed not
just older, but from a different planet. The 'generation gap' – in truth
a chasm – loomed large in popular consciousness; a game show by
that name lightheartedly exposed how little parents knew of their
children's world and vice versa.

It was an egocentric generation, and could afford to be. Few
outward worries encouraged reckless self-gratification. To say that
the young were spoiled would be unfair; to say that they believed the
world was their oyster would not be.

> We're right at the center of everything. You remember when
> you're a child and your older brother is the big star, or your
> big sister is doing all the things? Now it's us, we're right in the
> center reading about ourselves in the newspaper. It's youth.
> Everything is youth and us.[2]

Through rebellion, Sixties youths marked out the boundaries of their
milieu. For most, rebellion was short-lived, self-centred and tame,

---

1 Doug McAdam, *Freedom Summer* (Oxford, 1988), p. 14.
2 Thomas J. Cottle, *Time's Children* (Boston, MA, 1971), p. 267.

taking the form of growing sideburns, wearing jeans, smoking marijuana or listening to the Rolling Stones. Yet these gestures did not seem tame to parents. Alarm bells sounded when Bob Dylan proclaimed that the times were a'changing, and warned the older generation to get out of the way. But singing along to Dylan was not necessarily a political act. Potheads still voted Republican, and got misty-eyed when the Star Spangled Banner was played at baseball games or on the Fourth of July. As one perceptive student observed, 'You don't have to be radical to love rock music . . . Most of the record buying kids of today are about as aware as eggplants.'[3] The ramshackle edifice of youthful rebellion was built upon bedrock American values – democracy, capitalism and the moral righteousness of the United States. Polls consistently showed that those under 30 were the group most likely to support the Vietnam War.[4] Hippies and squares alike felt pride when America colonized the moon in 1969.

For a small number, rebellion was seriously political. Wini Breines believed 'we could achieve an egalitarian, free and participatory society. . . . we were going to make a revolution. We were convinced that we could transform America through our political activity and insights.'[5] Disenchantment with the world of their parents fuelled a desire to create a perfect world of their own. Political radicals congregated mainly in the universities. The correlation between protest and education is not distinct to the 1960s. There were notable student protest groups before that decade, and there have been important movements since.[6] But the 1960s was special because there were suddenly a lot of students and much to protest against.

Partly due to the baby boom, student numbers more than doubled during the decade. There were 7,852,000 students in 1970; they outnumbered farmers, construction workers, miners and transportation workers.[7] The second- and third-tier universities in the tripartite higher education system coped reasonably well with this influx. These educational factories were designed to process large numbers of students in impersonal but efficient environments and to expand relative to demand. The students themselves had low expectations which were

---

3 Terry H. Anderson, 'American popular music and the war in Vietnam', *Peace and Change* 11 (1986), p. 52.

4 William Lunch and Peter Sperlich, 'American public opinion and the war in Vietnam', *Western Political Quarterly* 32 (1979), p. 33. Those over 50 were least supportive of the war.

5 McAdam, *Freedom Summer*, p. 19.

6 See Gerard DeGroot, ed., *Student Protest: The Sixties and After* (London, 1998).

7 David Steigerwald, *The Sixties and the End of Modern America* (New York, NY, 1995), p. 134.

easily satisfied: they wanted a better standard of living than their parents had enjoyed, something a diploma usually provided. They were reluctant to topple their ladder of mobility by dabbling in political activism.

But at elite universities like Columbia, Michigan and Berkeley a combination of factors (among them a tradition of activism[8]) created real tension. These institutions were judged not by the quality of their graduates, but by the impressiveness of their research profile and their ability to land lucrative contracts. During the Cold War, those contracts were often defence-related, a sore point with sensitive students who dabbled in philosophical morality. At Michigan, for instance, 43 per cent of federal money took that form.[9] Research demands rendered the professor less accessible to the student, whose instruction was increasingly left to postgraduates only slightly older and marginally more mature. The mainly middle-class students at these universities sought intellectual fulfilment not simply social mobility. They were sensitive to perceived injustices and inclined to complain. They could agitate about the present because they did not have to worry about the future. Life on campus offered the time to plan the perfect world and the intellectual climate in which to do so, without the real world's bothersome practicalities.[10] Protest legitimized the student's natural inclination to skip studies; 'the war ate my homework' was a common refrain.[11]

In the early 1960s universities confidently assumed that since students were not adults, they needed to be chaperoned at well as educated. But there was an inherent contradiction in this role *in loco parentis*: universities wanted to monitor students' lives, but did not have time to do so properly. They aspired to be parents, but ended up neglectful ones. The assumption of quasi-parental authority led to the regulation of certain 'adult' pursuits, among them sex and politics. The regulation of sexual activity is beyond the scope of this book; suffice it to say that universities waged a diligent but futile campaign to curb the urge to merge. As for politics, universities proudly defended their status as ivory towers. Students, being youths, were not supposed to have political views and were not, therefore, allowed to engage in political activities on campus. The very first demonstrations

8 See Nella Van Dyke, 'The location of student protest: patterns of activism at American universities in the 1960s', in DeGroot, ed., *Student Protest*, pp. 27–36.

9 Kenneth J. Heineman, *Campus Wars* (New York, NY, 1993), p. 15.

10 See E.M. Schreiber, 'Opposition to the Vietnam War among American university students and faculty', *British Journal of Sociology* 24 (1973), pp. 289–91, 293, 296.

11 Myra MacPherson, *Long Time Passing* (New York, NY, 1984), p. 457.

of the 1960s, most notably the Free Speech Movement at the University of California, arose over the right to protest.[12]

Once that right was granted, students were keen to stretch the limits of their new freedoms. Alienation, that Sixties buzz-word, ran deep at the elite universities. The curricula seemed irrelevant, professors remote, classes crowded, dormitories shabby, food inedible and administrators arbitrarily authoritarian. The first protests were directed inward, toward changing the university environment. Indeed, throughout the 1960s, the most popular issues were not the Vietnam War or civil rights, but curfews, coed living, cafeteria food and the size and nature of classes. Immaturity was ever-present: the Filthy Speech Movement at Berkeley agitated diligently over the right to shout 'FUCK!' on campus. The most significant long-term accomplishments of the protesters were the changes wrought to the structure of higher education: new courses, new departments, new methods of teaching.

But many students were not satisfied with remodelling the ivory tower. They took seriously C. Wright Mills's advocacy of the educated as the 'radical agents of change'.[13] Radicalism was encouraged by leftist intellectuals who were only just resurfacing after years of McCarthyite persecution. They saw students as a new proletariat, much more promising than the working class who had failed them. The two groups shared a common alienation and a dismal, almost apocalyptic view of the world. 'We are the people of this generation, bred in at least modest comfort, housed now in universities, looking uncomfortably to the world we inherit', the melodramatic Port Huron Statement, charter of the Students for a Democratic Society (SDS), proclaimed. 'We may be the last generation in the experiment with living.'[14]

Some students learned the art of demonstrating by taking part in the civil rights marches and voter registration drives of Freedom Summer, 1964. But that movement subsequently turned toward black nationalism and violence, marginalizing white activists. Those who returned to university in September 1964 were rebels without a cause. Lyndon Johnson solved that problem by deciding to bomb North Vietnam. With strange serendipity, Vietnam became an issue at the very moment when the baby boomers of 1947 entered university. The

12 See W.J. Rorabaugh, *Berkeley at War: The 1960s* (Oxford, 1989), pp. 21–47.

13 Sandy Vogelgesang, *The Long Dark Night of the Soul: The American Intellectual Left and the Vietnam War* (New York, NY, 1974), p. 71.

14 James Miller, *'Democracy is in the Streets': From Port Huron to the Siege of Chicago* (New York, NY, 1987), pp. 329–30.

first major response came at Michigan where students organized a teach-in, supposedly designed to educate the ignorant about Vietnam. One student called it her 'first educational experience provided by the university during four years attendance'.[15] Within weeks, similar events took place at dozens of universities across the country. It was not lengthening casualty lists but the perceived immorality of American action which motivated protest. At this stage, American deaths in Vietnam remained well under 500.

In theory, teach-ins were appropriate since ignorance of Vietnam ran deep, but they were in truth platforms for proselytizing radicals. Students were exposed to the stalwarts of the American intellectual left – I.F. Stone, Staughton Lynd, Norman Thomas, etc. – for whom the teach-ins offered a ladder out of obscurity. Men unaccustomed to adoring crowds found that references to the United States as a 'bastard empire' provoked hysterical cheers more appropriate to a football game. But to the 'establishment' the teach-ins were little more than an annoyance – living proof of the marginality of the campus peace movement. The Johnson administration, keen to deprive them of credibility, ignored them. McGeorge Bundy briefly considered an invitation to speak at an event scheduled for 15 May 1965 in Washington, but then declined.[16]

Even though most students were protected from the draft, they felt the war personally in a way that civil rights had not affected them. It seemed close and, as it escalated, it drew closer. Male students realized that, but for the accident of intelligence, they might be facing the horrors of a jungle patrol. The war provided the perfect cause: personal *and* political. It was individually threatening and, in a wider sense, seemed to embody everything wrong with America. SDS president Carl Oglesby confessed in 1965 that the war 'broke my American heart'.[17]

Todd Gitlin, reflecting on his days as a student radical, concluded that 'only true believers in the promise of America could have felt so anti-American'.[18] The students' status as the gifted of their generation convinced them that they had a right and duty to lead their country away from the madness. Their goal was not confined to ending the war, since the war was but a symptom of wider malaise. Instead, the

---

15 Louis Menashe and Ronald Radosh, *Teach-Ins: USA* (New York, NY, 1967), p. 11.

16 Fred Halstead, *Out Now!* (New York, NY, 1978), p. 51.

17 Todd Gitlin, *The Sixties: Years of Hope, Days of Rage* (New York, NY, 1989), p. 263.

18 Ibid.

way to end the war (and all such wars) was through a comprehensive revolution in American politics. The sterile hypocrisy of their parents' generation would be swept away and replaced by a new dynamic, people-centred politics, a strange amalgam of European socialism, Jeffersonian democracy, and the participatory politics of the Greek city-state. This was a Utopian idea, but also a quintessentially American one in the importance assigned the individual. In practice, individualism and participatory democracy had a hard time thriving amidst the boundless egotism of the movement. The Marxist historian Eugene Genovese was not unfair when he dismissed student rebels as 'pseudo-revolutionary middle class totalitarians'.[19] Running through it all was the wide-eyed naiveté of young people who have just discovered 'eternal truths'. Read a speech made by Tom Hayden and it is not hard to guess the books he skimmed the night before.

There would have been campus unrest without the war, and there would have been an anti-war movement without the students. The merging of these two phenomena into one student anti-war movement was not necessarily good for the cause of peace. The campus protesters were too atypical to tap a populist vein. The Port Huron Statement proclaimed that the 'bridge to political power . . . will be built through genuine cooperation, locally, nationally and internationally, between a new left of young people and an awakening community of allies'.[20] In fact, students were better at building walls than bridges.

The United States has some 2,500 institutions of higher education. During the Vietnam War, serious anti-war disturbances occurred at about 10 per cent of them. At those institutions, less than 10 per cent of students actively participated in demonstrations.[21] Polls consistently revealed that the war was not a prominent concern among most students. This was precisely because university provided a refuge from the conflict. In October 1965 a football rally at Berkeley attracted a much bigger crowd than a long-planned teach-in.[22] Thus, the anti-war protesters were anomalies on the campuses, the elite campuses were anomalies within the higher education system, and higher education was an anomaly within American society.

Spiro Agnew once referred to student protesters as an 'effete corps of impudent snobs who consider themselves intellectuals'.[23] On that

19 John Morton Blum, *Years of Discord* (New York, NY, 1991), p. 360.
20 Miller, '*Democracy is in the Streets*', p. 374.
21 Schreiber, 'Opposition to the Vietnam War', pp. 289–91.
22 Gerard J. DeGroot, 'The limits of moral protest and participatory democracy: the Vietnam Day Committee', *Pacific Historical Review* 44 (1995), p. 114.
23 'Blood on Campus', *The Scotsman*, 18 May 1995.

occasion, he had a point. The protesters were impudent, they could be snobs and they did consider themselves intellectuals. (The effete part was probably unfair.) Student activists did believe that only the young *and* intelligent knew what was right for America. Their opposition arose from the belief 'that the war is immoral at its root, that it is fought alongside a regime with no claim to represent its people, and that *it is foreclosing the hope of making America a decent and truly democratic society*'.[24] Such an argument may have seemed logical to students taking Political Science 101 at Berkeley or Columbia, but was never likely to strike a chord with the American people. Middle Americans did not understand the campus protesters and the campus protesters did not understand middle America. Sam Brown recalled:

> We were young, smart, intellectual (so we thought) and committed to a moral cause. We believed ourselves patriots defending America's ideals. They (and by that time 'they' were almost always older) were, as far as we were concerned, narrow-minded, intolerant and unwilling to accept our patriotism. It was a time of intense certainty. The ideas espoused by either group were almost automatically opposed by the other. Each side held to its half-thoughts and unfounded assumptions. Each side hurt the other.[25]

Out of incomprehension grew contempt, which inhibited a united effort to end the war. In working-class bars across America, the peacenik and the communist guerrilla were equally reviled.

Campus activists saw themselves as 'psychic terrorists'; their aim was 'to create controversy where there is apathy'.[26] The obscenity, desecration of the American flag, espousal of socialist politics, counter-cultural values and violence which characterized protests alienated those outside the university.[27] 'I was thoughtless, arrogant, horrible, hysterical, and unbelievably selfish', one former protester confessed. 'I still will not forgive myself for the pain and agony I caused my family.' There was little common ground between student anti-war protest and mainstream American values, as Eugene McCarthy's fruitless presidential campaign revealed. Stephen Cohen, a young McCarthy

---

24 SDS press release, October 1965.

25 Sam Brown, 'The legacy of choices', in Grace Sevy, ed., *The American Experience in Vietnam* (Norman, OK, 1989), p. 196.

26 Jerry Rubin, *Do It!* (New York, NY, 1970), p. 38. Vietnam Day Committee press release, 13 September 1965, Social Protest Project, Bancroft Library, University of California.

27 J. Justin Gustainis and Dan Hahn, 'While the whole world watched: rhetorical failures of anti-war protest', *Communication Quarterly* 36 (1988), pp. 205–11.

activist, felt that campus protesters betrayed the cause by refusing to jettison selfish lifestyles:

> I fought hard against associating lifestyle issues – drugs, rock music, sex – with the peace movement because they so alienated and turned off people who would have been genuinely against the war. Students generally made a fundamental strategic error by not continuing the 'Clean for Gene' appeal to the middle class.[28]

Gitlin recalled the attitude of students certain of their moral virtue:

> The napalm had to be stopped for the correct reasons. Strategy-minded antiwar liberals rudely reminded us that we were forfeiting the respect of Americans who were turning against the war but were unwilling to do so at the price of their own sense of patriotism. But to hell with them! Which side were they on, anyway?[29]

Protests organized by immature students often achieved nothing more than mere spectacle. For instance, the March on Washington in October 1967 was, Dave Dellinger admitted, a mix of 'Gandhi and guerrilla'.[30] Some 100,000 descended upon Washington without plan, purpose or real leadership. Among the group were some hippie mystics bent on levitating the Pentagon, and sufficiently stoned to insist that it did rise.[31] The self-indulgent 'psychic terrorists', though relatively few in number, were sufficiently loud to drown out those who argued calmly and rationally against the war. Television cameras invariably focused on the freaks or on those women who somehow thought they could end the war by baring their breasts.[32]

Demonstrations were devised not for the message they conveyed but for the controversy they created. 'It was an important policy . . . of the movement to make no concessions to respectablity', wrote one organizer. Or, as Jerry Rubin, the self-proclaimed P.T. Barnum of student activism, confessed: 'We were fucking obnoxious and we dug every moment of it.'[33] Robert Nisbet, a Berkeley professor of socio-logy who opposed the war, commented: 'At their worst the actions of

28 MacPherson, *Long Time Passing*, pp. 126, 457.
29 Gitlin, *The Sixties*, p. 262.
30 Steigerwald, *Sixties and the End of Modern America*, p. 110.
31 'It Was Twenty Years Ago Today', LWT documentary, 1988.
32 Those who blame the media for defeat in Vietnam somehow conveniently forget how negative images of peace protesters dominated news broadcasts.
33 DeGroot, 'The limits of moral protest', p. 108.

the student rebels . . . resembled nothing so much as the jack-boot authoritarianism of Hitler Youth in the 1920s: complete with shouted obscenities, humiliation of teachers and scholars, desecration of buildings, and instigation of various forms of terror'.[34] By their excesses, students demonstrated that it is impossible to build a mass movement by thumbing one's nose at the masses. And the more bizarre the protests became, the more they seemed proof of extremist excess – a fact exploited by the political establishment.

Outside the campuses, anti-war sentiment did exist. It was rooted not in the immorality of the war, but in its futility. As casualty lists lengthened, doubts surfaced about whether the war could be won.[35] Student protesters never quite understood that most Americans were concerned only about the fate of their sons and the significance of their sacrifice. A typical evolution of anti-war sentiment was described by Clem Labine, former star pitcher for the Brooklyn Dodgers, whose son Jay lost a leg in Vietnam: 'First I guess I was a hawk. Then I was a dove. Then Jay went over and I went superhawk. Atom-bomb those Northern bastards for my kid. Now that he's back . . . what do you think? I'm super-dove.'[36]

The turning point came during the Tet Offensive when supposedly invulnerable Saigon came under attack. Though the PLAF was roundly defeated, Americans found television scenes of their boys hysterical with fear deeply unsettling. On 27 February 1968 CBS anchorman Walter Cronkite effectively sealed the fate of the Vietnam War when he argued that the sensible option was 'to negotiate, not as victors but as an honorable people who lived up to their pledge to defend democracy, and did the best they could'.[37] The American people trusted Cronkite more than they trusted Johnson or Westmoreland. After Tet a peace movement of substance, rooted in the anxieties of ordinary Americans, gained dominion. Egocentric campus activists could not bring themselves to merge with this deluge of popular protest, which eventually overwhelmed them. Polls showed that, while support for the war plummeted, so too did support for the students. In 1968 a poll rated them 28.4 on a scale from zero (very unfavourable) to 100 (very favourable).[38]

34 Robert Nisbet, 'Who killed the student revolution?', *Encounter* 32 (1970), p. 11.

35 See Howard Schuman, 'Two sources of antiwar sentiment in America', *American Journal of Sociology* 78 (1972).

36 Roger Kahn, *The Boys of Summer* (New York, NY, 1972), pp. 208–9.

37 Don Oberdorfer, *Tet!* (New York, NY, 1984), p. 251.

38 E.M. Schreiber, 'Antiwar demonstrations and American public opinion on the war in Vietnam', *British Journal of Sociology* 27 (1976), p. 229.

In the presidential election of 1968, Americans turned not to avowed peace candidates like McCarthy or McGovern, but to Nixon, who promised that he could end the war *and* salvage American credibility. Nixon's victory is perhaps the best indication of how little the campus peace movement had achieved in three turbulent years. The American people wanted the war over, but they did not buy the fundamental reconstruction of their society which student activists espoused.

The peace movement's finest hour was also its farewell concert. On 15 October 1969 the first Vietnam Moratorium Day was marked by small, largely mainstream demonstrations in 500 towns and cities across America. It was followed by a demonstration on 15 November which brought 250,000 protesters to Washington. The crowd was peaceful, orderly and fundamentally ordinary. Student protesters who attended were drowned in a sea of respectability. The November march was in truth a revolt of pragmatists who believed that the war could not be won and was no longer worth the sacrifice of their sons. Reacting to the spectacle of protesting stockbrokers, lawyers and middle-aged moms, Jerry Rubin sneered: 'peace has become respectable!'.[39]

The demonstration was impressive, but Nixon cleverly manipulated it to his own advantage. In his famous 'silent majority' speech of 24 November 1969, he warned that 'the more divided we are at home, the less likely the enemy is to negotiate in Paris'. He continued:

> And so tonight – to you, the great silent majority of my fellow Americans – I ask for your support. . . . Let us be united for peace. Let us also be united against defeat. Because let us understand: North Vietnam cannot defeat or humiliate the United States. Only Americans can do that.[40]

After the speech, Gallup found that 77 per cent agreed. Around 75 per cent thought that the term 'silent majority' referred to those people who believed that 'protesters have gone too far'.[41]

'One of the reasons the President can get away with such nonsense is that many of us in the peace movement failed to dissociate ourselves strongly enough from violence on the left', wrote a dejected Sam Brown, one of the Moratorium's organizers.[42] Nixon's subsequent policy epitomized middle American sentiment: a gradual withdrawal of troops was combined with virulent attacks upon the 'mob

---

39 Nisbet, 'Who killed the student revolution?', p. 16.
40 Richard Nixon, 'Silent Majority' speech, 24 November 1969.
41 *San Francisco Chronicle*, 26 November 1969.
42 Sam Brown, 'The politics of peace', *Washington Monthly* 2 (August 1970), pp. 41, 43.

at the gates' – namely campus dissenters. It was a hawk's solution to the war's dilemma: antagonism previously focused upon external foes was re-directed toward the enemy within. Despite the apparent success of the November demonstration, Gallup in December found a 6 per cent *rise* in public approval 'of the way President Nixon is handling the situation in Vietnam'.[43]

In the spring of 1970, the Moratorium committee shut its offices in Washington. There would be no more huge peace demonstrations. Yet the war would go on for another three years. Nixon, it appeared, had ended the demonstrations even if he had not ended the war. This suggests that the moral outrage was window-dressing for selfish fears – the winding down of the draft and gradual de-escalation was sufficient to silence protest. Activists explain things differently, citing the disillusionment which arose from five years of protest against a war which would not end. If that is the explanation, it merely reveals how shallow was their commitment.[44]

But then came the Cambodian invasion and with it a torrential resurgence of campus unrest. Nixon achieved what Johnson had avoided, namely the alienation of ordinary students at second-tier universities. Within four days of the invasion, over 100 campuses erupted. These protests lacked the radical bombast of earlier campus activism, when students sought to end the war *and* change the world. 'The overflow of emotion seemed barely containable', wrote the *Washington Post*. 'The nation was witnessing what amounted to a virtual general strike by its college youth.'[45] Kent State University was typical of the post-Cambodia protests and atypical of late 1960s activism. Since 1965 the campus had been comparatively quiet, with small bands of SDS activists going through the motions of futile protest. Then, on 4 May, thirteen seconds of wild over-reaction by the Ohio National Guard resulted in the death of four students. Nine others were injured. None of the slain protesters had previously demonstrated against the war.[46]

Ten days later, two students were killed in a similar incident at Jackson State University in Mississippi. In the following weeks, more than 4 million students protested the killings. For most, this was their first (and last) taste of activism. Protests occurred at over 1,300 colleges and universities, with 536 temporarily closed, 51 for the rest of

---

43 Schuman, 'Two sources of antiwar sentiment in America', p. 516.
44 MacPherson, *Long Time Passing*, p. 88.
45 *Washington Post*, 6 May 1970.
46 Fred Halstead, *Out Now!* (New York, NY, 1978), pp. 537–9; *The Scotsman*, 18 May 1995; Heineman, *Campus Wars*, pp. 237–56.

the academic year.[47] It appeared that Kent State had inspired a unified student movement of monumental power. But solidarity borne of anger could not be sustained; fissures quickly developed between true pacifists, anarchists, hippie pranksters, proto-terrorists and the habitually apathetic. Nixon found it easy to manipulate these divisions. His promise of a withdrawal from Cambodia by 30 June (not, strictly speaking, a departure from his original plans) cooled tempers. Most students returned to their books, while a small faction turned to violence. Almost two years later the last combat troops left Vietnam. Neither the campus protests of the mid-1960s nor the massive reaction to the Kent State killings had any measurable effect upon the way middle America ended its war.[48]

Sixties romantics often view the anti-war movement as a continuum which began on the campuses of Berkeley and Michigan, gained strength from Walter Cronkite's post-Tet commentary, coalesced in the March on Washington, and reached its apotheosis when the troops began to flood home.[49] If such a scenario were accurate, the student protesters would emerge as heroes of the war – true martyrs who endured scorn before recognition. But it is difficult to assign credit to the students for shaping the opinions of middle America, since each regarded the other with deep contempt. In any case, courage seems a prerequisite for martyrdom. Civil rights protesters in the South went into the lion's den, risking severe injury and death. Those not physically attacked faced constant psychological torment. In contrast, student anti-war protesters operated within the closed, protected and tolerant world of the university. They protested to each other more than to their enemies. The civil rights activist Bayard Rustin challenged a Berkeley crowd gathered in November 1965 to 'go out into the community instead of spending so much time talking to yourselves . . . Then when people read in the newspapers that you've been arrested, they'll know why.'[50] Draft deferments reveal the hypocrisy of the

47 Tom Wells, *The War Within* (Berheley, CA, 1994), p. 425.

48 See Schreiber, 'Antiwar demonstrations', p. 232; and W.R. Berkowitz, 'The impact of anti-Vietnam demonstrations upon national public opinion and military indicators', *Social Science Research* 2 (1973), p. 10.

49 My analysis of the effects of the student protest movement is, admittedly, not a popular one. Most books on the subject take an opposite view, namely that the protesters were largely responsible for bringing the war to an end. See, for instance, Charles DeBenedetti, *An American Ordeal: The Antiwar Movement of the Vietnam Era* (Syracuse, NY, 1990); Tom Wells, *The War Within*; and Nancy Zaroulis and Gerald Sullivan, *Who Spoke Up?* (New York, NY, 1984). On the other side, Adam Garfinkle, in *Telltale Hearts* (London, 1995) ploughs a lonely furrow.

50 *Berkeley Gazette*, 5 November 1965.

student movement; there seems something wrong with individuals who object to a political system and a war but accept the protection from that war which the system offers. A much more impressive moral stand would have been to refuse the deferment *and* refuse to serve. One student protester, looking back at the 1960s, admitted that history would probably judge the movement 'passionately hypocritical'.[51]

Perhaps the greatest error of the anti-war movement was its scorn for the one group of American who suffered most deeply from the war. Young men sent unwillingly to Vietnam because they had the misfortune to be poor, under-educated, black or hispanic were lumped together with McNamara and Johnson as war criminals. Many a veteran recalls being spat upon by protesters upon his return from Vietnam. Ivory tower existentialists failed to realize that the American GI, like the Vietnamese peasant, was a victim. When protesters made overtures to soldiers, they did so in a condescending fashion which under-scored class differences. Berkeley activists warned recruits that if they fought in Vietnam they might be liable to prosecution for war crimes. They also argued, with incredible effrontery, that it required more courage to protest than to fight.[52]

The various anti-war movements did affect the outcome of the war. Johnson and Nixon, two paranoid presidents, did formulate their military strategies with the public reaction in mind. The protest convinced Hanoi that it could win a protracted war and Washington that it could not. But two points deserve emphasis. First, Americans would have supported a war which was being won, therefore defeat had to become apparent before dissension could turn critical. Had American forces really been winning, as Westmoreland and Johnson repeatedly claimed, the protesters would have seemed only a noisy nuisance. Second, no one group should claim credit for mobilizing Americans against the war – certainly not the students. Success came because diverse and antagonistic groups eventually attained critical mass. It does not seem reckless to speculate that, with a bit less egotism on the part of some protesters, and a bit more political savvy, success could have come sooner.

THE DRAFT

Around 8.6 million men served in the military during the Vietnam War. Of those, 2.15 million went to Vietnam. Another 16 million

---

51 MacPherson, *Long Time Passing*, p. 151.
52 DeGroot, 'The limits of moral protest', p. 110.

311

avoided military service by one means or another. Among those who did not go to Vietnam, 60 per cent claimed that they took active steps to ensure this outcome. Avoiders sought to beat the system by finding a loophole which would foil the Selective Service board. They were mainly white, middle-class, well-educated young men who had the intelligence, imagination and wherewithal to challenge the system. In all, 8,769,000 permanent deferments were granted.[53]

At first, avoidance was easy for anyone with a sufficient brains to get into university and sufficient money to stay there. Educational deferments increased by 900 per cent between 1961 and 1966. One survey revealed that 20 per cent of college youths listed avoiding the draft as one of their three most important reasons for entering higher education.[54] Graduate student deferments were abolished in 1967, but the fact that they were still extended to men at divinity school or those in preparation for teaching influenced career choices. Yale president Kingman Brewster felt that the deferments led to a 'cynical avoidance of service, a tarnishing of the national spirit, . . . and a cops and robbers view of national obligation'.[55] Marital deferments, which ended in 1966, contributed to a 10 per cent rise in the marriage rate among those aged 20 or 21. Since fathers were less likely to be taken than those who had no dependents, a minor baby boom among baby boomers resulted. Some took the slogan 'make love not war' literally: three in ten fathers polled said that the draft had influenced their decision to begin a family.[56]

At the universities, counsellors and support groups advised would-be draftees on promising escape routes. Copies of *How to Lower Your Blood Pressure* were in great demand among male students nearing graduation. Supposedly foolproof ways to beat the draft circulated like urban myths. Everyone knew a friend of a friend who had discovered that eating large quantities of bananas could lower blood pressure sufficiently to gain a medical exemption.[57] The habitually overweight tried desperately to put on pounds, while waifs dieted, each in an effort to court rejection. Two thousand dollars and a dishonest dentist could secure orthodontic braces and a temporary

53 Lawrence M. Baskir and William A. Strauss, *Chance and Circumstance* (New York, NY, 1978), pp. 5, 7, 30–1. These figures are not universally accepted. The Veteran's Administration put the total who served in Vietnam at nearly 2.6 million. See 'Vietnam warriors: a statistical profile', Internet source.

54 MacPherson, *Long Time Passing*, p. 32.

55 Baskir and Strauss, *Chance and Circumstance*, p. 7.

56 MacPherson, *Long Time Passing*, p. 97.

57 Another version held that the bananas were not supposed to be eaten; their peels were supposed to be dried and smoked.

exemption.[58] The fact that obscene tattoos could earn one a medical exemption led to a brisk trade at tattoo parlours. Phil Ochs captured the spirit in 'Draft Dodger Rag':

> And I'm only 18
> I've got a ruptured spleen.
> And I always carry a purse
> I've got eyes like a bat
> And my feet are flat
> And my asthma's getting worse
> Yeah, think of my career,
> And my sweetheart, dear,
> And my poor, old invalid aunt –
> Cuz' I ain't no fool, I'm a going to school
> And working in a defense plant.[59]

A Berkeley group advised young men to pretend to be a homosexual, a bed-wetter, a 'psycho' or an addict. 'Use a common pin on your arm for a few weeks in advance. Check with your friends who "shoot" to see if the marks look good.' Great play should be made of a criminal past: 'Most of us aren't lucky enough to have a felony record, but . . . suspicion of burglary or robbery or murder are also nice bets'.[60]

In 1966 whites received twice as many medical exemptions as blacks, despite the fact that blacks had lower health standards generally.[61] There is no doubt that the selective service system was riddled with class and racial bias:

> One Republican lobbyist, comfortable in a US$500 suit in a palatial Georgetown house, brags about avoiding the war.
> 'I pled a hardship case – drove down in my brother's Mercedes.'
> . . . 'How could anyone feel guilty about not going to that war?' asks a congressman's son. 'Vietnam was a *mess*. Besides, it didn't fit into my career plans.' . . . A Princeton graduate and high-priced corporate lawyer says, 'I feel sorry others did not have my benefits, but I certainly feel no guilt.'[62]

For the Army and the country, the system was a double-edged sword. It protected the gifted and those with promise, but it also deprived the

---

58 Baskir and Strauss, *Chance and Circumstance*, p. 44.

59 Phil Ochs, 'Draft Dodger Rag', copyright 1964 by Appleseed Music Inc.

60 'Brief Notes on the Ways and Means of "Beating" and Defeating the Draft', reprinted in House Committee on Un-American Activities, *Hearings on Assistance to Enemies*, pp. 1133–5.

61 Baskir and Strauss, *Chance and Circumstance*, p. 47.

62 MacPherson, *Long Time Passing*, pp. 28–9.

military of some good men. On the other hand, it neutralized the potential opposition most feared by the government: that of middle-class parents who had the money and confidence to complain loudly. James Fallows, a Harvard graduate who found a medical loophole in 1969, reflected:

> Johnson and Nixon both knew that the fighting could continue only so long as the vague, hypothetical benefits of holding off Asian communism outweighed the immediate, palpable domestic pain. They knew that when the screaming grew too loud and too many sons had been killed, the game would be all over. That is why . . . our reluctance to say No helped prolong the war. The more we guaranteed that we would end up neither in uniform nor behind bars, the more we made sure that *our* class of people would be spared the real cost of the war. Not that we didn't suffer. There was, of course, the *angst*, the terrible moral malaise we liked to write about so much in the student newspapers and undergraduate novels.[63]

Many evaded the draft by volunteering for an alternative form of military service. Some joined the Navy, which had a low casualty rate, but competition for places was severe. The most popular way of escaping the war was to join the National Guard or Army Reserve. Of the million guardsmen and reservists of the Vietnam era, only 15,000 went to Vietnam. Between 1968 and 1970 the National Guard and Reserves had 28,000 more college-educated men than all of the other active forces combined. (When the National Guard was sent on a campus to quell an anti-war disturbance, cynics commented, not without accuracy, that one group of draft dodgers was fighting another.) Competition for places was stiff, but both services were expanding – the National Guard because of escalating civil disturbances, and the Reserve because Vietnam drained America's mobilizable strength. According to the National Guard, 90 per cent of its recruits were draft-motivated. In 1968 its waiting list numbered 100,000, yet three years later, when the war was winding down, it was 45,000 men under strength.[64]

Around 172,000 men successfully earned conscientious objector status.[65] Since this was the most difficult escape route, it is safe to say

---

63 James Fallows, 'What did you do in the class war, Daddy?', in W. Capps, ed., *The Vietnam Reader* (New York, NY, 1991), p. 217.
64 Baskir and Strauss, *Chance and Circumstance*, pp. 48–55.
65 Ibid., p. 41.

that the vast majority were sincere. Those who belonged to established pacifist religions, such as Quakers, Mennonites and Jehovah's Witnesses, had an easier time than those who argued on philosophical grounds. Perhaps 50,000 young men escaped to Canada or some other sympathetic country, before or after their induction. They were usually working-class, since middle-class men preferred an easier way out. Nearly 210,000 who defied the law in one way or another were reported to federal prosecutors. Of those, 10 per cent, or around 25,000, were indicted, around 8,750 convicted, and only 3,250 went to prison. This suggests that Muhammad Ali, who refused to obey a draft notice, was convicted and served a prison term, was either very unlucky or, more likely, a high-profile scapegoat. The average sentence for draft evasion rose from 21 months in 1965 to 37 months in 1968, though most were paroled within a year. Those convicted were often men who had been refused conscientious objector status on religious grounds and wished to make a political statement by going to prison, or those from uneducated backgrounds who fell victim to an incomprehensible legal system. In 1969 selective service violations constituted the fourth largest category of crime in the United States.[66]

The inequities of the draft were plain to everyone, but were revealed never more bluntly than in a 1970 study which examined the service record of the 234 draft-age sons of members of Congress. Only 28 went to Vietnam, of whom only 19 saw combat, and only one was wounded. Not a single son of a member of the House Armed Services Committee did duty in Vietnam. Barry Goldwater, Jr, whose father was one of the era's most outspoken hawks, did 'alternate service' in the House of Representatives.[67]

The ease with which those at the top of society escaped service forced the government to relax standards pertaining to those at the bottom, namely the mentally deficient. 'Project 100,000' was a Great Society manpower programme purportedly designed to help disadvantaged youths by providing military training. In truth, it was an attempt to draw more men into the military. Some with an IQ of 62 were taken, thus the cruel epithet 'the Moron Corps'. The original goal of 100,000 men was easily surpassed; eventually some 350,000 were recruited. Forty per cent of the Project 100,000 recruits were trained for combat, compared to just 25 per cent in the services generally. Four out of ten were black.[68]

---

66 Ibid., pp. 69, 169; Steigerwald, *Sixties and the End of Modern America*, p. 107.
67 MacPherson, *Long Time Passing*, p. 141.
68 Baskir and Strauss, *Chance and Circumstance*, pp. 122–31; MacPherson, *Long Time Passing*, pp. 558–62.

By the end of the war evading the draft had become a great deal more honourable than serving in Vietnam. A 1971 Harris survey found that a majority of Americans believed that those who had agreed to serve in Vietnam were 'suckers, having to risk their lives in the wrong war, in the wrong place, at the wrong time'.[69]

SOUNDS OF APATHY AND PROTEST

Listening to Bob Dylan can be dangerous. Play a few bars of 'Blowin' in the Wind' and suddenly the most apathetic imagine that they, too, manned the barricades in 1968. Music smothers all rational assessment of that confusing time. It is easy to forget that while Dylan and Joan Baez alerted listeners to injustice, militarism and hypocrisy, the Ohio Express made a great deal of money singing 'Yummy, yummy, yummy, I got lovey in my tummy'. Paul Simon and Art Garfunkel, two of the most gifted, sensitive and cerebral musicians of their generation, had more success with the embarrassingly inane '59th Street Bridge Song' ('Feelin' Groovy') than with 'Silent Night/Seven O'Clock News' which lambasted Nixon's handling of the war. Most compilations of the greatest hits of the 1960s contain no protest or anti-war songs. The reason is simple: those songs were not hits.

Rock music is a business. In the 1960s the profit motive allowed little room for songs which challenged the political status quo. Granted, a lot of Sixties music *was* 'counter-culture' – it did challenge social conventions, especially those pertaining to sex and drugs. It provided the theme music for a generation bent on challenging parental authority. But the popular charts also found room for blatantly counter-revolutionary songs like Merle Haggard's 'Okie from Muskogee':

We don't smoke marijuana in Muskogee;
We don't take our trips on LSD
We don't burn our draft cards down on Main Street;
We like livin' right, and bein' free.

I'm proud to be an Okie from Muskogee,
A place where even squares can have a ball –
We still wave Old Glory down at the courthouse,
And white lightin's still the biggest thrill of all.[70]

Vietnam, civil rights and student unrest were minority issues, and music was produced for a mass market. Less than 29 per cent of those

---

69 Baskir and Strauss, *Chance and Circumstance*, p. 6.
70 Merle Haggard, 'Okie From Muskogee', copyright 1970 by Blue Book Music.

under 29 opposed the war in 1966. A large market for anti-war music did not exist because opposition to the war did not exceed 50 per cent of the population until after the Tet Offensive. In fact, among those under 29, support for the war did not drop below 50 per cent until the autumn of 1968.[71] Before 1968, only one political protest song – Barry McGuire's 'Eve of Destruction' – was sufficiently successful to be termed a hit. In 1966 the most popular Vietnam-related song was the rousingly patriotic 'Ballad of the Green Berets', by Sergeant Barry Sadler:

> Back at home a young wife waits
> Her Green Beret has met his fate
> He has died for those oppressed
> Leaving her his last request.
>
> Put silver wings on my son's chest
> Make him one of America's best.
> He'll be a man they test one day
> Have him win the Green Beret.[72]

Sadler's song was in fact the most popular war-related song ever produced, selling seven million copies.[73] Country Western artists produced more pro-war songs, with greater success, than rock artists produced anti-war songs. No issue was too controversial for patriotic songwriters, as demonstrated by the success of 'Battle Hymn of William Calley', which became a gold record within a month of its release.[74]

In 1969 changing public opinion was reflected in the success of John Lennon's 'Give Peace a Chance', which rose to number 11 in the American Top 100 charts. Over the next five years, the rock industry produced 34 identifiably anti-war songs, of which 26 made it into the Top 100.[75] Even Motown artists, usually preoccupied with love and romance, got into the act, most notably with Edwin Starr's 'War'. 'The music business is a whore', one BMI executive admitted. 'It will make and market anything that it thinks will sell.' By 1970, the war was sufficiently unpopular for the Beach Boys to put aside their surf-boards and sing the eminently forgettable 'Student Demonstration

---

71 Lunch and Sperlich, 'American public opinion', p. 33.

72 Barry Sadler and Robin Moore, 'The Ballad of the Green Berets', copyright 1963 by Music, Music, Music, Inc.

73 Anderson, 'American popular music and the war in Vietnam', p. 56.

74 Ibid., pp. 58–62.

75 Kenneth J. Bindas and Craig Houston, '"Takin' care of business": rock music, Vietnam and the protest myth', *The Historian* 52 (1989), p. 14.

Time'. Protest songs had become commodities manufactured for profit. Country Joe MacDonald, whose 'I Feel Like I'm Fixin' to Die Rag' was a popular anthem at protest rallies, complained that he was 'selling peace . . . for US$3.98'.[76]

Thus, contrary to popular myth, protest songs did not inspire opposition to the war. They simply reflected that opposition. In fact, it seems that music was not a very effective medium for communicating an anti-war message. The lyrics (not to mention title) of Barry McGuire's 'Eve of Destruction' should leave little room for confusion, covering racism, militarism, and the hypocrisy of the space race. Yet a poll of students in 1965 revealed that only 14 per cent correctly understood the song. Around 70 per cent confessed to being attracted by the beat rather than the message.[77] Poor McGuire shouted all that anger into a vacuum.

There were, admittedly, institutional obstacles to the dissemination of protest rock. The Federal Communications Commission (FCC) vigilantly monitored the playlists of radio stations. CBS executives, fearful of official sanction, banned Pete Seeger from performing an anti-war song on the *Smothers Brothers Comedy Hour* in late 1967.[78] A great deal of self-censorship was practiced by station managers who knew better than to incur the wrath of the FCC. 'Eve of Destruction' was banned from some radio stations. And since all stations were commercial, those who paid the piper called the tune. Sponsors preferred inane drivel like 'Love Potion Number Nine' or harmlessly escapist songs like 'Surfin' USA' to the angry ballads of McGuire, Dylan or Baez.

But the main obstacle to the success of protest music was undoubtedly the music industry itself. In 1966 rock music became, for the first time, a billion dollar enterprise. Record producers may have considered themselves hip, but sideburns and shades could not hide a capitalist's mind. 'The difference between a rock star and a robber baron is six inches of hair', *Rolling Stone* commented.[79] Dylan once chided his listeners: 'Ya don't need a Weatherman to know which way the wind blows'. A more honest line would have been: 'Ya don't need a banker to know which way the money flows'.

---

76 Ibid., p. 9.

77 R. Serge Denisoff and Mark Levine, 'The popular protest song: the case of "Eve of Destruction"', *Public Opinion Quarterly* 35 (1971), pp. 117–22.

78 H. Ben Auslander, "'If ya wanna end the war and stuff, you gotta sing loud"– a survey of Vietnam-related protest music', *Journal of American Culture* 4 (1981), p. 109.

79 Bindas and Houston, 'Takin' care of business' p. 23.

MAKE LOVE NOT WAR

'Protesting was a great place to get laid, get high, and listen to some great rock.'[80] The enjoyment of sex was not one-sided. It is frequently argued that women were the casualties, not beneficiaries, of sexual revolution. While this has a grain of truth, 1990s prurience can be taken too far. There would not have been a sexual revolution if women had not been willing rebels. 'It was a wonderful time to be young', one woman reflected, 'Think how many times you got laid.'[81] A popular slogan among young women protesters was 'Girls only say yes to boys who say no'.

But beneath the veneer of free love, patriarchy remained monolithic. In early 1969 one SDS woman wrote:

> We were still the movement secretaries and the shit-workers; we served the food, prepared the mailings and made the best posters; we were the earth mothers and the sex objects for the movement men. We were the free movement 'chicks' – free to screw any man who demanded it, or if we chose not to – free to be called hung-up, middle-class, and up-tight. We were free to keep quiet at meetings – or if we chose not to, we were free to speak up in men's terms. . . . We found ourselves unable to influence the direction and scope of projects. We were dependent on the male for direction and recognition.[82]

Little incidents had profound importance, if not at the time, then years later. Marjery Tabankin, an activist at the University of Wisconsin and the first women president of the National Student Association, recalls that when Tom Hayden visited her campus, 'the first thing he handed me was his dirty laundry and asked if I would do it for him. I said, "I'll have it for you by tonight".' She later reflected: 'Most guys didn't take women seriously . . . They were things to fuck. . . . You went through this intense experience [at demonstrations], and you went back and had sex.'[83] In contrast to the later feminist movement, which trumpeted the slogan 'the personal is political', women antiwar activists found that thinking personally wasn't highly regarded. They were supposed to submerge their interests to those of the movement, always reassured (by men) that, since patriarchy was a product of capitalism, the revolution would bring sexual equality. Meanwhile,

80 MacPherson, *Long Time Passing*, p. 33.
81 Ibid., p. 458.
82 Kirkpatrick Sale, *SDS* (New York, NY, 1973), p. 526.
83 MacPherson, *Long Time Passing*, p. 467.

by doing the dishes, female activists would hasten the end of the war and bring closer the socialist millenium. Perhaps it was the drugs which made the road to Utopia seem so clear.

The anger of Valerie Solanis (who dreamt of an 'out-of-sight, groovy, all-female world') took expression in the formation of SCUM (the Society for Cutting Up Men) and in an attempted assassination of Andy Warhol.[84] Others channelled their anger in more productive directions. Women left the anti-war movement with their spirits fired by alienation and their protest skills honed by experience. 'In the midst of sexist movements, women were having experiences that transformed their consciousness and changed their lives', Breines concluded. 'When women acquired the experience and skills that enabled them to feel strong enough to move out on their own, it was with political ideas that they had inherited from the sixties.'[85]

THE MYTH OF 1968

The year 1968 is supposed to have been a turning point in history or, in the words of one chronicler, 'a terrible, wonderful year when everything seemed possible'.[86] It was the year of the Kennedy and King assassinations, the Tet Offensive, the Paris riots, the tragic Mexico Olympics, the toppling of Lyndon Johnson and the spectacle of Chicago. Thirty years later, those events seem to lack any coherence or logic. The dominant image of 1968 is anarchy, not progress. One is struck by a world which did not turn, or not in the direction many hoped. Everything may have seemed possible, but little was.

Before 1968, there was prosperity and idealism. The prosperity was real, the idealism probably misguided, but that is beside the point. Sixties radicals arose from this ethos of fluidity and tried to marshall it. They failed. Or, more accurately, they were defeated by a conservative counter-revolution. The year 1968 seems chaotic because, rather than being a time when 'the movement' came together, it was instead the year it was defeated and flew apart, the fragments scattering in weird idiosyncratic directions. After 1968 came recession, conservatism, cynicism and despair. There is no more potent or symbolic image of the futility of post-1968 activism than the explosion which ripped apart a townhouse in Greenwich Village on 6 March 1970,

84 Charles Kaiser, *1968 in America* (New York, NY, 1988), p. 186.

85 Wini Breines, 'Review essay', *Feminist Studies* 5 (1979), pp. 504–5. My thanks to Barbara Tischler for this reference.

86 'Fatal flaws in an ideal world', *Glasgow Herald*, 15 January 1994.

killing three would-be bombers of the Weather Underground, a deformed offshoot of the SDS stump.[87]

A generation later, it is the forces of reaction which seem most prominent and, certainly, most successful in 1968. The folk heroes of Sixties militancy – Hayden, Rubin, Daniel Cohn-Bendit, Rudi Dutschke and Tariq Ali – emerge as rather ineffectual figures out-classed and out-manoeuvred by an organized, powerful establishment. The counter-revolution was perhaps most impressive in California, not only because that was where militancy was particularly strong, but more importantly because the reaction was led by Ronald Reagan, who launched his career tilting at the windmills of Sixties radicalism and who came to symbolize, perhaps more than anyone, the conservative Eighties.

Reagan's counter-revolution began in 1966 with his defeat of the incumbent California governor, the liberal Democrat Edmund G. (Pat) Brown. The Reagan campaign drew its strength from the forces it sought to destroy. It was not the right which defeated Brown in 1966, but the far left; specifically, student radicals on California campuses. During the campaign, every outbreak of unrest improved Reagan's chances of victory because it suggested that Brown's liberal tolerance was dangerous. 'We jumped on [student unrest] as an issue', Stuart Spencer, a Reagan aide, later admitted.[88] Richard Kline, who worked for Brown, recalled that 'the university thing drove us nuts . . . It was just utterly strange. All these things happening around us and why couldn't they be controlled?'[89]

For Reagan, the problem of campus unrest highlighted the themes of his populist crusade: morality, law and order, strong leadership, traditional values. The state universities had become, he claimed, havens for communists, drug-addicts and sexual perverts. In very public statements, he urged Johnson to declare war on Vietnam, so that protest could be outlawed and traitorous dissidents jailed. He encouraged Californians to see the universities as a battlefront in the Cold War. In Berkeley as in Vietnam, the dominoes would not be allowed to fall. Police were sent on to the campuses in ever greater numbers and undercover operations proliferated. His war reached a peak in 1969 with the sixteen-day siege of People's Park, in which one protester was killed, another blinded and, at one stage, a National Guard helicopter, in a bizarre airstrike, sprayed CS gas indiscriminately on the campus. Even after an inquiry found that inappropriate force was

---

87 See Peter Collier and David Horowitz, *Destructive Generation* (New York, NY, 1990), chap. 2.

88 Stuart Spencer oral history transcript, Bancroft Library, p. 31.

89 Richard Kline oral history transcript, Bancroft Library, p. 46.

used, Reagan remained undefiant: 'there was no alternative.... once the dogs of war are unleashed, you must expect that things will happen and that people, being human, will make mistakes on both sides.'[90] When he shouted 'If it takes a blood bath to silence the demonstrators, let's get it over with', the public bellowed its approval.[91]

Reagan discovered a deep well of antagonism towards privileged university students. Among the blue-collar constituency which he so successfully courted, the campus kooks were an easy enemy to hate. He had a special way of plucking a chord with Mr and Mrs Blue Collar of Ordinaryville, who delighted in off-the-cuff remarks like: 'This last bunch of pickets were carrying signs that said "Make Love Not War". The only trouble was they didn't look like they were capable of doing either. Their hair was cut like Tarzan, and they acted like Jane, and they smelled like Cheetah.'[92]

Reagan was not conspicuously successful in finding a solution to student unrest. His toughness probably did more to radicalize students than to tame them. But the average Reagan supporter swallowed the myth of the uncompromising governor who got a difficult job done. By adroit manipulation of the problem Reagan achieved three significant objectives: he revived the Republican right, he defeated the radical left and he began the process which would push liberalism to the margins of American politics, where it remains to this day. He also, of course, laid the foundations of his own glorious career. Through his skill in turning a relatively small problem into a massive conspiracy to overthrow democracy, and then in meeting that threat with maximum force, Reagan established himself as a leader worthy of national attention. After 1971, student unrest declined and so did his popularity in California. But that hardly mattered to him, for he had begun to strut on a larger stage. By the time he left the governor's mansion, there was a growing band of supporters across America who saw in the battler of Berkeley a man ideally suited to restore a combative pride to America.

POSTSCRIPT

Vietnam gave the youth movement of the 1960s a cause through which it could pursue principle, morality and virtue. Some of the

90 Transcript of Reagan meeting with UC Berkeley professors, Sacramento, 21 May 1969, box 178, Reagan Papers.

91 *Berkeley Gazette*, 9 April 1970.

92 Gerard J. DeGroot, 'Ronald Reagan and student unrest in California, 1966–1970', *Pacific Historical Review* 65 (1996), p. 115.

protesters displayed noble commitment in their opposition to the war. But others failed to keep their immature exuberance in check – clever pranks overshadowed prudent politics. When Nixon took the war away, the movement lost its backbone. Some used the skills they had gained for the pursuit of new causes: feminism, environmentalism and civil liberties among them. Others grew frustrated at their inability to change the world and tried instead to mould it with bombs and bullets. It was a deeply worried Father Daniel Berrigan who wrote an open letter to the Weathermen in late 1970:

> the history of the movement, in the last years, it seems to me, shows how constantly and easily we are seduced by violence, not only as to method, but as to end in itself. With very little politics, very little ethics, very little direction, and only a minimum of moral sense, if any at all, it might lead one to conclude in despair: the movement is debased beyond recognition, I can't be part of it.[93]

Nihilists like the Weathermen attracted far more attention than their actual threat ever merited. They achieved little, but proved useful in the Republican resurgence. Most young people, when deprived of the political direction and moral purpose that the war had provided, turned not to violence but to self-absorption. Drugs, free love, long hair and extravagant clothes, which were once symbolic of a new political order, became instead mere manifestations of Seventies egotism.

William McGill, Chancellor of the University of California, San Diego, during the hardest years of the 1960s, felt that his most difficult task was to 'persuade students to use the brains God gave them instead of turning to mindless and self-destructive confrontation'.[94] He objects to the nostalgia merchants who have made the 1960s into a decade of hope and glorious achievement. He saw the suicides, the insanity, the lives ruined by anger and drugs.

> There is a special problem for participants in any era of dramatic upheaval when they attempt to distill the significance of what they lived through. Temptation is strong to rewrite history in order to justify our own beliefs and actions. Memory can be very deceptive. Unerringly it seeks respectability for things done in ignorance and confusion. We all prefer to think

93 Harrison Salisbury, ed., *The Eloquence of Protest: Voices of the 70s* (Boston, MA, 1972), p. 17.
94 William J. McGill, *The Year of the Monkey* (New York, NY, 1982), p. 188.

of ourselves as moral agents rather than muddled actors in a theater of the absurd.[95]

Eight Americans burned themselves to death in protest against the Vietnam War, among them a student from the University of California, San Diego, angered by the Kent State killings.[96] Martyrdom of this type seems fitting to an oppressive regime like South Vietnam, but out of place in a liberal democracy. No rational explanation of the homefront culture during the Vietnam War can ever come to grips with the madness ever present. 'It was important to explain to overwrought 18-year-olds that the world crushes naive idealists', writes McGill, who experienced the futility of trying to do so. He nevertheless felt that though 'Many students . . . were brutally damaged by their search for simplistic utopias . . . there was something undeniably beautiful about their crusade'.[97]

95 Ibid., pp. 216–17.
96 Steigerwald, *Sixties and the End of Modern America*, pp. 106–7.
97 McGill, *Year of the Monkey*, p. 225.

13 'A COUNTRY, NOT A WAR'

The Vietnamese people paid dearly for efforts on their behalf – be they to unite Vietnam or to save it from communism. According to one of the more conservative estimates, there were 1,435,000 civilian casualties in the period 1965–74, and well over 10 million refugees.[1] The United States, a nation of some 200 million people, lost nearly 60,000 men in the war. Vietnam, a country of around 36 million, lost perhaps 2 million soldiers and civilians.[2] A survey of eight provinces and cities in the North found 17,000 families with more than one dead, 2,000 with at least three dead, and 3,000 families in which all children were killed.[3] Soldiers missing in action (MIA) number around 300,000.[4] In Vietnam as a whole, 25 million acres of farmland, 12 million acres of forest, and 4,000 of 5,800 agricultural communes were destroyed, partly by the 19 million gallons of herbicide sprayed on the countryside.[5] Unexploded ordnance and mines continue to kill and maim.

RECONSTRUCTION

'Waging war is simple', Pham Van Dong told Stanley Karnow, 'but running a country is difficult.' The Politburo, whose direction of the

---

1 Guenter Lewy, *America in Vietnam* (Oxford, 1978), p. 445. Lewy rejects the estimates of the Senate committee chaired by Edward Kennedy, which placed the total at 1,435,000. Others have claimed, from very dubious evidence and suspicious accounting, that the figure exceeds 2.2 million. Gloria Emerson, in *Winners and Losers* (New York, NY, 1992) (p. 357), takes the Kennedy figure but changes the period covered to 1965–73, and then adds 339,882 civilian casualties suffered from 1973 to 1975. She gives no source for the latter figure.

2 In spite of huge losses, Vietnam's population (North and South) actually increased from around 35 million in 1965 to over 42 million in 1973. Lewy, *America in Vietnam*, p. 301.

3 Douglas Pike, *PAVN: People's Army of Vietnam* (Novato, CA, 1986), p. 309.

4 'A country, not a war', *The Economist*, 12 August 1995, p. 37.

5 Marilyn Young, *The Vietnam Wars, 1945–1990* (New York, NY, 1991), pp. 301–2.

war was often uncannily brilliant, proved inept at feeding the people, forging a government, uniting the country and encouraging economic growth. Slavish obedience to communist doctrine caused waste, inefficiency and injustice. 'We are plagued by problems', Pham Van Dong admitted. 'We do not have enough to eat. We are a poor, undeveloped nation.'[6] Yet in Malaysia, Singapore and South Korea the postwar period was one of astonishing growth. Vietnam, logic suggests, should not have been poor.

Many blamed the United States, with some justification. The Americans, it seems, are poor losers. They wreaked vast destruction upon Vietnam and then abruptly left, with no attempt to repair the damage. Vietnam became a pariah after 1973. Aid was promised at the Paris Peace Conference, but never delivered. An amendment to the Foreign Assistance Appropriation Act of 1976 prohibited aid to Vietnam, Laos and Cambodia. Membership in the UN was vetoed and assets were frozen. Hanoi's intervention in Cambodia further poisoned relations, reviving talk of toppling dominoes. Progress toward normalization was also inhibited by the highly emotive POW/MIA issue. Campaigners in the US, many of suspect virtue, kept the issue hot. Crude attempts by the Vietnamese to exploit the problem in order to gain favour, including the infamous 'bone-trading' episodes, merely fed American paranoia.[7] A classic Catch-22 resulted: normalization was tied to resolution of the issue, yet a resolution was difficult without normalization.

American aid and a relaxation of the trade embargo would have made a profound difference to Vietnam's postwar economic health. But greater magnanimity would not have made the difference between the dire poverty Vietnam has suffered and the economic miracles her neighbours have enjoyed. Her problems were mainly internal: she has been poorly governed and her economy has been mismanaged. Bad government arose in part from an arrogance of power which had not existed before the revolution, but resulted from it. Victory convinced the revolutionaries that they were both popular and right. Out of this delusion grew a dangerous assumption of unchallenged legitimacy and absolute power. They were, quite simply, drunk with victory.

The revolution succeeded because it was pragmatic, patient and humble. The leaders had recognized that the discontented were a broad church who could not be brought together by a single doctrine. Yet after they succeeded, they grew impatient, dogmatic and arrogant.

6 Stanley Karnow, *Vietnam: A History* (Harmondsworth, 1993), p. 9.
7 See Chapter 14, pp. 350–4.

Because victory had come as a result of the complete defeat of the Saigon regime, instead of a compromise, the communists were left with no credible opponents. They concluded that it would be sensible to speed ahead with unification and communist transformation. But the revolution, in the strictest sense, had not taken place, since victory was military, not political. The popular uprising had not materialized. Because it had not, the communists should have taken time to reassure the people and win their support, with a gradual transformation from capitalism to collectivism. But, as had happened after the 1954 victory, the Politburo moved too quickly, leaving in its wake untold hardship.

The results of this hasty transformation were predictable – except to its authors. In a manner typical of emerging communist nations, the government opted for big industrial projects instead of concentrating upon the light industry more suited to the Vietnamese economy. Inevitable Five Year Plans were devised, implemented and proudly trumpeted. Tractor factories made great propaganda but did not bring in much-needed foreign capital. Factory managers were paid according to how many workers they employed, not on productivity. It was all right to incur a deficit, as long as workers were employed. Bureaucracy clogged the system: in order to transport an insignificant product like an umbrella stand from Tay Ninh to Ho Chi Minh City, it was necessary to 'go through 17 agencies, obtain 15 seals, sign 5 contracts and pay many different types of tax'.[8]

Agricultural production dropped severely. 'Red landlords', as the new bureaucrats were called, proved as adept at alienating peasants as their predecessors had been. Trinh Duc, a former fisheries administrator, witnessed what happened when political theory took precedence over practical economics:

> starting in 1976 I began to hear open complaints about the way things were going. . . . The main thing they complained about was they couldn't do what they wanted with their land. They had to follow the program the administration got from the central government, a lot of which was absurd. For instance, they were ordered to grow more coffee on the land where they used to grow tea. But that land wasn't suitable for coffee . . . Also, they had to sell their produce to the government at the official price. In return, the government was supposed to sell them fertilizer and tools at the official price. But the reality

8 Melanie Beresford, *Vietnam: Politics, Economics and Society* (London, 1988), p. 170.

was that there was never enough supplies. So they had to go to the black market and buy what they needed at black market prices.[9]

Poor weather, supply shortages and mismanagement together caused bad harvests in 1977 and 1978. Vietnam continued to import massive quantities of rice. The introduction of food rationing alleviated, but did not prevent, widespread starvation.

Communist dogmatism proved enormously costly. When faced with a budgetary squeeze the government simply printed money. The currency became virtually worthless and shops were empty. Corrupt government officials used their travel privileges to buy commodities in areas where they were relatively plentiful and sell them where they were scarce. Inflation reached 600 to 700 per cent per year during the 1980s.[10] By the time Le Duan died in 1986, complete economic collapse threatened.

Amidst the economic chaos, some progressive reforms were made. Educational policies placed a greater emphasis upon vocational training to reflect actual labour requirements. Highly prescriptive Confucian precepts, which discouraged creativity and individual reasoning, declined in importance. Positive steps were taken to reduce the birth rate, including propaganda campaigns to encourage families to limit offspring to one or two, and progressive birth-control provision.[11] Much effort was devoted to tackling the massive prostitution and drug rackets in southern cities, a legacy of the American presence.

Economic regeneration was encouraged through New Economic Zones (NEZ). Urban dwellers, including former civil servants, were persuaded to move to the countryside with incentive bonuses, tax exemptions, housing and food allowances and exemption from conscription. Where incentives failed to persuade the reluctant, force often did. Around 2 million urban dwellers were moved to the countryside by 1985, an exodus sufficient to reduce the population of Saigon by 1 million residents.[12] Thus, urban over-population was tackled at the same time that valuable land abandoned during the war was brought back into production, with modern methods. But the greatest difficulty lay in convincing 'soft' urbanites to stay on the farms.

---

9 David Chanoff and Doan Van Toai, *Vietnam – A Portrait of Its People at War* (London, 1996), pp. 197–8.

10 Neil Sheehan, *Two Cities: Hanoi and Saigon* (London, 1992), pp. 16–17.

11 See G.W. Jones, 'Population trends and policies in Vietnam', *Population and Development Review* 8 (1982), p. 797.

12 Beresford, *Vietnam*, pp. 150–1; James P. Harrison, *The Endless War* (New York, NY, 1989), p. 306.

On the whole, the period up to 1986 was a dismal tale of failure. It does seem strange that leaders who had, for over 30 years, managed revolution and war so skilfully should so quickly lose their touch. The problem arose in part because victory in 1975 was unexpected, and Hanoi unprepared.[13] But that does not explain the faults in leadership which were so readily apparent. In truth, the failures have their roots in the revolution years. The biggest mistakes made during the period 1945–75 came when the Politburo overestimated the strength of the revolution and the support of the people for it. The catastrophes of Tet and the 1973 Easter Offensive all arose from an assumption that the revolution was more popular than in fact it was. The Politburo failed to appreciate that the revolution had been held together by the desire for an independent Vietnam. Once Saigon fell, this tie snapped. The popular front resumed its original form – a collection of disparate groups. Total war had concentrated minds on a single task. When peace came, minds wandered and chaos ensued. Sacrifices which had been tolerable were no longer so. It would have been difficult for any government to deal with this situation, given the widespread destruction. It became impossible when the government insisted upon imposing a political ideology which had little popular support or pragmatic sense.

DISSIDENTS AND BOAT PEOPLE

PAVN Colonel Bui Tin was in Doc Lap Palace in Saigon on 30 April 1975 when he encountered General Doung Van Minh, provisional head of the RVN. 'You have nothing to fear', he reassured Minh. 'Between Vietnamese, there are no victors and no vanquished. Only the Americans have been beaten. If you are patriots, consider this a moment of joy. The war for our country is over.'[14] Whether honest sentiment or cynical propaganda, Tin's assurances proved hollow. The vanquished had much to fear.

In their assault upon the capitalist economy, the communists demonstrated that they were just as adept at alienating the populace as their one-time enemies had been. Because power emanated predominantly from Hanoi, the new regime seemed essentially a foreign conqueror. Northern cadres in Saigon launched a crusade to root out and punish anyone displaying bourgeois trappings, such as long hair

---

13 This is the argument made at length by Gabriel Kolko in *Vietnam: Anatomy of a Peace* (New York, NY, 1997).
14 Karnow, *Vietnam*, p. 669.

or Western clothes.[15] Ethnic and religious persecution, which the revolutionaries had once exploited to great effect in their propaganda war against the RVN, continued under the new regime, the only difference being that Catholics now joined Buddhists among the ranks of the tormented.

Southern supporters of the revolution had long feared that victory would mean domination by the 'Tonkinese', but could do little to prevent this eventuality. What they did not accurately predict was how complete this domination would be. The NLF 'had no further role to play', Truong Nhu Tang recalled. It 'became a positive obstacle to the rapid consolidation of power'. All communist organizations were amalgamated into one Vietnamese Communist Party, tightly controlled by the Politburo. 'With total power in their hands, they began to show their cards in the most brutal fashion', Tang wrote. 'They made it understood that the Vietnam of the future would be a single monolithic bloc, collectivist and totalitarian, in which all the traditions and culture of the South would be ground and moulded by the political machine of the conquerors.'[16]

The bloodbath so feared in the South did not materialize. Those judged enemies of the revolution were ostracized, spied upon and prevented from taking employment, but not slaughtered. Many RVN politicians and military officers were sentenced to detention in re-education camps, the length of sentence proportionate to the individual's seniority. Estimates of the number sentenced vary from 700,000 to 1.3 million.[17] The treatment was cruel, and conditions harsh, but nearly 95 per cent survived the ordeal.

To many, the new government did not seem distinctly different from the old. After undergoing re-education, Nguyen Cong Hoan was told that he should stand for election to the Communist Assembly. A party official told him that the 'Fatherland Front has decided you should run, so it's your duty to run. It's not a matter of wanting to or not wanting to.' Hoan found himself one of twelve candidates for eleven seats in his district. He gathered 94.9 per cent of the vote, only enough for eleventh place.[18] The Assembly itself was a farce. When Hoan dared question government policy, a party goon carefully explained the difference between individual democracy and party democracy, extolling the virtues of the latter. References were made to the 'law of freedom' which, like the law of gravity, was immutable. The official

---

15 William J. Duiker, *Sacred War* (New York, NY, 1995), p. 261.
16 Truong Nhu Tang, *A Vietcong Memoir* (San Diego, CA, 1985), p. 268.
17 Harrison, *Endless War*, p. 306.
18 Chanoff and Toai, *Portrait*, pp. 189–91.

then explained just how immutable natural laws were by referring to the speed a human body would reach if thrown from an airplane without a parachute. 'The whole thing was unbelievable', Hoan reflected. 'This guy was just a thug. . . . Under Thieu there were plenty of thugs, but it had been much more interesting. At least there you were only bribed and beaten, it wasn't the immutable laws of nature . . . demanding your obedience.'[19]

Southerners were at first told that their property and money were secure. Then, in March 1978, Hanoi announced that, in order to root out the 'poisonous weeds of bourgeois capitalism', all industry above the family level would be nationalized. 'Capitalist trade' was summarily abolished, causing great suffering among the entrepreneurial class. By the end of the year, around 1,500 people were leaving the country each month, by whatever precarious means. Perhaps 1.4 million have left since 1975, with 50,000 dying *en route*.[20] Hanoi arrogantly assumed that, like rats leaving the sinking RVN ship, they were not the sort to make a contribution to the new Vietnam. Around 70 per cent of these economic refugees, known to the West as 'Boat People', were of Chinese extraction. Since the Chinese had long dominated industry and commerce, the government feared that they would not only impede progress in the South but threaten stability in the North. Trinh Duc, an ethnic Chinese, recalled how 'Some of the mass organizations began to launch campaigns denouncing the "Chinese betrayals". . . . The object was to create a hostile public atmosphere between Vietnamese and ethnic Chinese.'[21]

The remaining refugees were urban middle-class Vietnamese, with a sprinkling of peasants and urban workers. They were either pessimistic about the possibilities of maintaining a decent standard of living, or simply scared. For the nation as a whole, the loss was massive, since those leaving were highly skilled, intelligent and dynamic individuals essential to future prosperity. On the other hand, bribes paid to government authorities to enable escape (the going rate was US$2,700 in gold) were a significant source of revenue.[22]

The regime was correct in the assessment of the danger capitalist interests posed to socialist transformation. In the two decades since the end of the war, peaceful capitalist infiltration has done more to undermine communism than was ever achieved by the tanks, artillery and helicopters of the French or Americans. But the regime was wrong

19 Ibid., pp. 191–2.
20 George S. Herring, *America's Longest War* (New York, NY, 1986), p. 270.
21 Chanoff and Toai, *Portrait*, p. 200.
22 Harrison, *Endless War*, p. 303.

331

to believe that the capitalist ethos could be eradicated by nationalizing industry, collectivizing farms and forcing unrepentant bourgeoisie into boats.

FOREIGN ADVENTURES

According to Henry Kissinger, during the Paris talks Le Duc Tho derisively rejected proposals for a neutral Cambodia, remarking 'we will get it eventually anyway'.[23] The Vietnamese still believed in their right to dominate Indochinese affairs, and to use Cambodia and Laos for their own purposes, as they had during the war. This was, however, the wrong time to tangle with the Cambodian people. Their leader, Pol Pot, had come to power on a platform of xenophobic nationalism. Though the true level of his popularity is debatable, his hold over his people was real. He interpreted Hanoi's talk of a 'special relationship' as fancy wrapping for imperialism, and reacted by launching raids to regain border areas which, he claimed, had traditionally belonged to the Khmer people.

Pol Pot's rejection of the special relationship and his fierce backlash against pro-Vietnam sympathizers within the KCP fired Hanoi's anger. In December 1978 PAVN troops crossed the border and linked up with 10,000 Cambodian rebels led by the dissident Khmer Rouge officer Heng Samrin. They took Phnom Penh on 7 January 1979, forcing Pol Pot to flee into the mountains, along with remnants of his movement. A motley amalgam of communist and non-communist forces began a guerrilla campaign against the pro-Hanoi government installed in Phnom Penh. It was supported by the Chinese, who backed Pol Pot simply because he opposed Vietnam. The same obscene rationale governed American policy. PAVN troops remained in Cambodia for the entire decade, fighting a costly and demoralizing counter-insurgency campaign.

The Chinese invaded Vietnam in February 1979. China wanted to punish the Vietnamese for their invasion of Cambodia, their recent overtures to Russia, and their repression of ethnic Chinese. Beijing was also keen to reassert its hegemony, and to teach its former protégé a lesson in power politics. The conflict was everywhere destructive, bloody and expensive, seriously undermining Vietnamese reconstruction. In the face of international criticism and a stiffer than expected Vietnamese resistance, China withdrew its troops by the end of March. But frequent border clashes occurred over the next few years.

23 Henry Kissinger, *White House Years* (Boston, MA, 1979), p. 469.

Hanoi's quest for hegemony within Indochina had huge costs. PAVN became, in the 1980s, the third largest military force in the world, with more than 1.25 million regulars and 3 million reserves. In 1990, 25 per cent of Vietnam's gross national product was spent on the military.[24] This naturally depressed the domestic economy, stifling reconstruction. The American-sponsored trade boycott further impoverished the economy. Vital Chinese aid abruptly stopped in June 1979, and an international embargo prohibited Vietnamese access to International Monetary Fund, Asian Development Bank or World Bank relief funds. Only Sweden and Finland, alone among non-communist countries, continued to send aid.

In this situation, Vietnam became even more reliant upon the Soviet Union. Since she could no longer manipulate rivalries between her superpower allies, Soviet aid now came at a higher price. The USSR involved itself in internal Vietnamese politics to an extent unknown during the war. During the 1980s, 6,000 Soviet administrators serviced an aid programme worth between US$1 and US$2 billion per year.[25] Cam Ranh Bay became essentially a Soviet port, growing to quadruple its wartime size. The presence of Soviet warships and the estimated 2,500 military personnel around the country were stark reminders of Vietnamese dependence. The Soviets seemed yet another imperialist exploiter. While many Vietnamese resented their presence, the importance of Soviet aid became painfully apparent when it disappeared after the collapse of the Soviet Union in 1991. Once-friendly communist regimes of Eastern Europe also folded. As time passed, Vietnam found herself drawn reluctantly back toward China, one of the few remaining outposts of communism.

FREE MARKET COMMUNISM

The Politburo's sense of embattled isolation rendered it less likely to countenance dilution of the socialist mission. Meanwhile the people grew ever more discontented. A change of climate occurred in 1986, after the death of Le Duan. Around the same time, the old war horses of the revolution – Truong Chinh, Pham Van Dong and Le Duc Tho – were removed from the Politburo and politely retired. The new General Secretary, Nguyen Van Linh, initiated a Southeast Asian *perestroika*, which included an admission that serious errors had been made in the hasty collectivist revolution.

24 Michael Lanning and Dan Cragg, *Inside the VC and the NVA* (New York, NY, 1992), p. 298.
25 Herring, *America's Longest War*, p. 272.

The new policy was called *doi moi*, or market socialism. The government henceforth accepted that 'the private, individual, small owner and private capitalist economic forms are still necessary in the long run for the economy . . . for the advance toward socialism'.[26] The tax system was reformed, foreign investment encouraged, and welfare provision cut. Rationing and subsidies were abruptly ended, as were the big industrial projects. Energies were shifted to light industry, agriculture and consumer goods. By mid-1989, prices stabilized, store shelves were filled. Largely due to the development of the oil industry, the growth rate rose from 5.1 per cent in 1990 to 9.5 per cent in 1995, with inflation down to 13 per cent. For the first time since the 1930s, Vietnam exported rice.[27]

The capitalist nature of *doi moi* was a kick in the teeth to those who sacrificed so much for communism during the war. In order to reduce the costs of nationalized medicine, the government passed laws in 1989 allowing hospitals to charge wealthy patients and permitting doctors to set up private clinics. In place of the hard-working peasant or the noble worker, the new hero is the 'Red capitalist' – the factory manager who, though technically a state employee, is rewarded for his or her entrepreneurial skills by splitting profits with the state.

As a spur to recovery, Vietnam established one of the most liberal foreign investment laws in the region. Economic giants like Korea, Japan and Singapore licked their chops at the prospect of access to Vietnam's low wages and industrious workers. Foreign investment poured in, especially from investors keen to cash in on rich oil reserves. William Ehrhart, who returned to Vietnam in 1990, remarked:

> The Australians have built a luxurious floating hotel on the Saigon River. The Japanese are refurbishing the old Metropole in Hanoi. The British, Dutch, French and Russians are pumping oil from deposits in Vietnamese coastal waters. I traveled the roads of Vietnam in an air-conditioned Toyota mini-bus. The hotels I stayed in were stocked with soap from Thailand and beer from Holland. Stores and street stalls from Hanoi to Ho Chi Minh City sell Japanese tape decks, German film, Saudi Arabian bottled spring water, shampoo from Malaysia, toys from China and electric fans from Singapore. One can buy Rambo sew-on patches and Playboy belt buckles and even model F-16s made in Taiwan with 'US Air Force' stenciled on the sides.

26 Kolko, *Anatomy of a Peace*, p. 35.
27 Sheehan, *Two Cities*, pp. 18–19; Kolko, *Anatomy of a Peace*, pp. 11, 44–6.

'It is as if the Americans had never been there, which is especially ironic because everyone else is there *except* the Americans', Ehrhart remarked.[28] By the late 1980s the US embargo had little justification other than spite. The American Chamber of Commerce in Hong Kong repeatedly pointed out to the White House that US firms were losing out in the race to exploit Vietnam's economic potential.[29]

Worker exploitation, once a sin, became a remedy for low growth. 'We have to accept a certain level of exploitation', Linh candidly admitted to Neil Sheehan.[30] Workers and peasants began to wonder if foreign interests were now more important than their own. Wages were frozen (or reduced), while conditions of work deteriorated seriously. When strikes increased, the government took steps to curb trade union power. It is no wonder that, in the face of increased poverty, urban workers have again turned to drug dealing and prostitution. In the mid-1990s, there were 600,000 prostitutes and 185,000 drug addicts, figures not dissimilar to those of the war years.[31] With irony unintended, drug barons, black marketeers and assorted political criminals have used the old tunnel systems to hide contraband and escape detection. The Cu Chi tunnels are particularly popular given their proximity to Ho Chi Minh City. The militia and police have apparently had as little success clearing them as the Americans once did.[32]

Collectivization, which had produced so much discontent, was largely abandoned in 1988. In its place came a land market system, which essentially restored many of the grievous practices peasants had endured for centuries. The wealthy ended up with the most land, rediscovering opportunities to exploit poor peasants. The militia occasionally had to respond to violent rural discontent. By 1993, one-fifth of rural dwellers were described as 'rich', one-quarter as 'desperately poor'. Income distribution is more unequal than in many proudly non-socialist countries.[33] The decline of collectivization has also meant that the irrigation and transportation network has suffered dramatically since there is no longer the cooperative will to maintain the agricultural infrastructure.

The Communist Party has lost the faith of its potentially most ardent supporters, namely the peasants. Party cadres have taken

28 W.D. Ehrhart, *In the Shadow of Vietnam: Essays, 1997–1991* (Jefferson, NC, 1997), pp. 150–1.

29 Keith Richburg, 'Back to Vietnam', *Foreign Affairs* 70 (1991), p. 128.

30 Sheehan, *Two Cities*, p. 80.

31 Kolko, *Anatomy of a Peace*, p. 108.

32 My thanks to Eric Bergerud for this delightfully ironic anecdote.

33 Kolko, *Anatomy of a Peace*, pp. 102–3.

the place of French administrators or RVN officials in the catalogue of rural villains. They now regularly engage in corruption – leasing, renting or selling land for personal gain. Some 200,000 written complaints pertaining to land-use rights were lodged between 1988 and mid-1990. The unthinkable has arisen, namely a class struggle in the countryside, fostered by the Communist Party. The government now believes that the key to rural regeneration lies in the growth of a middle-class peasantry, through increased competition.[34]

Education, that great class leveller, has also suffered. Much of the education remit was carried out by rural cooperatives. Their disappearance has meant that the schooling of poor peasants has suffered. Cuts in public-sector spending (on the advice of the International Monetary Fund and World Bank) caused further damage. Toward the end of the 1980s, a sharp decline in student enrolment was evident at all levels. As with land distribution, class inequality has been institutionalized; the children of Communist Party officials are most likely to receive a good education. The same can be said for health care. A poor peasant has but a 10 per cent chance of being able to see a doctor, while those in the upper income bracket have a 90 per cent chance. No wonder, then, that health standards have declined. By 1995, 45 per cent of children under five suffered some form of malnutrition and half the student-age population suffered spinal deformities. Since the money to purchase insecticides or to fund water purification is scarce, malaria, cholera, dengue fever, diarrhoea and respiratory diseases have spread.[35]

In the mid-1990s the yearly growth rate reached 8 per cent. On the surface, it seemed that Linh had brought about the long-delayed reconstruction:

> the past is being ripped down or painted over everywhere you look in Vietnam's increasingly chaotic capital: from the bridge across the Red River, once a target for American bombers but now the site of two Coca Cola billboards that would do Time Square proud, to the 'Hanoi Hilton', once a jail for [American POWs] . . . but now being torn down to make way for a supermarket, a car park, some offices, and, yes, a real hotel.[36]

But those who struggled for the revolution in the South have to wonder whether their sacrifices were worthwhile. 'We spent our lives to

34 Ibid., pp. 93, 96–9.
35 Ibid., pp. 107–10.
36 'A country, not a war', *The Economist*, 12 August 1995, pp. 37–8.

have a Vietnam that was independent, free, and with happiness for everyone', a retired PLAF major complained. 'Now we have independence, but not happiness. The bureaucrats have the cars and the franchises, the mutilated are poor and have nothing.'[37] Behind the facade of fancy new hotels, Vietnam remains one of the poorest countries in the world.

To the average peasant and worker *doi moi* has meant a restoration of the gross inequalities which characterized colonial Vietnam. Corruption has returned with a vengeance. The party admits the predominance of 'deviant and decadent cadres'. Linh confessed that 'corruption, smuggling and bribery have reached such a widespread and alarming proportion that many people regard them as a national disaster'.[38] Visiting Vietnam in 1989, Sheehan was struck by how government officials tended to 'flaunt corruption so openly':

> a military security officer having an expensive lunch, a gold ball point pen in the breast pocket of his neatly laundered uniform . . . parked in the square out in front of the hotel – a white BMW sedan . . . the license plates, green with white lettering, were the kind issued to Vietnamese civilian government agencies. . . . The capital of the South may have been renamed Ho Chi Minh City, but . . . the ways of Saigon . . . [have] lingered.[39]

In 1996 a party-owned firm was the centre of a scandal in which managers were found to have embezzled nearly US$40 million. The director took US$5.5 million for himself, US$270,000 of which went to his mistress.[40]

Vietnam has demonstrated how difficult it is to be slightly capitalist. The relaxation of stringent rules regarding private enterprise has brought entrepreneurs out of the closet. Their success has made others desperate to share in the spoils. There is no shortage of individuals willing to work hard to improve their lot. For obvious reasons, this phenomenon has been more apparent in the South, where capitalism was never eradicated. Perhaps communism in the South was always a pipe dream, it is simply too alien to southern culture. The vibrancy of the South has deepened the geographical divide, exacerbating the jealousy and insecurity felt by northerners and the alienation felt by southerners. But because the capitalist transformation

37 Sheehan, *Two Cities*, pp. 107–8.
38 Kolko, *Anatomy of a Peace*, pp. 72, 76.
39 Sheehan, *Two Cities*, pp. 99–100.
40 Kolko, *Anatomy of a Peace*, p. 59.

has been kept carefully in check, Vietnam has not undergone the structural transformation of its economy which is so desperately needed. Though a few people have amassed huge fortunes, the conditions for a Malaysian-style industrial explosion have not been established. Yet the people apparently want just that. Every relaxation of economic policy is exploited to the full by an eager populace.

This suggests that the Vietnamese and American people have more in common than was ever realized. The belief in the free market and entrepreneurialism runs deep in both. So does a suspicion of the Chinese and their plans for Southeast Asia. It is ironic that the US went to war to defend the Vietnamese people from an irresistable tide of Chinese communism. Yet the most formidable obstacle to that tide since the war has been, and continues to be, Vietnam. One might speculate how much more formidable a bulwark Vietnam would have been had she received a bit more encouragement from the United States. In the absence of such encouragement, the sense of embattled isolationism found its own justification. While there is no doubt that Vietnamese communists made huge errors after 1975, it is also true that they were encouraged to do so by the actions of the United States.

In 1995 President Bill Clinton decided that the time had come for the United States to normalize relations. He argued that 'normalization and increased contact between Americans and Vietnamese will advance the cause of freedom in Vietnam, just as it did in Eastern Europe and the former Soviet Union'.[41] 'With the Cold War over, we view Vietnam as the product of its own history and the master of its own destiny', Secretary of State Warren Christopher announced in Hanoi on 6 August. 'As many of your countrymen and ours have urged, we look on Vietnam as a country, not a war.' In truth Vietnam's destiny was being shaped not by its people but by multinational corporations. Christopher hoped that 'many more Americans will join companies like Ford, Coca-Cola and Baskin Robbins in betting on Vietnam's future'.[42] The cause of freedom, to which the Americans once devoted men, money and munitions, would now be advanced with soft drinks, ice creams and cars.

It is easy to conclude that Vietnam won the war but lost the peace. In *Sorrow of War*, Bao Ninh describes the bitter harvest which followed victory:

> After 1975, all . . . had quieted. The wind of war had stopped. The branches of conflict had stopped rustling. As we had

41 White House press release, 11 July 1995.
42 State Department press release, 6 August 1995.

won ... then that meant justice had won; that had been some consolation. Or had it? Think carefully; look at your own existence. Look carefully now at the peace we have, painful bitter and sad. . . . this beautiful landscape of calm and peace is an appalling paradox. Justice may have won, but cruelty, death and inhuman violence had also won.[43]

'The ... losers were the people, the sad people, of South Vietnam', Tran Van Don concluded. 'Their future and interests and right of self-determination were ignored or waived away by everyone – Northern leaders, Southern leaders, allies and neutral nations, by a frightened world divided into irreconcilable and implacable blocs.'[44]

But the war did not destroy the spirit of the Vietnamese people, their ambitions and their love of freedom. Those emotions will eventually prove much more destructive of tyranny than bombs, bullets and napalm ever were. In the brave new world of *doi moi*, residents of Ho Chi Minh City have started to use the name 'Saigon' again.[45] Against the backdrop of hundreds of years of tradition, the communist period will some day seem a brief aberration.

43 Bao Ninh, *The Sorrow of War* (London, 1994), pp. 179–80.
44 Tran Van Don, *Our Endless War* (Novato, CA, 1978), pp. 220–1.
45 Sheehan, *Two Cities*, p. 62.

14   REMEMBERING AND FORGETTING

On 29 April 1975 President Gerald Ford announced that the fall of Saigon 'closes a chapter in the American experience'.[1] If so, it is a chapter with an ambiguous ending. At first Americans seemed not to care. 'Consider this', wrote William Ehrhart,

> eight years after I went to Vietnam to prevent the Domino Theory from tumbling into San Diego, the fall of South Vietnam to the communists was reported on the six o'clock news with hardly more impact than the story of a bad fire in Cleveland. The lives of Americans were not altered in any way. Kids continued to play ball in the park, mothers and fathers went to work, and all America geared up feverishly for the coming bicentennial celebration.[2]

'Today it is almost as though the war had never happened', a columnist remarked in late 1975. 'Americans have somehow blocked it out of their consciousness. They don't talk about it.'[3] But the weird silence did not last. Soon, a new Vietnam War, a war to determine its legacy, began. Combatants of various political persuasions battled over the interpretation of America's role, the assessment of her efforts, and the measurement of the war's consequences.

THE UNRETURNING ARMY

Just under 60,000 Americans died in Vietnam. By the standards of modern war, that is a small figure. Ten times as many were lost in the American Civil War, when the US population was much smaller. The war produced no demographic blip, no lost generation, no horde of lonely spinsters unable to find husbands. During the height of

1 Gloria Emerson, *Winners and Losers* (New York, NY, 1992), p. 36.
2 W.D. Ehrhart, *In the Shadow of Vietnam: Essays, 1977–1991* (Jefferson, NC, 1977), p. 49.
3 George Herring, *America's Longest War* (New York, NY, 1986), p. 273.

American involvement in the war (1965–73), over twice as many Americans died as a result of homicides in the US than were killed in Vietnam. It is the individual deaths, not the total, which are important. Sixty thousand separate losses had to be mourned. 'We remember sadly now the things that will not be', Louise Ransom commented about the death of her son; 'the weddings never attended; the children never born; the houses never built and the fields not ploughed; the books never written and the songs not sung.'[4]

Adjustment was all the more difficult because of the dubious meaning of this war. Eleanor Wimbush wrote:

> In our family, in our home, and in our lives, the Vietnam War will never end. There is no enemy that you can see. There are no weapons, no fighting, no hardships. Only an emptiness because a loved one is missing, and the never ending questions of Why? . . .
>
> So Vietnam, Vietnam, what did you take from me? You took my son Bill. You took part of my hopes and dreams. You broke my heart! You took something from me that most people don't even realize they have until they lose it, and that is a feeling of security. . . . You absolutely changed my life, and from then on, nothing was ever the same.[5]

In past wars, the dead were mourned according to a well-defined ritual of remembrance. A national memorial would be established in Washington, with lesser memorials in state capitals and individual cities. Ceremonies on Veteran's Day would pay homage to the dead from all America's wars. But previous wars had been victories, or at least defined as such. 'My grandfather's generation fought in the war to end all wars. My father's generation fought in the war to rid the world of fascists', writes Ehrhart. 'My generation fought in Vietnam to – to what?'[6] Vietnam was at best futile, at worst an outright defeat. The dead had to be remembered, but remembering them involved pain beyond the pain of loss. The remembrance ritual is supposed to aid healing, but because the meaning of the war remained obscure, the path toward healing was not clear.

Many Americans simply decided to forget. John Wheeler found that the 'shock for a lot of us coming home was the gradual realization . . . that there was a social taboo against our experience'. But silence made the wounds of war fester. Jan Scruggs, a Washington lawyer

4 Myra MacPherson, *Long Time Passing* (New York, NY, 1984), p. 411.
5 Eleanor Wimbush, 'In tribute to Bill', in Walter Capps, ed., *The Vietnam Reader* (New York, NY, 1991), pp. 267–8.
6 Ehrhart, *Shadow of Vietnam*, p. 119.

and Vietnam veteran, decided that a memorial could aid healing. He organized the Vietnam Veterans Memorial Fund, which eventually resulted in the dedication of the national memorial on 13 November 1982. The design by Maya Lin – a simple wall listing the names of the dead – was intended to force Americans to confront the war. Located in a prominent position on the Mall in Washington, its very existence affirms the fact that the war was an important episode in American history which deserves consideration. It also gives those who served and those who died something they had hitherto lacked – a sense that their service was recognized. The polished black granite of the wall is appropriately sombre, but also acts as a challenge to those who visit the memorial and see themselves reflected in it. 'No matter how you look at it, you always saw yourself reflected back among the names', Wheeler feels. 'No matter who you were, you could no longer deny that you shared responsibility. You realized that you had to learn from this war, that you could not escape its pain.'[7]

The V-shaped structure is a physical manifestation of the war's equivocal nature. But while the memorial does not prescribe a meaning for the war, it is supposed to aid the search for meaning. The two arms of the wall are symbolically closed by the presence of the observer. 'It is not meant to be cheerful or happy', Lin wrote, 'but to bring out in people the realization of loss and a cathartic healing process.'[8] This healing is both individual and collective. Visitors undergo a personal process of healing, but also participate in a collective purgation, thus counteracting the repression of war experience.

> The names of the dead wait here for the living to come close and touch them. But as the Wall gives them to us, it also takes them away again, for touching the names only makes us feel how far away they are. They must remain there, united by their shared catastrophe, while we, the living, must leave, united by our shared grief.[9]

The Wall's open-ended, deliberately ambiguous message did not suit everyone. Some felt that the war dead deserved an unequivocal display of gratitude and homage. One West Point graduate and Vietnam veteran called it an 'open urinal'.[10] The debate over the memorial is

7 John Wheeler, *Touched with Fire* (New York, NY, 1984), pp. 95, 155.

8 Lisa Capps, 'The Memorial as symbol and agent of healing', in Capps, ed., *Vietnam Reader*, p. 280.

9 James Quay, 'Epilogue', in Grace Sevy, ed., *The American Experience in Vietnam* (Norman, OK, 1989), p. 301.

10 Rick Atkinson, *The Long Grey Line* (London, 1989), p. 468.

a microcosm of the debate over the war. For James Webb, author of *Fields of Fire*, the wall is nothing more than a 'black ditch for the dead' which suggests a reluctance to accept the heroic sacrifice and nobility of the war. 'It was supposed to be a proper hero's edifice. It was *not* supposed to be the Vietnam *Dead* Memorial. It was supposed to be the Vietnam *War* Memorial.'[11]

Partly in response to critics like Webb, it was decided that Lin's original design would be altered, much to her disgust. A more traditional statue depicting three soldiers – one caucasian, one black, one hispanic – was added in a grove of trees 70 feet from the southwest corner of the wall. The statue, according to its sculptor, Frederick Hart, recognizes that 'in an age of doubt and selfishness, millions of Americans found their country worth fighting – and dying – for'.[12] Some would call the compromise a fudge. Indeed, the two memorials do not juxtapose well, but their incongruity symbolizes the war's mixed message: heroism and ignominy, nobility and futility. It is also a metaphor for the way the war continues to divide America.

The Wall has become a place of pilgrimage not just for those who lived through the war, but also for those born after it who are perplexed by its meaning. It provides, according to Scruggs, an opportunity for 'decompression':

> For remembering youth and innocence. For talking and thinking. For telling the story of the guy who walked point instead of you and died. For seeing a familiar face and shouting, 'Is that you! Is that really you?' . . . For finally breaking down. For finding that piece of yourself that had been missing.[13]

Some people go to touch the name of a lost loved one. Others go simply to absorb the enormity of the Vietnam experience. Some take rubbings of individual names, or leave letters, flowers, or mementos to the dead. Bruce Weigl visited 'to find the names of those we lost in the war, as if by tracing the letters cut into the granite we could find what was left of ourselves'.[14]

THE TROUBLED AND SCORNED

It is not uncommon to be approached, while walking in an American city, by a homeless person who strengthens his appeal for charity by

11 MacPherson, *Long Time Passing*, p. 549.
12 Jan Scruggs, *To Heal a Nation* (New York, NY, 1985), p. 125.
13 Ibid., p. 144.
14 Bruce Weigl, 'Welcome home', *The Nation* 235 (17 November 1982), p. 549.

claiming to be a Vietnam veteran. Some of these claims are genuine, but often it is obvious that the individual is not nearly old enough to have fought. Yet the gullible are taken in; the appeal is effective because the pathetic homeless person, unshaven and dressed in rags, accords with a common image of the Vietnam veteran.

This image has been exaggerrated in the popular media through films like *Taxi Driver* (1976), *Tracks* (1976), *Who'll Stop the Rain* (1978) and a host of TV movies in which service in Vietnam is effective shorthand for an erosion of sanity and self-respect. The depth of mental decay reinforces the war's futility. It is almost as if the public seems uncomfortable with the idea that a man might pass through the Vietnam experience and emerge sane and well-adjusted. One veteran complained how 'Whenever I go to any Vietnam function, it seems like the news media picks out the dirtiest, nastiest-looking vet they can find, and they use him to represent us. But that's not us.'[15]

It was not always so. In June 1968, when the war still retained some popularity, George Gallup published an article entitled 'What combat does to our men'. A survey of 140 Vietnam veterans led him to the conclude:

> These 18 to 25 year olds command respect because they
> respect themselves. They have gained self-confidence, firmed up
> their goals. They have learned to follow and to lead, to accept
> responsibility and to be responsible for others. While only
> 26 per cent wanted to go to Vietnam in the first place, 94 per
> cent, having returned, say they are glad for the experience.
> What kind of citizens will they be? Judging by the cross section
> we talked to, the answer is: superior.[16]

It seems then that the image of the troubled and scorned Vietnam veteran is itself a product of postwar disillusionment. A war so horrible, so devoid of purpose, and in the end so futile, must, in other words, have produced a bumper crop of psychological casualties.

The evidence for a ravaged generation of veterans is compelling. According to some psychologists, 80 per cent of veterans have not 'worked through' the experience and 15 per cent are seriously disordered.[17] Phillip Caputo was one of those mildly afflicted:

> I had all the symptoms of *combat veteranitis*: an inability to
> concentrate, a childlike fear of the darkness, a tendency to tire

---

15 Bergerud, *Red Thunder, Tropic Lightning* (New York, NY, 1994), p. 320.
16 Emerson, *Winners and Losers*, p. 196.
17 MacPherson, *Long Time Passing*, pp. 191–3.

easily, chronic nightmares, an intolerance of loud noises – especially doors slamming and cars backfiring – and alternating moods of depression and rage that came over me for no apparent reason. Recovery has been less than total.[18]

There has been a higher than normal incidence of crime, drug addiction, homelessness and suicide among veterans. In 1971 it was found that 26 per cent of veterans had used drugs after returning, with 7 per cent using heroin or cocaine. The Office for Veterans Action in New York City estimated that in the city alone 30,000 to 45,000 veterans were heroin addicts. Another study has suggested that, among those who saw combat, 24 per cent were subsequently imprisoned, often for a drug-related crime.[19]

> When I came back to America . . . I was doing a lot of stick-ups. Because I wanted that *thing*. Stuff didn't bother me, like what happens if you get shot. Fuck that. I been shot. Being in trouble doesn't bother you. Big fucking deal. How bad can it be? . . . It wasn't the money . . . It was like being in Nam again. I had a chance to get shot at and a chance to shoot other people. That was the only thing I knew. . . . So I was playing Russian Roulette with life here in America, racing toward the death wheel without even knowing it.[20]

The White House task force on veterans discovered that suicides among institutionalized Vietnam veterans was 23 per cent higher than among other institutionalized patients from the same age group.[21] It is claimed, albeit according to dubious accounting, that at least 60,000 veterans have committed suicide, more than were killed in the war itself.[22] But, given the notorious unreliability of such statistics, it is safe to conclude that the argument over suicides is a better indicator of the passions the war has aroused than of the damage it has actually caused.

By 1980 the American Psychiatric Association saw fit to give the condition a new name: post-traumatic stress disorder (PTSD). According to some estimates, over one-quarter of those who served in Vietnam, or around 829,000, are affected to varying degrees.[23] Yet less than 300,000 actually experienced combat. This fact alone raises

18 Phillip Caputo, *A Rumor of War* (New York, NY, 1977), p. 4.

19 MacPherson, *Long Time Passing*, p. 53.

20 Mark Baker, *Nam* (New York, NY, 1981), p. 248.

21 MacPherson, *Long Time Passing*, p. 252.

22 See, for instance, the 'Suicide wall' website at http://www.suicidewall.com/vets/.

23 R.A. Kulka *et al.*, *Trauma and the Vietnam War Generation* (New York, NY, 1990), p. v.

the possibility that many cases are bogus. Give an ailment a name and you assign it legitimacy. Today, victims of automobile accidents and witnesses to violent crimes also lay claim to PTSD. The ailment dovetails nicely with the 'victim culture' in which a sense of personal blame is avoided by looking outward for explanations for one's predicament. Testifying before the US Senate Committee on Veteran Affairs, Dr John F. Wilson, an expert on PTSD, outlined the factors particular to this war which contributed to this epidemic:

> send a young man fresh out of high school to an unpopular, controversial guerrilla war far away from home. Expose him to intensely stressful events, some so horrible that it would be impossible to really talk about them later to anyone else except fellow 'survivors'. To ensure maximal stress, you would create a one year tour of duty during which the combatant flies to and from the war zone singly, *without* a cohesive, intact, and emotionally supportive unit with high morale. You would also create the one year rotation to instill a 'survivor mentality' which would undercut the process of ideological commitment to winning the war and seeing it as a noble cause. Then . . . you would rapidly remove the combatant and *singly* return him to his front porch *without* an opportunity to sort out the meaning to the experiences with the men in his unit. No homecoming welcome or victory parades. Ah, but yet, since you are demonic enough, you make sure the veteran is stigmatized and portrayed to the public as a 'drug-crazed psychopathic killer'. By virtue of clever selection by the Selective Service System, the veteran would be unable to easily re-enter the mainstream of society because he is undereducated and lacks marketable job skills.
>
> Further, since the war itself was so difficult, you would want to make sure that there were no supportive systems in society for him, especially among health professionals at VA hospitals who would find his nightmares and residual war-related anxieties unintelligible. Finally you would want to establish a GI Bill with inadequate benefits to pay for education and training, coupled with an economy of high inflation and unemployment.
>
> Last, but not least, you would want him to *feel* isolated, stigmatized, unappreciated and exploited for volunteering to serve his country.[24]

24 MacPherson, *Long Time Passing*, p. 189.

Though the ailment undoubtedly exists, Wilson's explanation for it seems a bit too cut and dried. He criticizes the one-year tour, which other experts cite as one of the main factors which kept men sane.[25] Would a longer tour actually have improved mental health? Furthermore, since 1865 all American wars have been fought in strange faraway countries by young under-educated men. All wars involve horrible, stressful events. That is war.

A war recognized to be horrible produces a bumper harvest of psychological casualties. Each proves the other. Those who believe that this war produced a unique epidemic of PTSD are wont to quote statements from veterans like the following as proof of the war's corrosive effect upon the psyche:

> My wife was 22 and I was 29 when it all began. When it was over, five years later, my wife was 27 and I was an old man.[26]

> I had a sense of power. A sense of destruction . . . In the Nam you realized that you had the power to take a life. You had the power to rape a woman and nobody could say nothing to you. That godlike feeling you had was in the field. It was like I was a god.[27]

> I seen so much I just forgot how to cry. I can't cry about anything ever. And I can't get close to anyone ever.[28]

> Seven winters have slipped away,
> the war still follows me.
> Never in anything have I found
> a way to throw off the dead.[29]

But these statements could in truth have been made by any veteran of any war. Vietnam was not particularly unusual; only its perception is unique. War destroys not just lives, but also minds. Some minds heal, some do not. The apparent ubiquity of mental casualties may quite possibly relate not to the vile nature of this war, but to the fact that, because of the one-year tour, a very large number of men actually served, even if relatively few died.

Long Time Passing, by Myra MacPherson, is a eulogy to the 'haunted generation' of the Vietnam era. Naturally, sufferers of PTSD

---

25 See Chapter 11, p. 287.
26 Emerson, *Winners and Losers*, p. 25.
27 Loren Baritz, *Backfire* (New York, NY, 1985), p. 291.
28 MacPherson, *Long Time Passing*, p. 34.
29 Gerald McCarthy, 'The sound of guns', in Ehrhart, *Shadow of Vietnam*, p. 90.

347

who have endured 'years of neglect or harassment' figure large in her tale of martyrdom.[30] The book is dramatic and deeply disturbing, but its drama camouflages suspect evidence, warped analysis and excessive reliance upon anecdote. Bitter vignettes about ravaged veterans are presented as evidence of an epidemic of war-related torment. In contrast, Eric Dean, in *Shook Over Hell: Post-Traumatic Stress, Vietnam and the Civil War*, carefully sifts through the evidence of actual PTSD cases, and dispassionately assesses the treatment, assistance, reception and social programmes accorded to Vietnam veterans. By comparing them with veterans of the American Civil War, he demonstrates that the Vietnam experience was by no means unique. Recent veterans have, in many ways, received better treatment than that which was available to returning servicemen from any previous war. The apparent epidemic of PTSD, according to Dean, has arisen because of the unspecific nature of the disease, the postwar victim culture and the fact that the image of such a psychologically destructive war fits into the ideological agenda of certain groups. Yet despite the brilliance of Dean's book, it is likely that MacPherson's will continue to have a greater impact, for the simple reason that her myths harmonize with what many Americans want to believe about this war.[31]

Armchair psychiatrists who wring their hands at the epidemic of PTSD lack a sense of perspective. In the Second World War, only 800,000 US ground forces saw direct combat, but 1,393,000 men suffered psychiatric symptoms serious enough to keep them out of action for some period. In the Army, psychiatric ailments kept 504,000 men permanently out of the battle lines. Of these, 330,000 eventually received discharges for psychiatric reasons. In Korea, 17 per cent of the total American combat force was killed, but 24 per cent received treatment for psychiatric conditions. By a similar accounting, the figures for Vietnam are 16 per cent of the combat force killed, and just 12.6 per cent psychiatric casualties. In other words, in every war during this century *except* Vietnam, a soldier was more likely to become a psychiatric casualty than to be killed.[32]

30 MacPherson, *Long Time Passing*, p. 577.

31 See Eric T. Dean, *Shook Over Hell: Post-Traumatic Stress, Vietnam, and the Civil War* (Cambridge, MA, 1997), passim.

32 Joseph P. Martino, 'Vietnam and Desert Storm: learning the right lessons from Vietnam for the post-Cold War era', 1996 Vietnam Symposium, Texas Tech University Vietnam Center website. Martino further points out that 'This situation is not unique to U.S. forces. During the 1973 Yom Kippur war, 30% of the casualties suffered by the Israeli Defense Forces were psychiatric casualties.'

The above figures admittedly pertain to cases diagnosed and treated during the war, not to those which developed afterwards. It is in this area that Vietnam is most often cited as unique. The reasons for this postwar epidemic are very often put down to neglect and to the hostile environment which the soldier encountered upon return. But it is difficult to prove conclusively the uniqueness of the post-1973 period since adequate data is seldom available from other wars. But the observations of Major-General Smedley Butler of the US Marine Corps, written in 1936, are germane:

> I have visited 18 governmental hospitals for veterans. In them are a total of about 50,000 destroyed men . . . men who were the pick of the nation 18 years ago. . . . Boys with a normal viewpoint were taken out of the fields and offices and factories and classrooms and put into the ranks. There they were remolded; they were made over; they were made to 'about face'; to regard murder as the order of the day. They were put shoulder to shoulder and, through mass psychology, they were entirely changed. We used them for a couple of years and trained them to think nothing at all about killing or being killed.
>
> Then, suddenly, we discharged them and told them to make another 'about face!' This time they had to do their own readjusting, *sans* mass psychology, *sans* officers' aid and advice, *sans* nation-wide propaganda. We didn't need them anymore. So we scattered them about without any speeches or parades.
>
> Many, too many, of these fine young boys are eventually destroyed, mentally, because they could not make that final 'about face' alone.[33]

The more widespread recognition of psychiatric ailments which exists today in comparison to Smedley's time may ironically mean that the post-Vietnam 'epidemic' can be explained not by neglect but by greater concern for the veteran's welfare. Concentration on the casualties of the Vietnam War has also produced a skewed picture of its effects. A 1977 study revealed that Vietnam veterans had a higher median weekly income than their civilian peers, and a better standard of education than any veteran group from any previous war. They used the GI Bill to fund higher education to a larger extent than did veterans of Korea or the Second World War.[34] There is no doubt that Vietnam produced

33 Jo Knox and David Price, 'Healing America's warriors: vet centers and the social contract', 1996 Vietnam Symposium, Texas Tech University Vietnam Center website.
34 Eric T. Dean, 'The myth of the troubled and scorned Vietnam veteran', *Journal of American Studies* 26 (1992), pp. 64, 66.

a huge crop of men who were seriously damaged by their experience. But these casualties are proof only of war's horrible harvest, not of the peculiarly obscene nature of this war. In all wars a chasm of experience develops between those who served and those who did not. 'In return for all your terror, the prairies stretch out, arrogantly unchanged', wrote Tim O'Brien on his return to Minnesota.[35] A veteran of Gettysburg could have written the same thing.

THE MIA MYTH

On 17 July 1991 Americans opened their newspapers to find a photograph allegedly showing three American servicemen still held in Vietnam. Names were soon given to the individuals when three POW families each identified a relative. Computer imaging provided 'convincing' evidence that the men were indeed John Robertson, Albro Lundy Jr and Larry James Stevens, as the families claimed. The media gorged itself on the case for about six months. One poll found that 69 per cent of Americans believed that Vietnam was still holding live POWs; 52 per cent that the government was not doing enough to recover them. 'Bring on Rambo' went a headline in the *Wall Street Journal* on 2 August.[36]

The photo in fact came from an article about three Russian bakers published 60 years before in an obscure Soviet propaganda journal. Moustaches had been airbrushed in, and a sign proclaiming the benefits of collective farming airbrushed out. Further hoaxes surfaced around the same time. A photo purporting to show Daniel Borah Jr, another POW, turned out to be of a Laotian highlander; a second, supposedly of Donald Carr, was in fact of a German bird smuggler in a Bangkok bird sanctuary. The scams worked because the American public wanted to believe that POWs were still alive.

The 1973 Paris Peace Agreements committed the United States to 'healing the wounds of war'. It was understood that reconstruction aid would total at least US$3.25 billion, a figure confirmed in a secret letter from Nixon to Pham Van Dong on 1 February. But the Nixon administration was already constructing a route by which to escape its commitments. In early February, Kissinger presented the Vietnamese with 80 files of 'individuals who we had reason to believe had been captured', but were not included among the list of 587 POWs

---

35 Tim O'Brien, *If I Die in a Combat Zone* (London, 1989), p. 203.
36 H. Bruce Franklin, 'Who's behind the MIA scam – & why', *The Nation*, 7 December 1992, pp. 700–2.

who would come home under Operation Homecoming. In the following September, Kissinger told the Senate, during hearings to confirm his appointment as Secretary of State, that, because the Vietnamese had not responded satisfactorily to American demands for information on POWs, 'we cannot proceed in certain areas such as economic aid'. This was, it appears, a cleverly constructed trap. The figure of 80 was significantly higher than any earlier official estimates of unresolved cases – the highest previous total was 56. In an interview with the *New York Times* in 1992, Roger Shields, a Pentagon official who handled the issue in 1973, admitted that Kissinger had deliberately included some cases which he knew Hanoi could not resolve. By creating a problem which defied solution, the administration could continue to use the issue as justification for denying aid.[37]

Nixon and Kissinger failed to realize that they might eventually be caught in the trap they had themselves set for Hanoi. By keeping the issue alive, the government left itself (and future administrations) vulnerable to charges that it was failing American captives held illegally in Indochina. As H. Bruce Franklin writes, the bogus issue '[fed] the paranoia of true believers, thus turning the sleeping giant into a Frankenstein's monster'.[38] The monster began to stir in the 1980s. Curiosity was aroused when sensational articles in *Soldier of Fortune* magazine described efforts to rescue Americans held captive in Laotian prisons. Rumour, gossip and misinformation fed an avalanche of controversy. The frequency of such stories lent credence to their veracity; the gullible naturally concluded that there had to be some truth amid the rumour. Passions were kept stoked with a plethora of books and films on the subject, among them the *Rambo* fantasies. POW/MIA flags, which bloomed on homes across America, expressed a widespread patriotic distrust of the government. Modern-day snake oil merchants used sophisticated marketing techniques to fund fraudulent recovery raids.

The issue was given further credence by the National Security Council, the National League of POW/MIA Families, and the Defense Intelligence Agency (DIA), each of which derived advantage from manipulating the vulnerable and spreading rumour. The Reagan administration, always sensitive to the benefits of a 'good cause', joined the populist bandwagon. Sedgwick Tourison, who worked for the DIA at the time, felt that, under external pressure, 'the Defense Department changed its operative assumption from a position that all

37 Ibid., p. 703.
38 Ibid.

351

unaccounted-for Americans were dead to a position that someone, no one knew whom, might be alive somewhere, but no one knew where'.[39] In Vietnam and Laos, unscrupulous operators were quick to exploit the opportunity for financial gain. A roaring trade in 'bone selling' developed. Some Vietnamese purchased bones from corrupt traders in the mistaken belief that they would improve their chances of emigration to the US if they possessed evidence of missing servicemen. Reports of sightings or 'significant finds' increased 20-fold in a year. In 1983 six DIA full-time analysts each handled 150 unresolved cases. By 1988, the staff had increased to fourteen, each with the same case-load.[40]

Every case, no matter how incredible, had to be investigated. One Eurasian charlatan who called himself Johnny King made a small fortune selling wild stories about missing servicemen. According to Tourison, the paperwork King generated eventually filled an entire filing drawer at the DIA. There were inevitable tragedies and occasional farce. Hsu Hsu Bin, an ethnic Chinese resident in Vietnam, had the misfortune of appearing caucasian. Even though he never claimed to be an American, he was held in a prison for two years by Vietnamese officials who thought he might have some value. In another case, the DIA investigated claims that American POWS had been abducted in a flying saucer.

In April 1991 President George Bush offered Vietnam a two-year timetable for normalizing relations. This alarmed a group of right-wing Senators led by Jesse Helms, who were determined to block normalization. The following May, Helms, acting in the name of all Republicans on the Senate Foreign Relations Committee, released a 100-page report entitled *An Examination of US Policy Toward POW/MIAs*, which included the totally unfounded claim that 5,000 US prisoners had been abandoned in Indochina. It further alleged a complicated and sustained conspiracy to cover up this 'fact'. Deputy Assistant Secretary of Defense Carl Ford later claimed that 'to catalogue the inaccuracies [in the report] would require a document of equal length'. Yet by July, over 100,000 copies (bearing the seal of the US Senate) had been produced and distributed at taxpayers' expense.[41] Despite this blitz of misinformation, the Helms campaign was losing steam by mid-summer. It was then that the photo of Robertson, Lundy and Stevens was released to the media, an interesting coincidence.

The Senate stepped in, setting up the Select Committee on POW/MIA Affairs, chaired by the highly respected Vietnam veteran Senator

39 Sedgwick Tourison, 'Let's sell the bones: the marketing of America's missing in action', 1996 Vietnam Symposium, Texas Tech University Vietnam center website.
40 Ibid.
41 Franklin, 'Who's behind the MIA scam', pp. 685, 700, 702.

John Kerry. Helms managed to pack the committee with members sympathetic to his cause. Under enormous pressure to demonstrate his credibility to right-wingers, Kerry asked Tourison for a list of cases which presented the best possibility of survival on the part of the missing serviceman, based on information known in 1973. Kerry wanted to press the Vietnamese government for an accounting of these cases. Tourison eventually found that the cases which presented the best possibility for survival were without exception ones which concerned 'individuals who we now have a strong basis for believing had died long before 1973'. When Kerry received this report, the following conversation ensued:

> 'Wait a minute, Wick, I want to see the best cases, the very best ones.'
> 'That's what you're looking at, Senator.'
> 'But these guys are all dead! You don't understand, Wick, I want to see the ones about the guys that might still be alive.'
> 'Senator, these are the best.'

In June 1992 the Kerry committee came up with a figure of '244 Americans who did not return at Operation Homecoming, but who were or should have been recorded in captivity'. The figure appears to have been plucked from mid-air.[42]

By early 1992, the MIA lobby had been whipped into such a frenzy of indignation that only a live body of a POW would have quelled the disquiet. The government's failure to produce one left it open to charges of cover-up. What is ironic is that the Kerry committee eventually criticized former Nixon administration officials, including Kissinger, for pretending that there were no prisoners left in Vietnam after Operation Homecoming. Yet those very officials were responsible for creating the controversy in the first place.

The debate has proved another battle line between groups arguing the legacy of the war. Few seem to realize what a MIA actually is. Captain Douglas L. Clarke calls the term an 'accounting limbo':

> It reflects a lack of knowledge concerning an individual rather than being truly descriptive of his condition. In only the most isolated and bizarre cases ... are men able to evade capture in enemy territory for any length of time. Virtually all MIAs are either dead or in enemy hands from the day they disappear.[43]

42 Tourison, 'Let's sell the bones'.
43 Douglas L. Clarke, *The Missing Man* (Washington, DC, 1981), p. 1.

A soldier can be listed as MIA if he is the victim of a direct hit from an artillery shell and nothing remains of the body to establish identification. An airman whose plane explodes and plunges into the sea is so listed if his body is not found. It is well to remember that the officially accepted figure of 2,546 MIAs in 1973 represents just 4 per cent of those killed, a testimony to the diligent efforts taken to recover casualties. MIAs from the Second World War still unaccounted for total 78,750, or 19.4 per cent, and 8,300 from Korea, or 15 per cent.[44]

In 1975 the House Select Committee on Missing Persons in Southeast Asia asked the Pentagon and State Department to comb the list of 2,546 MIAs for individuals who might have been captured. A report came back listing just 36. The committee then concluded that there was evidence of capture for only eleven of the men, all of whom were probably dead, except for Robert Garwood, a shady figure who apparently defected to the North, then escaped from Vietnam in 1979.[45] From eleven men in 1975, the number of suspect MIA cases rose to 5,000 in 1991. The latter figure is an accurate measure of the unscrupulousness of many participants in the debate, who have cruelly manipulated the grief of POW/MIA families for political or monetary gain. Though the recent normalization of relations with Vietnam has defused much of the volatility of the issue, the problem will not go away as long as there is money to be made from it.[46]

A NOBLE CAUSE?

While this book was being written an argument raged, briefly but fiercely, on an e-mail discussion list devoted to the 1960s. Country Joe MacDonald, balladeer of the anti-war movement, proposed that Vietnam veterans should be invited to celebrations marking the 30th anniversary of the Summer of Love in 1997. MacDonald wanted former hippies, activists and soldiers to join hands in a symbolic healing. For this blasphemous suggestion, poor Country Joe was judged a traitor to the movement. A virulent debate about the nature of heroism in the Vietnam era unfolded. Most discussants argued that the

---

44 Frances Arlene Leonard, 'Prisoners of war, missing in action', in James S. Olson, ed., *The Vietnam War: Handbook of the Literature and Research* (Westport, CT, 1993), p. 476.

45 One inevitably finds Garwood, a publicity addict and notorious liar, at the bottom of many MIA hoaxes.

46 For an alternative (and much more sensationalist) view of the MIA controversy, see Monika Jensen-Stevenson and William Stevenson, *Kiss the Boys Goodbye* (London, 1990).

only real heroes were the peace protesters, thus presenting a case for their own inclusion in the noble pantheon. 'The war in Vietnam, as we said then . . . was a crime against humanity', one correspondent argued. 'And, like it or not . . . the US soldiers who fought in that war were all, to one degree or another, compliant accomplices to that crime.'[47] One has to be impressed with minds which, 30 years after the fact, are still able to see issues in black and white. The wounds of the Vietnam era are slow to heal because many insist upon picking the scabs.

As PAVN troops closed on Saigon, the US Secretary of Defence sent a message to all members of the American armed forces:

> For many of you, the tragedy of Southeast Asia is more than a distant and abstract event. You have fought there; you have lost comrades there; you have suffered there. In this hour of pain and reflection you may feel that your efforts and sacrifices have gone for naught.
>
> That is not the case. When the passions have muted and the history is written, Americans will recall that their armed forces served them well. Under circumstances more difficult than ever before faced by our military services, you accomplished the mission assigned to you by higher authority. In combat you were victorious and you left the field with honor.[48]

For most veterans of the war, these must have seemed, in retrospect, hollow words, promising compassion which proved elusive. For previous generations of soldiers, the nation's gratitude followed automatically after war. But Vietnam veterans had the misfortune of fighting an immoral war and also of losing. 'The left hated us for killing', one veteran remarked, 'and the right hated us for not killing enough.'[49]

This bitterness was echoed by other veterans. 'We went to Vietnam as frightened lonely young men', William Jayne, a Marine rifleman, recalls; 'We came back, alone again, as immigrants to a new world. For the culture we had known dissolved while we were in Vietnam, and the culture of combat we lived in so intensely for a year made us aliens when we returned.'[50] Many told of being spat upon by peace protesters upon their return:

47 Miles Z. Archer to Sixties-L discussion list, 18 August 1997.

48 Emerson, *Winners and Losers*, p. 36.

49 MacPherson, *Long Time Passing*, p. 29.

50 A.D. Horne, *The Wounded Generation: America After Vietnam* (Englewood Cliffs, NJ, 1981), p. 161.

> Walking down the streets of Berkeley, I felt like the man from
> Mars visiting the Earth. Everybody was looking at me. All kinds
> of comments. People spit at me. I was more scared walking
> down that street than I had been in Vietnam. There I had my
> weapon and I could protect myself. But they had taken my
> weapon away. These people looked like they wanted to kill me
> more than the Viet Cong did.[51]

Fred Downs tells of being confronted by a stranger who asked if his
amputated hand was the result of the Vietnam War. When Downs
answered in the affirmative, 'Serves you right!' came the reply.[52] Many
people found it impossible to divorce their opposition to the war from
their feelings toward those who had to fight it, even if, in some cases,
that opposition was a late developing thing. Others who used every
devious means to escape the draft assigned to themselves a mantle of
noble pacifism, as if joining the National Guard or fabricating a dis-
ability made one a modern-day Bertrand Russell.

Attitudes began to change in the 1980s. Recognition of the rav-
ages of PTSD, the commissioning of the Vietnam memorial, films like
Born on the Fourth of July and *Letters Home*, and the war novels of
Tim O'Brien, Larry Heinemann and Philip Caputo brought much-
needed exposure to the sacrifices soldiers had made and the suffering
they still endured. The veteran became an icon suited to the 1980s, an
underdog who, though let down by a nefarious government and a fickle
population, still manages to maintain his dignity and self-esteem. The
message was driven home in Billy Joel's 'Goodnight Saigon' and Bruce
Springsteen's 'Born in the USA', both of which tell of a rough-hewn
working-class patriotism cruelly exploited.

But the veteran still remained vulnerable to manipulation by right
and left. Ronald Reagan was not above this sort of manipulation,
though he would probably have resorted to his distinctive 'Aw, shucks'
innocence if so accused. During the 1980 presidential election campaign he told 5,000 delegates gathered at the Veterans of Foreign
Wars (VFW) Convention that 'It's time we recognized that ours was,
in truth, a noble cause'.[53] Delegates responded with sustained, enthusiastic applause. For the first time in its history, the VFW officially
endorsed a presidential candidate.

---

51 Baker, *Nam*, p. 221.
52 Frederick Downs, *The Killing Zone: My Life in the Vietnam War* (New York,
NY, 1978), p. 11.
53 *Washington Post*, 19 August 1980.

Reagan's advisers had counselled him not to pour salt on unhealed Vietnam wounds. But Reagan, the quintessential campaigner, trusted his populist instincts. The speech certainly pleased the constituency to which it was addressed and the millions of like-minded veterans of earlier wars. It also gave a signal, to the American people and the world beyond, of a new foreign policy. America, Reagan promised, would no longer be ashamed of her anti-communist instincts nor would she be afraid of following them forcefully. It is no coincidence that Rambo and Reagan were popular at the same time. Both suggested that America had recovered from the 'profound moral crisis' of the Carter years. As Sylvester Stallone explained:

> This country has really needed to flex its muscles. This country is like a child that developed too quickly and became self-conscious of its power. The other little nations were pulling at us, saying, 'You're bullying. Don't tread on us.' So we pulled back. . . . And what happened, as usual, is people took kindness for weakness, and America lost its esteem. Right now, it's just flexing. You might say America has gone back to the gym.[54]

During a ceremony at the White House in which he bestowed the Medal of Honor upon the Vietnam veteran Sergeant Roy Benavidez, Reagan said of the veterans, 'they were greeted by no parades, no bands, no waving of the flag they so nobly served . . . they came home without victory because they had been denied permission to win. . . . Never again do we send an active fighting force to a country unless it is for a cause we intend to win.'[55]

Reagan had made belligerence respectable again. It was acceptable once more to believe in America's right to enforce her will around the globe, since her cause was always 'noble'. The domino principle was again used to work its magic: 'the government of El Salvador', Reagan argued, 'is on the front line in a battle that is really aimed at the very heart of the Western hemisphere'.[56] But the bravado which he encouraged was in the end as dangerous as the neurotic insecurity of the immediate post-Vietnam era. The world did not need a weak America, but nor did it need an America so confident in itself that it could believe that a three-way deal involving arms, drugs and hostages was morally right if the cause was just. Nor did Reagan do

54 Kevin Hillstrom and Laurie Collier Hillstrom, *The Vietnam Experience* (Westport, CT, 1998), pp. 249–50.
55 Walter Capps, *The Unfinished War* (Boston, MA, 1990), p. 147.
56 Lloyd C. Gardner, *A Covenant with Power* (New York, NY, 1984), p. 231.

much for veterans beyond exploiting their martyrdom. 'Trickle down' Reaganomics had little to offer those on the margins of society. And veterans were not well-served by a reopening of the Vietnam debate. Their plight needed to be separated from argument over the meaning of and justification for the war.

Leaving aside those stubborn veterans of the protest movement, most Americans now respect those who fought in Vietnam, even if they do not respect the cause for which they fought. The soldiers themselves seem also to have progressed a long way along the painful road toward adjustment.

> I used to blame Vietnam for my problems, but I don't do that now. When I got back from Vietnam I tried to kill myself. . . . For a long time I was ashamed of being a Vietnam veteran, afraid of telling people I had been to the Nam. Not any more, though. I have a flag on my bike and decals saying I served in Vietnam. The truckers honk their horns at me. I am proud.[57]

At first, they did not feel comfortable joining the VFW or the American Legion, since their war stories did not seem heroic. But those veterans eventually realized that the qualities evident at Anzio were also evident at Khe Sanh, even if the end result was not the same. Their similarities to earlier generations of soldiers are more significant than their differences. By 1984, the American Legion had 750,000 Vietnam veterans on its rolls, one-quarter of its total membership. The VFW had another 500,000, a similar proportion.[58]

Coming to terms with the war has turned out to be much more difficult. In his inauguration address in 1989, Bush expressed regret at the way the Vietnam War 'cleaves us still. But, friends, that war began in earnest a quarter of a century ago; and surely the statute of limitations has been reached. This is a fact: the final lesson of Vietnam is that no great nation can long afford to be sundered by a memory.'[59] Bush was being either foolishly naive or cynically manipulative. A quarter century is not a long time for an individual or for a nation. Memories can be painful, but denying them does not eradicate their effect. Most Americans *want* to remember the war; it is their past, and has shaped their identity. Bush hoped to expunge a recent painful memory in order to revive an older, glorious myth of a triumphant America.

---

57 Stanley W. Beesley, ed., *Vietnam: The Heartland Remembers* (Norman, OK, 1987), pp. 155–6.

58 MacPherson, *Long Time Passing*, p. 55.

59 *New York Times*, 21 January 1989.

Americans remember the war vividly and read about it voraciously. They know a great deal about the conflict, but knowledge has not brought understanding. Nearly every American college and university includes within its curriculum a course on the war, but these vary widely in content and often reflect the political persuasion of the instructor. Some present the war as a morality tale exposing a monstrous criminal conspiracy by the imperialist United States, while others exclude all but right-wing interpretations from the syllabus and echo the time-worn complaint about a government stabbing its military in the back. It is perhaps too much to expect that a consensus should have emerged, or that it will ever do so. The debate over the Vietnam War will probably always provide a barometer of the political temper in the United States and of Americans' conception of themselves.

Within the United States, the actions of Vietnam after 1975 have made the wounds of the war harder to heal. In 1979, a group of former anti-war activists, among them Joan Baez, issued 'An Appeal to the Conscience of Vietnam' which criticized its repression and challenged stalwarts of the New Left to take a stand. A counter-appeal appeared in the *New York Times*, signed by, among others, Dave Dellinger and William Sloane Coffin, two of the most outspoken anti-war activists. It argued that 'The present government of Vietnam should be hailed for its moderation and for its extraordinary effort to achieve reconciliation among all of its peoples'. Baez and her crowd were, it was alleged, establishment stooges manipulated by the CIA. The Dellinger/Coffin group went on to claim that 'if the Vietnamese *had* chosen the course of mass executions and plunder, of political prisoners and torture, it would have been our own strategies of terror which drove them to it'.[60] Moral relativism is the sand in which the ostrich hides his head.

The left has invented a politically correct way to view the war. There are those who feel certain that the only explanation for communist evil is American devilry. Accepting blame for every vile aspect of the war and every injustice of the subsequent peace is apparently America's penance for becoming embroiled in the wrong war. America's guilt absolves the communists of all malfeasance. Their cause becomes noble, the way they achieved it pure. This is bunk. William Calley's guilt, Lyndon Johnson's subterfuge, Robert McNamara's absurdity and William Westmoreland's folly can never excuse the barbarity of Vietnamese communism.

60 Peter Collier and David Horowitz, *Destructive Generation* (New York, NY, 1990), p. 175.

That barbarity has convinced many of America's noble cause. But this is a hypocrite's refuge, since the fate of Vietnam was, in truth, always peripheral to most Americans. Vietnam was a place where the American people acted out their vision of the postwar world and their assumed mastery of it. As Bui Diem, former South Vietnamese ambassador to the United States, recognized:

> Vietnam was regarded primarily as a geopolitical abstraction, a factor in the play of American global interests. That was true about the way the United States intervened in the war with its land army. It was true about the way the United States conducted the war. And it was especially true about the way the United States left the war.[61]

The American vision lacked logic and was impossible to realize. Yankee riches could not buy a Vietnam which the Vietnamese people did not want. Americans were naive, but not evil. Their purpose was idealistic, but the ideals were distinctly American. In this sense, failure was therapeutic and the postwar sense of uncertainty healthy. The American people went to war expecting that they could shape the world in their image. It is fortunate that they did not succeed.

It was a horrible, wasteful, futile war. Defeat weakened the United States and set in motion a generation of self-doubt. But what would victory have brought? Suppose the United States had been able to find the magic formula for defeating the communist revolution. What then? Would the US have gone on to assert its triumphant liberal morality even more forcefully in Africa and Latin America? Defeat was damaging, but victory would have been dangerous. Vietnam brought to an end an era in foreign policy when the American people assumed automatically that they were both totally virtuous and absolutely powerful. Because, afterwards, victory no longer seemed automatic, the US has been more careful in its exercise of power. That is good. Lincoln Steffens once wrote that 'we need some great failures, especially we ever-successful Americans – conscious, intelligent, illuminating failures'.[62] Vietnam was a great, illuminating failure. The world is a better place because America lost. America is also a better place.

61 Robert J. McMahon, *Major Problems in the History of the Vietnam War* (Lexington, MA, 1990), p. 438.
62 Lincoln Steffens, *The Autobiography of Lincoln Steffens* (New York, NY, 1973), p. 788.

BIBLIOGRAPHY

Adair, Gilbert, *Hollywood's Vietnam*, London, 1989

Adams, Sam, *War of Numbers*, South Royalton, VT, 1994

Ambrose, Stephen, *Eisenhower: The President*, London, 1984

Anderson, David L., *Shadow on the White House*, Lawrence, KS, 1993

Anderson, David L., *Trapped by Success: The Eisenhower Administration and Vietnam, 1953–1961*, New York, NY, 1991

Anderson, Terry H., 'American popular music and the war in Vietnam', *Peace and Change* 11 (1986)

Anderson, Terry H., *The Movement and the Sixties*, New York, NY, 1995

Andrews, William R., *The Village War: Vietnam Communist Activities in Dinh Tuong Province, 1960–1964*, Colombus, MO, 1973

Armitage, M.J. and R.A. Mason, *Air Power in the Nuclear Age*, Chicago, IL, 1983

Atkinson, Rick, *The Long Gray Line*, London, 1989

Auslander, H. Ben, ' "If ya wanna end the war and stuff, you gotta sing loud" – a survey of Vietnam-related protest music', *Journal of American Culture* 4 (1981)

Bain, David Haward, *After-Shocks*, London, 1986

Baker, Mark, *Nam*, New York, NY, 1981

Ball, George, *The Past Has Another Pattern*, New York, NY, 1982

Ball, Moya Ann, *Vietnam-on-the-Potomac*, New York, NY, 1992

Bao Ninh, *The Sorrow of War*, London, 1994

Baritz, Loren, *Backfire*, New York, NY, 1985

Barnett, Arnold, *et al.*, 'America's Vietnam casualties: victims of a class war?', *Operations Research* 40 (1992)

Barrett, David M., ed., *Lyndon B. Johnson's Vietnam Papers*, College Station, TX, 1997

Barrett, David M., *Uncertain Warriors*, Lawrence, KS, 1993

Baskir, Lawrence M. and William A. Strauss, *Chance and Circumstance*, New York, NY, 1978

Beesley, Stanley W., ed., *Vietnam: The Heartland Remembers*, Norman, OK, 1987

Bellamy, Christopher, *The Evolution of Modern Land Warfare*, London, 1990

Beresford, Melanie, *Vietnam: Politics, Economics and Society*, London, 1988

Bergerud, Eric, *The Dynamics of Defeat*, Boulder, CO, 1991

Bergerud, Eric, *Red Thunder, Tropic Lightning*, New York, NY, 1994

Berkowitz, W.R., 'The impact of anti-Vietnam demonstrations upon national public opinion and military indicators', *Social Science Research* 2 (1973)

Berman, Larry, *Lyndon Johnson's War*, New York, NY, 1989

Berman, Larry, *Planning a Tragedy*, New York, NY, 1982

Bidwell, Shelford, *Modern Warfare: A Study of Men, Weapons and Theories*, London, 1973

Billings-Yun, Melanie, *Decision Against War: Eisenhower and Dien Bien Phu, 1954*, New York, NY, 1988

Bilton, Michael and Kevin Sim, *Four Hours in My Lai*, London, 1992

Bindas, Kenneth J. and Craig Houston, ' "Takin' care of business": rock music, Vietnam and the protest myth', *The Historian* 52 (1989)

Blum, John Morton, *Years of Discord*, New York, NY, 1991

Borch, Frederic, 'Judge advocates in combat', unpublished manuscript

Boyle, Richard, *Flower of the Dragon*, San Francisco, CA, 1972

Braestrup, Peter, *Big Story*, Novato, CA, 1994

Braestrup, Peter, ed., *Vietnam as History: Ten Years After the Paris Peace Accords*, Washington, DC, 1984

Brands, H.W., *The Wages of Globalism*, New York, NY, 1995

Breines, Wini, 'Review essay', *Feminist Studies* 5 (1979)

Brodie, Fawn, *Richard Nixon: The Shaping of His Character*, Cambridge, MA, 1983

Brower, Charles F., 'Strategic reassessment in Vietnam: the Westmoreland "Alternate Strategy" of 1967–1968', *Naval War College Review* 44 (1991)

Brown, Sam, 'The politics of peace', *Washington Monthly* 2 (August 1970)

Butler, David, *The Fall of Saigon*, New York, NY, 1985

Buttinger, Joseph, *Dragon Embattled*, 2 vols, Newton Abbot, 1973

Buzzanco, Bob, 'The American military's rationale against the Vietnam War', *Political Science Quarterly* 101 (1986)

Cable, Larry, *Unholy Grail*, London, 1991

Capps, Walter, *The Unfinished War*, Boston, MA, 1990

Capps, Walter, ed., *The Vietnam Reader*, New York, NY, 1991

Caputo, Philip, *A Rumor of War*, New York, NY, 1977

Carroll, James, *American Requiem*, Boston, MA, 1996

Charlton, Michael and Anthony Moncrieff, *Many Reasons Why*, New York, NY, 1978

Chanoff, David and Doan Van Toai, *'Vietnam' – A Portrait of its People at War*, London, 1996

Clarke, Douglas L., *The Missing Man*, Washington, DC, 1981

Clausewitz, Karl, *On War*, ed. Anatol Rapaport, Harmondsworth, 1980

Clayton, Anthony, *The Wars of French Decolonization*, London, 1994

Clifford, Clark M., 'A Vietnam reappraisal: the personal history of one man's view and how it evolved', *Foreign Affairs* 47 (July 1969)

Clodfelter, Mark, *The Limits of Air Power: The American Bombing of North Vietnam*, New York, NY, 1989

Collier, Peter and David Horowitz, *Destructive Generation*, New York, NY, 1990

Colson, Charles W., *Born Again*, Old Tappan, NJ, 1976.

Cottle, Thomas J., *Time's Children*, Boston, MA, 1971

Currey, Cecil B., *Edward Lansdale: The Unquiet American*, Boston, MA, 1988

Currey, Cecil B., *Victory at Any Cost*, Washington, DC, 1997

Dalloz, Jacques, *The War in Indochina, 1945–54*, Dublin, 1990

Davidson, Phillip B., *Vietnam at War*, Oxford, 1988

Dean, Eric T., 'The myth of the troubled and scorned Vietnam veteran', *Journal of American History* 26 (1992)

Dean, Eric T., *Shook Over Hell: Post-Traumatic Stress, Vietnam, and the Civil War*, Cambridge, MA, 1997

DeBenedetti, Charles, *An American Ordeal: The Antiwar Movement of the Vietnam Era*, Syracuse, NY, 1990

DeGroot, Gerard J., 'The limits of moral protest and participatory democracy: the Vietnam Day Committee', *Pacific Historical Review* 64 (1995)

DeGroot, Gerard J., 'Ronald Reagan and student unrest in California, 1966–1970', *Pacific Historical Review* 65 (1996)

DeGroot, Gerard J., *Student Protest: The Sixties and After*, London, 1998

Denisoff, R. Serge and Mark Levine, 'The popular protest song: the case of "Eve of Destruction"', *Public Opinion Quarterly* 35 (1971)

Dickstein, Morris, *Gates of Eden: American Culture in the Sixties*, New York, NY, 1977

Divine, Robert A., *The Johnson Years, Vol. II: Vietnam, the Environment and Science*, Lawrence, KS, 1987

Douhet, Giulio, *The Command of the Air*, trans. Dino Ferrari, New York, NY, 1942

Downs, Frederick, *The Killing Zone: My Life in the Vietnam War*, New York, NY, 1978

Duiker, William J., *Sacred War*, New York, NY, 1995

Duiker, William J., *The Communist Road to Power in Vietnam*, Boulder, CO, 1981

Duong Thu Huong, *Novel Without at Name*, London, 1995

Duncanson, Dennis J., *Government and Revolution in Vietnam*, New York, NY, 1968

Dunn, Peter M., *The First Vietnam War*, London, 1985

Edelman, Bernard, *Dear America: Letters Home from Vietnam*, New York, NY, 1985

Elegant, Robert 'How to lose a war', *Encounter* 57 (August 1981)

Emerson, Gloria, *Winners and Losers*, New York, NY, 1992

Ehrhart, W.D., *In the Shadow of Vietnam: Essays, 1977–1991*, Jefferson, NC, 1977

Errington, Elizabeth Jane and B.J.C. McKercher, eds, *The Vietnam War as History*, New York, NY, 1990

Ethell, Jeffrey and Alfred Price, *One Day in a Long War*, London, 1989

Fall, Bernard, *The Two Vietnams*, New York, NY, 1964

Fall, Bernard, *Hell in a Very Small Place*, New York, NY, 1967

Fitzgerald, Frances, *Fire in the Lake*, New York, NY, 1972

Ford, Ronnie E., *Tet 1968: Understanding the Surprise*, London, 1995

Franklin, H. Bruce, 'Who's behind the MIA scam – & why', *The Nation* (7 December 1992)

Freedman, Lawrence, 'Vietnam and the disillusioned strategist', *International Affairs* 72 (1996)

Freedman, Lawrence, *War*, Oxford, 1994

Fulbright, William, *The Arrogance of Power*, London, 1967

Gardner, Lloyd C., *Approaching Vietnam: From World War II through Dien Bien Phu*, New York, NY, 1988

Gardner, Lloyd C., *A Covenant with Power*, New York, NY, 1984

Gardner, Lloyd C., *Pay Any Price*, Chicago, IL, 1995

Garfinkle, Adam, *Telltale Hearts*, Basingstoke, 1995

Gelb, Leslie H. and Richard K. Betts, *The Irony of Vietnam: The System Worked*, Washington, DC, 1979

Gilbert, Marc Jason and William Head, eds, *The Tet Offensive*, Westport, CT, 1996

Gitlin, Todd, *The Sixties: Years of Hope, Days of Rage*, New York, NY, 1989

Goodman, Allan, *The Lost Peace, America's Search for a Negotiated Settlement of the Vietnam War*, Stanford, CA, 1978

Greene, Graham, *The Quiet American*, London, 1973

Grinter, Lawrence E. and Peter M. Dunn, *The American War in Vietnam*, Westport, CT, 1987

Gruner, Elliott, *Prisoners of Culture: Representing the Vietnam Pow*, New Brunswick, NJ, 1993

Gurtov, Melvin, *The First Vietnam Crisis*, New York, NY, 1967

Gustainis, J. Justin, *American Rhetoric and the Vietnam War*, Westport, CT, 1993

Gustainis, J. Justin and Dan Hahn, 'While the whole world watched: rhetorical failures of anti-war protest', *Communication Quarterly* 36 (1988)

Halberstam, David, *The Best and the Brightest*, New York, NY, 1972

Halberstam, David, *Ho*, New York, NY, 1993

Halberstam, David, *The Making of a Quagmire*, New York, NY, 1964

Haldeman, H.R., *The Ends of Power*, New York, NY, 1989

Hallin, Daniel C., *The Uncensored War*, New York, NY, 1986

Halstead, Fred, *Out Now!*, New York, NY, 1978

Hannah, Norman, *The Key to Failure: Laos and the Vietnam War*, Lanham, MD, 1987

Harrison, James P., *The Endless War*, New York, NY, 1989

Hauser, William, *America's Army in Crisis*, Baltimore, MD, 1973

Hayden, Tom, *Reunion*, New York, NY, 1988

Head, William and Lawrence Grinter, eds, *Looking Back on the Vietnam War*, Westport, CT, 1993

Heineman, Kenneth J., *Campus Wars*, New York, NY, 1993

Heinemann, Larry, *Close Quarters*, London, 1987

Heinemann, Larry, *Paco's Story*, London, 1989

Hellman, J., *American Myth and the Legacy of Vietnam*, New York, NY, 1986

Hendrickson, Paul, *The Living and the Dead*, London, 1996

Henggeller, Paul R., *In His Steps: Lyndon Johnson and the Kennedy Mystique*, Chicago, IL, 1991

Herr, Michael, *Dispatches*, New York, NY, 1977

Herring, George C., *America's Longest War*, New York, NY, 1986

Herring, George C., *LBJ and Vietnam*, Austin, TX, 1994

Herring, George C., ed., *The Pentagon Papers*, abridged edn, New York, NY, 1993

Herzog, Tobey C., *Vietnam War Stories: Innocence Lost*, London, 1992

Hess, Gary R., 'The first American commitment in Indochina: the acceptance of the "Bao Dai Solution"', *Diplomatic History* 2 (1978)

Hess, Gary R., 'Franklin D. Roosevelt and Indochina', *Journal of American History* 59 (1972)

Hess, Gary R., 'The military perspective on strategy in Vietnam: Harry G. Summers's *On Strategy* and Bruce Palmer's *The 25 Year War*', *Diplomatic History* 10 (1986)

Hillstrom, Kevin and Laurie Collier Hillstrom, *The Vietnam Experience*, Westport, CT, 1998

Ho Chi Minh, *Selected Writings*, Hanoi, 1973

Holmes, Richard, *Firing Line*, London, 1987

Horne, A.D., *The Wounded Generation: America After Vietnam*, Englewood Cliffs, NJ, 1981

Hunt, Michael, *Lyndon Johnson's War*, New York, NY, 1996

Hunt, Richard A., *Pacification*, Boulder, CO, 1995

Hunt, Richard A. and Richard Shultz, eds, *Lessons from an Unconventional War*, New York, NY, 1982

Huntington, Samuel, 'The bases of accommodation', *Foreign Affairs* 46 (June 1968)

Huntington, Samuel 'Vietnam reappraised', *International Security* 6 (Summer, 1981)

Isaacs, Arnold, *Without Honor: Defeat in Vietnam and Cambodia*, Baltimore, MD, 1983

Isaacson, Walter, *Kissinger*, New York, NY, 1992

Jensen-Stevenson, Monica and William Stevenson, *Kiss the Boys Goodbye*, London, 1990

Joes, Anthony James, *The War for South Viet Nam*, New York, NY, 1989

Johnson, Lady Bird, *White House Diary*, London, 1970

Johnson, Lyndon Baines, *The Vantage Point*, London, 1971

Jones, G.W., 'Population trends and policies in Vietnam', *Population and Development Review* 8 (1982)

Kahin, George McT., *Intervention*, New York, NY, 1986

Kahn, Roger, *The Boys of Summer*, New York, NY, 1972

Kaiser, Charles, *1968 in America*, New York, NY, 1988

Karnow, Stanley, *Vietnam: A History*, Harmondsworth, 1993

Kearns, Doris, *Lyndon Johnson and the American Dream*, London, 1976

Kendrick, Alexander, *The Wound Within*, Boston, MA, 1974

Kimball, Jeffrey P., *Nixon's Vietnam War*, Lawrence, KS, 1998

Kimball, Jeffrey P., ed., *To Reason Why*, New York, NY, 1990

Kinnard, Douglas, *The War Managers*, Wayne, NJ, 1985

Kissinger, Henry, *Diplomacy*, New York, NY, 1994

Kissinger, Henry, 'Domestic structure and foreign policy', *Daedalus* (Spring 1966)

Kissinger, Henry, 'The Viet Nam negotiations', *Foreign Affairs* 47 (January 1969)

Kissinger, Henry, *White House Years*, Boston, MA, 1979

Kitfield, James, *Prodigal Soldiers*, New York, NY, 1995

Klein, Michael, ed., *The Vietnam Era*, London, 1990

Koch, Christopher J., *Highways to a War*, London, 1995

Kolko, Gabriel, *Anatomy of a War*, New York, NY, 1994

Kolko, Gabriel, *Vietnam: Anatomy of a Peace*, London, 1997

Krepinevich, Andrew F., *The Army and Vietnam*, Baltimore, MD, 1986

Kulka, R.A. *et al.*, *Trauma and the Vietnam War Generation*, New York, NY, 1990

La Feber, Walter, 'Roosevelt, Churchill and Indochina, 1942–1945', *American Historical Review* 80 (1975)

Lanning, Michael and Dan Cragg, *Inside the VC and the NVA*, New York, NY, 1992

Lansdale, Edward, 'Vietnam: do we understand revolution?', *Foreign Affairs* 43 (1964)

Lederer, William J. and Eugene Burdick, *The Ugly American*, New York, NY, 1958

Lehrack, Otto, *No Shining Armor*, Lawrence, KS, 1992

Lewy, Guenter, *America in Vietnam*, Oxford, 1978

Littauer, Raphael and Norman Uphoff, eds, *The Air War in Indochina*, Boston, MA, 1972

Lomperis, Timothy J., *From People's War to People's Rule*, Chapel Hill, NC, 1996

Louvre, Alf and Jeffrey Walsh, eds, *Tell Me Lies About Vietnam*, Milton Keynes, 1988

Lunch, William and Peter Sperlich, 'American public opinion and the war in Vietnam', *Western Political Quarterly* 32 (1979)

Marr, David G., *Vietnamese Tradition on Trial, 1920–1945*, Berkeley, CA, 1981

McAdam, Doug, *Freedom Summer*, Oxford, 1988

MacDonald, Peter, *Giap*, London, 1993

McGill, William J., *The Year of the Monkey*, New York, NY, 1982

McMahon, Robert J., *Major Problems in the History of the Vietnam War*, Lexington, MA, 1990

McMaster, H.R., *Dereliction of Duty*, New York, NY, 1997

McNamara, Robert S., *In Retrospect*, New York, NY, 1995

MacPherson, Myra, *Long Time Passing*, New York, NY, 1984

McQuaid, Kim, *The Anxious Years*, New York, NY, 1989

Mangold, Tom and John Penycate, *The Tunnels of Cu Chi*, London, 1986

Mason, Robert, *Chickenhawk*, London, 1983

Melanson, Richard, *Reconstructing Consensus: American Foreign Policy since the Vietnam War*, New York, NY, 1991

Melling, Phil and Jon Roper, eds, *America, France and Vietnam: Cultural History and Ideas of Conflict*, Swansea, 1991

Menashe, Louis and Ronald Radosh, *Teach-Ins: USA*, New York, NY, 1967

Miller, James, *'Democracy is in the Streets': From Port Huron to the Siege of Chicago*, New York, NY, 1987

Moïse, Edwin, 'Land reform and land reform errors in North Vietnam', *Pacific Affairs* 49 (1976)

Moïse, Edwin, *Tonkin Gulf and the Escalation of the Vietnam War*, Chapel Hill, NC, 1996

Moore, Harold G., *We Were Soldiers Once ... and Young*, New York, NY, 1992

Moore, John Norton, ed., *The Vietnam Debate*, Lanham, MD, 1990

Morris, Roger, *An Uncertain Greatness: Henry Kissinger and American Foreign Policy*, New York, NY, 1977.

Moyar, Mark, *Phoenix and the Birds of Prey*, Annapolis, MD, 1997

Nalty, Bernard, ed., *The Vietnam War*, London, 1996

Navarre, Henri, *Agonie de l'Indochine*, Paris, 1956

Newfield, Jack, *Robert Kennedy, A Memoir*, New York, NY, 1988

Newman, John, *JFK and Vietnam*, New York, NY, 1992

Nguyen Cao Ky, *Twenty Years and Twenty Days*, New York, NY, 1976

Nisbet, Robert, 'Who killed the student revolution?', *Encounter* 32 (1970)

Nixon, Richard M., *A New Road for America: Major Policy Statements, March 1970 to October 1971*, New York, NY, 1972

Nixon, Richard M., *The Nixon Presidential Press Conferences*, ed. George W. Johnson, London, 1978

Nixon, Richard M., *RN: The Memoirs of Richard Nixon*, New York, NY, 1978

Nolan, Keith William, *Battle for Hue*, Novato, CA, 1996

Oberdorfer, Don, *Tet!*, New York, NY, 1984

O'Brien, Tim, *Going After Cacciato*, New York, NY, 1980

O'Brien, Tim, *If I Die in a Combat Zone*, London, 1989

O'Brien, Tim, *The Things They Carried*, London, 1991

O'Donnell, Kenneth P. and David F. Powers, *'Johnny, We Hardly Knew Ye'*, Boston, MA, 1970

Olson, James S., *The Vietnam War: Handbook of the Literature and Research*, Westport, CT, 1993

Oudes, Bruce, ed., *From: The President – Richard Nixon's Secret Files*, New York, NY, 1989

Page, Caroline, *US Official Propaganda During the Vietnam War, 1965–1973*, London, 1996

Palmer, Bruce, *The 25 Year War*, New York, NY, 1984

Palmer, David Richard, *Summons of the Trumpet*, Novato, CA, 1978

Paterson, Thomas G., 'Historical memory and illusive victories: Vietnam and Central America', *Diplomatic History* 12 (1988)

Paterson, Thomas G., ed., *Kennedy's Quest for Victory*, New York, NY, 1989

Pfeffer, Richard N., ed., *No More Vietnams: The War and the Future of American Foreign Policy*, New York, NY, 1968.

Pike, Douglas, *PAVN: People's Army of Vietnam*, Novato, CA, 1986

Pike, Douglas, *Viet Cong: The Organization and Techniques of the National Liberation Front of South Vietnam*, Cambridge, MA, 1966

Pimlott, John, *Vietnam: The Decisive Battles*, London, 1990

Pisor, Robert, *The End of the Line: The Siege of Khe Sanh*, New York, NY, 1982

Popkin, Samuel L., 'Pacification: politics and the village', *Asian Survey* 10 (August 1970)

Post, Ken, *Revolution, Socialism and Nationalism in Viet Nam*, 5 vols, Aldershot, 1989

Powers, Thomas, *Vietnam: The War at Home*, Boston, MA, 1984

Race, Jeffrey, *War Comes to Long An*, Berkeley, CA, 1972

Richburg, Keith, 'Back to Vietnam', *Foreign Affairs* 70 (1991)

Rorabaugh, W.J., *Berkeley at War: The 1960s*, Oxford, 1989

Rubin, Jerry, *Do It!*, New York, NY, 1970

Rusk, Dean, *As I Saw It*, New York, NY, 1990

Russell, Norman L., *Suicide Charlie*, Westport, CT, 1993

Safire, William, *Before the Fall*, New York, NY, 1975

Sale, Kirkpatrick, *SDS*, New York, NY, 1973

Salisbury, Harrison, *Behind the Lines*, New York, NY, 1968

Salisbury, Harrison, ed., *The Eloquence of Protest: Voices of the 70s*, Boston, MA, 1972

Santoli, Albert, *Everything We Had: An Oral History of the Vietnam War by Thirty-Three American Soldiers Who Fought It*, New York, NY, 1981

Schandler, Herbert Y., *The Unmaking of a President*, Princeton, NJ, 1977

Schlesinger, Arthur, *The Bitter Heritage: Vietnam and American Democracy, 1941–1966*, Boston, MA, 1967

Schlesinger, Arthur, *Robert Kennedy and His Times*, New York, NY, 1979

Schreiber, E.M., 'Antiwar demonstrations and American public opinion on the war in Vietnam', *British Journal of Sociology* 27 (1976)

Schreiber, E.M., 'Opposition to the Vietnam War among American university students and faculty', *British Journal of Sociology* 24 (1973)

Schuman, Howard, 'Two sources of antiwar sentiment in America', *American Journal of Sociology* 78 (1972)

Scott, Peter Dale, *Deep Politics and the Death of JFK*, Chicago, IL, 1996

Scruggs, Jan, *To Heal a Nation*, New York, NY, 1985

Sevy, Grace, ed., *The American Experience in Vietnam*, Norman, OK, 1989

Shaplen, Robert, *The Lost Revolution: The US in Vietnam 1945–1965*, New York, NY, 1966

Shaplen, Robert, *The Road From War*, New York, NY, 1970

Shapley, Deborah, *Promise and Power*, Boston, MA, 1993

Sharp, U.S.G., 'Airpower could have won in Vietnam', *Air Force Magazine* 54 (1971)

Sharp, U.S.G., *Strategy for Defeat*, Novato, CA, 1978

Shawcross, William, *Sideshow*, London, 1979

Sheehan, Neil, *A Bright Shining Lie*, London, 1990

Sheehan, Neil, *Two Cities: Hanoi and Saigon*, London, 1992

Sherry, Michael, *In the Shadow of War*, New Haven, CT, 1995

Shesol, Jeff, *Mutual Contempt: Lyndon Johnson, Robert Kennedy, and the Feud that Defined a Decade*, New York, NY, 1997

Short, Anthony, *The Origins of the Vietnam War*, London, 1989

Shulimson, Jack and Charles Johnson, *US Marines in Vietnam, 1965: The Landing and the Buildup*, Washington, DC, 1978

Simpson, Howard R., *Dien Bien Phu: The Epic Battle America Forgot*, Washington, DC, 1994

Small, Melvin and William D. Hoover, *Give Peace a Chance*, Syracuse, NY, 1992

Small, Melvin, *Johnson, Nixon and the Doves*, New Brunswick, NJ, 1988

Smith, John T., *Rolling Thunder*, Walton on Thames, 1994

Smith, Melden E., Jr, 'The strategic bombing debate: the Second World War and Vietnam', *Journal of Contemporary History* 12 (1977)

Smith, R.B., *An International History of the Vietnam War*, 3 vols, London, 1983

Smith, Winnie, *Daughter Gone to War*, London, 1992

Snepp, Frank, *Decent Interval*, New York, NY, 1977

Spanier, John, *American Foreign Policy Since World War II*, New York, NY, 1965

Spector, Ronald H., *Advice and Support*, New York, NY, 1985

Spector, Ronald H., *After Tet*, New York, NY, 1993

Stanton, Shelby, *The Rise and Fall of an American Army*, Novato, CA, 1985

Starr, Paul, *The Discarded Army*, New York, NY, 1973

Steffens, Lincoln, *The Autobiography of Lincoln Steffens*, New York, NY, 1973

Steigerwald, David, *The Sixties and the End of Modern America*, New York, NY, 1995

Stein, Jean and George Plimpton, eds, *American Journey. The Life and Times of Robert Kennedy*, New York, NY, 1970

Steinberg, Blema, *Shame and Humiliation*, Pittsburgh, PA, 1996

Summers, Harry G., *On Strategy: A Critical Analysis of the Vietnam War*, Novato, CA, 1982

Taylor, Maxwell, *Swords and Plowshares*, New York, NY, 1972

Terzani, Titziano, *Giai Phong: The Fall and Liberation of Saigon*, New York, NY, 1976

Thayer, Carlyle, *War by Other Means*, Sydney, 1989

Thompson, James Clay, *Rolling Thunder: Understanding Policy and Program Failure*, Chapel Hill, NC, 1980

Thompson, Robert, *No Exit from Vietnam*, New York, NY, 1969

Thompson, Robert, *Peace is Not at Hand*, London, 1974

Tilford, Earl H., 'Why and how the US Air Force lost in Vietnam', *Armed Forces and Society* 17 (Spring, 1991)

Tran Van Don, *Our Endless War*, Novato, CA, 1978

Treverton, Gregory F., *Covert Action: The Limits of Intervention in a Postwar World*, London, 1987.

Trewhitt, Henry, *McNamara*, New York, NY, 1971

Truong Chinh, *Primer for Revolt*, New York, NY, 1963

Truong Nhu Tang, *A Vietcong Memoir*, San Diego, CA, 1985

Turley, G.H., *The Easter Offensive*, Annapolis, MD, 1985

Turley, William, *The Second Indochina War*, New York, NY, 1986

Turner, Kathleen J., *Lyndon Johnson's Dual War*, Chicago, IL, 1985

Valenti, Jack, 'The night LBJ surrendered', *George* (March 1998)

Van Creveld, Martin, *The Transformation of War*, New York, NY, 1991

VanDeMark, Brian, *Into the Quagmire*, New York, NY, 1991

Van Tien Dung, *Our Great Spring Victory,* New York, NY, 1977

Vo Nguyen Giap, *The Military Art of People's War*, ed. Russell Stetler, New York, NY, 1970

Vogelgesang, Sandy, *The Long Dark Night of the Soul: The American Intellectual Left and the Vietnam War*, New York, NY, 1974.

Warbey, William, *Ho Chi Minh*, London, 1972

Weigl, Bruce, 'Welcome home', *The Nation* 235 (17 November 1982)

Wells, Tom, *The War Within*, Berkeley, CA, 1994

Werner, Jayne S. and Luu Doan Huynh, eds, *The Vietnam War: Vietnamese and American Perspectives*, Armonk, NY, 1993

Westmoreland, William, *A Soldier Reports*, Garden City, NY, 1976

Wheeler, John, *Touched with Fire*, New York, NY, 1984

White, Theodore H., *The Making of the President 1968*, New York, NY, 1969

Williams, William Appleman *et al.*, eds, *America in Vietnam: A Documentary History*, New York, NY, 1975

Wills, Gary, *The Kennedy Imprisonment*, New York, NY, 1982.

Windt, Theodore Otto Jr, *Presidents and Protesters*, Tuscaloosa, AL, 1990

Wirtz, James J., *The Tet Offensive: Intelligence Failure in War*, Ithaca, NY, 1991

Wolff, Tobias, *In Pharoah's Army*, London, 1994

Young, Marilyn, *The Vietnam Wars, 1945–1990*, New York, NY, 1991
Zaroulis, Nancy and Gerald Sullivan, *Who Spoke Up?*, New York, NY, 1984

PERIODICALS

Berkeley Gazette
The Economist
George
The Guardian
Newsweek
New York Times
Oakland Tribune
San Francisco Chronicle
Scotland on Sunday
Scotsman
Time
US News and World Report
Washington Post

DOCUMENT COLLECTIONS

Berkeley Chancellor Files, University of California, Berkeley
HUAC Hearings
Robert F. Kennedy Papers, JFK Library
Ronald Reagan Papers, Hoover Institution
Social Protest Project, University of California, Berkeley

WEBSITES

H-War
Minerva
People's Park
Texas Tech University
Vietnam Generation

Map 1　**Vietnam, 1944**

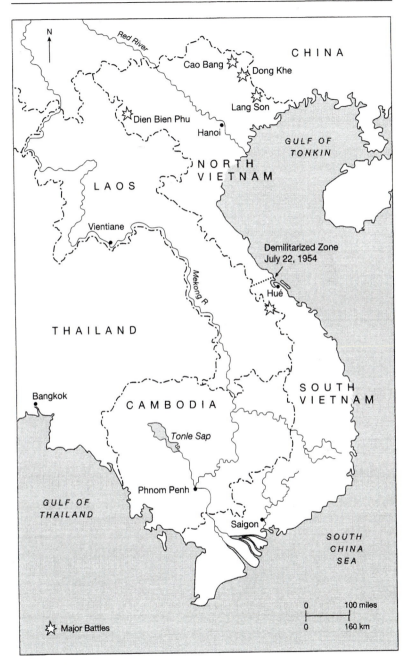

Map 2   **Indochina 1950–54**

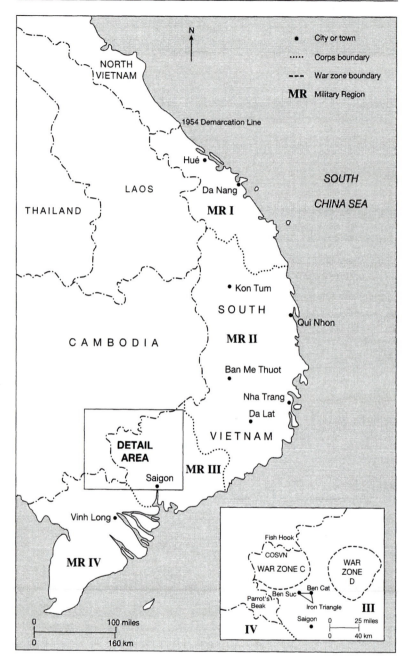

Map 3   US military operations in South Vietnam

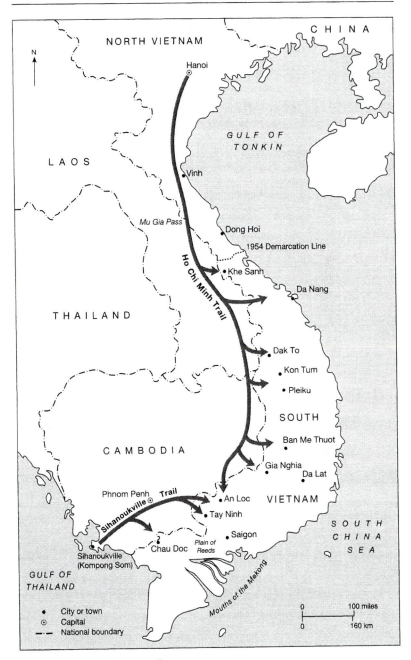

Map 4   **PAVN/PLAF supply routes**

Map 5   **Tet Offensive, 1968**

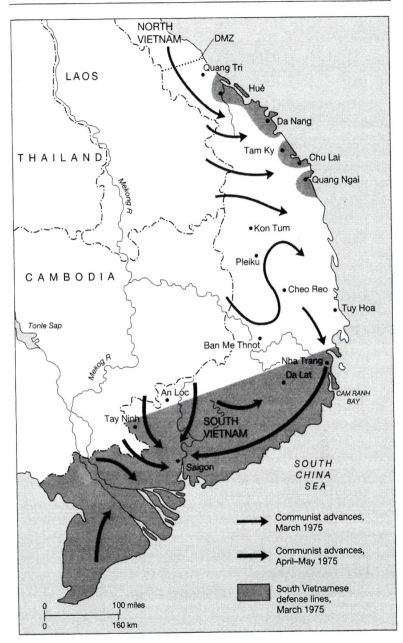

Map 6 **The final offensives**

377

INDEX